STRANGERS IN
THE FAMILY

STRANGERS IN THE FAMILY

Gender, Patriliny, and the Chinese in Colonial Indonesia

Guo-Quan Seng

SOUTHEAST ASIA PROGRAM PUBLICATIONS

AN IMPRINT OF CORNELL UNIVERSITY PRESS   ITHACA AND LONDON

Copyright © 2023 by Cornell University

All rights reserved. Except for brief quotations in a review, this book, or parts thereof, must not be reproduced in any form without permission in writing from the publisher. For information, address Cornell University Press, Sage House, 512 East State Street, Ithaca, New York 14850. Visit our website at cornellpress.cornell.edu.

First published 2023 by Cornell University Press

Library of Congress Cataloging-in-Publication Data

Names: Seng, Guo-Quan, 1981– author.
Title: Strangers in the family : gender, patriliny, and the Chinese in colonial Indonesia / Guo-Quan Seng.
Other titles: Gender, patriliny, and the Chinese in colonial Indonesia
Description: Ithaca [New York] : Southeast Asia Program Publications, an imprint of Cornell University Press, 2023. | Includes bibliographical references and index.
Identifiers: LCCN 2023022383 (print) | LCCN 2023022384 (ebook) | ISBN 9781501772504 (hardcover) | ISBN 9781501772511 (paperback) | ISBN 9781501772528 (pdf) | ISBN 9781501772535 (epub)
Subjects: LCSH: Chinese—Indonesia—History—20th century. | Chinese—Indonesia—History—19th century. | Women—Indonesia—Social conditions—History—20th century. | Women—Indonesia—Social conditions—History—19th century. | Interethnic marriage—Social aspects—Indonesia. | Indonesia—Ethnic relations.
Classification: LCC DS632.3.C5 S464 2023 (print) | LCC DS632.3.C5 (ebook) | DDC 305.48/89510598—dc23/eng/20230517
LC record available at https://lccn.loc.gov/2023022383
LC ebook record available at https://lccn.loc.gov/2023022384

To Pa, Mummy, and Nainai

Contents

List of Illustrations	ix
Acknowledgments	xi
Note on Transliteration	xv
Introduction	1
Part 1 NYAI, MARRIAGE, AND THE BIRTH OF A STRANGER PATRILINY	**15**
1. *Nyai* Liminality	17
2. Bourgeois Manhood and Racial Boundaries	33
Part 2 DIVORCE, WEALTH, AND CHINESE WOMANHOOD	**53**
3. Divorce and Women's Agency	55
4. Women's Wealth and Matriarchal Strategies	79
Part 3 RELIGION AND THE REINVENTION OF PATRILINEAL STRANGERHOOD	**101**
5. Confucianism, Marriage, and Sexuality	103
6. Love, Desire, and Race	119
Part 4 LEGALIZING DESCENT, RACIALIZING PATRILINY	**143**
7. The Civilizing Gift of Monogamy	145
8. Registering Births, Racializing Illegitimacy	169
Conclusion	188
Appendix. A Note on Divorce Cases and Patterns (Chinese Council of Batavia)	197
Abbreviations	199
Notes	199
Bibliography	229
Index	243

Illustrations

Map

0.1 Map of Java and Southeast Asia during the 1910s   xvi

Figures

I.1. Studio portrait of a Chinese man, his native concubine and their child   2

I.2. Photograph of an unnamed Chinese family   3

I.3. Studio portrait of a Peranakan family   4

2.1. Portrait of Tan Eng Goan, Major of the Chinese of Batavia   39

3.1. Photo of the interior of the Chinese Council of Batavia, 1930   58

3.2. Crude divorce rate among the Chinese in Batavia, 1820s–1890s   60

3.3. Proportion of divorce proceedings initiated by women, 1820s–1890s   61

3.4. Trends in cited reasons for divorce in wife-initiated proceedings   62

4.1. Marriage alliance of the Tan and Liem families of Tegal, Central Java   94

4.2. Two generations of cross-cousin marriages between the Ong and Oeij families of Batavia and Tangerang   95

4.3. Photo of Jo Heng Nio taken in the 1890s   98

4.4. Cross-cousin adoption within the uterine family alliance of Jo Heng Nio, her daughter Kan Oe Nio, and her son Kan Tjeng Soen   99

5.1. Portrait of Lie Kim Hok   104

8.1. Front cover of Kwee Tek Hoay's *Boenga roos dari Tjikembang* (1930)   183

8.2. Kin relations among major protagonists in Kwee Tek Hoay's *Bunga roos dari Cikembang* (1927)   186

Acknowledgments

Looking back on the evolution of this book, it has become clear that many questions that had driven its research and writing over the past twelve years or so can be traced to my own descent from a third-generation ethnic Chinese family in Singapore. One lasting image of (patrilineal) domesticity from my 1980s childhood is that of my mother (Mummy) reading letters from our relatives in China aloud to my illiterate grandmother (NaiNai) and great-grandmother (Lao Ma). It was rare to see the three women assembled in one place and conferring about the appropriate sum of my father's money to be remitted "back" to China for ancestral worship. In my own experience, women have been so central to the maintenance of this Chinese patrilineal identity that I always knew in my gut that the male-dominant histories I later read of the overseas Chinese in Southeast Asia were missing something.

Two moments—the first theoretical and the second empirical—gave me the conviction that there were serious intellectual reasons for addressing the missing gender dimension in histories of diasporic Chinese communities in Southeast Asia. When I encountered Gayatri Spivak's "Can the Subaltern Speak?" (1988), I was naively intent on proving her wrong through historical voices of women who did speak for themselves in the archival records. And then I chanced upon the published minutes of the Chinese Council of Batavia while doing preliminary research for another topic at Xiamen University. They were so full of women's voices from the nineteenth century that I was moved to change the direction of my research. The irony of women acting to reinforce a patriliny, even as they spoke up for themselves, is a conclusion I readily concede to Spivak, and one of the key stories I tell in this book.

The subject always remained close to home, but it took a long journey, and some necessary distance, for the questions to crystallize and the research to move along. At the University of Chicago, Mark Philip Bradley was the strong guiding hand that shepherded the project from its inception to its completion. John D. Kelly always had a way of making me interpret whatever I brought to him from three other angles. James Hevia led me to postcolonial theory and history. Prasenjit Duara and Kenneth Pomeranz read various drafts of my work and were as inspiring in dialogue as they are in their own work. Chicagoans I run into everywhere like to reminisce about the intense debates and conversations we never had after Hyde Park. I was lucky to have shared those formative moments in seminars, in workshops, and around dinner tables in the company of Chae Jun Hyung, Chen Wei-ti, Hanisah Binte Abdullah Sani, Hui Kwok-wai, Hwang Ingu, Hsia Ke-Chin, Tadashi Ishikawa, Stacey Kent, Kim Seong-un, Kim Taeju, Jeon Jaewoong, Lee Chengpang, Herbert Lin, Emily Marker, Covell Meyskens, Cameron Penwell, Song Nianshen, Teh Limin, Tian Geng, Wang Fei-Hsien, Jake Werner, Nicholas Wong, Noriko Yamaguchi, Zhao Hai, Zhang Lin, Zhang Yang, and Abraham Zhou Feng.

I am thankful for the grants and fellowships provided by the Department of History, the Department of East Asian Languages and Civilizations, and the Committee on Southern Asian Studies at the University of Chicago, and the International Dissertation Research Fellowship of the Social Science Research Council (New York). They funded research and writing stints in the Netherlands, in Indonesia, and back in Chicago. In Leiden, Marieke Bloembergen, Leonard Blussé, Chen Menghong, Koos Kuiper, Patricia Tjiook-Liem, Alicia Schrikker, Rene Wezel, Marijke van Wissen, Kan Sioe Yao, and Ems Zuidgeest warmly opened doors to help facilitate my research. It was on Professor Blussé's good advice that I found a social and intellectual home among fellow students from or studying Southeast Asia: Titas Chakraborty, Monique Erkelens, Farabi Fakih, Tom Hoogervorst, Intan Lidwina Wibisono, Ariel Lopez, Ravando, Sanne Ravensbergen, Klaas Stutje, Pimmanus Wibulsilp, and Widaratih Kamiso. In Jakarta, I am especially grateful to Dr. Thung Ju Lan of the Indonesian Institute of Sciences for sponsoring my research visa, and for the hospitality of her extended family in Bogor and the Netherlands. Ibu Myra Sidharta, the late Ibu Mona Lohanda, Didi Kwartanada, and the staff of the National Archives of Indonesia were instrumental in sharing their expertise and experience doing archival and library research in the city.

My current employer, the National University of Singapore (NUS), awarded me the Overseas Graduate Scholarship for dissertation writing in Chicago and the Overseas Postdoctoral Fellowship for a stint at Cornell University. I thank Eric Tagliacozzo for serving as my sponsor at the Southeast Asia Program at Cornell. Chiara Formichi, Tamara Loos, Kaja Maria McGowan, and Steve Sangren sparked inspiration in our conversations. At the famed Kahin Center, I was fortunate to find my community among budding Southeast Asianists like Ryan Buyco, Chan Cheow Thia, Jack Chia Meng Tat, Alexandra Dalferro, Nguyen Phi-Vân, Chairat Polmuk, Anissa Rahadiningtyas, Matthew Reeder, Emiko Stock, Alex Thai, and Erick White.

Along the way, the forking paths were lit by teachers, and my eventual journey was forged together with teachers and fellow travelers alike. You have all helped me in more ways than I can recount: Daniel Andrew Birchok Jr., Shelly Chan, Charles Coppel, Faizah Zakaria, Michael Gilsenen, Casey Hammond, Tim

Harper, Caroline Hau, Mary Somers Heidhues, Hong Lysa, Hui Yew-Foong, Koh Keng We, Kwee Hui Kian, Le Huy Anh, Peter Lee, Edgar Liao, Lim Cheng Tju, Loh Kah Seng, Sai Siew-Min, John Solomon, and Nurfadzilah Yahaya, among others.

I owe much to the following people for the final shape of this book. Framing the entire book with the "stranger" trope came from talking through chapter 6 with Cheow Thia and Matt. The two peer reviewers of the manuscript prodded me to further clarify the stakes in my argument. Robert Cribb, Rachel Leow, Charlotte Setjadi, and Zhou Taomo offered further insights in a manuscript revision workshop. My undergraduate research assistant Koh Hong Kai helped proofread an early draft. Sarah E. M. Grossman and her fabulous team at Cornell University Press deserve a special thanks for moving the manuscript through the editorial process with such care and efficiency. Their imprints are all over the book. Needless to say, any error is mine alone.

In the NUS History Department, it has been an honor to reconnect with my former teachers as colleagues—Brian Farrell, Huang Jianli, Albert Lau, and Bruce Lockhart. I thank Timothy P. Barnard, Donna Brunero, Ian Gordon, Medha Malik Kudaisya, Joey Long, and Wang Jinping, among the department's leadership, for giving me the necessary space and advice to grow as junior faculty. It has been my good fortune to count Maitrii Aung-Thwin, Sayaka Chatani, Jack Chia, Priya Jaradi, Kung Chien Wen, Kelvin Lawrence, Lee Seungjoon, Hajimu Masuda, Sharon Low Su-Ling, and Portia Reyes among my neighbors in the office corridor.

My academic pursuits have taken me far away from home for much of the past two decades. It is to Pa, Mummy, and Nainai that I dedicate this book, for their indulgence and support of their absentee (grand)son over the years. Ping Jie deserves a special mention for stepping up as the "only child" in my physical absence. While I have been telling Michelle that I will dedicate the next book to her, she and I know that this one could not have gone past the finishing line without the sacrifices she, Julien, and Chloe made over many a weekend. To many more good things in life!

Note on Transliteration

The book cites many extracts of texts in English translation from their original languages. I have provided the key terms in their original language wherever necessary. The relevant languages will be labeled as "M" for Malay, "D" for Dutch, "C" for Chinese in the original script or Hanyu Pinyin, and "Hk" for Hokkien (southern Fujianese dialect). Either the original word or the translation may appear in parentheses; for instance, the text might mention the creole Chinese concept of love (M: *cinta*) or the creole Chinese concept of *cinta* (M: love). Sino-Malay (or Chinese Malay) is now the standard term used to refer to the creole Malay language used by the Chinese of Java. In certain contexts, it might have been more apt to refer to it as Bahasa, or the Indonesian national language. For simplicity's sake, I have uniformly labeled these words as Malay. In my citation of Malay words from primary sources, I have generally avoided converting them to the modern orthography agreed on by Malaysia and Indonesia in 1973. Hence, "kelakoean" rather than "kelakuan," and "goendik" rather than "gundik." I only adopt the modern spelling when I discuss them as concepts in the main text: for instance, "cinta" rather than "tjinta."

FIGURE 0.1. Map of Java and Southeast Asia during the 1910s, with locations mentioned in this book.

INTRODUCTION

This book unravels the structure of intimate interethnic relations in the Dutch East Indies in the early twentieth century, a structure demonstrated in the subtle contrast between photographs taken from that time (see figures I.1 and I.2). The first is a rare studio photograph, most likely taken in Java during the 1920s or 1930s, of a Chinese man holding an infant he had with his Indonesian partner. The second conforms to a more general pattern of domesticity represented in many photos of ethnic Chinese families from late colonial Indonesia. Here, the Chinese wife-cum-mother sits among the children, while the Indonesian servant's place is on the floor; the man is standing (see also figure I.3). The native woman in the first image appears to be more intimately connected with the family unit, yet she remains on the floor. She was most likely a native concubine (*nyai*) of the Chinese man. While many photos of ethnic Chinese couples and their children from the early twentieth century have survived in private and public collections, rarely does one encounter one of a Chinese man and his *nyai*. Its chance survival in a museum collection centered on the theme of cultural hybridity is a reminder not only of the relative absence of Asian women in the historiography of the European empires but of the native wives and mothers who gave birth to creolized Asian settler communities in nineteenth- and twentieth-century colonial Southeast Asia.

Such an image of interethnic intimacy would not have been unfamiliar to any person living in the Dutch East Indies in the early decades of the twentieth century, as a whole subgenre of love stories in the Chinese-Indies print market was devoted to it.[1] The following excerpt from *The Rose of Cikembang*—a

FIGURE I.1. Untitled.

Source: Collection of the Peranakan Museum. Gift of Mr. and Mrs. Lee Kip Lee.

best-selling novel written in 1927 by Kwee Tek Hoay, the foremost religious reformer and writer among the Chinese in colonial-era Indonesia—adds sociological depth to this image of race and gender relations:

> Even though he was thirty years old, Ay Cheng had not yet married and had no wish to marry. . . . He loved with all his heart his *nyai*, his concubine, Marsiti. . . . He did not want to take the risk of changing

FIGURE I.2. Photograph from an album (B3973).

Source: Collection of the Peranakan Museum.

such a satisfying life by marrying a "modern" girl filled with aspirations, desires and demands, which he feared he didn't have the means to meet.

... Although she knew that Ay Cheng loved her intensely and enjoyed indulging her every wish, Marsiti always held him in high respect and honor as a *tuan*, and whenever she spoke with him she would address him as "*juragan*"—which, like "*tuan*," meant "lord and master"—and refer to herself as "*abdi*," that is "slave" or "servant."[2]

FIGURE I.3. Studio portrait of a Peranakan family (Padang, Sumatra).

Source: Collection of the Peranakan Museum. Gift of Mr. and Mrs. Lee Kip Lee.

The family in the photograph might very well have been Ay Cheng, Marsiti, and their child. Set in a rubber plantation in the highlands of Dutch colonial Java, the capitalist owner and his manager were not, as standard histories of colonial capitalism might lead us to think, members of the white ruling elite. Rather, they were Chinese migrants, who had, for two or more generations, made Java their adopted homeland. While Indonesian male coolies worked the plantation grounds, young Indonesian women like Marsiti served as domestic servants and sometimes formed intimate relationships with their European or Chinese male employers. Reading the novel today, a person without some knowledge of Indonesia's colonial past might be forgiven for mistaking the Chinese as the settler-colonizer.

It was along such colonial divisions of race, class, and gender that Kwee, the reformer and writer, set up his male protagonist to fall in love in succession with two women: an Indonesian servant concubine and an educated Indonesian Chinese woman. The story was a play on misrecognized identities that dramatized and challenged Chinese notions of patrilineal descent. Marsiti died in self-imposed exile to let Ay Cheng marry the Chinese woman. But both their mixed-race daughter, unknown to him at the point of separation, and Marsiti's soul would return to redeem and haunt Ay Cheng's preconceived understandings of descent and wealth succession.[3] The novel was ahead of its time for critiquing Chinese patriliny's exclusionary tendencies even as it failed to fundamentally challenge the colonial-structured racial hierarchy. Today, in postcolonial Indonesia and Southeast Asia, it continues to speak to a cultural condition of migrant-to-settler Chineseness that remains insufficiently aware of its own patrilineal past and present at a time when the postcolonial inversion of racial hierarchies have in turn solidified the colonial-invented categories of race.

Strangers in the Family historicizes the making of a Chinese settler patrilineal society on the northern coast of Dutch-colonized Java between the late eighteenth and mid-twentieth centuries. Through the lenses of gender and race, this book brings questions from empire and Chinese migration studies into a singular field of analysis. Anne McClintock and Ann L. Stoler have shown how bourgeois white settlers constructed new notions of race through the affective governance of domesticity on the colonial frontier.[4] Male Chinese migrants did not have sovereign control over colonial society, but they did order their families and communities under the colonial rubric of private or family law. Uncovering the intimate dynamics of race-making, this book shows how a creolized Chinese identity was born and reinvented in Java under more than a century of Dutch colonial rule (1816–1942).

Gender and Inter-Asian Intimacies in Colonial Societies

Perspectives regarding gender and sexuality have radically altered our understanding of Euro-American global imperial projects in recent times. If Marxist approaches previously stressed the metropole's exploitation of colonial resources on the periphery, they left the more palpably felt white superiority social complexes underexplained.[5] In writing about his homeland, French colonial

Martinique, early Freudian critic Frantz Fanon located the site of colonial racial alienation in a "sexual myth" that fueled the Black ego's "obsession with white flesh": white men could exploit Black women's sexuality with impunity, while white women were made taboo to Black men.[6] Later on, Foucault's insights about the hypernormalization of sexuality discourses in the modern West were extended by Ann Stoler to show how bourgeois whiteness consolidated itself in intimate and domestic spaces across colonial Asia.[7] Given Europe's dominance in global imperialism, the field's preoccupation with the colonizer-colonized sexual encounter is understandable. Yet Europeans—or, more precisely, white men— were not the only settler group who sought sexual opportunities across colonized Asia for much of the modern period. In Southeast Asia, male traders and laborers (and, only much later, women) from the Middle East, India, and China have long traditions of sojourning and settling in port cities in the region. With some important exceptions, the literature has mostly been silent on the gender and sexuality dimensions of these settlers' long encounter with local societies.

Situated at the crossroads of Eurasian and inter-Asian maritime trading routes, indigenous and colonial port cities in early modern Southeast Asia have thrived historically on hosting foreign male traders within their respective enclave communities. Most Southeast Asian societies were more flexible than their European and South or East Asian counterparts in their practice of bilateral rather than patrilineal kinship. Women played a greater role in wealth transmission across generations and in the hosting of their husbands at their parents' residence—what anthropologists call matrilocal marriages. In the maritime port cities, foreign visitors observed a general tolerance toward divorce, remarriage, and participation by women in the marketplace. In this context, it was common for women to enter temporary marriages with foreign men and trade on their husbands' behalf when they were absent in between monsoon seasons.[8]

A gendered approach to history in maritime Southeast Asia has revealed the salience of women in giving birth to and anchoring the most dynamic dynasties or creolized political orders in the early modern period. As historian Jean Gelman Taylor shows, behind the official line of governors the Vereenigde Oost-Indie Compagnie sent to Batavia (present-day Jakarta) to rule over its eastern empire (1600s–1800) were creolized Eurasian women, who often remarried new officeholders to keep wealth and power within their multigenerational, culturally hybrid families. Enterprising queens in seventeenth century Aceh (northern Sumatra) and Bantam (western Java) proved more adept than their husbands, fathers, and sons at stabilizing their political regimes in the face of challenges from their Dutch and English allies/competitors.[9] Until the eighteenth century in Java and up to the nineteenth in Siam, indigenous rulers absorbed the bicultural sons of Chinese traders and local women not only in recognition of their prominence in trade but as the de facto regional power brokers.[10] The practice of "temporary marriages" with foreign men stood at the heart of Southeast Asia's social encounter with the world in its early modern "age of commerce."[11]

In contrast to the voluminous scholarship on Eurasian intimate encounters, the study of interethnic Asian relationships has barely begun. The disparity is understandable since Eurasian communities bore the brunt of colonial racializing or "whitening" policies in the late colonial era (1890s–1940s).[12] However, historian Tamara Loos notes that "the arguably far more numerous international intra-Asian liaisons between local Southeast Asian women and Chinese or South Asian male laborers" remains understudied. They "often remained under the radar of the colonial state (and therefore scholars) because they did not threaten to blur the lines between ruler and ruled." Research on these inter-Asian forms of gender history, she argues, "will move the analysis of colonial-era power and race relations beyond a focus on Western colonial encounters in Asia."[13] In her own work on transcolonial family law reform, Loos shows how becoming "civilized" became the political currency of the semicolonized and polygynous Siamese royal elite, as they more readily "granted" the protection of Muslim personal law to their southern vassal states than choose to adopt monogamy for themselves.[14]

Strangers in the Family joins new scholarly efforts in uncovering transnational histories of intimate encounters, previously thought to have become insignificant by the twentieth century, in both inter-Asian and hybridized colonial terms. One of the most enduring views of race relations in colonized Southeast Asia is that colonial free-market policies in the nineteenth century gave rise to a "medley" of races, in Furnivall's phrasing, that "mix[ed] but d[id] not combine."[15] Writing in the 1920s and 1930s in colonial Southeast Asia, earlier local modes of interethnic acculturation had been obscured by the rise of European imperial race management. New works suggests that overlapping inter-Asian ethnic categories survived into the late nineteenth and possibly the early twentieth century or even later: *kabya* in Burma, *peranakan* in the Malay-Javanese world, and *lukjin* and *minh hương*—specific to the mixed descendants of Chinese settler fathers—in Siam and Vietnam, respectively.[16] Chie Ikeya shows that it was not until the rise of a more masculine form of modern Burmese nationalism in the 1920s and 1930s that chauvinists began to frame intermarriage between South Asian men and Burmese women as sources of cultural contamination.[17] The rise of racial discourse also changed perceptions of preexisting forms of inter-Asian marriage taboos. As Engseng Ho shows, local Muslim communities did not see the creole Hadrami Arab practice of *kaa'fa* (rule of sufficiency), which prohibited daughters of sayyids (descendants of the prophet) from marrying non-sayyid Muslims, as a form of Arab racism until the twentieth century.[18] Bao Jiemin's gender-based ethnography of the Chinese Thai in the 1990s indicates that some second- and third-generation *lukjin* men subscribed, like their fellow Thai middle class, to *chaochu* (womanizer) masculine norms, which were in turn supercharged with the Chinese patrilineal ideal of bearing sons and providing for a big family.

The period of high imperialism (1880s–1940s) may have been a brief episode in Asia's longer history, but the changes it wrought—the formation of modern colonial states and their postcolonial successors, the birth of anticolonial nationalism, the racialization of populations, the institutionalization of Asian religions, and the facilitation of mass migrations, to name a few—set in motion state and social dynamics that postcolonial societies continue to grapple with today. The colonial construction of race alone, and the concomitant problem of eugenics-informed policies, cannot fully unravel the intricacies of how Asian groups conceived of identities and intimacies. The phenomenon is older than European colonial race management yet cannot be understood apart from it. Equally important was how colonial states governed religion and how that became the grounds on which Asians settled private familial matters among themselves and between groups.

Engendering the Stranger: Patriliny and the Rules of Intimacy

The stranger, as Georg Simmel famously puts it, is a social structural feature "not of the wanderer who comes today and goes tomorrow, but rather the person who comes today and stays tomorrow.... He has not quite overcome the freedom of coming and going. He is fixed within a particular spatial group, or within a group whose boundaries are similar to spatial boundaries." As Simmel reminds us, the barriers need not be spatial (or legally formal), but their affective construction was at least bidirectional. "Although in more intimate relations, he may develop all kinds of charm and significance," Simmel continues, "as long as he is considered a stranger in the eyes of the other, he is not an 'owner of soil.'"[19] Simmel's stranger theory was ahead of its time in its attention to questions of intimacy, but the stranger was also always a gendered person (a "he"). How might unpacking the masculine assumptions of the "stranger" reframe the history of inter-Asian intimate relations?

Until recently, scholars have tracked interethnic intimate relations among Asians for demographic trends rather than study them for their effects on gender and racial identity. Combining Simmel's stranger theory with Robert Park's race relations survey method, G. William Skinner's assimilationist study of the Chinese in Thailand in the 1950s and 1960s treated the presence or absence of interethnic marriages as indicators of acculturation or isolation (or alienation from the local majority). As was common among Skinner's generation of Sinologists and anthropologists, patriliny, or the perpetuation of the male lineage for the purpose of Confucian ancestral worship, formed the essential core of Chineseness—a protoracial form of identity.[20] "Marriage with Thai women was the rule for Chinese immigrants when occupation and financial status permitted. The next question concerns the offspring of such marriages: was the influence of the father or of the mother supreme?"[21] Patriliny was both a natural given and the control variable for tracing whether the Chinese were moving culturally toward assimilation or isolation.

Strangers in the Family sets the older analytical trope of the diasporic male "stranger" on its head by telling the story of the creolization and reproduction of a patrilineal community over time from the perspective of women. For colonial Java, I adapt Steve Sangren's theorization of traditional Chinese patriliny, as an institution "specific to China [that] produce[d] characteristic filial sentiments in Chinese sons and daughters that are not altogether resonant with the normative demands of the family system itself." Rather than view filiality alone as intrinsic to Chinese patriliny, Sangren argues that there were "endogenous resistances at the level of sentiments and desires to the roles society prescribes. Sons desire autonomy, which, in the Chinese context, can mean escape from the intense identification with their fathers . . . ; daughters, in contrast, desire recognition and inclusion from a patrilineal system that excludes them."[22] Less concerned with the problem of intergenerational filiality and more with race, gender, and sexuality, this book historicizes the "sentiments and desires" Chinese settler men prescribed for and projected onto women, and specific legal and ethno-kinship inclusionary and exclusionary strategies that turned women in general, and native Indonesian women in particular, into strangers in the family.

It is only from the vantage point of women, this book argues, that the emotional and ideological strategies of patrilineal familial reproduction—and, by extension, modern kinship-inflected notions of race—become clear. Women spoke back but, as Spivak reminds us, seldom in ways patriarchal society recognized.[23] When women's bodies and sexuality were at stake in the late colonial period, diasporic Asian nationalists, as John Kelly shows, fought discursively over a "politics of virtue" framed in reformed religious forms.[24] *Strangers in the Family* uncovers the sentimentalist and moral structures within patrilineal and patriarchal society that permitted women to speak back to men and act in their own interests, if seldom against patriliny itself. With a focus on marriage and sexuality, the book is a history of how creole Chinese patriliny, in its traditional and reformed guises, kept itself alienated from the indigenous majority by adapting and adjusting its intimate rules of inclusion and exclusion over time. It historicizes the patriliny, as far as possible, through the contemporary voices of women as native concubines, daughters, wives, widows, matriarchs, and feminist advocates. At the heart of the birth of a modern Chinese Indonesian identity, the book argues, lies the transformation of a discourse of love that equalized husband-and-wife relations but replicated the older exclusion of Indonesian women from Confucian marriage.

Becoming Strangers in the Indonesian Family: Context and Chapter Outline

In a larger sense, this book is also about how communal patrilineal politics during the colonial era turned the Chinese into strangers in the new Indonesian nation. In 1959, the writer Pramoedya Ananta Toer famously called the Chinese in Indonesia "strangers who are not foreign."[25] In his penetrating analysis of diasporic nationalist ideology among the Chinese in West Kalimantan, anthropologist Hui Yew-Foong referred to them as "strangers at home."[26] In Hui's view, their political projection of a progressive diasporic homeland in China was, ironically, their way of negotiating a politics of belonging in an anti-imperialist Indonesia. In this book, I view the analytical trope of the stranger through an affective lens to refer to the gendered discursive processes of recognition, identification, and alienation that were at the heart of the formation of a creolized Chinese patrilineal community between 1816 and 1942.

Serious maritime contact between China and Indonesia goes back to the fourteenth century. However, today's Chinese-identifying Indonesians can trace their ancestors' migration to Java only as far back as the latter half of the eighteenth century. Between the 1750s and the 1830s, during a period of Southeast Asian history Anthony Reid has called the "Chinese century," new waves of male Chinese traders, artisans, and laborers landed on the shores of northern coastal Java and elsewhere across Southeast Asia.[27] Dutch colonial restriction of immigration and its system of religious plurality created the conditions for the growth of island Southeast Asia's largest creolized Chinese communities. In contrast to their creole counterparts in the British Straits Settlements, new immigrants from China never swamped Java to an extent that the numerical superiority of the indigenous group would be threatened. It was on Java, in closer proximity to the indigenous groups, that Confucian reformers assumed the racializing task of inventing new moralities to discipline the everyday sexual micropolitics of the creole bourgeois subject.

The moral economy of Java's creole Chinese communities was formed in the middle decades of the nineteenth century, when new immigration to the island was tightly restricted. Under the Cultivation System (1830–70), the Dutch collaborated with Java's feudal elites to monopolize the agrarian production of coffee and sugar crops through the peasantry. Java thus missed the large waves of immigrant Chinese laborers who poured into Southeast Asia's plantations and mines during these decades. Originating mostly from southern Fujian, earlier generations of traders, artisans, and laborers settled in their colonial-designated ethnic enclaves with "separate quarters, dress, administrative structures, and recognized religions."[28] Their acculturated descendants spoke mostly Malay, the trade lingua franca of the maritime world, but maintained the religious practices of their forefathers. In 1857, there were between 3,000 and 4,000 immigrant men, as compared to 76,000 local-born adult men and women among the Chinese of Java.[29] In 1883, thirteen years after Java began to open up to new immigration, Chinese male immigrant numbers increased to about 19,000, while the local born constituted 200,000 men and women.[30] This contrasts with elsewhere in the region—particularly the British colonies, where new labor migrants swamped the new settlements to become the far larger constituents among the Chinese.[31]

In this book, I focus primarily on the local-born creolized Chinese group. By 1900, despite the gradual loosening of migration controls, there were an estimated 250,000 local born on Java as opposed to 24,000 immigrant Chinese, or a ratio of 10 to 1.[32] Chinese immigration thereafter increased rapidly, but the creoles remained in the majority. According to the 1930 census, the ratio of local born to immigrant narrowed to 462,000 to 120,000, or 3.9 to 1.[33] As Chinese medium schools expanded in the early twentieth century, a cultural-linguistic divide formed between the so-called *peranakan* (M: local born) and *totok* (pure-blooded or immigrant) groups, which, by the 1930s, could not always be distinguished by place of birth. The term "*peranakan*" was politicized in the assimilationist politics of the 1950s and 1960s.[34] Until the 1930s, it was still more common for the acculturated Chinese to refer to themselves as *baba* rather than *peranakan*.[35] For these reasons, I prefer to use the more analytically impartial term "creole" rather than "*peranakan*." Toward the end of the book, I devote some attention to the creole-immigrant divide, but it is not of central concern here.

I refer readers to important historical and socio-ethnographic research on the Chinese in colonial Java/Indonesia, which has laid out the changing social, linguistic, religious, and political-economic landscapes. These works demonstrate how settlers acculturated over the last four hundred years. Control of the China trade, close entrepreneurial collaboration with the local colonial authorities, and the Kapitan system of communal self-rule, as the studies of Leonard Blussé, William G. Skinner, Peter Carey, James Rush, Chen Menghong, Kwee Hui Kian, Alexander Claver, and Mona Lohanda show, created the early modern socioeconomic conditions for the growth of creolized or *peranakan* Chinese settlements.[36] Lohanda, Lea Williams, Leo Suryadinata, Charles Coppel, Claudine Salmon, Myra Sidharta, Faye Chan Yik-Wei, Patricia Tjiook-Liem, Elizabeth Chandra, Hui Yew-Foong, Sai Siew-Min, Didi Kwartanada, Zhou Taomo, and Tom Hoogervorst have detailed transformations to their political and cultural identities as nationalism and the newer immigrants swept through Java after 1900.[37]

Building on this existing scholarship, *Strangers in the Family* tells the gendered history of the formation and reformation of a Chinese patrilineal community in Java through eight chapters grouped into four thematic parts. Part 1 accounts for the legal and discursive formation that gave birth to a creolized Chinese society. Chapter 1 historicizes the slave women and native concubines who had intimate relations with Chinese male migrants and settlers. It locates their agentic liminality in the contradiction between their categorical exclusion from Confucian marriage and their role as the mestizo children's mothers, who were responsible for raising the children as Chinese. Chapter 2 shows how the middle-class Chinese marriage system was premised on a profoundly unequal sexual exchange, in which men were celebrated for their virility and polygyny, whereas women were valued for their chastity. Part 2 pivots from the vantage point of the native concubine to that of creole Chinese daughters, wives, and matriarchs. Chapter 3 shows that, borrowed from local Islamic norms, creole Chinese women spoke back to the patriarchy in divorce pleas that articulated their gendered moral expectation of material maintenance and conjugal love. Chapter 4 demonstrates how matriarchs (often widows) were able to protect the interests of their immediate uterine family (sisters, brothers, and their children), even as a more stringent interpretation of Chinese family law in colonial jurisprudence put an end to women's freedom to contract.

The next two parts turn to twentieth-century transformations and resistances. Part 3 analyzes the alienating interethnic dynamics of marriage reform debates as Confucian reformers reconstituted a new patriliny to counter the Dutch colonial civilizing mission. Chapter 5 traces the rise of the modern creole Chinese subject in Java to the reformers' attempts to appropriate and "naturalize" Western sexology in the name of a monotheistic God. Chapter 6 shows how reformist male writers internalized and popularized the new discourse of love and love marriage, only to exclude extramarital relationships with indigenous women as a problem of lust. The two chapters of part 4 detail the moral ambivalence with which the Chinese of Java received family law reforms imposed on them by the

Dutch colonial state. Chapter 7 shows how Confucian reformist leaders resisted the notion of gender equality and women's rights championed by colonial reformers and their Dutch-educated elite Chinese allies. Chapter 8 traces how colonial birth registration inadvertently created a legal category of illegitimacy for children born to native mothers, given the persistent Chinese reluctance to marry native women in civil law or by custom.

In the conclusion, I compare my gendered history of the Chinese in colonial Indonesia with other ethnic Chinese communities in the British colonial Straits Settlements, semicolonial Thailand, and the American colonial Philippines. I then reflect on the immediate and longer-term effects of colonial-era race and gender policies on Chinese identity in postcolonial Indonesia.

A Note on Sources

This is a book about gender and race relations. To describe how identities coalesced around the late colonial legal-racial categories I use the terms "Chinese" and "Native" as they circulated in colonial society, but it is no longer acceptable in today's Indonesia, and has not been since at least the early 2000s, to single out individuals or groups by these labels in most social and political settings. This does not, of course, deny ethnic Chinese Indonesians their universally recognized right to identify with and celebrate their creolized cultural heritage.

The first three chapters of the book makes extensive use of the minutes of the proceedings of the Chinese Council of Batavia. Dutch colonial authorities have appointed merchants to be the intermediating leaders of the Chinese communities on Java since their colonization of Batavia in the seventeenth century. Historians have traced official recognition of the council's communal functions to a correspondence in April 1747.[38] These include marriage and divorce registration, management of communal cemeteries, and resolution of conflicts among Chinese. In its most routinized form, the officers met twice a week to handle these matters, while also playing an intermediary role between the authorities and the Chinese community. The archives of the council's biweekly minutes for the period 1787 to 1920 have mostly survived, with the exception of a thirty-one-year gap (1792–1823). The minutes were recorded in classical Chinese but contained many transliterated Hokkien, Malay, and Dutch terms of local usage. The proceedings were most likely conducted mainly in creole Malay—the lingua franca of the marketplace and the mother tongue of the local born officers—and supplemented with Hokkien and some Dutch. In the 1990s, the archives were salvaged from a warehouse in Jakarta and relocated to Leiden University. A team of researchers from Leiden University and Xiamen University collaborated to transcribe, annotate, and publish the entire set of Chinese minutes, which, running into fifteen volumes, began to appear in 2002.[39] Since 2018, the entire archives have been digitized and made accessible to the world through Leiden University's online catalog, under the title "Collection Guide Archive of the Kong Koan of Batavia (吧城公館)."[40] I have referred to both published (transcribed) and digitized (manuscript) versions of the minutes for my research. I will be citing these minutes throughout the text in the following format: "Chinese Council Minutes, Day Month Year." Readers who wish to verify my interpretation of the materials can easily consult either the transcribed version or the online manuscript version, both of which are chronologically organized by the date of the meeting provided.

Readers should note that although the book makes broad general claims for urban Java, chapters 1 to 3 on the nineteenth century have a Batavia or West Java bias due to their reliance on the council's sources. This bias is in part mitigated by the fact that Chinese councils in Semarang and Surabaya had similar functions and were modeled after their Batavia counterpart. Chinese officers in these two cities would have had the same authority to formulate their own patrilineal racial border. It cannot be assumed, however, that the gender-mediated interethnic relations followed the same patterns as those in Batavia. My own evidence from the twentieth century (in chapters 7 and 8) suggests that the consolidation of a patriarchal Confucian proto-racial boundary in the prior century probably did not proceed in Semarang and Surabaya as strongly as it did in Batavia. Unfortunately, the archives of the Chinese councils in these two major urban settlements have not survived. Beyond the first three chapters, much of this history continued to unfold from Batavia. It was, after all, the capital city of the Dutch empire in the East. Both the Indies Supreme Court and the General Secretariat were headquartered there. It was no accident that the Confucian revivalist movement was first born in the city before it spread to the rest of Java and beyond.

Chapter 3, "Divorce and Women's Agency," is based on my assembly of a database of 739 divorce trials recorded in the council's minutes from the 1820s to the 1890s. The chapter makes a specific argument about creole women's moral agency. I refer readers to the appendix for a more technical explanation of how the raw data was assembled and the methodology behind deriving the trends discussed in the chapter.

Part 1
NYAI, MARRIAGE, AND THE BIRTH OF A STRANGER PATRILINY

Male Chinese settlers in colonial urban Java established racially endogamous communities by both producing heirs through their relationships with slave women and limiting the institution of Confucian marriage to the descendants of Chinese fathers. The two chapters in part 1 explore the race and gender dynamics of this patriliny's founding between the 1780s and the 1880s. The turn of the nineteenth century was a tumultuous period in the political history of Java. The collapse of the Dutch Vereenigde Oost-Indie Compagnie in Europe in 1799 created a power vacuum on the island. Batavia and other northern coast port cities (and their hinterlands) were briefly taken over by the French (1806–11) and British (1811–16) before the island was recolonized by the Netherlands in 1816. The coastal port cities had been in the hands of the successive European powers since the early 1700s. But the co-optation of the Javanese aristocratic elite, centered at Yogyakarta and Solo in Central Java, was only completed after the Dutch defeated Diponegoro in the Java War (1825–30).

Concentrated in the port cities and focused on trade, more settled creole Chinese communities formed in the course of this period. The *nyai*—a native concubine—was an important feminine figure in the birth of a rooted creole Chinese society in Java. Chapter 1 historicizes the agency of slave women in their unstable relationships with the migrant Chinese. It showcases how the nyai was a liminal ethno-gendered category: excluded from Confucian marriage, they were nevertheless expected to raise their mestizo children as Chinese. Chapter 2 demonstrates how creolized Chinese manhood was born toward the end of this period at the intersection of wealthy merchants' cult of virility (and their practice of polygamy), middle-class men's marital expectation of virginity in their bride, and the Kapitan elites' policing of racial borders in their treatment of runaway Chinese mestiza brides.

1

NYAI LIMINALITY

Between the 1750s and 1850s, the sojourning Chinese communities of northern coast Java sank tentative roots in their adopted home cities. In the aftermath of the Chinese massacre of 1740 and the wars that raged on until 1755, junks from southern Fujian (and some from Guangdong) and neighboring port cities in the region continued to visit the port cities of Java. Men from Fujian and Guangdong poured forth into the port cities and their environs in search of opportunities for trade and work. Some formed relationships with local slave and free women with the intention, at least at first, of returning to their villages in southern China. Many did not return. Out of these unions, stable creolized Chinese communities had emerged by the end of the century. The Dutch recolonization of Java in 1816, along with the restrictions put on Chinese immigration in the 1830s, gave further impetus to the formation of localized Chinese societies.

This chapter historizes the ethno-gendered figure of the Chinese male settler's native concubine—the *nyai*. The migration and marital patterns of these eighteenth- and early-nineteenth-century Chinese have been described in the existing scholarship in broad brushstrokes from a patrilineal standpoint.[1] Historian Barbara Andaya has shown that the local "temporary wives" of foreign merchants in the region's port cities were influential women, who served as trading agents of their male partners when the latter were absent for trade. She argues that with the onset of larger waves of migration in the nineteenth century, "the temporary wife [did] not disappea[r] . . . but the respect she once enjoyed . . . slipped away."[2] Throughout this period, patterns of both the sexual exploitation and social elevation of (former) slave women were evident. This chapter reads patriarchal local Chinese sources against the grain to reconstruct the social, sexual, and quasi-marital lives of the native concubines of Chinese men in urban Java. Between the 1750s and the 1850s, the nyai was a liminal ethno-gendered historical figure in two ways. First, these women were essential to the reproduction of Chinese communities as mothers of mestizo children, yet they remained marginal to the community, as they were excluded from full Confucian ritual marriages. Second, both they and their mestiza daughters often crossed ethnic borders erected by men in their marital and sexual choices.

From Slave to Nyai

The historical figure of the nyai has its roots in the indigenous system of slavery. As the Dutch VOC established its hegemony over the entire length of the northern coast of Java, it channeled all trade—and the slave trade in particular—through Batavia. By the same logic, Chinese maritime trade and labor migration bound for Java were funneled through the port city. It was there that male migrants and slave women met. Before Confucian marriages became the established norm, the nyai was the dominant female head of the Chinese settler household in colonial port cities in Java.

For much of its history, Batavia was the slave town of the Dutch VOC trading empire. Slaves bought in Bali and southern Sulawesi were brought first to the city's slave market for sale. At its peak in the seventeenth century, more than half of Batavia's population was made up of slaves. As late as 1790, one in four people in the city and its environs were slaves.[3] The slave population declined drastically during the British interregnum (1811–16) to 12,500 (3 percent of the population) in Batavia, 4,488 in Semarang, and 3,682 in Surabaya.[4] The Dutch would ban the import of slaves to Java in 1818 and prohibit slavery in 1860. By the 1850s, only about three thousand slaves remained in Batavia.[5] Throughout the region, slavery was not, as in the Caribbean islands and the Americas, yoked to the capitalistic production of plantation crops. The wealthiest elite families kept domestic slaves for pomp and prestige rather than for agrarian production. In the biggest households, they were engaged in minor domestic work, craftwork, or entertainment (as musicians, Chinese opera actors, and so on). It was thus a more forgiving form of servitude that saw many manumitted within their lifetime.[6] Many were free to work and save in order to redeem themselves. Slaves and their children were inheritable by law, but most owners, especially Eurasians, emancipated slaves and their children in their final wills after having enjoyed a lifetime of their service. Yet at all times they were liable to be, and frequently were, bought and sold as property.

Among the Chinese, besides the wealthiest merchants, middling traders, craftsmen, and housewives also held female slaves for domestic service. A slave register from 1816, a time when slavery had drastically declined, reveals some distinctive Chinese patterns of slave ownership. Only three out of a hundred Chinese owned slaves, whereas one-third of Europeans were slave owners. More precisely, 627 European owners held 8,641 slaves (13.8 each on average) compared with 691 Chinese holding 2,281 slaves (3.3 each). As Susan Abeyasekere notes, "Very few of the Chinese listed were wealthy, to judge from the numbers of slaves owned."[7] When there were three times as many slaves back in the 1780s, probably one in ten Chinese would have held slaves, with slave numbers spread equally thin, especially among the middling urban male artisans and housewives. For the middling urban artisans and small traders, the one or two slaves they held for domestic service would have doubled as temporary wives.

Female slaves were priced beyond the income of the average coolie. It was left to the urban artisans, middling traders, and workers' foremen to compete for one or two slave-concubines during their sojourn in Batavia. In the late 1780s, Chinese men in Batavia bought or kept slave girls for around 200–250 guilders.[8] According to civil trial records, those who bought or kept slave-concubines and revealed their occupations included two traders who plied the Bali-Batavia route, a trader who owned a junk boat, and a wood sculptor.[9] It would take a new carpenter more than five years—if he spent time on nothing else—to save enough for a slave-concubine.[10] For a year or a season of work on a sugar plantation, 45 workers were paid an average of thirty-one guilders each compared with their sole foreman, who received 243 guilders.[11] Twenty-six workers who sailed on a Dutch ship to the Netherlands and back over a period of twenty months were paid one guilder per month each.[12] Owning a domestic slave girl was a luxury the working-class Chinese sojourners simply could not afford.

Anecdotal evidence shows that Chinese men treated slave women as sex slaves. They profited from these women's sex work by leasing and subleasing them as chattel, or reselling them after a short period of ownership. A barber leased a slave girl for five guilders and two stivers a month before matching her with a buyer when the owner tried to raise the rent.[13] The presence of slave girls in their midst often triggered jealous brawls, molestation, or abduction. Tan Beng, a textile peddler, lured and harbored a slave girl belonging to another Chinese.[14] A conflict between two furniture makers—one accused the other of molesting his slave girl—almost escalated into a gang fight.[15] As the autobiographical narrative of the slave girl leased by the previously mentioned barber shows, slave women, even those who bore their male owners a child, were sometimes treated no differently than sex slaves:

> I was originally a slave of Tjao Tjoen Sie. I bore a daughter for him. When he was still alive, he pawned me to Nyai Kapitan Liem (Han Tan). After Tjao died, I was sold to several owners. After being sold to Jao Tong, he leased me to Lie Sie (the barber) for 50 guilders and 2 stivers per month. Later on, Jao Tong wanted to increase the rent. Lishi wouldn't lease me anymore. Jao Tong wanted me to save money to redeem my status. For this reason, I was trying to earn money everywhere. Later on, I was lucky to come across Joe Tjeng, who was willing to redeem me, hence he negotiated to buy me from Jao Tong.[16]

The insecurity and transactional nature of domestic slavery gave the women involved no reason to stay and remain loyal to their masters. Historian Eric Jones has shown that the runaway slave woman was a recurrent problem for city authorities in late eighteenth-century Batavia.[17] According to the slave testimony, Tjao leased his female slave for rental income even after she had born him a child. But she would face even more uncertainty after Tjao died and failed to emancipate her. Even in a case like Ong Hae's, in which he claimed to have lived with his Buginese former slave "as husband and wife for over twenty years," it is not hard to imagine why his former slave-concubine left under the "seduction" of another Chinese man: "Ong has leprosy, that's why I can't live with him. My ex-husband . . . has a Chinese son named Sam Hok, who asked me to live with Tjong, and I agreed."[18] While the men saw their partners' flight as an affront to their masculinity, the slaves themselves often revealed more grounded concerns about personal safety and longer-term economic security.

The fate of the nyai stood in sharp contrast to the average female domestic slave. In the Chinese records, "nyai" referred to the more senior indigenous women who acquired a degree of respectability through more enduring relationships with their partners. The Balinese etymology of the word suggests that many of the early wives of the foreign traders hailed from among the female slaves from the island adjacent to Java. In Balinese, "nyai" is the second-person pronoun for a woman of lower status.[19] In Java, it evolved to become "the honorable title of a respectable woman of age, [and] of equal standing with *kyai* for men."[20] The Chinese appropriation of the term was closer to its Javanese variant. Its phonetic transcription was conjugated by appending the character for elegance, 雅 (pronounced *ŋã* in Hokkien), with the female radical 女 to form 婔—a creole Chinese neologism. Younger slave-partners like Wati and Buloti, who were involved in the previously mentioned jealous brawl of the furniture makers, were referred to by their personal names.[21] As the young domestic slave matured to become the female head of her partner's household, people began to identify her formally as the nyai of her partner, such as in the cases of Nyai Tjia

Hoe or Nyai Gwat Sei.²² Interestingly, the colonial legal disabilities of slavery did not prevent a domestic slave from acquiring social esteem. Nyai Gicit was going to testify in the Chinese Council until she was informed that her status as slave disqualified her to stand as witness for a third party.²³

Almost all the nyai of Chinese men who turned up at the Chinese Council in the late eighteenth century were at least of middling standing in society. They were mostly widows who had inherited their husbands' businesses and assumed control of household finances. The most entrepreneurial of them was Nyai The Hwie, who continued to run an indigo dyeing shop with the help of a dyer and her son-in-law.²⁴ More frequently, the nyai operated retail shops (*warung*) in their street-fronting houses or stalls in the market, or followed up on debts and deliveries due to their deceased husbands' long-distance commodity trading arrangements.²⁵ At the very least, most of them inherited a house, a slave, or significant sums of money, which they then leased out or loaned to earn a rental or interest income.²⁶ Yet such wealth was often not enough to support a nyai for long. Two or three temporary marriages after emancipation would not have been rare, as Nyai Siri Gambir testified in 1825: "I was a slave of the Tjoa family. I followed Sim A Beng for five years, and had a son and a daughter. The son died, and I am left with my daughter Sim Bang Nio. . . . Then Sim A Beng died. Three years later, I followed Lie A Gan, he had two sons, one died, while the other is Lie Boen Seh. Gan died when Lie was 7. Two years later [1808], I followed the native Siri Gambir. It has been 17 years since."²⁷ After she was emancipated, Nyai Gambir "followed" (M: *ikut*) two Chinese men and had children with both before settling more permanently with a native husband. In this patriarchal framing of her life, Nyai Gambir made her marriages with men and the bearing of their children the key milestones of her familial life. Yet as further details from her case reveal, she in fact formed the matriarchal center around which children and grandchildren from her multiple marriages revolved.

A very small minority of slave girls were among those whose Chinese partners rose to the highest echelons of colonial society. While they would not have to endure the fate of being resold to multiple owner-partners, they were almost certain to suffer a decline in status at home through their partner's subsequent marriage(s) with other slaves or Chinese mestiza women. The case of the Dutch-appointed Lieutenant Ko Kimko's (C: Gao Genge) contested estate offers a rare glimpse at the status of the nyai vis-à-vis the Chinese mestizo wife. A native of Xiamen, Ko had most likely been plying the spice trade between the Banda islands, Batavia, and China before settling in the VOC capital in the 1750s or 1760s. Ko's testament mentioned eight women (see table 1.1). He left something for all the women who survived him, mentioning them according to the birth order of the children he had with them.

TABLE 1.1. Lieutenant Ko Kimko's testament (28 June 1787)

WIFE/CONCUBINE(ETHNICITY)	INHERITANCE	NAME OF CHILD (GENDER, MARITAL STATUS, YEAR OF BIRTH)	INHERITANCE
Unstated	NIL	Tjengnio (daughter, widowed, 1766)	2,500 guilders
Roget (Buginese, Pintu Barat, Batavia)	Lifelong rental for her house	Iknio (daughter, single, 1767)	7,500 guilders
Lie Innio (Chinese, predeceased)	NIL	Tiennio (daughter, single, 1769)	7,500 guilders
Tan Siemnio (Chinese, Patekoan, Batavia)	12,500 guilders	Pienio (daughter, single, 1772)	7,500 guilders
Kwie Swienio (Chinese, Glodok, Batavia)	To purchase the house belonging to Abu Bakar	Jongkiat (son, minor, 1775)	50,000 guilders
Name forgotten (Chinese)	NIL	Jonghwie (son, minor, 1780)	50,000 guilders
Tjoenbwey (Native)	Emancipated, 250 guilders	Jongtjwan (son, minor, 1781)	50,000 guilders
Mani (Native)	Emancipated, 250 guilders	Jongtiap (son, minor, 1784)	50,000 guilders
Tang-in (Native)	Emancipated, 250 guilders	NIL	
Oeij Tjinio (Chinese, Banda)	62.5 guilders	NIL	

Source: Chinese Council Minutes, 22 Nov. 1787.

This ordering suggests that Ko had two slave partners before he married Chinese women. Lie Innio was most likely a primary wife, who died young and whose role was replaced by Tan Siemnio. As matriarch of the family, Tan Siemnio was given the most money. She would be followed by three more Chinese and three indigenous concubines. We know that Ko's status in Batavian society was confirmed when the governor-general appointed him a Probate Council member in 1770 and then lieutenant of the Chinese in 1775—a position he held until his death in 1787.[28] His rise in status coincided with his marriages to Chinese women.

His testament shows that there was a clear status distinction among the primary Chinese wife, the Chinese concubines, and the senior and more junior nyai. The Chinese wife and concubine inherited property and significant sums. The nyai were simply emancipated and paid smaller but not insignificant sums of money. Two anomalies need further explanation. First, Oeij Tjinio, the Chinese wife from or still living in Banda, was given a pittance. But she knew her rights, and the case has survived in the archives because she sued the estate for more. Interestingly, Roget, as Ko's most senior surviving female partner in

Batavia, was treated better than the younger slave-concubines. She was supported for life in her rented house.

Given the Chinese preference for sons, those nyai who bore their partners male offspring would likely have been more secure in their old age. Chinese men made no distinction among their children in terms of ethnicity. Ko Kimko gave all his children Chinese names and treated them equally within their gender categories. Ko had most likely taken more wives and concubines to try for sons after Roget, Innio, and Siemnio gave him daughters. Sons received a lot more inheritance than daughters or their mothers. But as minors, they were all put under the charge of the primary Chinese wife, Tan Siemnio, who was delegated the authority and resources to raise them.

While the Kapitan's indigenous concubine had the securest of tenure, the middling trader's nyai probably had a more fulfilling life, for she remained the sole female head of the household and would have learned to co-manage with or even inherited some business from him. In a city dominated by transient men and a system of slavery, the odds were stacked against them in their search for security, personal well-being, and the warmth of familial life. To understand how the nyai exercised their agency within and against the creole Chinese patriarchy, let us first try to situate their predicament within the context of Java's patriarchal colonial and ethno-religious segregations.

Confucian Marriage and the Exclusion of Native Women

Since 1717, the VOC authorities had officially recognized Chinese customary marriage by ordering Chinese Kapitans to register them. The earliest records of Kapitan-registered marriages date to the 1770s. With the exception of the French and British interregnum (1800–16), Kapitan-certified Chinese marriages were registered continuously from the late eighteenth century until 1919, when marriage law reform placed registration under civil law and the authority of the European-staffed colonial bureaucracy. Not a single indigenous woman's name can be found on these Kapitan-certified marriage registers. Structured by the concept of patriliny in ancestral worship, only those who practiced the rituals *by descent* could contract marriages, usually for their children. Throughout the nineteenth century, the ethnic divide in families was experienced not so much as colonial racial prohibition but as patrimonial discrimination, reinforced with colonial legal sanction, against women without demonstrable descent from Chinese fathers.

The men who left China in the eighteenth century brought with them what historian Susan Mann has called a "new discourse on marriage, . . . part of the

Confucian revival ... that reached down through the ranks of the commoner classes and focused on the family."[29] In its bare outlines, as laid out in the *Book of Rites*, the Six Rites of marriage involved the groom's and the bride's families engaging a go-between as negotiator-cum-ritual-specialist to propose a match, verify the suitability of the couple's astrological birth dates, exchange gifts, and perform the ceremonies—including ancestral worship—involved in the groom's fetching of the bride.

The Dutch VOC authorities turned Chinese marriage into a legal-customary institution by requiring registration on the one hand and forbidding interreligious unions on the other. Since 1717, the company had stipulated that Chinese marriages had to be registered with the Chinese officers in order to be legal.[30] In the late 1750s, a secretary at the VOC's aldermen court compiled a nonbinding compendium of Chinese law by interviewing Oeij Tsi Lauw, the first and only secretary to be promoted to an officership in the history of Batavia's Chinese Council. Oeij was described by a contemporary as "truly having the style of a poet and a scholar, although he did not know how to manage the Company's affairs."[31] This sojourning member of the literati defined a "legal marriage" as one that went through Confucian rites: "That the young man, both wealthy and poor, puts up six visits to his prospective bride, and according to his ability, offering some gift, be it women's adornments or money, so that some necessities can be purchased; those six meetings are named 'Diokle' [C: Six rites]."[32] An examination of the registers of Batavia kept intermittently since 1772 show that both bride and groom had to bear Chinese names, have Chinese patrilineal ascendants, and have ceremonial go-betweens serve as witnesses to authenticate the customary marriage.[33] This ritual-legal setup was confirmed by the colonial state in an 1828 statute that made marriages valid only if they were registered by their respective ethnic chiefs and approved by the municipal Orphans and Probate Council.[34]

In 1766, the VOC instituted a "ban for Chinese and Muslim men and women to marry 'outside their nation.'"[35] The company had consulted the officers about interreligious marriages in China. The reply that it was punishable by death enabled the company to claim that its policy respected the Chinese regulation. This company-era ban on marriage between Chinese and Muslim subjects remained in force until it was superseded by the Mixed Marriages Law of 1898. This ritually inflected racial discrimination against indigenous women, as chapter 6 will show, would be fortified by modern notions of race and marriage in the twentieth century.

To what extent was the religiously couched interethnic marriage prohibition upheld by the community? Leonard Blussé has argued that the officers on the ground were flexible in their enforcement of the prohibition.[36] The evidence from before 1800 is thin, but representations from the Chinese merchant leaders suggest that a racial notion of Chinese patrilineal marriage had emerged to distinguish eligible Chinese from slave and indigenous women. In 1788, Tjoa Kiat Beng had tried to register a marriage with Rokit, a slave girl gifted to him by an Indo (Eurasian) Dutch man, by claiming that she was the daughter of a Chinese friend. Blussé uses this case to argue that the Chinese "bridegroom first had to manumit the desired bride free before she could be 'turned into a Chinese' by having her adopted into a Chinese family."[37] In fact, the protest note put up by the Chinese mercantile community leaders on this occasion was revealing. Forced by the company's aldermen court to register the marriage, the Chinese officers defended their long-standing role in enforcing a patriliny rule among applicants for marriage:

> Since time immemorial, as determined by our lords, all Chinese men and women who are marrying require the Chinese Kapitan to check on the family background of both parties. They may be issued the marriage certificate to become kin only when it has been verified that there was no rape, abduction or bigamy. There was never any mention of issuing certificates to people of other colors or slaves of various hues. Moreover, the Company had issued an order several years ago forbidding Native and Chinese from marrying.
>
> Because [Tjoa Kiat Beng] had a letter from Sinyo Gerritt, he wanted to use it to cut corners. We carefully perused our archives, found no such precedent from past Kapitans, and could not render our assistance, because we did not dare to make a unilateral judgement and break the state's laws.[38]

In the absence of women playing the role of the go-between, the men themselves became the ad hoc "ritual specialists" in negotiating and officiating over the Six Rites marriage. Historian Chen Menghong notes that "at the beginning of the nineteenth century, 15% of matchmakers were male but ... no male matchmakers could be found in the 1890s."[39] Further back in time, as many as half of the Chinese marriages registered in Batavia between 1772 and 1790 listed men as their matchmakers.[40] Given the fact that their names appeared no more than three or four times, they were perhaps more amateurs than specialists. The name Lo Hup was on record for successfully negotiating two matches in 1784 and 1790. By 1790, he must have been in his late forties or early fifties. In November, he was a witness for his own twenty-seven-year-old son's marriage, which had been arranged by another male matchmaker.[41] Testimonies given before the Chinese Council show that all parties, even the nyai mothers at times, were well acquainted with the Confucian marriage rituals. However, a third match Lo Hup tried to make in May that year failed. In this case, the frustrated groom claimed that he "had asked Lo Hup to be [his] go-between, to seek the hand of Nyai Han Kao's daughter. The nyai's approval was supposed to have been sealed with her return of a ring, but when [he] proceeded to present the ritual gifts for engagement [C: 訂盟禮儀], she would not accept them."[42] Knowledge about Confucian marriage rituals was being passed from male settlers to native and first-generation mestiza women.[43]

By the closing decades of the eighteenth century, creole Chinese women had learned enough about Confucian marriage rituals to begin to specialize as go-betweens. In contrast to men, Liem Hien Nio (ninety-two marriages) and Tan Kim Nio (forty-one marriages) alone arranged one-third of all female matchmaker-negotiated marriages between 1772 and 1790. At times, even nyai were entrusted to serve as go-betweens. In Jan Pit Kong's betrothal dispute with Tey Ling Soa, the former had arranged a marriage for his younger brother by "asking the go-between Nyai Lo Tin to propose to Tey's daughter. Tey agreed, and they became engaged after bridal gifts were paid."[44] By the 1820s and 1830s, creole Chinese women had almost fully taken over the ritual-laden business of matchmaking, negotiating 85 percent (2,482 out of 2,950) of all marriages.[45]

The Six Rites marriage had become a patriliny-perpetuating institution by no later than the 1850s. In defining what counted as marriage for the Chinese, the officers in Batavia allowed for simplified rituals but insisted on parents on both sides being ritually involved. In 1856, asked by the assistant resident of Banten to determine whether an unregistered couple could count as married, the Chinese Council replied:

> According to Chinese rules, both lineages need to uphold the Six Rites, with a marriage contract [C: *hunshu*] and list of gifts [C: *litie*]. All rich and official families do that. As for poor families, performing the engagement rites will do. [In such cases,] the husband's promise is the contract. Parents from both sides need to officiate at the ceremony, and it will only count after the engagement letters [C: *mengtie*] are exchanged. Batavia has had 150 years of marriage certification. That serves the same purpose as the marriage contract. The founding fathers were farsighted, knowing that we're shorthanded, and cannot fulfill all six rites, hence they used the certificate to replace the contract. We Chinese take the certificate more seriously. As for this particular couple, if they don't have one, they may be forgiven since they live in an isolated place. As long as their parents officiated, and engagement letters were exchanged and agreed on, that will count.[46]

What they implied but left unsaid was that only people who practiced those rituals could pair up their children in Chinese marriages.

By the mid-nineteenth century, not only had the Six Rites marriage become a communal expectation, but it also served as a status differentiator among the rich and the poor. This popularization of patrilineal Confucian ritual marriage must have further entrenched the status distinction between the men who ritually married Chinese women and those who cohabited with indigenous women. There was, however, one important way for indigenous women to exercise their historical agency in an ambiguous status within the creole Chinese family, despite their ritual exclusion from marriage: as mothers of children meant to be brought up Chinese.

Nyai as Mother: Reproducing and Resisting Chinese Patriarchy

Jean Gelman Taylor writes that "women could sometimes pass between ethnic communities, cross lines drawn by color and caste, and enter slots for which they had no birth right, depending on their alliances with men."[47] The nyai of Chinese men inhabited this liminal zone that connected the world of the indigenous kampongs (villages) with the bustling shophouse dwellings in the Chinese quarters of Java's colonial cities. In no other familial role was their liminality felt more palpably than as nyai-mothers of their own mestizo Chinese children. By colonial law, but more so by patriarchal Chinese customary preference, the nyai was expected to raise her children to belong to a patrilineal family and racial group in which she herself remained an outsider. It was in contestations with the nyai over the custody rights of mestizo sons that a religious discourse of patriliny began to map onto that of race and law.

The concept of Chinese patriliny has been used to explain the basic demographic patterns of creole Chinese settler family formation and population growth. As William Skinner notes, "Chinese immigrants who remained overseas formed alliances with either locally born mestizo or indigenous women, but in either case the offspring were absorbed by the intermediate [creole Chinese] community. Mestizo men who did not marry within their own community took indigenes as wives, and their children, too, were absorbed into mestizo society."[48] Although Skinner admits that there were "exceptions" to this rule, he attributes this "leakage" as being among those men who were "less successful, within the lower classes, and generally in rural as against urban families."[49] Skinner saw, admittedly for demographic analysis, the "absorption" or "leakage" of mestizo children as due purely to the socioeconomic success or failure of the Chinese father.

Cases from the Chinese Council archives both affirm and complicate Skinner's account of interracial "leakage." The patrilineal gender bias of the Chinese settlers was clear. After the father's death, Chinese relatives contested the nyai's custody rights of their mestizo children only when she tried to take minor-age sons, not daughters, back to her own indigenous family. In the first half of the nineteenth century, the Chinese Kapitans of Batavia consistently rejected the nyai's plea to take her mestizo sons and grandsons across racial borders. Such retention of males in the community was achieved, however, through a colonial mechanism of adjudication. Although only three cases can be found in the archives of the Chinese Council, a close reading of the process of legal settlement show a deepening awareness by all parties of the colonial state's religion-based interethnic divide.

The first point to note is the ethno-spatial structure of Dutch Chinese patriarchal authority. Chinese men, with the support of local Chinese officers in the colonial system of indirect rule, prevented nyai from removing mestizo sons and grandsons from the local community. While the nyai appealed to the Dutch assistant resident, on both occasions the latter most likely deferred to the authority of the Chinese Kapitans. Such disputes over custody tended to happen in cases where mestizo children's Chinese fathers had died. In mid-1834, Nyai Tang Kwie, who had come to Batavia from Lampung in South Sumatra to fetch her grandson from her widowed daughter, was stopped from doing so by the child's paternal uncle.[50] In May 1848, Emak Kwieswa, a Balinese former slave–widow, tried but failed to retrieve her eight-year-old son from Koo A-Sam, her husband's younger brother.[51] The third case demonstrated the same ethno-spatial pattern, except in reverse: a Chinese father removed his two mestizo sons from their mother, Nauru, to Semarang "to learn Chinese customs and manners."[52] Nauru, who, in her own words, had been "unofficially married" to Jo A-Go in Batavia for fifteen years, accepted significant compensation in exchange for giving up any further claim to her sons.[53]

The second point to note is that the Chinese contestants framed their claims in terms that demonstrated a religious understanding of racial boundaries. Nyai Tang's disputant was an elder patrilineal uncle of her grandson. He had alleged that the mother and grandmother were conspiring to take the boy to Lampung and have him converted to Islam. He pleaded for the return of his nephew so that "there will be an heir for worshipping my (deceased) cousin and the ascendants in his line."[54] Agreeing, the officers ordered the mother to "return [the son] to the Tjam family. Although your late husband is now in the netherworld, he remains dependent on the generations that follow." In their reply to the Dutch assistant resident, the Kapitans stressed that a son is needed to "carry on the line," without which the father's lineage "will be extinguished."[55] In the second case, Koo A-Sam framed his right to retain the custody of his nephew with the same discourse of lineage-derived culture: "The boy is the son of my elder brother. He is my lineage-nephew [C: 胞侄]. I should be the one to raise and educate him to be human [C: 教篤成人]. This Emak Kwieswa is a native woman. How would she know anything about Chinese customs and behavior?"[56]

The escalation of these three cases to the Dutch assistant resident should be read in the context of a broader range of lineage-based racial strategies Chinese men deployed to guard against the assimilation of their nyai-reared children. Higher mortality rates for men and the mobile nature of maritime trade easily left mestizo children under the custody of the nyai by default. Chinese fathers took precautions to prevent this from happening in their household arrangements and wills. There was a tendency for them to place their nyai and their children with their patrilineal kin prior to their departure. A small trader going away for weeks or months deposited his nyai and his children in the Chinese wife-headed household of the junk owner or with his patrilineal relatives.[57] A dying man, whose indigenous partner was still young and eligible for remarriage, transferred custody of his children, especially his sons, to a patrilineal kin or a close friend.[58] At divorce or separation, Chinese fathers often wanted all the children, or if they were selective, preferred sons over daughters. They had rights to all the children but would often pay or be asked to compensate their nyai.

Thus, Nyai were more likely to bring their Chinese mestizo daughters than their sons to their subsequent households. Even if they remarried indigenous men, it was not uncommon for nyai to arrange marriages with Chinese men for their mestiza daughters and granddaughters. The previously discussed case of Nyai Siri Gambir is revealing for how a matriarch could successively raise a multiracial household consisting of children and grandchildren from her partnership with two Chinese and an Indonesian.[59] Nyai Gambir lived in a house left by her second Chinese husband on the outskirts of Batavia, most likely near Pekojan, the Arab quarter. The house belonged by title to her son by the second Chinese partner. As the matriarch of the household, however, her children and grandchildren from her previous marriages continued to live with her and her indigenous husband Siri Gambir, from whom her appellation was then derived. Her complex familial background was recorded because of a dispute over her granddaughter's marriage. A daughter from the nyai's first Chinese partner married a Chinese man. This young couple left their daughter with the nyai, who raised her together with Gambir, presumably in a more indigenous setting. When the nyai tried to marry this granddaughter to another Chinese man, she rebelled and ran away.

A second dispute reveals how the Kapitans themselves acknowledged the porosity of racial-religious boundaries, especially when they were under pressure to do so by the Dutch authorities. In this case, the seeds of discord were sown by the Chinese father's decision to place his mestiza daughter, Tjoe Sie Tan, under the care of his nyai's sister, Bibi (Aunt) Kasih, while keeping the elder son with his own father.[60] Both parents died young. Bibi Kasih raised Sie Tan in an indigenous kampong, where she converted to Islam under the name Senen. The length of time she had spent in the kampong was disputed. The native side claimed to have had her for fourteen years; the Chinese side claimed it was only four. In 1849, when Senen turned sixteen, her elder brother brought her back to Batavia to arrange a Chinese marriage for her. At the Chinese Council, she was clear about her own sense of belonging: "I do not wish to follow my [Chinese] grandmother. . . . I wish to enter Islam. Moreover, I am engaged to a Muslim man. I wish to go back to the kampong, and assume my Muslim status. . . . I do not wish to be Chinese. I want to enter Islam, return to the kampong . . . and live with Bibi Kasih." The Chinese Council determined that "according to our Chinese customs, Tjoe Sie Tan, being a maiden, cannot decide by herself to enter Islam. Moreover, since her mother is dead, she should be under the custody of her elder brother." On this occasion, the Dutch assistant resident appeared to be sympathetic with Senen's plea. He wrote back to the Chinese Council to ask if a convert like Senen needed the "approval of one's relatives." More generally, "What customs and laws govern such a situation, and how does one actually follow through on them?" The officers softened their stance but cited laws that went back to the company era to justify their decision:

> We Chinese need to follow Chinese laws and customs. In China [it is more straightforward] because there is no other race [C: *ji* / 籍]. As for the various races in Batavia, we need to obey the power and decisions of the Resident, in order that people will follow their separate laws and customs. If someone wants to enter Islam without reporting, the person may do so as s/he pleases. If s/he wishes to seek permission, s/he should check with his/her parents, father's brothers, and brothers before proceeding. Even if s/he wanted to change his/her family name, that is possible. If we go by the governor's statute of 23 July 1766, it was specified there that following the [earlier] statute of 9 February 1717, we Chinese cannot enter Islam.[61]

It is not known how the resident eventually decided on the case. But the Chinese officers' equivocal reply reflected an admission that ultimately Chinese individuals might change their name and religion with their family's approval, and that the officers could do nothing to stop an individual from doing so if nobody reported on it.

An 1849 custody dispute between a young indigenous woman and her Chinese partner triggered a debate within the Dutch officialdom. In this case, Dutch officials and jurists began to raise doubt about the customary legal expertise of the Chinese officers.[62] Sena, a young native woman who had served as a housekeeper for a Chinese man for three years and bore a child for him, had been expelled for no apparent reason. Sena wanted to keep the child but had no independent means of livelihood. At the local Batavia police court chaired by the Dutch resident, the native prosecutor and Chinese officer each recommended custody for their own racial group. "According to true Chinese customs," said the unnamed Chinese officer, "the woman, although she brings the child to the world, exercises no authority over it, and is considered to be like a sack, whose contents belong to the person who fills it." The Dutch jurists publicized the case in *Het Regt van Nederlandsch-Indië* to show how the resident dismissed the Chinese patriarchal doctrine but awarded custody to the Chinese father by the pragmatic reasoning that his paternity had been proven and that the mother had no means to raise the child. For the editor of the recently inaugurated Dutch Indies law journal, the precedence of Chinese over native customs in this case was mistaken: "We believe, by conscience, that [Sena's] right . . . to further maintenance was surrendered, principally on the grounds of the consideration, that the aforementioned Chinese doctrines, are only considered to be in effect in this country, among the Chinese, but in no sense for Chinese living with Native, such as Sena, the Mohammadan religion avowing woman. This is so that The Atauw [the Chinese father], without her express permission, is not authorized to raise a child born by her or to withdraw her maternal care from said child."[63] In other words, Dutch colonial law should acknowledge both Chinese and native sources of law in conflicts that involved litigants of different religious backgrounds. A system that applied both sets of laws would have compelled The Atauw to maintain Sena and to let her keep her child.

The legal precedence of Chinese paternity for mixed families presented no easy legal solution for custody disputes between the nyai and her Chinese relatives. Some nyai, especially those who inherited from their Chinese husbands, tried to raise their children as Chinese. Mestiza daughters raised in an indigenous setting, however, were not themselves keen to return to Chinese society via marriage. Dutch officials and jurists encountering the problem anew in the 1840s had only scratched the surface when they believed a mixed jurisdiction might bring justice for indigenous women.

This chapter has reconstructed the historical agency of the nyai in the formative years of creole Chinese society on the northern coast of Java between the 1750s and the 1850s. It traces the nyai's origins to the system of slavery in island Southeast Asia. Slave women were expensive to acquire, and many were treated and leased as sex slaves by their owners. The nyai in this period were the fortunate minority of indigenous women who had enduring relationships with their Chinese partners. They acquired respectability from Chinese society for having brought up their mestizo children as Chinese, and from everyone else for their relative wealth (inherited or through their own entrepreneurial efforts). Yet the nyai remained throughout this period a liminal ethno-gendered figure. She was central to the creation and reproduction of creolized Chinese communities but remained structurally excluded from Confucian marriage. Her historical role was to raise the next generation of mestizo children as Chinese, who could then claim descent from their fathers for the purpose of customary marriage. Yet this did not always work out according to the patrilineal order of things. Mestiza daughters were more likely than sons to "return" to their mother's kin group. Gender-inflected racial/religious borders remained porous. It was toward the end of this period, around the 1850s, that fluid identities began to be more rigidly defined. Let us now turn to examine how such Chinese notions of patriliny, patriarchy, manhood, and womanhood were stabilized among the local-born creoles toward the middle of the nineteenth century.

2

BOURGEOIS MANHOOD AND RACIAL BOUNDARIES

Chapter 1 noted that Chinese marriage rites in colonial urban Java followed a Confucian pattern, whose patrilineal ideology gave it an exclusionary edge against the native partners of Chinese men. This chapter turns to look at manhood itself and, more specifically, how the rudimentary Confucian literacy (rather than learning) of upper-class business families shared, came to indirectly shape, and justified the class- and race-inflected gender and sexual norms of the entire community. It begins by demonstrating how basic Confucian and Chinese literacy was expected of boys and young men of middle and upper-class family backgrounds. There is no intrinsic theological connection, however, between book-based Confucian learning and the moral norms that shaped gender and sexuality expectations.[1] Rather, creolized Confucian masculine and sexual norms were morally determined in three mutually constitutive ways around the institution of marriage. First, it was through success in business that wealthy men and their cult of virility, as embodied in the polygynous ways of the male Kapitan elite, came to represent the peak of Chinese manhood. Second, the brideprice put Confucian marriage and a Chinese bride beyond the reach of the urban working class. Middle-class men came to value this marital premium through their sense of entitlement to a virgin bride. These patriarchal norms were not imposed without interethnic tensions. A final section demonstrates that middle-class Chinese men could often only keep their "Chinese" brides from running away—and crossing ethnic boundaries—by enlisting the moral policing aid of their Kapitan leaders.

Creolized Confucian Manhood: Wealth, Culture, Virility

Chinese officers, their sons, and new aspirants to their lucrative businesses and political status collectively embodied the ideal shape of manhood in creole society. As the expanding colonial bureaucracy absorbed many of their previous functions, the Chinese officers' role as advisers for Chinese customary law come to the fore. Although best known for their accumulation of extensive wealth, they were not completely uneducated community leaders. The standard of manhood for the creole Chinese of Java was determined in part by the upholding of Confucian-colonial family law and in part by the officers' conduct of their own sexual and marital lives.

The wealthier the creole Chinese family, the more likely was the son to be given some grounding in the Confucian classics. In contrast to their counterparts in late imperial China, learning was not so much valued for climbing the Confucian bureaucratic ladder as for business literacy and for the conduct of one's family. In Java, the basic written language for business among the creole Chinese traders was Chinese. Merchants needed basic literacy for bookkeeping, record-keeping in temples and native-place lodges, and communications with other Chinese merchants. For trade purposes, accounts were still mostly kept in Chinese for much of the nineteenth century.[2] The trend among creole elites was acculturation toward Malay and Dutch literacy.[3] But classical Chinese was still needed to groom men who aspired to be officers, for vetting contracts and minutes kept by their secretaries, clerks, and treasurers.

In his 1879 survey of classical Confucian schools in Batavia, the Dutch sinology–trained interpreter J. E. Albrecht found eleven sojourning tutors teaching in the city, each with fifteen to fifty male students, whose ages ranged from seven to nineteen years old.[4] Albrecht found that these full-time sojourning tutors taught the full classical curriculum—from reading, memorizing, and copying the entry level Four Books, to the more advanced Five Classics, and finally to literary composition. Of all the creole students of Confucian classics, only one Surabaya-born Chinese followed the literati career of their tutors.[5] Albrecht made a stinging criticism of Chinese classical education in Java when he compared their achievements with educational standards set in post-Enlightenment Europe and China's imperial examination-bound system:

> Among many here, the possession of some property by the parents contributes to the idea that serious study is unnecessary and useless. Many boys were placed in their fathers' business to work from a young age. In short, most of them leave the school very early. They have not

gained very much literary knowledge from there. They learned to read and write a little, but the majority, the chiefs not excepted, are nearly unable to read or write a simple letter, not to mention their total ignorance of the literature, the laws and institutions of the motherland. They even lack the competence to keep accounts; that is why traders running businesses of some scale hire from China their accountants, who also maintain their Chinese correspondence.[6]

Their inadequacies by Western standards notwithstanding, what was remarkable was the scale of creole Chinese boys' exposure to classical education. Across Java, there were 176 tutors teaching 3,211 students in the late 1880s, and 250 tutors with more than 5,000 students in the 1890s.[7] At its peak in the 1890s, the numbers equaled the enrollment in Dutch-language ethnic Chinese schools in its first decade (1908–17) of establishment. I estimate that perhaps one in every seven local-born Chinese boys in Java had some encounter with classical Chinese education at the end of the nineteenth century.[8] There was enough popular demand such that imported classics were "always available in the tokos [M: shops] selling Chinese commodities."[9]

Such exposure laid the basis for Confucian patriarchal ritual order among creolized Chinese men. The boys not only memorized the classics but were trained to address a fellow Chinese in writing for business and major life-cycle events. One heavily used collection of model letters from the Go lineage of classical tutors in Surabaya included templates for proposing marriage for a son, rejecting a marriage proposal, asking a friend to edit a poem, requesting a go-between to propose a wedding date, asking for a debt-repayment extension, composing a congratulatory note for a father's birthday, convening a business meeting with a friend, and inviting a friend to go overseas for business.[10] Business, literature, learning, and practicing kinship were part of the same ritual order of affairs run by men. Albrecht himself admitted that "the lesson to love one's parents, and to show them respect, was not in vain" among these boys.[11]

The officer elite had high expectations in the upbringing of sons of good and wealthy familial background. A basic Confucian orientation was requisite. In 1869, a dispute in Batavia over the legal guardianship of Ong Pit Tjek, a third-generation heir of the deceased lieutenant Ong Boen Hien, attests to some of the difficulties mentioned by Albrecht in sustaining knowledge and interest about the classics. Ong Pit Tjek's elder brother sued their paternal uncle for failing in his "duties in education and guardianship." The young man had grown up "knowing neither Chinese nor Dutch characters even at the age of sixteen. He knew neither manners nor righteousness [C: *Liyi*], moreover he took opium, gambled, and was addicted to cockfighting."[12] If "even the poor wished to educate and guide their sons and nephews as they grew," the elder brother complained, "what more Ong Pit Tjek, who had inherited his father's wealthy estate." In the record of his interrogation before the Batavia Kapitans, Ong Pit Tjek's upbringing was tested against a Confucian standard, up to which he clearly failed to measure. The Kapitans noted their questions for him and recorded his replies:

> ONG PIT TJEK: I received seven years of education, from age seven to thirteen. Four teachers taught me. I began with the *Analects*, followed by the *Mencius*, and the four volumes of *Poems of a Thousand Authors*.
>
> THE KAPITANS NOTED: We asked him to dictate what he's learnt, but he could only barely manage the first three lines of the first chapter of *Analects*. When he got to *Mencius*, it only got worse. As for the *Poems*, he could only recite one. When he was asked to write his own name, he wrote them with the strokes in the inverse order. We asked what he did after school ended, if he took opium or engaged in cockfighting.
>
> ONG PIT TJEK: After stopping school, I reared chickens and ducks, watched opera, and fooled around. But I did not take opium. Cockfighting wise, I set my roosters to fight among themselves, but never set them against others.
>
> THE KAPITANS NOTED: We asked for how long had he learnt Dutch.
>
> ONG PIT TJEK: Three to four days.
>
> THE KAPITANS NOTED: When asked to write, he could not make out a word.[13]

Young men did not choose their own brides. Among the Cabang Atas (highest branch) of creole Chinese society, marriages were occasions for forming alliances among the wealthy and political families of the localities. James Rush has shown how business partnerships among the Chinese were cemented by marriage alliances. In Semarang, Major Tan Hong Yan, a third-generation creole, married his daughter to the son of his opium *kongsi* (company) partner Be Ing Tjioe. Both the elder and younger Be would succeed Tan Hong Yan as Chinese major of Semarang in the 1850s and 1860s.[14] Using genealogical sources, Steve Haryono has meticulously reconstructed the complex multigenerational marriage links among the families of nineteenth-century Chinese officers. Between three and six wealthy families monopolized the revenue-farming operations and officerships and, by extension, oversaw the patriarchal moral order of each major city. All were connected through marriage within the same region.[15]

Wealth did not immediately qualify a young heir to marry a daughter of the circle of elite families. Batavia's most famous philanderer, Oey Tambah, was one example. The younger son of a wealthy Chinese immigrant, Oey Tambah had not had a match made for him before his parents died young. Despite his wealth, his philandering disqualified him as a potential candidate for the daughters of the big officer families in town. He eventually settled for Nyonya Siem Hong Nio—the creole daughter of a bankrupted small trader.[16] At the same time, Oey Tambah's reprisal against Major Tan Eng Goan was indicative of how conspicuous display of wealth through the Six Rites ceremonies had become closely interlinked to status differentiation among the Chinese. "No other wedding was as celebrated with such crowds" as Oey Tambah's monthlong wedding, which was said to have cost 35,000 guilders to stage and triggered consternation in Major Tan.[17]

Outside the super-wealthy elite, close to three-quarters of the Chinese population made up urban Java's middle class. In the 1875 colonial annual report, the 302 village chiefs, 18,721 small traders, 962 small industrial entrepreneurs, 2,976 revenue farmers and small contractors, 206 chiefs of agricultural enterprises, 410 employees of agricultural enterprises, 3,657 craftsmen, 28 shipbuilders, 408 shippers, 207 fishermen, and 344 cattle breeders were all part of this newly emerging urban bourgeoisie.[18] These men distinguished themselves from the working class by their possession of enough capital to own a stall, a small shop, a fishing boat, a small farm, or a skill that gave them a measure of economic independence, if not security. They were also economically in demand. Although Chinese immigration was officially banned between 1837 and 1866, the Dutch made special exemptions to admit craftsmen as early as 1844.[19] Below them, working-class men floated among public works, peddling, domestic service, and working the farms of landowners: 7,903 daily-wage workers, 3,467 agricultural workers, 270 house servants, and 720 working for other companies.[20]

A groom and his parents made it to middle-class respectability if the groom could afford to marry a Chinese woman by the Six Rites. From the 1820s to 1860s, the average groom or his family had to set aside between 100 and 200 guilders in bridal gift expenses for a customary marriage.[21] This sum paid for the matchmaking proposal fees, the engagement rings, and the final package of gifts at the wedding—a pair of candles, pig's trotters, shoes, socks, and clothing for the wedding.[22] Bourgeois men outside the elite had to work to save for their own marriage and consequently had more freedom in choosing their bride. The owner of a blacksmith shop, Oei Sin Ing, promised 200 guilders worth of gifts to the mother of his bride.[23] Ho A Moa paid 50 guilders for his proposal but had his engagement dissolved when the bride's stepfather could not agree to the "poor man's" plans for a "hasty and simple wedding." "There should be a maiden for you," the Kapitans consoled him, "if you can afford 50 guilders for your marriage fees."[24] These ritual gifts essentially priced a Chinese customary marriage beyond the means of the working class—a quarter of the economically active Chinese men—and probably the lower end of the middle class as well.[25]

The colonial Chinese marriage tax reflected this distinction of ceremonially derived status. To obtain a marriage certificate, a couple had to register with the Chinese Council before applying to the colonial Probate Court and paying a tax. The sons of Chinese officers paid 40 guilders, a rich Chinese 20, and all other Chinese 5. The super-wealthy would not have flinched at a tax between 80 and 100 guilders for an elaborate bridal convoy.[26] The urban middle class would have been happy to apply for the 5 guilders marriage license.

Akin to aristocratic manhood in Java, to be an elite Chinese man was to show off one's virility in the form of the big family he kept and maintained. Creole men acculturated the Chinese form of polygyny to Javanese conditions. The primary and secondary wives were called *bini kahwin* (married wife) and *bini muda* (younger wife), respectively, while only women of Chinese descent qualified for either role. Heather Sutherland writes that "almost all nineteenth century [Javanese aristocratic] Regents were polygamous."[27] In this regard, the practice of polygyny by Chinese officers, whose positions were of a semi-hereditary nature, was not unlike that of their Javanese counterparts. Their social power, however, was founded more on wealth than on the feudal right to extract corvée (unpaid labor). Daughters of poorer Chinese and indigenous families were thus more likely to be bought or acquired through their parents' indebtedness than through tribute by lower-ranked aristocrats. It may not be unreasonable to assume that until young men began to receive Dutch education in the 1890s, men of wealth, including those of officer lineages, were generally polygynous.

The precise extent of elite polygyny is hard to estimate.[28] Anecdotally, the wealthiest or highest-ranked Chinese officers flaunted their entourage of wives and train of descendants. Major Tan Eng Goan, head of the Chinese of Batavia from 1837 to 1865, had four wives registered (see figure 2.1).[29] In 1853, a complaint for abuse of authority was lodged against the fifty-three-year-old Tan for "trying by all means to obtain the daughter of a certain Liem Sok Gie as concubine."[30] Lieutenant Tjoa Sien Hie of Surabaya (in office 1869–84) left behind thirteen sons and twelve daughters when he passed away in 1904.[31] In a later period, the Chinese major of Batavia, Lie Tjoe Hong (in office 1872–96), had four wives and two concubines who produced for him fifteen children.[32] When Major Oei Tiong Ham of Semarang—Java's "Sugar King" and wealthiest Chinese—died in 1924, he was on record for having eight wives (who bore him twenty-six children) and eighteen other acknowledged concubines.[33]

The only time the colonial state counted polygamous relationships was in the census of 1920—a year after polygamy was legally abolished for the Chinese of Java. Remarkably, although the indigenous population was surveyed separately from the "Foreign Orientals," of whom the majority were Chinese (alongside a significant minority of Arabs), the rate of polygyny was consistent among all

FIGURE 2.1. Portrait of Tan Eng Goan, Major of the Chinese of Batavia (in office: 1837–65).

Source: Kong Koan Collection, Leiden University.

Asian groups: about 15 per 1,000 married men had more than one wife. And for every 15 polygynous men in this group, 14 of them had only two wives. Only 20 out of 87,441 married Chinese or Arab men had four or more wives, according to the 1920 official count.[34] These figures almost certainly underestimated the rate of polygyny among the Chinese, but they nevertheless put in perspective how the superrich and highly ranked could and did indulge in the practice.

Dutch influence did, however, begin to change the attitudes of some Chinese men. The contrast between the writer Lie Kim Hok and his father is instructive. The younger Lie's view on marriage represented the Dutch-educated baba's ideal of familial life in the latter half of the nineteenth century. According to Lie's biographer, the father, Lie Hian Tjouw—a second- or third-generation Chinese of Bogor—was "fluent in Sundanese, good in conversation and refined in manners, so that he had many friends from various strata of society."[35] Although not of elite officer standing, the elder Lie—who sold paint from a European-style shop, held a license to run a pawnshop in Bogor, and had ten children by two consecutive wives—was certainly richer than most in the urban middling class. Born in 1853, Lie Kim Hok was the eldest child by the second wife. The younger Lie "received teachings from his father, who practiced traditional Chinese culture." He had three years (1866–69) of rote-learning Chinese classical instruction before spending the next fourteen years learning from and teaching alongside Dutch Christian missionaries. Although he never picked up the ability to read Chinese, he "realized later in life that the lessons obtained in those three years gave him something of value."[36] In 1876, having had seven years of Dutch education and having read many Western novels, Lie was "worried" that his parents' choice of a girl would not be the "good nyonya of the household and thoughtful wife" he had begun to imagine.[37]

His worries proved unfounded. The sixteen-year-old bride Oey Pek Nio, alias Roti, gave him "a peaceful life, whether he was resting at home or being busy learning and teaching in school, and doing work." The happy marriage ended after five years in 1881, when Oey Pek Nio died while giving birth to their second child.[38] Lie did not remarry until ten years later. For several years, he continued to write poems in Dutch to his wife.[39] In 1889, he published the *syair* (poem) *Orang Prampoewan* (*Women*), the only known creole Chinese literary depiction of the inner dimensions of husband-wife relations within a traditional arranged marriage.[40] Following are excerpts showing how the ideal baba of the late nineteenth century conceived of his relationship with the nyonya:

> **(On status)**
> Let us be frank,
> Women and men are of equal rank:
> If a woman "owns the capital city,"
> Then a man must "own the crown property."
>
> **(On attraction and love)**
> And what more you. Lady! The female race;
> Your demeanor so full of grace.
> It arouses feelings of confusion.
> Your manners so refined, it demands love and veneration.

(On companionship)
A man's best friend in this life,
Is none other than his very own wife.
Love well, and hide nothing from each other,
When one errs, the other forgives.

(On fidelity)
Because loyalty will surely till death hold,
Wherever goes the husband, the wife will follow;

(On filial piety)
His parents are not her parents,
Yet to them she shows deference;
When these parents from this world depart,
With him she grieves from her heart.

(On child-bearing and parenting)
When the wife is pregnant with child,
The husband too carries in him the child;

. . . .
If it is a good child who does no evil,
in it together the husband and wife revel,
If it is a child who does godless deeds,
together will their hearts bleed.[41]

Some basic Confucian learning and literacy in the Chinese language was requisite for young men who aspired to a career in business and perhaps even being appointed an officer by the Dutch. Although only a small proportion of Chinese men had the means to take additional concubines, it was commonly practiced among the wealthiest. A proper ritual marriage was something only the urban middle class could easily afford. With the bride-price came physical and moral expectations of women, expressed both in money terms and in the language of shame.

Pricing Chastity, Secluding Chinese Women

Historian Myra Sidharta writes, "Until the 1920s, a girl who had reached adolescence had to go into confinement."[42] Yet when and how such an attitude became normalized has remained unclear. I trace this shift in the patriarchal regulation of young women's sexuality to the mid-century rise of an urban male bourgeoisie and their attachment of middling status to ritual marriage. The high prices paid for a ritual marriage turned women's virginity into something that both men *and women* thought could be bought, bargained for, and rejected upon examination on the wedding night. Thereafter, a longer period of *pingitan*—the seclusion of post-puberty young women—became an ethno-gender norm that distinguished the Chinese from their urban indigenous peers. This shift took place sometime between the 1830s and 1860s. We catch a glimpse of such changing attitudes to sexuality when the occasional dispute over the bride's virginity made its way into the purview of the Batavia Chinese officers' moral jurisdiction.

Rising bride-prices amid competition for a Chinese bride delayed the age of first marriage among men and women. The bride-price barrier explains Batavia Chinese men's relatively late marriage age—between twenty-five and twenty-six in the latter half of the nineteenth century.[43] For men saving to marry a Chinese nyonya, cohabitation with native women became a temporary and pragmatic alternative. As late as the early 1950s, the anthropologist Leslie Palmier observed in urban Central Java that it was a "custom for Chinese young men to take mistresses from among the village women during their bachelorhood—and after."[44] Hildred Geertz's anthropological study of gender and kinship in a market town in East Java shows that Javanese girls were married off as soon as they received their first menstruation (between the ages of twelve and fifteen).[45] Early marriage combined with a high rate of divorce and the generally permissive attitude among the urban poor toward women's cohabitation with wealthier foreign men created the social conditions for a racially skewed marriage market in Java.

In contrast, pingitan lasted an average of five to seven years for Chinese girls in Java. Chen Menghong's study of the Batavia Chinese marriage registry shows that on average, Chinese women married between the ages of eighteen and nineteen in every decade in the nineteenth century.[46] One mid-twentieth-century ethnographer of urban Java remarked that "great emphasis [was placed] on the chastity and fidelity of Chinese women."[47] For the middle-class urban Chinese in Java, the practice of pingitan set them apart from "the acceptance the Javanese gave to women of twenty-two or twenty-three living with their fourth or fifth husband."[48]

This racial divide between women and class divide between Chinese men was expressed in the language of shame against those men who could not afford the bride-price to marry virgin brides and those women who could not keep themselves or their daughters chaste. As young men delayed their marriage (but not their sexual careers) and girls were shielded from potential male lovers, the bride-price that stood between them came to be regarded as the price to be paid for the Chinese bride's virginity. Women internalized the creole Chinese patriarchy's virginity complex. It might have been uttered in a moment of exasperation, but Jo Ping Nio, in her divorce plea filed in 1856, conceived of her matrimonial property as something she earned with her chaste body:

> Tan Oei: I can grant her wish to divorce, but my wife took my golden buckle, a pair of earrings, a hairpin, six Dutch-style chairs, a cupboard, and a bed. She should return them.
>
> Jo Ping Nio: Besides the pair of earrings, I never took anything else. The other things, he willingly gave to me. If he wants them back, what about my virginity? Who will compensate me for that?[49]

Yet until the 1860s, mestiza Chinese girls were occasionally caught evading pingitan to go out with their male lovers. Close reading of four cases that have survived from the 1830s to the 1860s suggests that pingitan was not restrictive enough in everyday urban life to prevent the girls from encountering and becoming attached to male strangers. Although the girls later accused their lovers of abduction and rape, in all four cases, the girls themselves had fled home on their own initiative. The fourteen-year-old Tan O Nio, alias Nyaha, often visited a particularly efficacious shophouse shrine in the city to make offerings. It was there that she met a Chinese man who "teased me, and asked me to go live with him."[50] Pang Fo Nio, also fourteen, left home for a Dutchman's household, led by the latter's native servant.[51] Nineteen-year-old Go Tjoe Nio packed her things and left home with Rarona, her native servant.[52] Another nineteen-year-old, Tio Teng Nio, reported, "I used to be neighbors with Kong Seng Goan. He always teased and joked with me, so I had a liking for him. He asked me to wait for him to set up a household. On the evening of the 18th, he really came for me, so I went and we've had a temporary union."[53]

While the Kapitans sought pragmatic solutions in the interests of the affected nyonya, the parents' reactions varied, ranging from simply seeking the return of the daughter (Tan O Nio) to refraining from further complaints in shame (Pang Fo Nio) to seeking punishment for "rape" (Go Tjoe Nio), to acquiescing to a makeup marriage (Tio Teng Nio). Only where there was a clear case of swindling (Tan O Nio) did the Kapitans recommend criminal penalties for the male lover. Otherwise, the tendency was to counsel marriage between the lovers and leave the final decision to the nyonya's parents. Even in the case of Go Tjoe Nio's relationship with her native servant, the Kapitans had initially suggested marriage, only settling for a harsher penalty when her father insisted on it.[54] In Tio Teng Nio's case, her lover was repentant and offered to atone for their wrongs with a full ritual marriage: "I did rent a carriage to take her to my house. As for our temporary union, she was a willing party. I plead guilty. Please be lenient. I'm willing to pay the bride price of 100 guilders, apply for a certificate, do the necessary rites, and live together with her to old age."[55] In acquitting Tio Teng Nio and her lover, the Kapitans explained to the Dutch resident how for the Chinese, ultimate authority lay with the parents and not with state law: "In Chinese marriages, one always follows the wishes of the parents. Digging tunnels and scaling walls to go on dates in the dark cause shame to one's parents. Such acts should be reprimanded. But since Kong is thirty-nine and has no family, Teng Nio is eighteen and is unmarried, and since their secret dating is also due to the parents' lack of supervision, and [the father] has now agreed, they can be forgiven. The law need not be applied here."

A moralistic insistence on chastity consolidated in the latter half of the nineteenth century. All five cases of Chinese men challenging their nyonya bride's virginity in public occurred in 1848 or later.[56] The virginity test—the staining of a white cloth on the bridal bed—became common enough for matchmakers to bother to invent forgery procedures.[57] Husbands probed into their newlywed wives' sexual pasts on the bridal bed. The language used to challenge or defend the nyonya's chastity points to the entrenchment of a patriarchal virginity complex, which was not present in public discourses about Chinese matrimony in the earlier decades. Particularly tragic were the fate of nyonya brides who had suffered rape earlier in life.[58] The discovery by one husband of such an occurrence prompted him to call her an "inferior quality good" in the Chinese Council. Tan Ho Nio's guilt-ridden confession shows how far that complex had entrenched itself among the women themselves: "I've been orphaned since young, and had to depend on and live with a female cousin. I was raped by her husband and lost my chastity. I know I'm inferior to others. I bear shame beyond expression. If my husband wants to divorce me, I dare not defy him."[59]

For the increasing numbers of socially mobile male Chinese settlers in Java, going through a Confucian marriage came to be associated with middle-class respectability over the course of the nineteenth century. While they could not afford the great fanfare with which the wealthy elites married their sons and daughters, it did set them apart from the working class—a full one-quarter of the male Chinese population who were priced out of the ability to secure Six Rites marriage. For the urban middle-class men, marriage itself was just the beginning of a lifetime of struggle to keep household fortunes afloat and the wife homebound.

Indigenous Men and the Runaway Chinese Bride

The average Chinese household lived in a shophouse in the Chinese quarter, or Pecinan—a regular fixture in every colonial town across Java. Middle-class Chinese built their homes within a physical and moral space that was racially segregated by colonial legality. Until it was abolished in 1916, people of the three official racial groupings—European, Foreign Oriental, and Native—were required by law to reside within their designated quarters and carry a passport whenever they traveled elsewhere. Before the 1850s, it was not uncommon for Chinese women to run away to their lovers in the native kampong. As heads of households and communities, Chinese husbands, fathers, and patriarchal officers tried to stop this. These mid-century moral exhortations worked in tandem with the colonial-imposed ethnic segregationist policies to encircle mestiza Chinese women and keep them within their town's Chinese quarter.

The hard colonial boundaries were meant to keep social change among the natives to a bare minimum and to prevent the emergence of intermarriage among the political elite. As one colonial scholar explained, exposure to Chinese traders brought more Javanese into the commercial sector: "The more developed (Natives) imitate him (the Chinese).... The native peddlers and craftsmen overprice excessively to a large degree." Intermarriage created a new creole elite, which threatened the commercial interests of the Dutch: "The higher natives bind themselves with the rich Chinese through marriage. A number of native chiefs are kin, and also descendants, of Chinese."[60] In 1835, the first pass and quarters system (D: *passen- en wijkenstelsel*) law alluded to rising trends of intermarriage and assimilation of foreign Asians, including the Chinese, with the Javanese as the main rationale for separate residential quarters: "To the local authorities in Java is declared, that here and there the tendency has been observed, that Foreign Orientals such as Malays, Buginese, Chinese, and so forth, are amalgamating among the Javanese population; that the Government considers this to be inappropriate and on the contrary wishes, that the ancient customs [D: *aloude gewoonten*] of these foreigners be maintained in separate quarters and neighborhoods, and (for them) to live under a Chief of their own national character [D: *landaard*]."[61]

By 1871, there were a total of 174 officially designated Chinese quarters across Java. Their locations were an indication of the pattern of Chinese mercantile penetration into the Java's hinterland. In the northern coastal residencies stretching across Cheribon, Tegal, Pekalongan, Semarang, Japara, and Rembang in West-Central Java, there were often Chinese quarters down to the district level. These residencies had an average of 13.8 quarters as compared to 5.4 in the rest of West and East Java, where the quarters usually did not spread beyond the regency capitals. The state's segregationist tendencies were, however, constantly undermined by its own economic imperatives. Residents often cited "the interest of agriculture and industry" to grant new settlements "Foreign Orientals quarters" status.[62] In 1893, a survey of the pass-and-quarter system found almost one-third of the Chinese in Java and Madura living outside the designated Chinese quarters (see table 2.1). The spillage across borders suggests that the segregation of residential spaces might not always be effective. But it also reveals that the colonial state's surveillance ambitions and its attempts to return people to their rightful spaces and categories were real. To police the border crossing of Chinese women, the state also had to rely on its Chinese intermediaries.

It was not an easy task. In physical terms, it was not always possible to tell an indigenous person from a creole Chinese. The distinctions were even more subtle among women. Unlike the baba who kept the queue and wore the skullcap, Chinese mestiza women shared the same dress code (*kebaya* or *kurung* blouse and sarong bottom) as all local-born women.[63] Mestiza daughters were also more likely than sons to be raised by the native side of the family. As the custody disputes in chapter 1 show, daughters raised by nyai mothers did not always accept arranged marriages with Chinese men.

The matrimonial disputes adjudicated at the Chinese Council of Batavia show that between the 1780s and 1850s, young Chinese women were, with the exception of one decade, more likely to form extramarital ties with native men than with the Chinese, Dutch, or Europeans (see table 2.2). In this period, the most frequent form of illicit interethnic affair was a Chinese woman's elopement with an indigenous man:

The higher rate of illicit relations with indigenous men reflected the social proximity shared between young Chinese women and native men in everyday life encounters in the city. By the 1820s, the Chinese had a certain notion of how a nyonya should comport herself, but as I argued in the previous section, many nyonya raised in mixed families very likely fell short of these new standards of

TABLE 2.1. Pattern of Chinese residence in Java and Madura according to the Fokkens Report (1894)

	NUMBER OF CHINESE
Inside 218 Chinese quarters in Java	174,980
Outside Chinese quarters without permission	6,551
Outside Chinese quarters with permission	13,376
Outside Chinese quarters by way of settlement before 1866	50,978 (33,092 on private feudal lands, of which 25,478 are in Tangerang)
Total	245,885

Source: "Het onderzoek naar de economische toestand der Vreemde Oosterlingen op Java en Madoera" [Research on the economic situation of the Foreign Orientals on Java and Madura] (more popularly known as "Rapport Fokkens"), chap. 2, 276–78, inv. 5037, MR 17 July 1896, no. 27, AMK, NA.

TABLE 2.2. Ethnicity of male lovers of eloped Chinese women tried before Batavia Chinese Council by ethnicity

	NATIVE	CHINESE	DUTCH/EUROPEAN
1788–90	7	5	1
1824–27	6	3	1
1832–34	1	7	1
1843–49	7	3	3
1850–59	5	2	1

Source: Compiled from Chinese Council Minutes, 1788–1859.

Chinese womanhood. The case of Ko Tan's runaway nyonya brings some of the contradictory social-familial pressures into sharp relief. When Ko Tan's wife, Siauw Joe Nio, appeared before the Chinese Council, the officers were shocked that she "came in Native dress, and had not half an iota of a Chinese woman's ways."[64] Siauw Joe Nio had run away and married a native, but in Ko's divorce plea, he "ask[ed] that as a woman, she continue to look after the children." The officers, however, intervened. Pointing out that "Joe Nio had changed her morals to belong to the Natives," the officers asked if "Ko Tan could raise the children himself." The council minutes do not record Ko's answer, but men like Ko, who was most likely a recent arrival or a poor settler, were clearly not as invested as the wealthy officers in raising their children as Chinese.

When put to trial, the nyonya often claimed that they were seduced or drugged into fleeing their marriages. Liem Djan Nio claimed that the "native [man] fed her coffee, which made her so confused that she fled with him."[65] Historian Eric Jones has argued that early modern Batavia as a "big city with its transient and teeming population provided the requisite anonymity for a *slavin* [slave girl] to slip away, pose as free," at the same time as it "left underclass women vulnerable to abduction and abuse from predators."[66] Likewise, the wives who ran away from their Chinese husbands were equally vulnerable to the temptations and dangers of Batavia.

Some of these indigenous men in the city or suburban kampongs simply offered a more stable and better life as compared to the runaway women's poorer and often abusive Chinese husbands. Kong Hie Nio allegedly began an affair with a native man when her husband was so poor he could not afford orange peel to boil for her when she was ill.[67] Thee Hie Nio was married for fifteen years but had been subjected to "frequent beatings and scolding," especially when her Chinese husband lost money at the gambling den. When she finally pleaded for divorce, her husband revealed that "she was already living with a native."⁶⁸ Oei Kiauw Nio's husband had been imprisoned for four years. During that time, she took her children and "eloped" with a Chinese man for a year before settling down with and bearing more children for her indigenous male lover.⁶⁹

The transactional nature of Chinese marriages, especially when they were hastily arranged, gave women a greater impetus to seize hold of their fates (and some property) when better opportunities became available. In 1790, the morals of Lie Jan Nio—who had been previously "abducted" by a Dutch pig slaughterer—were so much in suspect that the Chinese officer ordered her brother-in-law and guardian to "quickly find a partner for her to prevent a recurrence of the same event."⁷⁰ She was married to a Chinese man, but within three months, Lie "was seduced into elopement with a Native florist, and took money and property with her." The fact that eloping women had money and property to steal from their households shows that they were not escaping poverty or hardship. Liem Djan Nio, who had claimed she had her coffee drugged, allegedly carried away 100 guilders when she fled.⁷¹

Oei Hau Nio's elopement with the merchant Noorudin in 1846 reveals how such interethnic relationships were viewed from the indigenous side of officially endorsed racial endogamy. Like the abovementioned cases, Oei Hau Nio had been pushed to the brink of escape from Chinese society by a bad marriage and unsupportive parents.⁷² At that point, she met Noorudin, who agreed to take her as his second wife. Noorudin's later testimony suggests that he was aware of the prohibition but thought consent from the Chinese father and native official authorities would have legitimized their marriage:

> I live at Cikau. I have a wife and children. I am a trader. I came on boat with my father to Krawang to trade with Oei Hien. That was how I got to know Hau Nio. Hau Nio told me she's not been paid for eight months, she's divorced. She loves me, wants to go home with me, and be a married couple. At first I didn't take it seriously. The second time she wanted to follow me, I reported to my father, and my father asked Oei Hien [her father], who agreed. On the second day, at 6.30 in the morning, Hau Nio came down to my boat, and went off with me. We slept in the boat for a night, and arrived the next day at dusk in Cikau. I thought Hau Nio belonged to the Chinese people, so I was worried there might be problems. I prepared the horse saddle, and wanted to go to Ulu Kacau to report to the Jaksa, but the Pangeran arrived at that moment to take Hau Nio back. I was thinking, why take her from me when her father had given his permission? So I brought Hau Nio to see the Jaksa. My father Jasiba Bajaludin can serve as witness.⁷³

Often, the upbringing of Indonesian mothers or guardians shielded their mestiza daughters from prejudices the Chinese harbored toward native society. The externally imposed colonial-Chinese endogamy made little sense to these young women. This becomes clear in the rare cases when their own voices were recorded in the trials. In 1847, when Lau Jie Nio's proposed remarriage with a Muslim neighbor in Kampong Canton was opposed by her father, she gave the following testimony to the Chinese Council: "I love very much the 'Selam' [Islam] man Kayu, who lives in the same kampong. My father refused to let me become a Muslim to marry Kayu, but previously I've been married to a Chinese, then to a Dutch. Moreover my mother is a Muslim, named Sayulao. From this, I think this has nothing to do with my father, and I am brave enough to make my own decision."[74] Here, Lau Jie Nio was citing the Chinese rule that granted remarrying women the freedom to decide their own match. But as we will see, the officers did not agree with her.

For the wealthier Chinese, the presence of younger native male servants (M: *bujang*) in the same household sometimes formed a real or imagined threat to the integrity of the Chinese patriarchal families. Although there was no concrete evidence, Ko Giok Nio's husband beat her up for "visiting a bujang's house alone" and "lending him money."[75] In another case, Go Oen had evicted his native coolie, Rarona, for a suspected affair with his wife. To avenge the perceived injustice, Rarona ran away with his daughter.[76] The Chinese widow, especially if she inherited property, was guarded by her children and her husband's family against such relationships. An adult son could challenge the widow-mother's leadership of the household if she did not keep chaste, especially if the romance crossed ethno-religious boundaries. In April 1845, Tan O Ha went to the Dutch resident to sue his mother for "betraying her race by cohabiting with a Native [C: 背籍從番] even before our father's dead body had turned cold."[77] Tsu Moi Nio had inherited the estate and was raising the children alone. After the father's death, the male servant Ribu took his place by opening a coffee shop (*warung*) in her inherited house. The conflict between the stepfather and the mestizo children was economic, but its escalation took a religious form. "Upon seeing that we prayed with pork," Tan O Ha testified, "Ribu threw it on the ground, scolded us, and strangled me." Ribu countered that Tan O Ha sold pork in the house, and it contravened a taboo not so much of his own but of his native customers. The Kapitans advised the resident that "since Moi Nio had acknowledged her affair, the four children should be given to [their patrilineal cousin] to be raised in case she entered Islam."[78]

In the closing decades of the eighteenth century, creole Chinese women became the target of punishment and correction. "There was nothing more damaging to morals," proclaimed the Kapitans, than Chinese women's elopement with native men. Occasionally, Chinese adulterers were let off the hook, but never their female Chinese and male Indonesian counterparts.[79] With the approval of the Dutch magistrate, the Kapitans called for a gathering of officers in the Chinese kampong at Angke for Lim Jan Nio "to be caned in the streets as a warning to the public."[80] Liem Djan Nio, on the other hand, was caned in the Kong Koan and allowed to reconcile with her husband.[81] Chinese men also had the right on the occasion of divorce to forbid their wives from remarrying native men. Loa Kah Nio had to promise to "[re]marry a Chinese, [and] if not, if [she] married a native, to be punished" as her ex-husband had demanded.[82] It is not clear whether such promises were enforceable, but the Dutch authorities were notified of them.[83] In the nineteenth century, such endogamous vows would disappear from the Kong Koan trials.

In the nineteenth century, Chinese officers' recommendations for punishing both Chinese women and native men under the rubric of "Chinese law and customs" were heard by the Dutch resident but were not always legally binding. Interethnic extramarital affairs were tried as adultery cases at the *landraad* (D: native court), where they were presided over by the Dutch resident, with the legal advice of the native prosecutor, the penghulu (M: Islamic official), and, when Chinese parties were involved, the local Chinese officers to determine the appropriate verdict and punishment. Until the passing of the Native Criminal Code in 1872, verdicts and penalties were decided by the majority vote among the legal advisers.[84]

The officers recommended harsher penalties for the native *bujang* for transgressing both their servile and lower racial status. For Rarona, who flirted with his Chinese master's wife and fled with his daughter, the officers recommended "doubl[e] the penalty when a servant wrongs his master." The Chinese girl's punishment was "for not awaiting the wishes of her parents." Although rape victims were given the choice to marry the rapist, this option was not granted in interethnic relationships, since "it w[ould] cause sexual chaos, and be a major blow to Chinese customs and rules."[85] More commonly, they recommended the age-old punishment for all Chinese adulterers: public caning and parade in the kampong.[86] For Oei Hau Nio and Noorudin, the same publicly administered punishment came with the additional "warning to others, to prevent the Chinese and natives from mixing."[87] These official condemnations of interracial unions percolated into the public consciousness. Oei Hau Nio's uncle, Oei Hien, who was likely culpable of condoning if not profiting from her elopement, became a racial endogamist during the trial, perhaps to compensate for his own involvement in the affair: "What [Noorudin] said are lies! Don't listen to him. I'm ashamed to see my niece Hau Nio become a native woman! If she's divorced from her husband, I beg that she stays in Batavia, and not be allowed to go back to Krawang, to avoid more trouble. If she stays in Batavia, I'll ask the widow Nyonya Lie Kiamto [to] live with her, and pay enough for her upkeep."[88]

Women who were divorced or widows were spared the whip, but they were expressly forbidden from remarrying Indonesian men. By Chinese custom, the divorced woman was free to choose her second husband, but in the context of colonial Batavia, the officers made sure that these women could only remarry Chinese. These claims to women's morality were framed in the interests of the ancestral cult or, more simply, in the name of "Chinese customs." For Lauw Djienio, whose father had arranged another Chinese match for her, changing her family name, changing her racial status (C: 籍), and entering Islam would "tarnish the ancestors' name." In pleading against her wishes, the officers begged the resident to let "Chinese and native follow their own ways, in order to prevent the confusion of registration statuses, and damaging the customs."[89] This patrilineal and endogamous discourse was not the preserve of the officer elite. As the affair of Tsu Moi Nio and Ribu shows, sons, brothers-in-law, and ward masters would accuse their mothers, sisters-in-law, and neighbors of "losing their virtues," "entering Islam," and, by implication, forgoing their custody and inheritance rights when they had relationships with Indonesian men.[90] Even if the husband was willing to give up early childhood custody rights, as in the case of Ko Tan, remarrying an Indonesian man "changed [the mother's] morals," and thus disqualified her for the seven years of child-rearing a Chinese mother normally performed even after divorce.[91]

The Chinese officers' enforcement of the colonial prohibition against interreligious marriage reveals the patriarchal basis of emerging racial boundaries on Java. Until the mid-nineteenth century, as the runaway Chinese brides demonstrate, the ethno-religious boundaries, especially those among women in Java, were still relatively porous. The need to enforce racial and religious difference among their womenfolk was not limited to the elite officers; the average Chinese denizen of Batavia made similar claims.

Creole Chinese manhood in the middle to latter half of the nineteenth century was formulated around a Confucian patriarchal morality that accorded wealthier men more sexual privilege. At its heart, this gendered privilege was expressed through men's expectation of a virgin bride if they could afford Confucian marriages, whereas there was no reciprocal restraint on men's sexual ventures either before or after marriage. The not uncommon phenomenon of the runaway Chinese bride or bride-to-be, coupled with the fact that they often ran across ethnic boundaries, reveals the social and ethnic tensions that the creole Chinese patriarchy-in-formation faced in keeping women in their gendered and racialized place. A theme that connects this chapter with chapter 1 is the fact that the patriarchy was not formed without resistance from women. An even bigger compromise that the Chinese patriarchy had to make was on the issue of divorce. The prevalence of women appearing before the Kapitans to plea for divorce, not to mention their relatively high success rate, speaks volumes about the moral agency of women in Java's patriarchal Chinese society.

Part 2
DIVORCE, WEALTH, AND CHINESE WOMANHOOD

Part 2 shifts the analytical focus from Chinese men and their native concubines to creole Chinese womanhood in their capacity as wives, matriarchs, and widows in Dutch colonial society. The period from the 1850s to the 1890s saw creolized notions of Chinese womanhood emerge in contention with two forms of patriarchy. Chapter 3 looks at middle-class married women's assumptions and expectations about marriage through the customary legal institution of Kapitan-patriarchy adjudicated divorce. Chapter 4 locates the strategic wealth transmission interests of creole Chinese matriarchs within the uterine family group—sister-brother siblings and their children—a form of feminine action that confounded Dutch colonial jurisprudential assumptions about Chinese patriliny.

3

DIVORCE AND WOMEN'S AGENCY

In this chapter, I turn to the moral and emotional to examine how creole Chinese wives radically reconstructed the Confucian notion of womanhood by seizing on divorce—a customary institution widely recognized and practiced by Southeast Asian women and men—to admonish their husbands, reassert their status, and break free from oppressive marriages if need be. Minutes from divorce trials at the Chinese Council of Batavia show that the overwhelming majority of petitioners were women. The five most commonly asserted complaints, by order of frequency, were desertion, abuse, jealousy, eviction, and tensions with in-laws (predominantly mothers-in-law). Based on my study of all 738 divorce trials from the 1830s to the 1890s, I begin by showing that creole Chinese customary divorce procedures were largely improvised from local Muslim legal practices.[1] The rest of the chapter analyzes two particular types of pleas: desertion and jealousy (against another woman). In both, women were able to discursively bargain for their personal autonomy by staging claims about their husband's moral duty as breadwinner and emotional obligation as exclusive lover.

Wife-Initiated Creole Confucian Divorces: Procedure and Patterns

The relative ease with which a creole Chinese woman in Java could dissolve her marriage in the nineteenth century would have shocked any contemporary visitor from China or Europe. There is no comparative study of the dissolution of marriages for the Chinese overseas prior to the twentieth century.[2] Within Java, there was a long tradition among Muslims of women-initiated divorce under Islamic law. The actual procedures and relatively high rate of women-initiated applications suggest a creolized Muslim Confucian communal pattern of divorce.

There is no record of how the institution of divorce first came about among the Chinese of Batavia (or elsewhere in Java). Divorce applications and trials became a routine event in the minutes of the Chinese Council of Batavia in the 1830s and 1840s. As mentioned in chapters 1 and 2, it was easier for women than men to cross ethno-religious boundaries in urban colonial Java. It is hence conceivable that creole Chinese women carried with them assumptions about marriage and divorce closer to those of the local majority Muslim population than to some of the newly arrived Chinese men or their male descendants. In imperial China since the first millennium, husbands could end marriages for the seven conditions that had been prescribed in ritual manuals during the classical era and written into successive dynastic law codes: disobedience to a husband's parents, barrenness, adultery, jealousy, incurable disease, loquacity, and theft. There were no legal grounds for wives to file for divorce.[3] Conjugal conflicts were primarily mediated by the patrilineal authorities of the husband's and wife's respective families. All parties aimed for reconciliation rather than litigation. Only in the final resort, usually when wives had been beaten to death or had committed suicide in protest, did the patrimonial state's magistrate intervene to impose penalties prescribed by the dynastic law code.[4]

In contrast, Islamic law, as practiced in Java and across island Southeast Asia, had clear institutional procedures for women to end their marriages. Aside from the well-known male-pronounced *talak* procedure, in which the husband simply announces that he rejects his wife, the law provides two routes for Muslim women to initiate divorce—either through the exercise of escape clauses attached by the bride's parents to the marriage contract, known as the *taklik*, or by compensating the husband a pre-agreed on sum, known as the *khula*.[5] Stamford Raffles, in his encyclopedic *History of Java* (1817), was referring to the *khula* option when he noted that "in no part of the world are divorces more frequent than on Java; for besides the facilities afforded by the Mahometan ordinances, a woman may at any time, when dissatisfied with her husband, demand a dissolution of the marriage contract, by paying him a sum established by custom."[6] He was describing the terms of the *taklik* when he observed the bride's father announce to the groom at the marriage ceremony before the penghulu, or mosque administrator, "If you should happen to be absent from her for the space of seven months on shore, or one year at sea, without giving her any subsistence, . . . your marriage shall be dissolved, if your wife requires it, without any further form or process."[7]

Unlike elsewhere in the Muslim world, women in Southeast Asia made ample use of these legal facilities to end unrewarding or unhappy marriages. As Nurfadzilah Yahaya shows, Arab male settler elites in Singapore successfully petitioned the British colonial government for a centralized marriage registry in 1880, claiming that the local "*qadi* [judges] were granting many divorces to women too easily."[8] In describing the role of the penghulu in Java in the 1930s, G. F. Pijper, a Dutch colonial native affairs adviser, ranked the duties of the state-salaried religious "priest" under the religious courts as (1) registering marriages and adjudicating women's divorce applications, (2) interpreting Islamic law, (3) administering mosques, and (4) leading religious festivals.[9] Pijper described a Batavia woman's divorce application process that, from the woman's point of view and with a few procedural differences, sounded similar to that of creole Chinese women. In this case, Sofijah brought her marriage certificate and two neighbors as witnesses with her to court—that is, to the penghulu's house—and sued for divorce, claiming that her husband had not given her household allowance (M: *belanja*) for a year and a half. Sofijah turned down an offer by the penghulu to negotiate for a settlement (D: *accord*, M: *akur*) or to hold out for reconciliation (M: *rujuk*). The penghulu noted in turn that the man's desertion had exceeded the duration (of six months) stipulated in the *taklik*. After the witnesses and Sofijah swore oaths to declare the verity of their claims, the penghulu granted her plea by issuing her a certificate of divorce.[10]

The divorce procedure for Chinese women in nineteenth-century urban Java was more cumbersome but not much different in essence. Any applicant for divorce, male or female, had to make a preliminary report with the two officers on daily duty. At this pretrial meeting, which both parties attended, the officers would try to achieve some form of settlement or reconciliation between the estranged spouses. Only if reconciliation failed would a date be scheduled for trial at the official twice-weekly Chinese council meetings. One important concession to the defendants, usually men, was that they had to be present for the trial to proceed. Only after repeated absences would the trial proceed in their absence. As far as the records go, no oath was sworn by the litigants and their witnesses. A photo taken of the interior of the Chinese Council in Batavia in 1930 shows a setup similar to how the colonial native court (*landraad*) was set up (see figure 3.1). When divorce trials were held there between 1816 and 1919, the plaintiff and the defendant would have faced a panel of assembled Chinese officers seated in the row of chairs.[11] When the officers granted the divorce, the marriage certificate of the couple would be torn on the spot, and both parties would leave their signatures or a mark on the divorce registry. The wife did not have to pay the husband a compensation fee, but a divorce judgment from the officers was not final if either party did not agree to it. In those instances, the case would

FIGURE 3.1. Photo of the interior of the Chinese Council of Batavia, 1930.
Source: Kong Koan Collection, Leiden University.

then be submitted to the Dutch assistant resident. Dutch residents were more likely to side with women's appeals against the Kapitans' reconciliation orders than with men's appeals against divorce judgments. For the most part, however, the officers' decisions were accepted by all parties.

Tjeng Tjoe Nio's attempt to divorce her husband, Lauw Boen Tek, in 1874 illustrates how she had to navigate a few more hurdles than Sofijah to break free from her unhappy marriage. In her pretrial meeting, Tjeng Tjoe Nio filed the following complaint with Kapitan Ni Boentjiang and Lieutenant Lie Tjoetjiang: "My husband has been away from home for the past 6 to 7 years. He married a concubine, ignored me and did not provide half a cent for me. He sometimes comes home for less than a month and then he will be gone again. I have tolerated all this up to now. I have been dependent on my father. Recently my son fell ill. I got someone to inform him but he did not care. Conscience [C: 良] has never been more lacking in humanity than this. I plead to be divorced."[12] At the pretrial, her husband denied the allegations: "What my wife said is false. Had I not provided for her, how would she have survived to this day? It is all because Mother-in-law does not like the sight of me. She always only has angry words for me, [because] she is not happy that I have married into and live in her household. I have now rented a house, and wish to invite my wife to live there with me. I will take care of her. I do not wish to divorce."

When Kapitan Ni and Lieutenant Lie tried to persuade Tjeng Tjoe Nio into returning to her husband, she steadfastly refused. She denied having been paid "half a cent for many years." She also could not trust that he had rented a house, since he was unemployed. When the Chinese Council, presided over by Major Tan Tjoentiat, held the official divorce trial on 2 July 1874, they sided with Lauw Boen Tek and asked Tjeng Tjoe Nio to go back to her husband. Three months later, on 1 October, she was back at the Chinese Council for a third time. She had not gone back to her husband as counseled by the Kapitans, but neither had Lauw Boen Tek resumed paying the allowances she was due. The officers faulted him on this point: "If you have any feelings for your wife, you should know to provide for her yourself. Why do you need to wait to be asked? Since you don't have an income, why take another wife?" They proceeded to investigate his financial situation by summoning his employer, a medicine hall owner, who contradicted his testimony when it was revealed that he had "no fixed salary." Still, Lauw Boen Tek would not agree to grant his wife the divorce. Tjeng Tjoe Nio made one last impassioned plea to the Chinese officers:

> My husband has been away from home and has not been able to forgo [C: 留戀] his concubine over the last six to seven years. Although he sometimes comes to see me out of kindness, he behaves like a guest in the inn. He stays and leaves in a few days. There has been no news from him since the second lunar month. I am not making a false report. All my neighbors know this. I can tolerate it if he lives outside [with his concubine] but pays for my maintenance. I can bear with it [if] we were short on clothing or meals, so long as he did not marry another wife, and so long as we depended on each other. Yet he is not up to either. He left me with no choice but to come time and again before the public [C: 屢踵公門], regardless of all the shame that comes with it. I plead for a fair judgment.[13]

This time around, the Chinese Council sided with Tjeng Tjoe Nio. But as her husband still refused to sign the divorce papers, the council had to submit the case to the Dutch assistant resident of Batavia for resolution. Two weeks later, the assistant resident replied that the Chinese Council's decision was to be followed.[14] The divorce was granted and deemed legal.

Beyond the procedural similarities, it was the rate of divorce, the high frequency of female plaintiffs, and the reasons they cited that made this a creolized Muslim Confucian pattern. Besides anecdotal nineteenth-century observations about the ease of divorce for Muslim women, Muslim marriage registries from the region in the 1920s through the 1960s recorded crude divorce rates (total number of divorces over marriages in a single year) of between 15 and 60 percent, usually nearer the higher end of the range.[15] Creole Chinese divorce rates in Batavia were lower: they were under 1 percent at the restart of colonial rule in the 1820s, peaked at just over 10 percent in the 1860s, then declined to about 3 percent in the 1890s (see figure 3.2).[16] This translates, by a conservative estimate, to 6.5 divorces per 1,000 married creole Chinese couples in the 1850s, and 4.1 in the 1860s.[17] The comparable figures were 0.0092 (1857) and 0.02 (1909) in England, 0.47 (1887) and 0.86 (1909) in the United States, and 1 (1930s) in Shanghai.[18] In other words, although somewhat lower than their indigenous counterparts, creole Chinese divorce rates were much higher when compared to western European and twentieth-century urban-mainland Chinese norms.

For most of the nineteenth century, the proportion of Chinese divorce applicants who were female ranged from 60 to 80 percent (see figure 3.3). Although tried under the colonial rubric of Chinese law, this pattern and the pragmatic way the creole Chinese officers granted divorce judgments point to a Confucian marriage system that was hybridized by the practice of Islamic marriage law in general and Javanese Muslim gender norms in particular. The Chinese officers ultimately granted 84 percent of all women-initiated divorce pleas across the nineteenth century.[19] Since the council minutes only put on record those pleas that proceeded to trial (those for which pretrial reconciliation attempts had

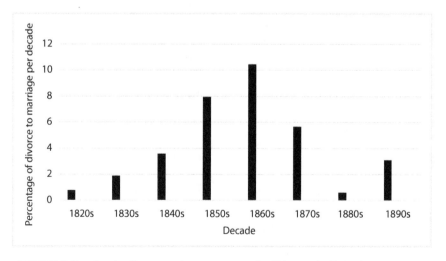

FIGURE 3.2. Crude divorce rate among creole Chinese in Batavia, 1820s–1890s.

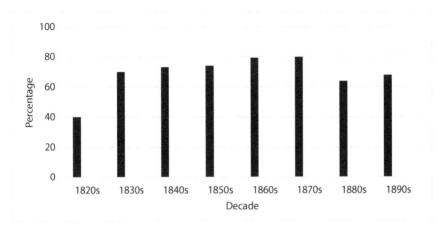

FIGURE 3.3. Proportion of divorce proceedings initiated by women, 1820s–1890s.

failed), it is possible—and the relatively lower crude divorce rate among the Chinese does support this likelihood—that the actual success rate was lower. But given how tenacious and resigned most of these women sounded in their pleas, and how there was a public shame element associated with heading to the Chinese Council to complain about one's husband, I suspect that the actual success rate for obtaining a divorce was not much lower. The commensurate figures are not available for nineteenth- and twentieth-century Muslim divorces, but as previously stated, contemporary observers found the ease of divorce for women remarkable.

The five most commonly cited reasons by creole Chinese women for divorce were desertion, abuse, jealousy (of concubine), eviction from the matrimonial house, and conflict with the mother-in-law (see figure 3.4). Women cited their husband's desertion in approximately six to eight out of every ten divorce pleas across the century. This pattern is consistent with the presumably high rates of *taklik* divorces among local women. On closer examination, however, desertion was sometimes a consequence rather than a cause of the breakdown of conjugal relations. In Tjeng Tjoe Nio's case, for example, it was her husband's preference for the concubine that led to her being neglected. Yet even if such cases were subtracted from the total desertion tally, cases citing desertion as the sole reason for divorce remain one of the big three categories, alongside abuse and concubine jealousy.

The rest of the chapter examines more closely how creole Chinese women framed their divorce pleas as moral statements about their failed marriages. Wife

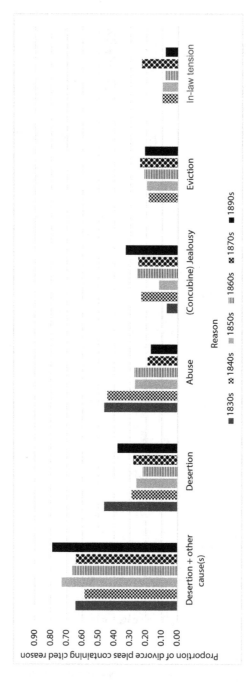

FIGURE 3.4. Trends in cited reasons for divorce in wife-initiated proceedings.

abuse was unfortunately a universal facet of patriarchy. Tellingly, the nineteenth-century European codification of cruelty as a cause for the dissolution of marriage was adopted and put to ample use by modernizing societies in Asia.[20] I chose the equally universal "desertion" and distinctively local "concubine jealousy" cases for further study. The former gave me an insight into how women articulated their moral sense of entitlement to material support from their husbands, the latter into the emotional content of their conjugal relationship. Hildred Geertz argued that the higher rate of women-initiated divorces was the result of not only Islamic law-related practices but the "matrifocal" kinship organization among the Javanese. To be "matrifocal mean[t] that the persons of greatest influence [we]re women, and that the relationships of greatest solidarity [we]re those between women, or those between persons linked by a woman." Because the "woman ha[d] more authority, influence and responsibility than her husband, and at the same time receive[d] more affection and loyalty," she was also more likely to initiate divorce proceedings.[21] A closer look at their divorce pleas reveals similar patterns of material support from the natal families and, more importantly, a jealous safeguarding of their conjugal love relationship.

Desertion and Women's Conception of Spousal Dependence

No marriage is a material transaction between two people or two kin groups. Yet when Chinese men in Java failed to provide for the household, the way women articulated the material debt they were owed made it sound as if it were just that. Although the Chinese in Batavia remained a mobile settlers' community, the failure of long-distance diasporic and extra-local marriages formed a surprisingly small proportion of desertion cases. It was not so much long-distance travel as poverty that led Chinese men to desert their wives. At its base, Chinese women expected three things from their husbands: rental for a roof over their household, a healthy work ethic, and an allowance stemming not from obligation but love. Since women mostly kept their own property separate from the household's, and since some men in fact resided with the wife's family, husbands who infringed on their wives' property received an extra moral rebuke.

To begin with, men who returned to China formed a surprisingly small proportion of husbands sued by their wives for desertion. One-third of Chinese marriages in Batavia were, after all, between newcomer grooms and local-born brides.[22] Only 7 out of 135 desertion cases across the decades involved sojourners forsaking their creole wives. As I indicated in chapter 2, the less well-off newcomers either cohabited with slave girls or were priced out of the Confucian marriage market. Still, even for those *sinkeh* sojourners who had "made it" in Java, there was no guarantee that their fortunes would continue to prosper. All seven returnee-desertion cases involved men who could no longer afford to support their Batavia-based wives.[23] These men typically disappeared for two to four years when they went back to their home village and families in China.

Because the husbands had to be present at the trial, women could not and probably also did not want to begin divorce proceedings until sometime after their return to Java. Creole Chinese women often waited to see if their sojourner husbands' desertion intent was final before they applied for divorce. In the fifth lunar month of 1845, Tan Tjai "returned the marriage license" to his Batavia wife of two years, Oei Boen Nio, before going back to China. But Oei Boen Nio did not give up. She waited, and indeed, he returned two years later. Yet, in her own words, not only did "he not come back to take care of me, but he did not even ask of me. How can one be unfeeling to this degree?"[24] In February 1868, Tjam Seng Nio waited four years for the return of her sojourner husband of twenty-six years, Koo Kiem Seng. When he finally returned to Batavia, she waited another two months, until it became clear that she "was not going to be paid, and that he was leaving for China again." Tjam Seng Nio had always known that her husband had "wife and children in China," but now it seemed to hold more sway, as Koo Kiem Seng himself confessed, "It is not clear if I will be coming back."[25]

In Java's urban money economy, it was not always easy for working-class men to support a Chinese wife in an autonomous household. Fragmentary data from the divorce trials show that Chinese working as coolies in this period were earning roughly the same daily wage as their counterparts in the Public Works Department, who were paid between one-third and one-half of a guilder a day, or roughly ten to twenty guilders a month, in the Batavia and West Java region.[26] One of the most frequent complaints by deserted wives, besides their loss of money allowances, was their husbands' inability or unwillingness to rent a separate space for the household. The rental for a room (presumably in a shophouse) or a house in an urban village (kampong), which cost about five guilders a month, would have taken up half or one-quarter of a coolie's monthly wage.[27]

Ong Tjeng Nio felt humiliated when her husband, who could not afford to rent a separate house, lodged the family with a friend. "If a husband can afford to marry," claimed Ong Tjeng Nio in her plea, "there should at least be an attap house for the wife, even if it is not a majestic house. How could he house his wife with someone else? I am so ashamed."[28] The Han Nio's plea was a typical list of material consequences women experienced when their men failed them: "My husband is an idler, he doesn't try to do any business, pay for the family, or rent a room, so that I've had to go back to live in my mother's house. This marriage will have no good ending, please grant me a divorce."[29] In granting a woman her divorce plea, the officers often noted that her "husband cannot afford to set up his own household, or rent a separate space[;] a husband should not be like this."[30]

Desertion by working-class men often began from their need to travel and reside in another part of the city or beyond as part of their seasonal wage-paying work. Batavia Chinese women disdained to follow their husbands to live in the "countryside" (C: 山顶, literally "mountaintop"). An administrator for a temple at Tanjong Kait (Tangerang) and a worker on a pig farm in Krawang offered to take their Batavia wives with them to their workplace, but they were refused.[31] Even within the city, where employers often provided lodging within the work premises, husbands who "want[ed] to live together with [their] wife in the towkay's [boss's] house" were turned down.[32] The long distance, their low wages, and the expenses of maintaining a household in the city created tremendous financial and emotional stress for the average family. Women whose husbands stopped sending them money had to vacate their rooms or houses and move back in with their parents. (Note, however, that despite the patrilineal Confucian rites, a significant minority of Chinese marriages were, from the beginning, uxorilocal, meaning that the groom lived with the bride's family.)

Where desertion was the only complaint, the Kapitans occasionally deemed the poorer men "too poor to take care of [their] wi[ves]" while approving the application on the spot.[33] Generally, though, the Kapitans tried to delay the wives' divorce pleas by ordering the husbands to pay their wives. The officers ordered working-class men to pay 2.5 to 6 guilders, or about a quarter to half of their monthly wages, and more well-off men, usually traders, to pay 8 to 15 guilders to placate their forsaken wives.[34] Aware of working men's limitations, the officers counseled women to accept these payments while awaiting the day their husbands could afford to pay rent again. In the case of the temple administrator, who "only earned 130 guilders a year managing the accounts of the Tanjong Kait temple," they wondered aloud "how [his wife] could follow him." Still, they turned down the woman's divorce plea and ordered the husband to pay his wife 5.5 guilders a month and her to reside with her father until such time as her husband could afford to rent a place.[35] More often than not, the wives would return a few months later to complain about noncompliance, and the Kapitans would then approve their pleas.[36] In 1849, Tan Tie Nio complained that her "husband had agreed before the Kapitans in June that he would pay me 3 guilders a week, but it has been seven weeks and I have not received a single stuiver." When she finally went to trial in October, the officers freed her from her marriage.[37]

These patriarchal bureaucratic hurdles prevented creole Chinese women from obtaining their divorces earlier than the women themselves wished. Deserted women waited an average of twenty-five months before they filed successfully for divorce.[38] The actual numbers ranged from a few days to twelve years of desertion at both extremes. The median figure, perhaps a better indicator, was a twelve-month wait. In contrast to the contemporary Javanese Muslim custom of divorce by default after six to seven months of desertion, it appears at first sight that creole Chinese women waited longer to file for divorce by desertion. In fact, it was likely the Kapitans who delayed the process and, for better or worse, saved an unknown number of marriages.

Yet for the most part, the Kapitans were pragmatic in their judgments. Nearly nine out of ten women (86.7 percent, or 111 out of 128 cases) who cited desertion as the main reason for their divorce application won their plea. The financially sunken husbands who resisted their wives' pleas did so to little avail when they could not back up their counterpleas with proven sources of income. Their testimonies reveal the frustration of the patriarchal male ego at its moment of reckoning with the material basis of colonial Confucian family formations. In January 1851, Oei Kong Hor, who had lost everything and had not paid his wife of five years in about a year, sought, in his own defense, to disconnect wealth from his moral standing as a husband: "I am a coolie for someone else, but I have never done anything wrong. I refuse to divorce. I am now staying with my father's younger brother. Please ask my wife to return with me."[39] Neither the Kapitans, who granted the divorce, nor the assistant resident, who overturned Oei Kong Hor's objections, agreed with him. In March 1864, the wife of Liem Tjong Jam, who had not held any job for a year, accused him of taking her jewelry and sarongs to pawn. Liem insisted that he "had not done anything wrong" and refused to end the marriage.[40] The officers chastised him for "knowing no sense of shame" before granting his wife her divorce plea.[41] For the most part, impoverished husbands were resigned to their wives' determination to divorce. By the 1890s, husbands had internalized the inferior status of hired workers. The admission that one was not only poor but "hired to work for others" (C: 为人傭工) became a standard refrain in husbands' acceptance of their wives' divorce pleas.[42]

In front of the community's patriarchs, women were just slightly more likely to speak of their husbands' desertion as a plain matter of fact than as a moral failure. Desertion itself was sufficient cause for divorce. Many who had waited for twelve months or more no longer saw the need to embellish their pleas with moral criticism. Take the case of Tan Djie Nio, a twenty-seven-year-old who had been married for nine years. In October 1856, she made the following report: "On May 17th, the Kapitan of the Gonggoan ordered me to return to Husband, with 8 guilders of maintenance. He agreed at the time, but he has only given 5 guilders and only once. He hasn't paid me a cent for five months, and he hasn't come home. I have no one to depend on. Please grant me a divorce."[43] Likewise, Liem Yam Nio, who was nineteen and had been married for a year, made the following plea in October 1869: "I fell ill since the third lunar month, but he never got anyone to treat me. I had to go back to my mother's house. For seven months, he never asked me to return, nor paid me. Please grant me a divorce."[44] Others framed their pleas with moral commentary, judgments, and accusations against their men's dereliction of husbandly duty. From these women's point of view, men's faults can roughly be categorized, by ascending order of seriousness, as follows: (1) moral failure to be a dependable husband; (2) lack of work ethic, often associated with a vice; (3) misappropriation of the wife's personal property; and (4) infringement of prior household arrangements (in the case of an uxorilocal situation).

Predictably, the most basic moral charge was to accuse men of failing in their duty to provide for the household and care for their wives (26 out of 59 cases). In these women's pleas, we hear what the majority of deserted wives must have thought and felt but, for one reason or other, refrained from articulating before the officers. In 1846, one Tjoe Ban Nio asked rhetorically in her plea, "What am I as a woman to do? Who should I depend on?" Another deserted woman, her namesake, likewise asked, "What can I as a woman survive on?"[45] Jap Sieuw Nio complained in 1891, "I have no one to depend on."[46] Lo Tie Nio exceeded the patriarchal submission expected of women in Confucian society when she said "women treat their husbands like Heaven [C: 天] and rely on them to stay alive. How can I live on without being paid?"[47]

Yet women expected to be provided for not only out of moral duty but also out of conjugal empathy and love. Others described their deserter-husbands as lacking in "feeling" (C: *qing*, 情), "conjugal feeling" (C: 夫妻之情), or "conscience" (C: 良). In June 1846, O Soen Nio pleaded for divorce by alleging that her husband had "failed to provide" for her: "We have been separated for very long, so that we no longer have feelings for each other."[48] Since O Soen Nio's *qing* (feeling) was likely translated from *rasa* or *perasaan*, the record of the twenty-two-year-old Gan Ho Nio's use of the term *qing* was probably closer to *cinta*, the word for "love" in creole Malay. In August 1872, she stated:

> GAN HO NIO: The Chinese Council had ordered [six months ago] for our reconciliation, yet my husband neither requested my return, nor provided for my maintenance. This proves that his *qing* [love] for me has ended.
>
> OFFICERS: Why did you not go back to him yourself?
>
> GAN HO NIO: I am a lone woman. The journey is far. I can't travel alone. Seeing that my husband no longer thought of me, I was determined to stop submitting myself to him, and to request instead for a divorce.[49]

Gan Ho Nio's reluctance to sue for divorce was clearly premised not only on her husband's morally bound material support but on the hope that he would think of her and think of asking her to return to their matrimonial household.

Deserted wives also faulted negligent husbands for addictions or laziness that prevented them from seeking work (17 out of 59 cases). They complained that these delinquent husbands were "always drunk," "only care[d] about gambling," or "consume[d] opium all day all."[50] Others "idle[d] around without trying to pick up some business" or "laze[d] at home and refuse[d] to go look for a job."[51] Husbands were expected to go out and work, then come home, especially at night. Men who "[went] out to roam at night," "treat[ed] the [neighborhood] guardhouse as home," "loiter[ed] around," or whose "whereabouts [were] never certain" were also faults recorded in wives' plea applications.[52]

The third kind of desertion plea involved complaints about negligence stemming from the husband's misappropriation of the wife's personal property (9 out of 59 cases).[53] All these cases involved husbands taking their wives' money and pawning their jewelry, clothes, and other valuables, or intending to do so, without their permission. Chapter 2 discussed Dutch colonial legal doubts about married Chinese women's title to their own separate property. It is interesting to note that in divorce trials at Batavia's Chinese Council, husbands' infringement of their wives' property constituted sufficient cause for divorce. Women clearly kept their parents' bridal trousseau as their own personal property. They might lend their property to their husbands for investments, but failure to repay could lead to a divorce plea. Take the well-recorded case of Tan Kiok Nio from 1846. She was married for just over a year when she sued for divorce, claiming that her husband "neither support[ed] nor care[d] for me." Her plea was backed up by the following allegation: "My husband secretly opened my cabinet, and took thirty-eight of my gold coins, 125 silver guilders, two Spanish real, . . . eight 2.50 silver guilder coins, 11 silver daalders, a golden bangle, . . . five diamond studded rings, three diamond rings, six pairs of silver pillow casings, a pair of earrings, a diamond needle, bronze coins worth 102 guilders, and a Makassar blouse."[54] Interviewed by the officers, the husband did not dispute taking her things but claimed she had agreed to loan them as capital for his native medicinal business. Assessing her "stolen" property to be worth 741.85 guilders, the council ordered him to set up a notarial deed to acknowledge his debt to his wife. The officers judged that "their feelings ha[d] ended" and would have granted the divorce had the husband not objected. The case was escalated to the resident. Although we do not know the resident's final decision, it is likely that they followed the officers' advice.

The fourth type of desertion plea, filed by women in an uxorilocal marriage, further accentuates how separate property ownership reinforced women's moral agency vis-à-vis their husbands in creole Chinese households (6 out of 59 cases). For such women, their parents often remained managers of a joint household, to which the "married-in" (C: 进赘) groom contributed his income until such time as he could afford to set up a separate residence. A closer examination of these cases shows that the delinquent husbands had not left on their own accord but were more often than not (4 out of 6 cases) expelled by their mothers-in-law.[55] In other words, when these women approached the Chinese Council, they were seeking to formalize a separation initiated by their parents (often mothers) through their divorce pleas.

The case of Tjia Hong Nio's divorce plea in March 1870 illustrates how in uxorilocal marriages, women could claim "desertion" from a position of relative economic strength. Barely married for five months, Tjia Hong Nio made this report: "[My husband has abandoned me for two and a half months. He neither cared nor paid for me. When I was ill he did not hire a doctor to treat me."[56] Up to this point, Tjia Hong Nio's plea would have sounded like those of most of her peers. But she continued, "When I went to the Chinese Council to report on him, [my husband] turned up to scold me, saying that . . . [I] wanted to recruit two to three or even ten more husbands for marriage. He really has no shame." The dispute, it turned out, had started over money. Her poorer husband had tried to borrow 100 guilders as capital for his medicinal business, but when she "refused to give anything," he allegedly said, "How could you not have 100 guilders as a rich man's daughter?" The incident most likely made Tjia Hong Nio's mother decide that this groom was a wrong match, and she had him expelled from the household. Three other cases involved the bride's parents intervening to expel grooms over mismatched expectations about his income-earning capacity.[57] Nowhere was men's dependence on their wives' familial wealth clearer than in the case of Oeij Lai Nio, who had been married for twelve years when she filed her plea: "Since my husband married into my family, he has never contributed to the household. He has often been disobedient. Since our marriage we have only cohabited for six years, out of which we did not enjoy peace for more than three. Sometimes he asks for money. If you give it to him, he will be nice, if not he will turn angry."[58]

Although small in number, the desertion pleas of women in uxorilocal marriages point to a broader pattern of creole Chinese women's continued reliance on and collaboration with their natal families after marriage. This relative strength in creole women's status softened the hard edges of the patriarchal Chinese family, but in other ways it served to entrench the institution of Confucian marriage in colonial urban Java. As Oeij Lai Nio's case suggests, women, because they could rely on their natal families, often waited many years before they went to the officers to formalize their already failed marriages. Tjia Hong Nio's testimony further shows that women's remarriage was deemed shameful. Not every married woman had natal families who were wealthy enough or willing to take them back. We catch glimpses of how deserted wives survived on their own through some of the testimonies in the divorce trials. A few mentioned working on embroidery pieces, wrapping tobacco, making and selling snacks (M: *kuih*), working as a servant-cum-nanny, and selling personal jewelry to tide things over.[59] But the overwhelming majority of deserted wives returned to their natal families. There, in the Chinatown shophouses or attap huts of nearby kampungs belonging to their parents, they waited an average of twenty-five months before they made their way to the Chinese Council to formalize their divorce in colonial Chinese customary law.

Deserted wives recounted their husband's dereliction of duty as often in factual terms as in moral terms. Tried as the officers did to reconcile these couples, they were pragmatic in granting the overwhelming majority of these women their pleas when it became clear that the men had no means or that the conjugal relationship had deteriorated to an irreversible condition. Just as important in these decisions was the fact that the women themselves and their natal families held out for the deserting men's return. Let us now turn to those women who could not tolerate their husband's keeping of a concubine.

Concubine Jealousy: Women's Interracial Discourses of Shame

In his observations of the Chinese in Singapore during the late 1940s, Maurice Freedman noted that "the acceptance of the right of men to enjoy women other than their wives . . . by no means excludes the institution of female jealousy . . . yet a wife has no right to feel (or rather, express) jealousy as long as her husband's adventures with other women are unsystematised."[60] In Java, not only did the creole Chinese wife express her jealousy, but she also acquired the right from the Kapitans to dissolve her marriage. In the second half of the nineteenth century, "forsaking the wife to dote on the concubine" (C: 弃妻宠妾) became an accepted reason for Chinese wives to sue for divorce and a common refrain the Kapitans used to admonish men who neglected their primary wives. After desertion and physical abuse, concubine-induced negligence was the most commonly cited cause for women's divorce application. About one in every seven women who pleaded for divorce complained about their husbands favoring concubines over themselves. Four out of every five such women (or 81 of 102 cases) won their divorce pleas. Bearing in mind that polygyny was legal among all Asian groups in urban colonial Java, it was remarkable that the wife's jealousy over the concubine became a legitimate cause for divorce applications. The high rate of jealousy-induced divorces shows that, like their Southeast Asian counterparts, the average creole Chinese woman in the nineteenth century treated marriage as a monogamous relationship despite the customary law dictating otherwise. This tension between women's monogamous conjugal ideal and the persistence of men's practice of polygyny created an interracial discourse of jealousy-induced shame between Chinese women and their native concubine competitors.

Anthony Reid attributes the "relative autonomy of women" in Southeast Asia to a few key traits in gender and sexual relations unique to the region. Women's autonomy in marriage was ensured by wealth "pass[ing] from the male to the female side in marriage."[61] Outside of the royal elite, the "dominant marriage pattern was one of monogamy, with divorce relatively easy for both sides."[62] In everyday life, "women took a very active part in courtship and lovemaking, and demanded as much as they gave by way of sexual and emotional gratification."[63] Women would terminate their marriage fairly easily if they were dissatisfied in sexual and emotional terms.

The phrase "forsaking the wife to dote on the concubine" appeared so routinely in the discourse of divorce trials that it must have developed into a customary legal norm. The standard formula appears in one form or another in the discourse of both women and officers in at least one-third of the cases involving a complaint against a concubine favoritism. In these pleas, the distinction between desertion and concubine favoritism was not always clear-cut. Some women complained of desertion, bringing up the concubine only incidentally. For the majority, however, the operative word in the pleas was the "doting" of another woman, rather than the "forsaking" of themselves. This customary norm for divorce application was so well established that women sometimes did not have to furnish further details.[64] For instance, in November 1862, when Jap Kapak Nio sued her husband by this norm, her plea simply read: "Husband dotes on his concubine, while neglecting his wife. He does not treat me as Wife anymore. Please grant me a divorce."[65] More often than not, a woman would open her plea with this stock phrase, and then go on to enumerate the various ways the concubine had been favored while she herself had been neglected, shamed, and sometimes even abused. In March 1860, Voon Boen Kie Nio made the following plea:

> Husband dotes on his concubine at the expense of his wife. He has stopped paying me. He is enjoying himself with his concubine, while forgetting about his family. Last September, the Chinese Council ordered him to abandon his concubine and go back to his wife, but he ignored the order. He has not been back for six months, and he never

paid. Last December, I went back to my mother's house . . . to visit my ailing younger sister. He approved of it and reminded me to be back before the new year. When I came back within half a month, he was gone. I informed Mother-in-law before I went home to see my sister again. In January, when I came back he was still away. I cannot tolerate this anymore. Please grant me a divorce.[66]

A case that involved more severe consequences for the primary wife was that of Souw Tok Nio, who made this plea in September 1863: "Husband forsook me for the sake of his concubine. He takes his anger out on me to please her. I have very often been evicted from home for no reason. I went back home to mother's house in Banten. This time, I have been back for 10 months. He has not paid me in a year and a half, and he has been treating me like a stranger at home. Please grant me a divorce."[67] The almost standard judgment given by the officers in such cases went like this, "This husband dotes on concubine at expense of his wife. . . . He should be reprimanded. The divorce is granted."[68] In December 1847, the Chinese Council even noted in one judgment that a husband who "abandons the wife to dote on the concubine, goes against the laws [C: 律理], and thus has to be punished," to be detained for a day and night, and then retried.[69] In almost every case, the Kapitans would have tried at first to reconcile the concubine-favoring husband with his jealous wife. In the end, however, they granted 80 percent of jealous wives' pleas for divorce.

By recognizing concubine favoritism as a valid reason for wife-initiated divorce, the officers reinvented a gender-familial norm in China as a customary legal right for Chinese women in colonial Java. In late imperial China, the status precedence of primary wives as the head-mother of the entire household and, in the afterlife, of the entire line of male descendants that followed was practiced in the realm of Confucian kinship organization. More precisely, primary wives served as the titular and fictive mothers of all concubine-born children, so that they always enjoyed one or two degrees of precedence over the concubine in mourning rites, or as victims, in the severity of penalties the state imposed on the perpetrators.[70] Upheld by patriarchal lineages within the Confucian social order, the suffering primary wife had no extrafamilial authority to turn to beyond her husband's lineage elders and, in the final resort, her own natal family. Extreme as it may sound, suffering wives could obtain legal remedy only when their deaths by suicide or homicide took their grievances to the county magistrate.[71] In urban Java, the jealous Chinese wife always had the option of walking a few blocks, usually from her parents' house, to the Kapitan's court to complain about her concubine-doting husband.

Within this reinvented Confucian customary legal framework, women expressed their ideas about conjugal love and their jealousy at having been deprived of it by the concubine. Women had conjugal love expectations related to sexual intimacy, companionship, and their status as (pending) female head of the household. Interestingly, because of the racial division of domestic and sexual labor in colonial society, Chinese women tended to reserve sharper, sexually charged, and status-conscious comments for their native concubine competitors. With their fellow Chinese women, the grudging acceptance of their status transferred the competition to the realm of property.

Despite the small sample size, the known racial distribution of Chinese men's concubines suggests a close co-relation with the racial division of gendered domestic and sexual labor in colonial society. Out of the thirty-five cases in which the race or occupation of the concubine is known, there were nineteen native and eight Chinese concubines, and eight native opera slaves/actresses (women slaves who were bought and trained to perform in Chinese opera troupes) (see table 3.1).

The largest category of native concubines reflected a practice I discussed in Chapter 1—of men taking native domestic women as their concubine-servants. Native women, both concubines and opera slaves/actresses, were very likely overrepresented in the jealousy suits, given their relatively uncertain status as concubines. Conversely, Chinese concubines, with the strongest claim to customary legal legitimacy, were likely underrepresented. Their relatively stronger status was apparently not affected by the fact that they were mostly set up in separate residences from the primary wife. Among native women, the Chinese made a clear distinction between the ordinary native concubine and opera slaves/actresses. Native women were more likely to be recognized as concubines

TABLE 3.1. Known race and occupation of concubines in divorce proceedings, 1840s–1890s

	NATIVE CONCUBINES	CHINESE CONCUBINES	NATIVE OPERA SLAVES/ ACTRESSES (CONCUBINES)
1840s	4	2	1
1850s	4	3	0
1860s	7	3	5
1870s	2	0	2
1890s	2	0	0
Total	19	8	8

Source: Compiled from Chinese Council Minutes, 1840s–1890s.

than their opera slave/actress counterparts. Only half the opera slaves/actresses were mentioned as being "concubines" (*qie*, C: 妾) or being "married" (*qu*, C: 娶) into the family, in contrast to sixteen of the nineteen native women. In the latter half of the century, there was a trend for the Chinese to reject the term "nyai" in favor of *"sundal"* (prostitute, immoral women) when referring to native women kept outside the matrimonial household.[72] This corresponded, in the 1860s and 1870s, with the appearance of opera actresses kept by men outside the matrimonial household.

Chinese Concubines

Men bought Chinese concubines from poorer families through marriage brokers. Unlike the primary-wife marriage, which was arranged by parents of equal social status, men approached matchmakers themselves to find concubines. Like primary-wife marriages, a concubine's marriage in Batavia was sealed with a contract, the groom's gifts, and fanfare to fetch the concubine-bride, although she probably received little to no trousseau from her parents and entered the groom's family with less elaborate rites. Impoverished parents or relatives of orphaned girls sold their girls into concubinage. In 1838, Tan Peng and his wife, in a custody dispute over an orphaned niece, defended the "sale of their own daughter to a European man" by admitting that they "were poor." Yet six years later, they contracted the niece to be sold as a concubine to a married Chinese man. This time, however, a relative had them reported, and the officers punished them for "breaking the promise of arranging a marriage for her according to Chinese rituals and law [C: Lifa]."[73]

Competition between the wealthiest men for the most beautiful concubine brides could inflate prices. As historian Hsieh Bao Hua notes, for late imperial China, the "price for a concubine depended on her age, beauty, virginity, artistic skills, size of feet and sometimes the social background of her natal family or former owner."[74] In colonial Java, foot binding was not in fashion, and Chinese men added race to the equation. A dispute between the landlord Tan Kong Soeij and Kapitan Tan Kam Long of Cheribon over a prospective concubine-bride in 1846 reveals how married men handled their own concubine choices. Tan Kong Soeij was "looking for someone to manage the household outside the city, so . . . [he] asked go-between Nyonya Oeij Kong Tjioe to check out Lie Soea's daughter, Lie Kwie Nio."[75] On hearing that she had "beautiful looks," the suitor paid thirty gulden to arrange for a viewing. Lie Kwie Nio and her mother came to his house in a carriage, and seeing that her "looks were indeed as reported . . . [he] immediately . . . paid her [the balance of] 170 guilders" and a pair of gold rings. Lie Kwie Nio's mother, however, went back on her word when she sold her daughter to Kapitan Tan for 600 guilders. Tan Kong Soeij was shocked when he heard about the "great festivities" that attended Kapitan Tan's and Lie Kwie Nio's wedding and that her mother had "given her to Kapitan Tan Kam Long as concubine." The officers admonished both men for not using a marriage contract to bind their agreement and annulled the latter concubine marriage.

Chinese women were the only concubine-brides who married with some fanfare, and even then, not all enjoyed this ritual privilege. Maiden concubine-brides, whose parents were sending them out for their first marriage, were more likely than divorcées or widows to go through a reduced form of the Six Rites ceremonies. The fanfare, however, could not exceed what the primary wife experienced. In May 1851, Oeij Wie Nio sued her husband for divorce, claiming that he "even married a concubine with drums and music, such lack of righteousness!"[76] Primary wife Jap Lan Nio complained in her divorce plea that her husband married another girl "with a horse carriage, colored flags, lights, trumpets, . . . as he left Pasar Senen, and he married into Kampong Melayu, where it was bustling."[77] In this case, the officers judged that "although there was no official certificate, this was like a new marriage, so it is no wonder Lan Nio is ashamed. This upsets the customs and laws of the Chinese Probate Council." In their usual pragmatic stance, they granted Jap Lan Nio her divorce and advised her husband to officially register his second wife.

Men mostly kept their Chinese concubines in separate residences from their primary wives. This was an important departure from the Chinese practice of keeping the entire (polygynous) family under one roof, with the Chinese term for primary wife and concubine—*zhengshi* (main chamber) and *pianfang* (side chamber)—giving literal expression to this status distinction in intra-household space-delineation terms. In five out of the seven known cases, primary wives complained about husbands who favored Chinese concubines residing "outside" the household.[78] As in the case of landlord Tan Kong Soeij, Jo Tiong had his main residence in Batavia, but, as his primary wife complained, he set up a second one "outside the city," where he "kept the concubine Lie Tio Nio."[79] Oeij Djoen Nio, in her plea, noted how she was doubly neglected by a husband who "doted on the native woman Zani at home, and kept the concubine Liem Djong Nio, who bore him a son outside." Even in the remaining two cases, where men set up their Chinese concubines at home, this happened only after their primary wives had been absent for some time.[80] The Jam Nio complained that her husband had "evicted her from the house . . . stopped coming to visit and stopped paying. Now he has married a Chinese concubine at home."[81]

Set up in different households, primary wives were particularly sensitive to their husbands' unequal distribution of resources and respect in relation to the Chinese concubine he kept outside. In May 1844, Liem Kip Nio attributed the lack of support from her husband to "a concubine he kept outside named Tjai Nio, who has no marriage certificate, and to whom he gives 50 guilders a month, whereas he only gave me 3 guilders for a year and nothing more since." Materially, Liem Kip Nio was taken care of, for she continued to receive an allowance from her father, but in the end, it was her husband's disregard of her position as primary wife of a Chinese officer that offended her. "He treats me like a servant, hitting me for no reason, how can I bear with it?" She continued, "As a Lieutenant, how could he only give his wife 3 guilders?"[82] In May 1851, Oeij Djoen Nio complained, "Husband took my things and gave them to his concubine."[83] And The Yam Nio reported, "Husband stopped coming to visit, and [stopped] paying, now that he has married a Chinese concubine at home."[84]

Native Concubines

Jealous primary wives tended to speak in far more emotional and intimate terms of the native concubine's alleged transgressions. This was in part because they usually lived in the same residence. Among the sixteen known cases, eleven resided in the main matrimonial household together with the Chinese primary wife.[85] In December 1843, Loa Tjam Nio complained about a husband who "married a native woman as concubine, loves and dotes on her to the extreme, while treating me like weed. He scolds and insults me for no reason, and has sent me to live away from the city."[86] In April 1860, Koe Tjoei Nio reported that her husband "dotes on a native woman, with whom he cannot bear to part." In the same month, Voon Djie Moi was tired of a husband who was "dependent all day on the native woman. For three years, they do everything together, while he has not slept with me for a single night."[87] These underlying sexual and companionate tensions explain why Chinese wives often headed to the Kapitans' office to file for divorce over seemingly trivial insults and innuendos from the native concubine.

The conflicts were often over precedence in the everyday context of domestic labor. A native concubine who had gained the favor of her husband could afford to stand by and watch the Chinese wife labor. In October 1867, Lie Tjoen Nio was "going to have her meal, when Husband's beloved concubine Shiba threw rice on the floor. He kept quiet and never said a word." When her husband accused her of "picking fights . . . for no reason," she retorted that it was "all because of that native woman. She should be placed in another house."[88] If things had begun to go bad with the husband, it was often the mother-in-law's condoning of the challenger's transgressions that made the situation intolerable. In September 1846, Tjia Hok Nio "went out to catch earthworms for feeding the ducks, but was made a joke by Husband's concubine. I couldn't bear it anymore. I had not bothered her, yet Mother-in-law came out, and without asking a question, insulted and beat me up."[89] In November 1871, Oeij Teng Nio gave the clearest description of how such inversion of status triggered shame and anger in the Chinese wife: "Husband married a native woman in the same household. I worked alone in the kitchen, while the native woman, my husband and mother-in-law ate together. My duty as a wife is limited to serving my mother-in-law. How could the native woman share a meal with her? I was so unbearably embarrassed and angered that I asked to go back to my parents' home. Husband actually hired a carriage to send me off. He even said, 'Once you leave, consider yourself divorced.'"[90]

Opera Slaves/Actresses

In nineteenth-century Java, Chinese-owned female opera troupes were trained and leased for religious and festive occasions, although they also performed sex work on the side. A contemporary Dutch observer noted that "at festivals they generally set up a kind of theatre (*wajang*) in which mostly various heroic deeds are presented, by actors and actresses, who (at least on Java) are servants or slaves, and mechanically learn their roles, without knowing Chinese."[91] Josh Stenberg surmises that these troupes performed a hybrid form of Chinese and Sundanese opera singing, dancing, and clowning, or an early variant of *ronggeng*, which included sexual services.[92] In October 1846, one such Batavia-based troupe, owned by the widowed Nyonya Lao Jiak (Festivity Nyonya), was hired by Baba Oeij Ing Sieuw to perform for five days on his estate in Karawaci, in the Ommelanden. Referred to as Opera Singer Slaves (C: 戏童唱曲, most likely translated as Budak Wayang Ciokek), a passenger list from a capsized boat shows that the troupe consisted of six slave actresses, who were in turn accompanied by two senior women, three male musicians, and one or two Chinese female overseers.[93] Baba Oeij Ing Sieuw paid 160 guilders, two pails of kerosene, and a picul of rice for the five days of opera performance. Trying to recover her loss, Nyonya Lao Jiak estimated that the costumes, jewelry, and musical instruments cost her close to 7,500 guilders. A resourceful entrepreneur she must have been to earn the epithet Festivity Nyonya. Back in the city, it is not hard to imagine Nyonya Lao Jiak running a *ronggeng* house and leasing her slave girls to men during their time off.

Unlike the native servant-concubines, opera slave girls were seldom kept at home; they were either set up in a separate house or visited by their male patrons at the house of the opera troupe itself. Accused by his wife of ill treatment and favoritism toward the concubine, one defensive husband countered that the latter was "kept in the house of the opera troupe owner, and not brought home."[94]

Women kept outside the matrimonial household were often suspected, rightly or wrongly, by their neighbors of prostitution. One ward master, called to testify for the alleged existence of a kept woman, referred to her as a "prostitute."[95] Many native concubines, probably through their hard work and submissiveness, were able to gain the favor of their mothers-in-law at the expense of the Chinese wife. Opera slave concubines did not share the same domestic space, and even if they did, they were probably unsuited for domestic labor. Mothers-in-law were not a factor in triggering the Chinese wife to leave her matrimonial household.

Against the opera/actresses, the Chinese wife's jealousy was more purely sexual and emotional. Oeij Tsin Nio felt "ashamed to the extreme, when seven days after marriage, Husband made me sleep together with him and his [opera slave] concubine."[96] A year into her marriage, Liem Tat Nio remarked, "Husband dotes on the concubine Gwei Lie, an opera actress. After the wedding, I have only slept two nights with him."[97] In September 1863, Tjioe Yam Nio noted, "Husband took my things and gave them to the Opera Slave, Gwei Tjoen. He has forgotten himself at her place."[98] And Go Soei Nio recounted, "Husband only has feelings for the opera slave, not any more for me. My heart ached too much."[99]

This chapter explored the moral and emotional claims creole Chinese wives made about marriage when they applied for divorce before their patriarchal community leaders. While divorce pleas by women before lineage elders or the magistrate were unheard of in contemporary China, divorce had always been law in Islam, and it occurred at a fairly high frequency among the Muslims of Southeast Asia. By granting women their pleas, the Confucian-literate Kapitan leaders inadvertently acknowledged creole women's material entitlement to maintenance and emotional claims about exclusive love. As an improvised form of colonial customary legal norm, the moral hypocrisy of polygynous Kapitans recognizing women's claims for monogamous love was a contradiction the patriarchy did not need to account for to any higher authority. Having looked at how creole Chinese wives asserted their moral and emotional agency against the communal patriarchy, let us now turn to how, as mothers, grandmothers, matriarchs, and widows, they manipulated marriage alliances and property holdings in a colonial jurisprudence that increasingly could not tolerate women's freedom to contract in the latter half of the century.

4
WOMEN'S WEALTH AND MATRIARCHAL STRATEGIES

Chapter 3 explored middle-class women's agency within a patriarchal creole Chinese society through the customary institution of divorce. This chapter shows how wealthy matriarchs, usually widows, exercised their "bilateralized" patrilineal authority through colonial legal instruments in a way that made the colonial state clamp down on their contractual freedom. William Skinner has argued that the creolized Chinese of Java had "shifted away from the patrilineal, virilocal, and patriarchal bias of the traditional Hokkien (Fujian) system" into an "essentially bilateral . . . system," where there was a "distinct tendency in the ancestral cult to worship the lineal ascendants of the mother as well as of the father."[1] With an important qualification, I use Skinner's anthropological insight to explain both the bilaterally weighted wealth succession strategies of the matriarchs and how they confounded Dutch colonial sinologists, who could only view them as a corruption of "pure" Chinese patrilineal behavior. Jack Goody has noted that "the existence of bilateral inheritance or devolution is perfectly compatible with a certain type of patrilineal clans."[2] Creole Chinese family formations in nineteenth-century Java were in fact essentially patrilineal, although they showed distinct bilateral tendencies in inheritance practices.

How wealth could go down the bilateral route yet be made to serve patrilineal interests becomes clear when we place the matriarch's concerns at the heart of the story. The chapter begins by locating matriarchal interest *in between* patrilineal family alliances. In a strictly patrilineal setting, women, exchanged by exogamous lineage groups in marriage, became permanently alienated from their natal families. In the colonial context, I show that matriarchs manipulated wills and contracts to help further the wealth succession goals of both their husbands and their brothers. From the 1850s, colonial legal authorities began to treat such bilaterally oriented modes of wealth transmission with suspicion. This orientalist approach to Chinese family law brought an end to married Chinese women's autonomy to contract in the 1890s. A final section reveals how the creole matriarchs continued to find new ways to circumvent colonial legal strictures in the interests of their bilaterally descended patrilineal kin.

Sources of Women's Wealth

Skinner saw that Chinese women in urban Java inherited some wealth from their fathers. Based mainly on this fact, he argued that the Chinese had become "essentially bilateral" in their kinship, assuming that women then passed on that wealth to their own children.[3] In fact, wealth inherited from their fathers often went back to their natal families through what Margery Wolf calls "uterine family alliances." In her study of gender and Chinese patriliny in rural Taiwan, Wolf notes that "the group that has the most lasting ties is the smaller, more cohesive unit centering on her mother, i.e., the uterine family—her mother and her mother's children. Father is important to the group, just as grandmother is important to some of the children, but he is not quite a member of it, and for some uterine families he may even be 'the enemy.'"[4] In colonial Java, the married woman's freedom to contract further accentuated her capacity to act, usually as a custodian, in the interests of both her brother and her husband.

First, women were wealthy, and they actively made use of colonial legal instruments to manipulate that wealth. It is significant to note that in the decades between the 1840s and the 1930s, 10 to 15 percent of the existing Chinese probate cases in the Indonesian archives were set up for women (see table 4.1).

Women usually acquired their first pot of wealth through their father's bridal trousseau. In response to official inquiries, the Chinese officers of Batavia acknowledged the daughter's right to inherit at least a share for her bridal gift. In 1861, the Dutch resident of Batavia asked if daughters inherited, and if so, if it came with ancestral worshipping duties. The Kapitans noted that women in China had no need to attend to their father's ancestral worship after marriage, but that this was not always true for the Chinese in Batavia: "There are some [daughters] who inherit. If the deceased has male descendants, then they pay for the ancestral offerings. The daughters may contribute if they so wish. It is fine if they do not, but they definitely have to obey the wishes of their husbands."[5] The Kapitans' reply was indicative of the supplementary nature of creole women's obligation toward their natal families. It was with the absence of male heirs that

TABLE 4.1. Female Chinese probate cases as a proportion of the total number of Chinese probate cases

PERIOD	FEMALE/TOTAL NUMBER OF PROBATE PAPERS	PROPORTION
1840s–1870s	3/19	15.8%
1880s	20/141	14.1%
1890s	28/262	10.6%
1900s	33/273	12.1%
1910s	62/448	13.8%
1920s	50/350	14.2%
1930s	69/527	13.0%

Source: Catalog of the Orphans and Probate Chamber, National Archives of Indonesia.

daughters were expected to step in. A daughter's share in her father's estate was more clearly expressed by the patriarchal community leaders four years later, in response to another inquiry on general inheritance norms. The officers urged respect for whatever was laid down in testaments, but in the absence of the father's will, an unmarried daughter would inherit one-sixth the share of the primary wife's son, one-third the share of the secondary wife's son, or one-half the share of the primary wife.[6] Note that the legacy was for an unmarried daughter, who was owed a bridal gift. Even then, it was far from equal from what sons of various grades or the surviving widow was expected to inherit. In this case, the officers did not distinguish between the marriage gift and a further inheritance at the point of the father's (or mother's) death.

In practice, wealthy Chinese fathers expected sons to jointly succeed them in the family enterprise, while giving their daughters a significant bridal gift of cash and seldom more. Chinese men's testaments in the Batavia Orphans and Probate Council (D: Wees- en Boedelkamer) archives across the latter half of the nineteenth century show this to be the ideal pattern of wealth succession for Chinese men. When he died on 18 January 1861, Oeij Kioksoei left behind three sons (aged 25, 21, and 15 years old) and eight daughters (aged 1–20). In a will set up on 1 March 1859, he named his three sons as joint heirs, but gave only 200 guilders each to the six younger daughters who were unmarried.[7] Set up in 1863, before any of his six children had attained adulthood, Tan Tjoeiseng named his four sons as joint heirs, and gave both daughters 3000 guilders each.[8] In a testament written four days before his death on 28 October 1899, Lim Soei Hien named his two sons as joint heirs and set aside 10,000 guilders for his six-year-old daughter, to be gifted upon her marriage.[9] In 1915, the honorary Kapitan The Tjoen Sek died with a minor son and two daughters in tow. He had appointed his only son heir. The married daughter was to keep "all jewelry given to her for her wedding," while the unmarried one, eight months old, was to be brought up by her mother with an allowance of 15 guilders a month, then given 2000 guilders for her marriage.[10]

Having received their bridal gift, it was a customary practice, recognized by law, for Chinese women to keep their private wealth separate from their husband's entrepreneurial capital and any household finances provided by the latter. As for the role of the law, the validity of married Chinese women's separate property holdings had been recognized since the eighteenth century out of pragmatic concerns for the women's welfare on the one hand and acknowledgment that this was an Islamic law-influenced local custom on the other. When passed on 23 May 1766, the Company Statute for Batavia emphasized its enforcement of the existing status quo regarding Chinese women's default right to separate estates from their husband's and the latter's debts. The Dutch, as I will explain, always harbored the suspicion that Chinese men kept property under their wife's name to protect themselves from debt. In the 1766 statute, the keeping of separate holdings was allowed as a concession because "not so many wealthy Chinese are to be found, and so not much [money] can be misappropriated by the surviving widow." More importantly, the statute acknowledged that this was a norm influenced by "Mohammaden laws, the doctrine to which many Chinese are bound through conversion [D: *overgang*] or by marriage with women..., whereby community property is completely excluded."[11] In 1855, the exclusion of "community property" for the Chinese was explicitly retained when the recently introduced European commercial code (1848) was applied to the Chinese, but with a caveat stipulating that "profits accruing to the wife, in a standing marriage, from her own affairs or trade, cannot be otherwise proven than by proper written evidence."[12]

By custom, the Chinese officers of Batavia recognized gifts not only from fathers but from husbands as well, as the private wealth of married women. Men inevitably lost when they tried to fight their wives over the latter's personal property in court. Three cases heard at the Batavia residency *landraad* were referred to the Chinese Council for adjudication. In 1848, Ong Ka Nio, who demanded her divorced husband reimburse her for a list of jewelry, won her case before the Chinese Council. While accepting the man's defense that the jewelry had been given to him to repay debts when they were "in love," the officers stated that "it was common for men to hand their wealth to women, but not necessary for women to hand their wealth over to men."[13] In 1850, a man who tried to deny his stepdaughter, Oeij Swie Nio, of his deceased ex-wife's (her mother's) personal property was likewise castigated by the officers. Witnesses testified that the girl's mother had brought the property to the household from her "previous marriage."

"As a man," the officers scolded, "how could you harbor designs over women's things? Women's accessories, once they have been worn by a lady, even if it was the husband who paid for them, they belong to the lady."[14] In 1863, officers tried to clarify with an aggrieved Tjoe Tan Nio the origin of two sarongs and a gold ring: "[Were they] brought with you as [a] bridal gift or did your husband give them to you?" Tellingly, while the husband was the giver, he did not dispute that they belonged to her.[15]

There were two more ways for the creole Chinese woman to add to her personal bridal gift after marriage: through business or through inheritance from her husband. Among the urban middle class, a small minority of women ran small-scale businesses, although seldom as autonomous entrepreneurs. In two randomly chosen years (1864 and 1869–70), only six out of eighty sureties for forty loan applications at the Chinese Council were given to women.[16] Among these six Chinese women of good credit reputation, only two were "entrepreneurial." In an application for a f2,000 loan, a certain Oei Kit Nio, who ran a sugar store, was put up as a guarantor. And Liem Tan Nio, who owned her own house, operated a *warung* (M: small stall) under the name of her husband.[17] The other four were wealthy women who owned immovable property. In one case, Kan Bing, an arak wine seller applying for a loan of f6,000, called on his wife to guarantee his loan. While she owned three houses under her name, she had also delegated the power of attorney to her husband.[18] Abuses in this form of intrafamilial loan securitization, exposed in the sugar crisis of the 1880s, would force jurists to rethink the question of Chinese women's autonomy to contract.

Chinese women could also inherit more than their fathers had intended through the colonial probate process. Whenever non-Christian subjects died without leaving a will (*ab intestato*), the probate council applied Dutch inheritance law, which guaranteed each son or daughter an equal share of the legal portion (D: *legitieme portie*).[19] Given the reluctance of many Chinese to set up wills before it was too late, or their failure to update them in time, a significant number of estates were subject to the gender equal *legitieme portie*. Without the social organization of a co-residential lineage formation, less wealthy men simply did not have the means to ensure that they left behind sons, not to mention set up wills to favor them over daughters. In these cases, it was straightforward for the probate authorities to grant the surviving widows and daughters what little was left behind. When the rice merchant Tan A Hoen died in Krawang in June 1869, the council appointed his widow Tjiam Molek executor and guardian of the estate for their minor daughter Tan Enong Nio. But his estate, amounting to a one-twelfth share in a gambier plantation (valued at f216.66) and half a share of an attap house (f10.40), was not enough to cover the f1,244.50 of debt he owed in the rice trade.[20] The intervention was deeper and more clearly beneficial to women in the case of Tan Ginko's estate. When Ginko died in 1854, his will, set up in 1837, had named a son and a nephew as his joint heirs. But he had in fact added another son and two more daughters in the intervening years. The probate authorities intervened to ensure that the estate would be divided equally among the son, the nephew, and the three later-born children—a gender equal provision the patriarch might not have thought of had it been left to him to decide. [21]

From the Chinese Council records, it appears that wealthy women were inclined to pass down their wealth only to their own children. But as I explain in the next section, in instances where the uterine family was allied for business, they often intervened to act on behalf of their brother's (and father's) patrilineal descendants. Between 1844 and 1862, there were twelve cases of inheritance disputes referred to the Batavia Chinese Council involving women's testaments.[22] All except one made plans for inheritance, usually of immovable property, following a patrilineal pattern.[23] The patrilineality of their wealth succession plans were not disputed; rather, disputes occurred from within the patrilineal descent group. For instance, in a will set up on 3 September 1835, Sing Sie Nio had divided three parcels of land equally among her twelve-year-old grandson, Tan Kie Tjoan, and what appears to be three sons, the boy's uncles. She appointed the three uncles as administrators of the parcels until such day as Tan Kie Tjoan could assume his role as legal co-owner. When he did in the late 1840s, he disagreed with how his uncles had managed the lands and sued to have the lands auctioned and divided.[24]

Chinese women in colonial Java inherited wealth from both their fathers and their husbands. Looking at wills alone, it may appear that they served as custodians of wealth mainly for their own children and grandchildren. I will demonstrate in the final section how the matriarch's interests in fact straddled both her brother's and her husband's families. Before that, let us turn, in the next two sections, to changes in the legislative and jurisprudential spheres, whose effects were increasingly felt in the everyday exercise of women's freedom to contract in the latter half of the nineteenth century.

Property and the Woman Question in Orientalist Chinese Family Law

The transfer of wealth from husband to wife among the Chinese became a contested colonial Chinese legal problem in the latter half of the nineteenth century. Confined to a small circle of legal and orientalist experts, this debate took place amid a broader move to codify a racialized private (family) law status for the

Chinese of Java between the 1850s and 1919. The rights of women animated the imagination of jurists and sinology experts throughout the entire period, although with very different emphases. Before the 1890s, the move to define women's rights revolved around questions of property and "legal certainty."[25] Since then, as I will show in chapter 7, a civilizing logic centered on race and sexuality became the main driver of family law reform. The earlier debate constructed a notion of racial Chineseness based on orientalist understandings of religion that ultimately subjected women to an abstract form of patriliny.

Mitra Sharafi argues that "the construction of Parsi law in British India differed sharply from the text-dependent process that forged Anglo-Hindu and -Islamic law."[26] Sharafi shows that the Parsis in western India, through their relative wealth, their precocious legal self-professionalization, and the absence of Zoroastrian religious texts, were able to lobby and win a separate personal law code based on patriarchal customary legal norms in 1865. In Dutch Java, the colonial state replaced legal advice from Chinese officers with "text-dependent" sinology-trained Dutch officials. In the Indonesian context, this conflation of the Confucian textual tradition with Chinese law contrasts with the colonial decision to de-emphasize an Islamic textual approach to native law in favor of customary (*adat*) law. How did religion, race, and law come to be defined from so many different sources for colonial subjects?

From the 1840s onward, Dutch and other European merchants petitioned the colonial government against the alleged Chinese abuse of the wife's separate estate in bankruptcy cases. From 1856 to 1942, between one-half and three-quarters of all bankruptcies involved ethnic Chinese merchants.[27] While admitting that Arab and Chinese "intermediation [was] a necessary evil in the commerce between the European and the actual native," the state-owned Netherlands Trading Company informed the government that Chinese and Arab merchants "have ... struck such deep roots of bad faith [D: *kwade trouw*], that strong legal regulations to extirpate the evil are needed in order that commerce will not be allowed to languish."[28] If Arabs and Chinese were the main "Foreign Oriental" traders in the colony, it was the Chinese who were singled out for regulation: "We are referring here mainly to the Chinese, whose institutions presuppose that their marriages are excluded from community property.... [It] was often the occasion that when insolvencies were discovered, the suspected properties of the husband had been transferred to the wife, [so that] creditors could assert no rights on them on the grounds that her marriage was said to be contracted with the exclusion of community property."[29] In Dutch civil law, husband and wife had a community property marriage by default, unless a prenuptial agreement had been contracted. While community marital property entitled divorcées and widows to a definite portion of the couple's estate, it also bound her to her husband's debt.[30] The European merchants requested that Chinese "marriages [be] contracted in such a way that the rights of the third party cannot be defrauded." More specifically, they wanted the same civil law rights and duties for the Chinese, so that "every Chinese who intends to be married but be excluded from community property marriage be obliged to consider the formalities that the law prescribes for Europeans, and that by default of those formalities, the property of the wife, in case of insolvency, will be considered to belong to the [marital] community."[31]

The colonial state met the merchants' demands in the middle. In 1855, even as the Chinese were subject to the Dutch commercial code for business purposes, the state continued to exempt the Chinese from community property marriage. To prevent fraudulent transfers, however, the 1855 law specified that "the acquisition of movable property at marriage by the woman cannot otherwise be proven than by an authentic deed, laid down *before* or at the point of marriage; property acquired during marriage, by inheritance, bequest or donation to the woman, must be demonstrated by a notarial description."[32] Between 1855 and the 1890s, this halfway-house legislative solution formed the starting point of many a debate over a Chinese woman's property rights in relation to her father's and her husband's patrilineal families.

The arrival of sinology-educated interpreters in the 1860s introduced an orientalist expert element to the debate. Koos Kuiper's study traces how, between 1854 and 1896, twenty-four government-selected young Dutchmen were trained in the written classical Chinese language, classical texts, and southern Chinese spoken languages in Leiden University and in South China before being deployed to cities with substantial Chinese populations in the Dutch East Indies as official "translators of the Chinese language" and "extraordinary members" of local probate courts.[33] These sinology-trained official translators and legal advisers brought a new ethnographic sensibility to bear on colonial legal questions about Chinese women's property rights.[34] Although locally appointed Chinese officers were still consulted, the sinologists' ethnographic opinions would increasingly become the authoritative positions on questions of family law and Chinese women's property rights in particular.

Under the orientalist mode of lawmaking, the Dutch came up with five drafts (1865, 1867, 1872, 1892, and 1897) of Chinese private legal status before finally aborting the project in the name of the new civilizing mission. Jurists drew up the first three successive drafts under the advice of Gustaaf Schlegel, the first sinology professor appointed at Leiden University. W. P. Groeneveldt, the only sinology-trained interpreter to rise to the rank of the Dutch Indies Council, personally drafted the 1892 draft. Finally, although not trained in Chinese, the Indies Supreme Court jurist P. H. Fromberg drew on the most up-to-date sinological knowledge to design a legal status that, he was ordered, "had to be in the spirit of Chinese morals and customs."[35] In a thorough study of these vacillating and ultimately futile orientalist legislative efforts, Patricia Tjiook-Liem argues that the rubric of "legal certainty for the Chinese was . . . a sophism for the regulation of inheritance law and a cloak for the limitation of land ownership."[36] While Chinese landownership in West Java was a sharp concern in the 1850s, the fact that these laws were drafted but never passed suggests, at the very least, that landownership was not as urgent in subsequent decades. I argue that these legislative efforts tried to balance Chinese women's property rights with the interests of the third-party European creditors of their Chinese husbands.

Colonial references to China's laws for adjudicating intra-Chinese disputes on Java were not new.[37] In the mid-nineteenth century, what was new was the move away from consulting the local Chinese themselves toward an orientalist construction of comparative women's rights through legal ethnographic studies of Chinese religion. Some signs of this shift were already apparent, as the colonial state made inquiries in preparation for the introduction of the Dutch Civil Code in the Indies. In 1847, as H. L. Wichers, the Dutch president of the Batavia Probate Chamber (Collegie van Boedelmeesteren) for non-Christians, reported, "We have tried in vain to persuade [our Chinese members] of the more natural and fair ideas of the Christians, in relation to the rights of the female sex and in general to those of one's own legal children."[38] The sinology-trained experts would bring with them a more text-dependent approach to this comparative religious-legal project.

In the first three drafts (1865–72), Gustaaf Schlegel constructed Chinese law by supplementing concepts abstracted from the Qing legal code with orthodox Confucianist ritual treatises and ethnographic observations in South China.[39] Deployed to Batavia as its first Chinese interpreter in 1862, Schlegel argued that studies of the Qing Code alone were insufficient, as it was a criminal code. This had to be complemented with studies of "customary ceremonies . . . [that] are altogether civil." To understand Chinese legal norms for marriage and marital property, then, it would be "necessary to render that part of the physical law code . . . before going over to the description of the [marriage] ceremonies."[40] Schlegel noted in his ethnographic description that the bride's "family prepares . . . her bridal gift, consisting of clothes, jewelry, tables and stools, furniture and such articles."[41] This practice did not constitute a right in Schlegel's interpretation. Concerning Chinese inheritance practices, he noted that "daughters received nothing. The testator can however give his unmarried daughters a small legacy as bridal gift."[42]

Schlegel relied on a purist notion of Confucianist social logic when he testified in court on the question of Chinese women's property rights. "The [Chinese] woman is seen rather as an object [D: *zaak*] and a means for the reproduction of the male lineage, than an independent personality with her own destiny and rights."[43] In his report, Schlegel cited neither the Qing Code nor marriage ceremonies but a popular Confucianist adage that prescribed women's lifelong subjection to the authority of fathers, husbands, and sons. To claim "that a Chinese woman can possess something is, according to Chinese ethics, an absurdity.... A Chinese woman has nothing; her diamonds, clothes, in short, all that she brings with her to her marriage, by the fact of her marriage itself comes to the possession of her husband."[44]

In contrast to Schlegel, W. P. Groeneveldt was a pragmatic orientalist, who tried to recognize localized Chinese practices that favored women. His 1892 draft legislation applied community property to Chinese marriages. As early as 1876, Groeneveldt testified in court that the father's bridal gift could be interpreted as the daughter's inheritance right.[45] The male heir in China, Groeneveldt argued, had "the duty to provide maintenance and to give [his sister] a trousseau in proportion with her status and with the property he inherited." He admitted that this "right of the unmarried daughter to the inheritance of the father is not further regulated" by law. But "if the brothers are found to be negligent, it is the duty of other family members to induce [D: *anndringen*] him, failing which the judge [in China] is empowered to see to it that . . . he lives up to the duty." "The recognition of [this] slightest right already dispels" Schlegel's claim that "she exists as an object."[46] Groeneveldt's argument for greater legal recognition of Chinese women's property rights, especially in marital property law, was based on his observations of Chinese social life in Java. This was later expressed in a memorandum criticizing the Schlegel-advised draft private law code (1872), which would have denied women any rights to separate marital property.[47] He pointed out that most Chinese in Java started out as "small shopkeepers or craftsmen," who would not have had the means to worry about marital property anyway. But in cases where couples did accumulate some wealth over time, "it was certainly also for a good part to the credit of [the wife's] labor." It was only fair for Chinese women to enjoy the protection of community property marriage.

At about the same time, the translator P. Meeter injected an alarmist streak into the purist view of Chinese womanhood. "The Indies-Chinese woman," he warned, "is . . . much less capable of exercising rights than her sister in China. She is usually a scantly developed, very sensual being, who becomes the tool of her male relatives after the death of her husband.[48] Meeter's realist standpoint stemmed from his observation that the Chinese often contrived to circumvent probate and bankruptcy proceedings. For instance, he claimed it was common for dying husbands to transfer property to their wives in order to prevent probate administration of their estates for minor heirs. A more serious abuse involved the transfer of property to the wife's name before the merchant's fraudulent declaration of insolvency. Meeter thought colonial law had to go out of its way to enforce patriarchal norms like the Confucianist state in China. For him, Chinese patriarchal power was prescribed by the classical text *Li Ki* (Hk: *Book of Rites*), which served as the "political ethics of Confucius" and the "basis for the state religion" (D: *staatsgodsdienst*). Wherever the Qing Code remained silent on women's status or "when[ever] the advice of the legal experts conflicted," it became "necessary to go to the source and consult the *Book of Rites*."[49]

The purist view prevailed, if only momentarily, in the legislative project. Groeneveldt's more Indies-oriented Chinese law code (1892) was replaced by Fromberg's "New Regulation of the Private Legal Status of the Chinese" (1897).[50] The latter departed from the former on the question of community property marriage. Groeneveldt's code included every title in Book I of the Dutch Civil Code regulating property holdings between husband and wife (Titles 6–9), whereas Fromberg's excluded them all. The reason behind this decision was that Fromberg had concluded, after an extensive review of both schools of thought on "the legal status of women," that the answer lay in the question, "[Had] the [Indies-Chinese] custom [of separate marital property] ever really existed? . . . No, when one distinguishes between appearance and essence."[51] For the purist view to stand, he not only had to be philosophical but anti-factual, as he explained: "Notaries [since 1766] have allowed married Chinese women to make contracts without the authorization of their husbands, for instance to sell a house, [so in such cases] one has to assume that such authorization had been given, despite there not being any outward sign of it."[52] This assumption had to stand, for Fromberg thought it was "almost unthinkable that the Chinese here will ever . . . let the power of the *paterfamilias* [Latin: male head of the household] lapse relative to his wife, to let go of the *hiao* [Hk: 孝, filial piety] principle between the wife and the husband."[53] The essence of Chineseness, in spite of appearances (or facts) to the contrary, had to prevail.

In the end, Fromberg's draft code never made it into law. No sooner had his draft been published for commentary than the political grounds for colonial lawmaking shifted under his feet. Both Groenvedlt's and Fromberg's draft codes recognized polygamy by exempting the Chinese from civil law marriage in Title 4. As I will show in chapter 7, with the onset of the Dutch civilizing mission, the colonial gendered imagination of Chinese women was turning in the 1890s from the question of property to marriage and sexuality. Of contemporary officials, Fromberg went the furthest in acknowledging the contrarian factual context, even if he still fell back on the essentialist approach. He had in fact been shown the way by lawyers and judges in court. "Jurisprudence had already set the problem in the correct direction" in 1891, when the Semarang-based lawyer

C. Th. van Deventer, the soon-to-be reformist voice of the Dutch civilizing mission, intervened as a lawyer on behalf of Tan Paginio to save her property by denying Chinese women the freedom to contract.[54]

Race and the End of Women's Contractual Freedom

Tan Paginio's quest during the 1880s to regain her house from her deceased husband's creditors served as the test case for lawyers and judges to bring their differing ideas about the Chinese race and women's property rights into open conflict. It was perhaps no accident that C. Th. van Deventer, one of the key voices of the ethical movement in the colony, found his way to serve as Paginio's advocate. Taking sides in the ongoing orientalist debate about women's rights, the trial revolved around the question of how to constitute the racial jurisdiction of the law itself to judge a set of facts that were not disputed. If jurists had until then understood married women's freedom to contract as part of a broader Indies pattern of gender relations, the case represented a turning point for women's rights to be defined more strictly according to the emergent racial-civilizational hierarchy.

Tan Paginio's suit was a rare plea that factually upheld what purists like P. Meeter had been arguing about Chinese fraud. There was now a woman who would openly claim she had been the victim of fraud by her male relatives. In 1879, Paginio had, on paper, borrowed ƒ10,000 from a certain Liem Eng Tjay by mortgaging a house she owned in the Chinese quarter of Tegal, Central Java. The contract was signed in the local resident's office. She later claimed it was only in 1883, when her husband died, that she found out about this loan. To prevent the local bailiff from selling the house to settle her husband's debts, she claimed it was "a fraud committed by her spouse in consultation with her brother" for debts they had jointly incurred in their operation of the opium revenue farm in Cheribon that year.[55] Her first two bids to void the contract were successful at the Semarang Court of Justice, but twice they were rejected by Justice Sibenius Trip at the Indies Supreme Court upon appeal by Liem. Contested over four years (1886–90), her lawyers had framed her claim around a contract law technicality and the nullity of contracts made by dependents in civil law. It was difficult to annul a contract one had signed after the fact. The Supreme Court argued that civil law's concept of personal dependency did not apply to the Chinese. This set the stage for a two-year trial (1890–92) over what constituted law for the Chinese on the question of married women's right to contract.

By the 1880s, lawyers and judges, like their sinologist colleagues, were split into two camps on this question. This was evident in a contemporary survey of the published jurisprudential record, which showed jurists differing over terms like "pure Chinese law" (since 1865) and "law as it is applied in China" (since 1867), as opposed to "Indies-Chinese law" (since 1875) or "Chinese law that is valid in the Netherlands Indies" (since 1867).[56] The two lawyers representing either side were advocates not only for their clients but for their ideologically opposed stance on Chinese racial-legal identity. C. W. van Heekeren took an Indies-centered approach to Chinese law in the Indies. He defended the creditor, Liem Eng Tjay, and his son, and would go on to have a lucrative career collaborating with Oei Tiong Ham to build the biggest Chinese enterprise in Southeast Asia.[57] C. Th. van Deventer represented Paginio and the view that the law of the Chinese nation should be applied to the Chinese subjects in Java.

The debate between the two lawyers pitted two views of race and law against each other. For Van Heekeren, who won the first round in the landraad, the Chinese of Java were a mixed race whose social norms had developed with legal changes in their adopted homeland.[58] Van Heekeren added historical depth to Groeneveldt's observations of Chinese social life in the Indies. Settlement, intermarriage, and living under Dutch company laws for the Chinese had created a set of unique "Javanese-Chinese laws." This history of legal development included company-era statutes that granted the Chinese their own probate officials (1642), granted unmarried Chinese women in Java autonomy at the age of twenty-five (1693), and sanctioned separate marital property for women (1766). Most innovatively, Van Heekeren also cited a survey of the archives of four public notaries in Batavia, where he found "deeds wherein married Chinese women, without the endorsement of their spouses, appear [before the law] and buy and sell in autonomy; issue powers of attorney, seal contracts of loans, etc." Like in Justinian's Roman digests, he argued that four hundred years of statutory and customary legal norms had formed a body of law for the Chinese in the Dutch Indies that supported women's right to separate estates and contractual freedom.

At the Raad van Justitie (high court), Van Deventer dismissed Van Heekeren's "Javanese-Chinese law" as a lawyer's fiction.[59] He cited P. Meeter to characterize the concept of an Indies-Chinese customary law as "a fiction, thought out by the clever Chinese chiefs or their handy lawyers." Moreover, his own survey of public notaries "in Tegal, Pekalongan and Semarang [showed that] all notarial deeds, to which married Chinese women bound themselves, were invariably endorsed by their spouses." For Van Deventer, the 1855 statute gave Chinese women the right to own separate property, but the right of management and disposal remained in the hands of the husband. Tan Paginio might have owned her house, but the disposal of it was not in her authority as a married woman. It could "simply be sought ... in the legal status of the married Chinese woman according to religious laws, folk institutions and usages valid in China." In short, citing Meeter again, Chinese "legal conceptions" can be found in the "pronouncement[s] of Confucius." Siding with Van Deventer, the judge added a racial-civilizational twist: "In the year of 1891, most European legislatures had still not accorded European married woman the authority," so subjects in the colony must be "unfit" for such rights.

The Supreme Court judge Sibenius Trip affirmed the Semarang Court of Justice ruling that a Chinese woman in the Dutch Indies was not authorized to sign contracts without the assistance of her husband.[60] This decision was all the more significant, for the judge had been a proponent not only of married Chinese women's freedom to contract but also of their right to own separate matrimonial property.[61] By affirming Paginio's claim that her husband and brother had defrauded her by selling her house without her knowledge, the judicial decision saved Tan Paginio's house from confiscation, but it also ended married Chinese women's right to separate estates and contractual autonomy.

Throughout both the legislative and jurisprudential debates, sinologists and jurists zeroed in on Chinese women's subordinate position to her husband in China. In the final analysis, the courts ruled that Chinese women could not possibly be allowed to contract, because even women of a higher civilizational and racial plane in Europe did not have such freedom. In this way, orientalist legal knowledge production percolated into jurisprudence, with real consequences on the everyday life of colonial subjects in law courts and beyond. The orientalist image of patrilineal Chinese power reached beyond the walls of bureaucratic drawing rooms and law courts to affect the lives and property holdings of women in society. Notaries following legal developments in the late 1880s and 1890s would have taken note and stopped married Chinese women from making any further transactions of property on their own accord.

Keeping Wealth within the Uterine Family: The Matriarch's Agency and Arsenal

Colonial jurisprudence could only frame Tan Paginio's rights in relation to her husband's authority. Yet the trial inadvertently revealed that her brother was in fact more involved in the transaction than her husband. It was stated on the mortgage contract that "she would be represented solely by the Captain of the Chinese Tan Kok Kiem, her brother, but not by her spouse."[62] Such uterine family alliances between matriarchs and their brothers were a key feature of the "active presence of bilateral kinship" within creole Chinese patrilineal descent groups.[63] In what follows, I use a combination of genealogical records and legal sources to illustrate how three matriarchs protected the interests of their own uterine family group, essentially their own and their brother's children, using a combination of kinship-credit-legal instruments: (a) adoption, (b) cross-cousin marriage, (c) fraudulent loan security, and (d) women's freedom to will their property. While they did not set out to do so, creole Chinese matriarchs had no qualms in contravening Chinese patrilineal rules or colonial legality when the core interests of the uterine family alliance were threatened.

Tan Paginio of the Liem-Tan Alliance in Tegal: Legal Action for Self-Protection against a Marriage Alliance Gone Sour

Mapping the actors imbricated in the Tan Paginio lawsuit onto the genealogical record, a more complex entanglement of interests between the creditor (Liem Eng Tjay) and the debtor (Tan Kok Kiem) is revealed. Both men and their families were in fact allied by marriage (see figure 4.1). Tan Kok Kiem's daughter was married to Liem Eng Tjay's son. By the 1870s and 1880s, the Tan family's business fortunes were on the decline, while those of the Liem family were on the rise. According to the genealogist Steve Haryono, the fortunes of the Tan family peaked during the time of Kok Kiem's and Paginio's father—Tan Siong Kang. Besides trading rice and other crops, Tan Siong Kang had made huge profits from sugar. The Dutch appointed Tan Siong Kang the Chinese Kapitan of Tegal from 1834 to 1863. It was an indication of his political influence that upon his death, he was able to pass on the Kapitan-ship to his son, who in turn held it for another twenty years (1863–82). The son, however, was "less capable at trading, so that the businesses of the Tans one by one declined."[64] In 1882, the Dutch "honorably discharged" Kok Kiem from his officership (officers had to be in good credit standing to remain appointed) and replaced him with Liem Boen Hie—a brother of his creditor, Liem Eng Tjay, who was also his daughter's father-in-law.[65]

Based on these genealogical facts, it is hard to believe that Tan Paginio had not authorized her brother to take care of the property she must have inherited from their father. Furthermore, the loan was taken out from a brother-in-law, whose family was on the rise in Tegal. The genealogical records on the Tans are patchy. We do know to whom Kok Kiem and Paginio were married, but it would not be surprising if either or both were married to a Liem. The relentless legal actions by the Liems to recover the debt suggests that their alliance with the Tans had gone sour. Paginio successfully extracted herself from the legal obligation to sell her

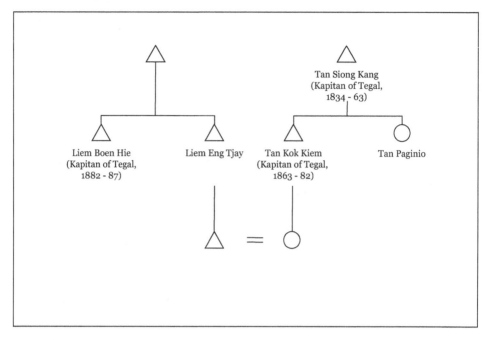

FIGURE 4.1. Marriage alliance of the Tan and Liem families of Tegal, Central Java.

house, but this does not imply that she withdrew from the uterine family alliance. She most likely found other means to support her brother and his children.

Ong Kwie Nio of the Ong-Oeij Alliance of Tangerang, Batavia: An All-Out Feud with the Colonial Probate Authorities to Retain Control of Uterine Familial Property

Ong Kwie Nio struggled against the Dutch colonial probate authority's attempt to assume guardianship over her brother's sons and, by extension, their uterine family's lands in Tangerang. Her brother Ong Boen Seng had died unexpectedly in 1881, leaving behind two underaged sons. In order to keep the lands under her control, she arranged for a cross-cousin marriage within the uterine family and activated a dormant fraudulent loan. The probate authorities sued, but she prevailed in a decade-long struggle that saw her successfully presiding over the patrilineal succession of wealth within both her natal and her own families.

Ong Kwie Nio was a second-generation member of an interlocking alliance between the Ong and Oeij families of Batavia (see figure 4.2). Her father, Ong Sieuw Ko, was a first(?)-generation Batavia Chinese who had owned a lucrative

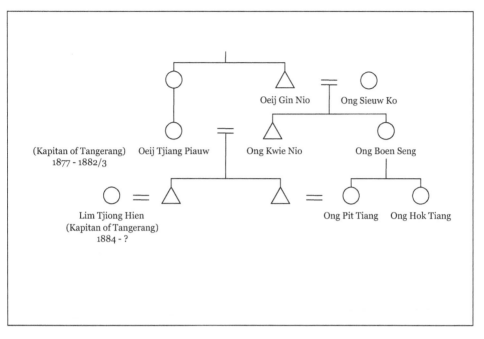

FIGURE 4.2. Two generations of cross-cousin marriages between the Ong and Oeij families of Batavia and Tangerang.

market license and several parcels of land in Tangerang since 1823. The alliance with the Oeij family developed through his marriage with a secondary wife, Oeij Gin Nio. The marriage produced a son and a daughter (Boen Seng and Kwie Nio). A cross-cousin marriage cemented the alliance in the second generation. Oeij Gin Nio arranged for a brother's son to marry her daughter. This turned out to be a good business decision because Oeij Tjiang Piauw, the nephew-cum-son-in-law, was later appointed Kapitan of Tangerang (in office 1877–83).[66] He was so competent, he leased and lived on the lands of his brother-in-law, Ong Boen Seng (hence a uxorilocal marriage) and was legally authorized to serve as his brother-in-law's general agent for twenty years.

This uterine family alliance, under the leadership of Oeij Tjiang Piauw, was not recognized by the colonial probate authorities when Ong Boen Seng died unexpectedly in 1881. The probate council turned down his application to serve as legal guardian of Ong Boen Seng's children, or his wife's nieces and nephews.[67] His reply to the council—a Dutch language letter probably drafted in translation by his lawyer—indicated how the elite creole Chinese were conscious of Dutch legal strictures but were convinced that their moral obligations superseded the law. Kapitan Oeij felt offended to be "reproached for intervening in Ong Boen Seng's estate, to which [he was told] he did not have the least right."

Feeling "very sore" (D: *zeer gevoelig*) about it, Oeij declared that "while he might not have the legal rights, . . . he felt obliged [D: *verpligt*] and well-grounded [in his claims] from a moral viewpoint [D: *zedelijke oogpunt*]" to claim guardianship.[68] He sued the probate council. But the native landraad, helmed by a Dutch judge and advised on Chinese "religious concepts" by "experts" (including Groeneveldt), rejected his plea and ordered the probate council to serve as guardian for Ong Boen Seng's two sons, both minors.[69] Oeij Tjiang Piauw died, leaving Ong Kwie Nio to lead the uterine family. By this point, she was ready to be aided by her own son-in-law, Kapitan Lim Tjiong Hien, who liaised with the probate council for her.

To prevent the authorities from splitting up the uterine family's properties, the matriarch Ong Kwie Nio tried to recover Ong Boen Seng's lands by extralegal means. First, she arranged a second generation of cross-cousin marriage between her own daughter and her elder nephew, Ong Pit Tiang.[70] Marriage conferred automatic adulthood and the legal right to withdraw one's inherited portion from guardianship.[71] The matriarch was clearly the master manipulator, for within six months of the marriage, Ong Pit Tiang had sold his lands to his aunt, now also his mother-in-law.[72] The two then tried to recover control of the younger boy's lands via Ong Pit Tiang's guardianship but failed on account of Ong Pit Tiang's inexperience.[73] It was for this reason that a fraudulent loan was reactivated.

Determined to take back control of her brother's properties, Ong Kwie Nio recalled a loan that most likely only existed on paper and was never transacted with money. In 1878, she "lent" her brother 290,000 guilders in a loan contract drawn up before a public notary.[74] Such fictitious loans served the purpose of hedging against a relative's bankruptcy, in which event the uterine family could then at least retain the lion's share of claims among debtors.[75] In this event, the default never happened, so there was no need for Ong Kwie Nio to recall her "loan" during her brother's lifetime. Refusing to buckle, the colonial probate council sued Ong Kwie Nio for colluding with her brother to make up the fraudulent loan. Citing Schlegel's and Meeter's Confucianist dictum about women's incapacity to own property, they challenged her to prove that "she had withdrawn her own money out of her purse" for the loan.[76] Knowing that it was her husband who managed their uterine family's properties, the lawyer demanded proof of her personal conscious authorization of the mortgage loan of 1878. Cross-examined and under an oath administered in the main Chinese temple in Batavia, she made the following statement: "I remember my husband . . . informing me in 1878 that he had loaned a sum of 290,000 guilders of my money, which was under his care, to my brother, and that later on he let me know that Ong Boen Seng had bound his immovable property as security to the repayment of that sum."⁷⁷ This amounted to a confession that she did not sign the mortgage contract herself back in 1878. More importantly, she did not see any boundary between herself and her brother in terms of property management—a key trait of uterine families. She said so in court under oath. The judges at both the Raad van Justitie and the Supreme Court decided in her favor. At this point, the Dutch judges maintained their prevailing doctrinal stance that married Chinese women were free to contract in their own names.⁷⁸ The Supreme Court ordered the probate court to pay Ong Kwie Nio ƒ145,000 (half the loan) out of Ong Boen Seng's estate on behalf of his second son.

Despite her oath in the Chinese temple, Ong Kwie Nio might have been suspected of actually cheating her nephew out of his inheritance. Her real intention, however, was revealed in her will when she died in 1899. She forgave her nephew of the 145,000 guilders debt awarded by the judgment. This fact supports my argument that the loan of 1878 was indeed fictitious as the probate council had alleged, and that she recalled the money only to keep the uterine family properties under her control.⁷⁹ She clearly saw her own role as that of a custodian and manager of wealth not only for her own children but also for her brother's. The bulk of her estate consisted of jewelry and a few houses that did not amount to 145,000 guilders. She did, however, hold her own property separate from her husband's. Her division of her property shows how she identified equally with both patrilineal descent groups. Remarkably, her own children, presumably already the heirs of Oeij Tjiang Piauw's significant wealth, were bypassed in favor of Oeij and Ong nieces and nephews.

Jo Heng Nio of the Han-Kan alliance in Batavia: A Cross-Cousin Adoption to Protect Her Own Son's Patrilineal Inheritance

Jo Heng Nio arranged for a cross-cousin adoption of a grandchild within her uterine family kin group to prevent her husband's wealth from being wholly inherited by the son of another wife.⁸⁰ This case did not involve any legal dispute, but the prominence of the family and the fact that the adopted grandson, Han Khing Tjiang turned Kan Hoek Hoei (H. H. Kan), later became the first and longest serving (1917–42) Chinese member of the quasi-legislature Volksraad (People's Council) in the Dutch East Indies made it a celebrated case of creole Chinese adat.

When she died in Batavia in November 1900, Jo Heng Nio was probably the richest woman in Dutch colonial Java, with an estate worth 1 million Dutch Indies guilders (see figure 4.3).⁸¹ She had inherited her wealth from her husband. In 1848, she was twenty-two years old when she married fifty-one-year-old Kan

FIGURE 4.3. Photo of Jo Heng Nio taken in the 1890s.
Source: Collection of Kan Sioe Yao.

Keng Tiong, becoming the youngest of his three wives. Kan Keng Tiong was a self-made first-generation immigrant in Batavia. He made his fortune from trading rice and producing sugar in Batavia and its environs. When he died in 1871, he divided his estate equally between his surviving widow and two sons: Kan Tjeng Sie (son by his first wife) and Kan Tjeng Soen (Jo Heng Nio's elder surviving son).[82] Crisis struck in 1896, when Kan Tjeng Soen predeceased his mother with no heir.

Family lore has it that Jo Heng Nio adopted a male heir for her deceased son to prevent Kan Tjeng Sie from becoming the sole inheritor. Strictly speaking, it was a joint action within a uterine family alliance headed by Jo Heng Nio, but principally made up of her eldest daughter (Kan Oe Nio) and son. Kan Oe Nio "gave" one of her two sons (Han Khing Tjiang) up for adoption to her deceased brother—a cross-cousin adoption (see figure 4.4). When Jo Heng Nio died in

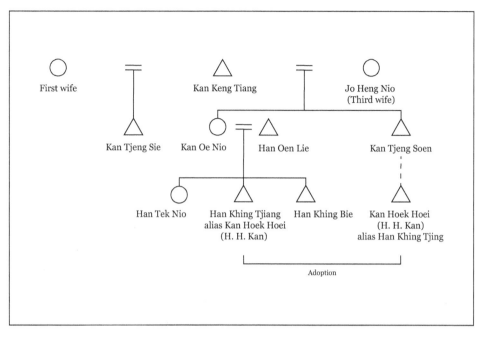

FIGURE 4.4. Cross-cousin adoption within the uterine family alliance of Jo Heng Nio, her daughter Kan Oe Nio, and her son Kan Tjeng Soen.

1901, she divided her own assets equally among her four daughters, Kan Tjeng Sie (stepson), and the adopted grandson. A colonial newspaper claimed that giving daughters equal shares as sons went against "Chinese adat," but the son did not challenge the will "out of the great respect he had for his mother."[83] It appears that the Kan siblings did not split up their mother's estate but instead set up a Jo Heng Nio Operations Company to jointly manage their inherited wealth. As late as 1954, the Kan siblings and their Kan/Han (and Tan) descendants had not split up the company. It was the grand matriarch's name and memory rather than any Kan, Han, or Tan patriarch that held the family alliance together.[84]

This chapter traced the social power of creole Chinese matriarchs to the wealth they inherited from their fathers and husbands and located their agency within uterine family alliances nestled in between patrilineal families. An enabling factor in colonial society was the freedom of Chinese women to dispose of property in their own names, independent of their husbands. As a more sinological approach to governing the Chinese matured in the latter half of the nineteenth century, this freedom was taken away. Examining the matriarchal actions of some of the more powerful Chinese elites, it becomes clear that while they were ultimately reproductive of their natal and their own families' patrilinies, they were themselves allied with their brothers, sons, and daughters and, through cross-cousin marriages/adoptions, primarily protective of the interests of their uterine families. From the 1890s, the first signs of change to that older familial world dominated by creole matriarchs appeared in the form of Dutch education for the young Chinese boys and girls of wealthy backgrounds. In the latter half of the book, we turn to examining how the onset of colonial modernity wrought momentous changes to these preexisting notions of gender and race among the Chinese of Java.

Part 3
RELIGION AND THE REINVENTION OF PATRILINEAL STRANGERHOOD

At the turn of the twentieth century, a group of creole Chinese reformers advocated sweeping changes to Chinese society in Java in the name of a renewed Confucian religion. They started newspapers, wrote novels, championed new marriage rituals, and above all built new schools across the island to propagate their new vision Chineseness to their compatriots. The advent of this form of creole religion-based reformism turned gender issues into open topics of public discourse that demanded mass attention and action. In dialogue with Dutch colonial civilizing discourses, a new Confucian religion-based patrilineal ideology was formulated surrounding the questions of race, marriage, family, and women. The two chapters in part 3 trace how, between 1900 and the 1920s, reformers and writers at the center of this movement imagined a new creole Chinese racial identity for Java by experimenting with and advocating new forms of marriage rituals, desire, sexuality, and love—both in the popular print medium and in practice.

5

CONFUCIANISM, MARRIAGE, AND SEXUALITY

In 1900, a group of reformers in Batavia set up Tiong Hoa Hwee Koan (THHK, or the Chinese Association) to reform religious practices and organize modern education. The THHK movement quickly spread across the rest of Java not only in terms of religious reform and education but in an explosion of publications, newspapers, and penny novels in the creole Malay vernacular. A newly imagined Chinese patriliny was born through the creolization of Western forms of God, religion, marriage, desire, sex, and love. This chapter begins by retracing how reformers constructed a modern creole Chinese patriliny through their dialogic encounters with the Christian God, marriage, and sexuality. Chapter 6 then turns to the birth of creole Chinese racial discourse through their patriarchal appropriation of Westerns forms of desire and love.

Reforming the Confucian Moral Subject: Marriage and Modern Rites

The growth of a reformed Confucian religion in urban Java at the turn of the twentieth century has attracted much scholarly attention. Scholars generally agree that the formation of the THHK marked the onset of a sinicizing move by creole reformers to make their communities more Chinese through the teaching of Mandarin in schools and the launching of campaigns to extirpate Indonesian influences in religious practices.[1] Yet the gender dimensions of this religious renewal movement remain underexplored. I retrace the moral formation of the modern creole Confucian (male) subject to the movement's countercolonial discourse on religion and marriage. Proclaiming Confucianism to be the answer to Western Christianity and natural science (or natural law), the reformers, I show, yoked the male ego of this new Chinese moral subject to Christianized marriage rites, thereby subjecting it to equality with its female counterpart in symbolic if not yet discursive terms.

It is well known that the Confucian reformers borrowed heavily from Dutch forms of Christianity they encountered on the ground. Historian Charles Coppel has shown that the birth of the THHK in 1900 was both a product of and a reaction against Dutch missionary efforts to convert the Chinese of West Java. Important members of the founding group, including Phoa Keng Hek (president) and Lie Kim Hok, and editors of the THHK Malay Confucian weekly, *Li Po*, were all students of the Dutch missionary school in Bogor (see figure 5.1). Early on, the reformers had to fend off their monotheistic conception of Chinese religion

FIGURE 5.1. Portrait of Lie Kim Hok.

Source: Nio Joe Lan, Riwajat 40 Taon dari T.H.H.K., 276.

from charges of having invented a "false religion" by the Dutch missionary L. Tiemersma. Lie Kim Hok and a precocious Kwee Tek Hoay, who was sixteen years old at this time, engaged in a yearlong (1902–3) polemical debate with Tiemersma in *Li Po*.[2] They defended the Confucian concept of Tian (C: Heavens) as "an impersonal force, a source of energy and life, rather than the Christian one of a God with human characteristics." After abolishing the more "superstitious" popular practices, they argued, Chinese religion could be more rational and suitable for modern times than Christianity, "which tried to enjoin moral behavior through a combination of bribery and fear with promises of Heaven and threats of Hell."[3]

From its very first public announcement, "A Letter to all Chinese . . . ," it was clear that the THHK's goal was to achieve parity with Europeans in the domains of morality and knowledge. Drafted by Lie Kim Hok and issued in July 1900 in Batavia, the opening paragraphs of the movement's first public declaration cited passages from his *Hikayat Khonghoetjoe* (M: Story of Confucius, published in 1897) that traced the "transcendental goodness and truth" of Confucius's teachings to intellectuals and political leaders "of the well-known European civilized race."[4] In a telling passage, the reformers attributed the relevance of the Confucian classics as "holy books" to the authority and opinion of European sinologists:

> It is not only us of the Chinese race who are saying (that the teachings of the Prophet Confucius are true and good), like the "sea calling itself salty," even among Europeans who are famous for being the civilized race [M: *bangsa sopan*], there are many who say the same.
>
> There is a gentleman of the European race, who knows the classics of China well, and even translated the holy books of *Taij Hak* [Hk: Great Learning; C: Da Xue], *Tiong Iong* [Hk: Doctrine of the Mean; C: Zhong Yong], *Siang Beng* [Hk: Analects Part I; C: Shang Ming] and *He Beng* [Hk: Analects Part II; C: Xia Ming] into the Dutch language. He said that among all the books that have spread since knowledge was printed on paper, there is perhaps not one that can be the equal of the essays of Confucius.[5]

It was telling that Lie had to rely on European sinologists to assert the theological superiority of these classical Confucian texts. Aside from the fact that he could not access the text in its original language, it was even more remarkable that his subsequent outline of a moral subject made no reference to any Confucian saying, not to mention these more esoteric texts.

Having pronounced the parity of European and Chinese classical or religious texts, Lie Kim Hok went on to provide a programmatic vision of what moral enlightenment should be like for the average person. As a brief explanation of what the broader project would entail, this statement of moral reform provided no intrinsic quality or even method to showcase how the celebrated religious texts would help enable such change. It was an enticement to let Confucius's teachings bring about moral change toward enlightenment, refinement, and parity with Europeans. What resembled Christianity more than Confucianism in this formulation was the centrality of desire, sin, and evil in Lie's conception of the moral ego, and how enlightenment could only be attained by being constantly on watch:

> People who obtain these good teachings, will surely become good in their consciousness [M: *ingatan*], thoughts [M: *pikiran*], manners [M: *adat*], heart-mind [M: *hati*] and behavior [M: *kelakoean*]. . . . Because of these teachings, one's consciousness will become enlightened [M: *terang*], he will forget all bad and ugly affairs, and remember only the good. He will no longer think about deceiving others, and think instead of fighting all forms of desire [M: *napsoe*] that are not good. His manners will no longer be coarse and arrogant, so as to bring shame [M: *ketjelahan*] to himself, but he will only lower himself and be sweet in manners. His heart will no longer be haughty and blurred, but become capable of judging with justice, hating what is unjust, and become generous. His actions will no longer be sinful [M: *hina*] or evil [M: *djahat*], but will only encompass what is appropriate. In short, people who obtain good teachings, will have culture and manners, be able to tend to his own affairs with his own sense of respect, and live with a good name among humanity. His parents will not live in shame.[6]

No doubt the inclusion of the parents' sense of shame as a sanction against the ego's moral actions was key, but it was the only Confucian modifier to this Christian notion of an ego suspended between sin and salvation (or self-enlightenment).

What in fact did Lie mean by the moral enlightening potential of Confucius's teachings? His most profound thoughts on these teachings can be found in his translation of an orientalist biography of the sage. Evi Sutrisno has demonstrated that Lie translated the main text of *Hikayat Khonghoetjoe* (1897) into Malay from a Dutch translation (1862) of an earlier French rendition of Confucius's biography.[7] In contrast to the Enlightenment thinker Montesquieu's classification of China's law and politics as despotic, this early nineteenth-century French interpretation of Confucius curiously retained the pre-Enlightenment French thinkers' admiration of Confucian political thought as the acme of human reason. It was this enlightened Confucian thought that Lie subscribed to and sought to convey to his creole Chinese readers. Rather than stressing the subject's filial piety to parents, husbands, or kings, Lie must have been taken by the text's emphasis on his moral freedom. Translating a passage that explained Confucius's philosophy in the author's own voice, Lie must have agreed with how, in this interpretation, the Confucian moral will was free: "with the reason [M: *boedi* = D: *rede*] and moral freedom [M: *kemerdekaan hati* = D: *zedelijke vrijheid*] one possesses, ... [One] knows and feels through the heart [M: *hati*], good and evil, and feels that one has great duties that has to be performed for God/Heaven, for oneself and for humanity."[8] Lie's translation established for himself, as it did for the movement after 1900, the creolized moral epistemic basis for reformist change. Note that he translated "reason" with the Malay-Indonesian word *boedi*, which encompasses the meanings of "character," "sensibleness," and "cunning" alongside "mind" and "reason."[9] More critically, this passage indicated to Lie how a Chinese person could be morally emancipated, unfettered from the moral authority of other humans or institutions as long as that person was accountable to "God/Heaven" and humanity. By contemporary European terms, this was no doubt a quaint pre-Montesquieuian gloss of the rationality of the Confucian project. But this affirmation of change based on reason—and, by extension, natural science—justified to THHK and their local Chinese audience both the historical necessity and respectability of their call for change.

Lie in fact left the doctrinal work of linking the Confucian texts to Christianity and science to his more esoterically inclined colleagues. In a nuanced reading of Yoe Tjai Siang's and Tan Ging Tiong's Malay translation of the Confucian *Great Learning* (C: *Daxue*) and *Doctrine of the Mean* (C: *Zhongyong*) (1902), historian Liu Oiyan shows that the Dutch-missionary-educated Yoe in particular tried to theologically synthesize Confucianism with Christianity. If Lie Kim Hok had demonstrated the monotheist potential of Confucianism by equating the heavens (C: Tian, M: Allah) with God, Yoe went a step further by regarding the sublime Confucian idea of sincerity (or purity) in the heart (C: Zhi Cheng, 至诚) as homologous or even synonymous with Jesus Christ.[10] Although the *Doctrine of the Mean* does render Zhi Cheng in such a way as to make its mystical connection with Tian/God plausible, nowhere does it personify Zhi Cheng as God's son sent to redeem humankind's sins. It was in a mystically framed afterword titled "The Heavenly Way" (C: Tiandao) that Yoe made the claim for equivalence while also declaring that the Confucian God's way was "nature"—the "universal natural law of origins" within which was encompassed "the knowledge of nature, physics, astronomy, cosmogony, geology with the end being Knowledge of Religion."[11]

Lie himself was more attracted to the pragmatic means of forming the new Confucian moral subject through a rites reform campaign. He had announced this ambition in July 1900, when he identified one of the reformist group's missions as "advancing [M: *bikin majoe*] or improving Chinese customs [M: *istiadat*] ... with rules [M: *atoeran-atoeran*] that would agree with the teachings or character of the Prophet Confucius."[12] These reforms have been cited for their sinicizing tendency.[13] But the racializing pressures were also coming from the Dutch sinologists and from the colonial state in the form of its civilizing mission, which had been in place since at least the 1890s. As two Dutch sinologists' China-focused studies of "Chinese marriage" in the 1890s demonstrate, the creolized marriage customs of Java were not deemed worthy of ethnographic study. J. W. Young's *Het huwelijk en de wetgeving hierop in China* was a text-based comparative legal study of marriage in late imperial China from four broad civil law approaches: (1) required conditions, (2) engagement and solemnization, (3) rights and duties of husband and wife, and (4) dissolution and remarriage.[14] This was translated into Malay by the Batavia-based Albrecht & Rusche as *Boekoe adat-adat kawin dan ondang-ondangnja di tanah Tjina* (M: Book on marriage customs and laws on marriage in China).[15] Likewise, Godfried von Faber's *Het familie- en erfrecht der Chineezen in Nederlandsch-Indië* was not so much about creolized customary practices as the constitutional status of Chinese family law in the Dutch Indies. It revealed that at its base, family law was about race management. Whether a group was classified as European or native depended on "the difference between their general state of civilization [D: *beschavingstoestand*]."[16]

Read against this colonial context, the symbolic counter-colonial meanings behind the THHK's marriage rites reform were as important as their substance. In its very first official meeting, THHK directors appointed two committees to look into marriage and funeral rites reform. Among all members, only Khoe Siauw Eng, a Chinese-literate secretary of the Batavia Chinese Council, and Lie Kim Hok were appointed to both committees.[17] While the sinologists had characterized Chinese marriage as an institution prescribed by rules from the classical texts and laws of imperial China, these creole reformers were demonstrating not only that the rites could be changed but that they could approximate Western civilized standards. The substance of the reforms has been well studied. Essentially, in notices issued to THHK branches island-wide, they encouraged Chinese to stop the more "superstitious" (M: *tachajoel*) or more crassly symbolic elements of the marriage rites. Divination by horoscope to determine the suitability of the bride, whether through the mediation of ancestors, the household deity (Hk: toapekkong) or fortune tellers, was discouraged.

But just as important as the content of these reforms, I argue, is the mode of communication and the political-symbolic discursive effect it had among its audience. The fact that reformers sitting in a committee in Batavia could redesign marriage rites and convey these as decisions *for all Chinese* to THHK branches across Java was indicative of the social power the printed word had acquired. In 1906, Lie Kim Hok and Tan Kim Bo, both editors of the THHK's newspaper *Kabar Perniagaan* (M: Commercial news, founded 1903), formed the two-man committee to recommend rites reforms.[18] These new rules were issued at a point when the THHK was rapidly expanding its school and branch network across West Java, elsewhere on the island, and beyond.[19] "In places where there is a branch of Batavia's Tiong Hoa Hwe Koan," the directors declared, "these rules will also be implemented, so that people residing in these places can perform their marriage in the branch houses." After the application, "THHK managers would decide whether the applications were approved or not."[20]

Substantively, they came closest to mimicking Christian marriage solemnization. The implication that a man, rather than his parents, could initiate proceedings for his own marriage was revolutionary: "Whoever wishes to follow these rules, be they members of the Tiong Hoa Kwe Koan or not, may express so in writing to the Directors of this association by giving your name, place of residence and occupation, [and the name of] the person whose child you are marrying, with the date when it will happen, which cannot be sooner than within a month."[21] With solemnization as the key rite, other traditional customs, like the matching of horoscopes, hair combing, bed setting, and the fetching of the bride, were relegated secondary to the solemnization ceremony. As an involved observer at the time, Kwee Tek Hoay later recalled that the new ceremonies were drawn up "at the request of several Directors who sought to make the THHK building into a sort of church and to provide a model for marriage that would be moderately modern, yet proper."[22]

THHK's marriage rites reform has been deemed a failure mainly for its disconnect from marriage practices on the ground. Lea Williams argued that these reforms "scratched the surface of the overseas Chinese cultural complex by proposing seemingly meaningless reforms in etiquette and ceremonials."[23] According to Kwee Tek Hoay, THHK "records show that only about a half dozen couples were married according to the THHK regulations and for many years there has been no mention of weddings in the THHK building."[24] He speculated that this "was probably due to the establishment of the Civil Registry for Chinese and to the shift in emphasis of THHK away from the reform of customs to an exclusive concern with the Chinese educational movement." Writing from the late 1930s, Kwee could by then say that the "reformist group [M: *kaum moeda*] has progressed to the point when marriages without religious or traditional practices are performed with bride and groom simply signing their names in front of the Civil Registry." But the colonial Civil Registry for Chinese marriages, as I will show in chapter 7, was not enacted until thirteen years after the THHK rules were set.

The Chinese Council of Batavia did in fact continue some version of this reformed marriage ceremony during the 1910s, which in turn prepared the local Chinese for the colonial Chinese Civil Registry. Some of the more activist founders of the THHK—reformers such as Khoe A Fan (the vice president), Lie Hin Liang, and Khoe Siauw Eng—were concurrently officers on the Chinese Council. Lieutenant Khoe A Fan's daughter was presumably married in this new-style wedding in the THHK building in May 1907.[25] The Chinese Council picked up the mantle when the THHK turned its focus to education, but its authority as ritual master of the Chinese remained unchallenged, at least among the creole Chinese of Batavia. In October 1913, Major Khouw Kim An, a less active director, consulted the THHK on the colonial government's plan to introduce a Civil Registry for the Chinese. The directors of the THHK replied that the plan was good for the Chinese, then left the matter to be managed by the Chinese Council.[26] Echoing the reformist calls for simplicity and economy, the Batavia Chinese Council marriage register stopped recording the names of go-betweens in 1912. Although still in the minority among marriages registered, the Chinese Council began to receive couples and their parents for "wedding celebrations" in the same year.[27]

The reform movement created the Confucian (male) moral subject as both an ideal and a contestable figure in creole Chinese public discourse for the first time. Confucius's teachings, it was believed, would serve to point this moral ego to an enlightened and civilized future, in which the Chinese race would be recognized as equals with Europeans. Although not explicitly stated, marriage rites reform was important for Lie Kim Hok and the THHK insofar as a significant element of the ego's structure of desire would ultimately have to be moderated within the institution of marriage. In fact, once these public-facing pronouncements and experiments went out, they made it discursively possible to imagine change in the moral-sexual lives of individuals. Before we get to that, however, a brief sociological context of these writers and editors is in order.

Print Revolution and Creole Chinese Bourgeois Morality

It is by now common knowledge that the advent of mass-market print materials heralded radically new forms of political imagination across colonial Asia in the late nineteenth and early twentieth centuries.[28] But the scholarship is only just beginning to turn to the affective dimensions of this nation- or ethnic-community-formation process.[29] The ethnic Chinese revivalist movement that began in Batavia spread across the island not only through organizing committees but also through the medium of print in the form of newspapers, printed manuals, and novels, the latter of which included a new genre of love stories. In contrast to the centralized dissemination of reformulated Confucian thought in their religious reform endeavors, a more loosely connected network of writers would be at the forefront of translating and appropriating popular Western ideas of sexuality and love in the remaking of ethnic Chinese bourgeois morality. Who were these writers, and how far and wide did their network spread?

Between 1900 and 1920, Sino-Malay newspapers and printing presses circulated an ethno-moral discourse of Chinese subjectivity in the form of popular manuals and mass-market novels. The local-born *peranakan* Chinese in Java began to publish their own newspapers and translations of literary classics from their homeland in the romanized Malay script from the 1880s. But at the turn of the twentieth century, several transformations signaled the rise of a new Sino-Malay printing sphere with a more distinctive Chinese identity. Editorial teams became more exclusively Chinese. Newspapers acquired Chinese names. Original novels surrounding the semi-fictionalized life stories of the local Chinese began to be composed. In contrast to the top-down religious reform pronouncements, reformist journalists and editors generated popular manuals and dime novels, whose mass circulation gave structure to new notions of ethno-moralities.

The Chinese of Java entered the vernacular Malay news and printing market in the mid-1880s, in the midst of a global sugar crisis that hit Java. Pioneered by Eurasians in the major cities of colonial Java, the news periodicals *Selompret Melajoe* (founded 1860) in Semarang, *Bintang Timur* (f. 1862) in Surabaya, and *Bintang Barat* (f. 1869) published a mix of commercial news; news translated from the Dutch newspapers; local issues concerning the common people, like rising rice prices; and advertisements. Written in "low" or "bazaar" Malay—the lingua franca of the marketplace—each paper attracted a circulation of between four hundred and six hundred subscribers.[30] As Chinese entrepreneurs and publishers took over printing presses and newspapers, they also devoted more attention to local Chinese news.[31] It was also on these pages that the Eurasians, followed by Chinese editors and writers, began composing Malay novelettes and lyric poetry (M: *syair*) for the Indonesian, Eurasian, Chinese, and Arab residents of the port cities.[32]

The rise of the Chinese reform movement on Java in 1900 "prompted a sudden flowering of 'organs' or mouthpieces" for its organizing body, which were "heavily Chinese in orientation and character."[33] As the THHK spread its education mission across the island, local vernacular Malay newspapers bearing Chinese titles and some Chinese characters sprung up. In Sukabumi, Tan Ging Tiong and Yoe Tjai Siang founded the Confucianist *Li Po* in 1901 to debate religion with Dutch Reformed Church missionaries. Other officially or unofficially THHK-affiliated newspapers included Tan Soe Djwan's *Sien Po* (f. 1902) in Surakarta, Lo Swie Tek's *Loen Boen* (f. 1902), Kwa Wan Hong's *Warna Warta* (f. 1902) in Semarang, H. F. R. Kommer's *Pewarta Soerabaja* (1903), and F. Wiggers and Lie Kim Hok's *Kabar Perniagaan* (later, *Perniagaan*) in Batavia (1903). For the first ten years of the twentieth century, at least one new Chinese Malay newspaper would appear each year on Java.[34]

Until 1917, Sino-Malay newspapers held a nationalist orientation that was reformist without contradicting colonial policy. This culturally nationalistic and reformist stance meant that the papers could accommodate editors and journalists drawn from both the pro-colonial wealthier Kapitan elite families and the urban middle class. What united these writers was their exposure to Dutch education and a commitment to a modern reformist outlook. Among those from elite Kapitan families include the brothers Tan Ging Tiong (1870–1935) and Tan Tjhan Hie (1870s?–?) of Juwana (East Java), and Phoa Tjoen Hoat (1883–1928) and Phoa Tjoen Hoay (1890–1966) of Bogor (West Java). The Phoa brothers were at various times associated with the *Perniagaan* of Batavia and *Li Po* of Sukabumi as editors or journalists.[35] All would have attended at least the elementary schools reserved for Europeans (Europeesche Lagere School). Some, like the Tan brothers, were taught classical Chinese by a private tutor and would be involved in translating Confucian classics into Malay in the reform movement.

Many more of the early reformist writer-editors came from average bourgeois backgrounds. In the early years, they were aligned with the *Perniagaan* group or with other Confucian periodicals in Semarang or Surabaya. Lie Kim Hok, for instance, contributed to *Bintang Djohar, Pembrita Betawi, Perniagaan,* and *Li Po*. Self-made men like Gouw Peng Liang (1869–1928) and Thio Tjin Boen (1885–1940) contributed to various local newspapers and edited *Perniagaan* in the 1910s and 1920s. Sie Hian Ling (1860s?–1928) of Semarang—the first Chinese journalist in the city (since 1885)—would have been tutored in the Chinese classics, with a self-taught knowledge of written Malay and Dutch. He founded his own weekly *Sinar Djawa* in 1900, which he published for thirteen years.[36] Even Tan Boen Kim (1887–1959), born in Batavia and a renegade among his generation of writers, never worked for *Perniagaan* but edited the Confucian *Tjoen Tjhioe* briefly in 1916.[37]

In contrast to the older generation of reformist writer-editors, the more radically nationalist *Sin Po* group would be less concerned with the moral formation of its readers. In the mid-1910s, Chinese public opinion in Java split over the questions of nationality and colonial militia duty. This younger *Sin Po* editorial group, who rejected Dutch nationality outright, did not dabble in fiction or moral tracts. Early editors Hauw Tek Kong and Kwee Hing Tjiat, for example, never wrote any.[38] Tjoe Bou San (1892–1925), became the first *Sin Po* editor to write a love story, although this was while he was editing the Confucian periodical *Tjhoen Tjhioe* of Surabaya.[39] Tan Tjin Kang (1900–1932), for a time an editor for *Sin Po*, would publish his first novel with the *Sin Po* press in 1922.[40]

The generation of reformist writer-editors at the helm of Chinese Malay newspapers between 1900 and 1920 hailed largely from elitist and middling social backgrounds. Like the THHK-Batavia reformers, many went to Dutch schools and, broadly speaking, shared the THHK's vision of trying to improve the Chinese race-nation through religious reform. While not all were deeply involved in the Confucian religious revivalist movement, they shared with the THHK the vision that Western (or Dutch) notions of the modern self could be creolized in an Indies Chinese form. How did these writers collectively reshape the affective elements of creole Chinese identity in the first decade of the twentieth century?

Sexual Hygiene and Reproductive Moral Duty

In the early twentieth century, a more self-consciously Chinese public sphere, preoccupied with frontline news of international political events in China, took root among the creoles of Java. Through the same newspaper and publishing networks, creole writers with a Confucian reformist bent appropriated the contemporary Western discourse on "social purity" to turn sexuality into a matter of moral duty. These sexual hygiene manuals were marketed for a broader Asian cosmopolitan milieu, although on issues like the reproductive preference for sons, they betrayed distinctively Chinese traits. As the pragmatic and popular front of the reformers' formation of modern moral subjects, Western sexual hygiene knowledge was reinvented as a mystical medium of an all-encompassing (subtly Confucian) God and Nature.

In the last quarter of the nineteenth century, secular feminist activists like Annie Besant in London redefined the meaning of love and marriage through their campaigns to popularize ethically responsible understandings of sex and the human reproductive system. In America and western Europe, medical doctors, psychologists, public health campaigners, biologists, and educators published manuals and guides about the human anatomy and sex, which were grounded in discourses of secular morality and concepts of purity and the natural. These campaigns unmoored Western marriage from its institutional base in the Christian church by reimagining it as a partnership in mutually responsible, exclusive, and hygienic sexual endeavors.

This secular sexuality movement reached the Chinese in Java indirectly via the Dutch metropole. A decade behind their British and American counterparts, the Dutch campaigns and debates reached their peak in the 1890s. Spearheaded by public health campaigner and leader of the neo-Malthusian society, Jacobus Schoondermark, sexual hygiene and sex education made inroads into Dutch society via the circulation of marriage guides, sex manuals, and polemical pamphlets. While the campaign did not enter the Indies public sphere, its literature was readily available and circulated widely among the Dutch-reading public from the 1890s on.[41] The bookstore H. M. van Dorp & Co. regularly placed advertisements for such popular guides and manuals. One 1896 advertisement included Dr. T. R. Allison's *The Book for Married Women*, Dr. E. Clement's *Hygiene for Marriage*, Dr. F. S. Kamp's *The Sexual Contraceptives*, Dr. A. Lesser's *Love without Children*, and *The Red Book: On the Sexual Relationship between Husband and Wife*.[42]

The Sino-Malay translators and collators of these marriage and sexuality manuals belonged to the network of intelligentsia who set up the Confucian-nationalist THHK schools and published the first explicitly nationalist and political newspapers in Java: the *Perniagaan* and *Sin Po*. I have been able to trace three such translated creole Sino-Malay texts—all published in the 1910s. The first of the three, *Laws and Mysteries: On the Relationship between Women and Men, or Knowledge about Humanity People Have to Know*, was published in 1913 by the Tjiong Koen Bie press of Batavia and "translated and collated" under the pseudonyms Butatuli and Hemeling.[43] Butatuli was most likely the Hakka-*peranakan* editor-writer Lauw Giok Lan (1882–1952).[44] Lauw edited the reformist newspaper *Perniagaan* from 1907 to 1909 before he passed the editorship to Gouw Peng Liang. Both Lauw and Gouw became actively involved in the THHK movement in Batavia and elsewhere in Java.

Gouw Peng Liang showed a broader social concern about sex and gender issues that went beyond the immediate familial context of marriage. He might have been one of the translators of the second text, *What a Woman Has to Know: For the Use of Whoever Wants to Prosper and Be Happy and Healthy* (1916?).[45] The third text was a marriage guide, *The Life of Husband and Wife* (1918?), which contained a mix of translated sexual hygiene and parental advice for the young.[46] Besides these, he also translated a prostitution abolitionist text, *The Sale of Women and Girls: An Advice for Curing the Sin of Adultery* (1919).[47] Like Lauw, Gouw went to a Dutch primary school and built a career in the Sino-Malay newspapers beginning in the 1890s. As I will discuss in chapter 6, he was the first author to publish a love story with *peranakan* Chinese characters (1906). As editor-in-chief of *Perniagaan* from 1909 to 1916 and as a reformer with the

THHK from its early years, his was the leading voice for the conservative wing of the reformist movement among the Chinese.

Akin to the contemporary "purity crusades" in the West, Lauw and Gouw framed sexual knowledge as a function of moral and spiritual hygiene.[48] In their translations, they stressed the "natural" and the God-divined bases of the new knowledge of the human anatomy and sexual desires. The appeal to God and Nature was not new to the reform movement. This was the pragmatic manifestation of the broader mystical Confucian revivalist move, as exemplified in Yoe Tjai Siang's equation of the Confucian God with Nature, to reinvent the moral subject for modernity. It is remarkable, however, that in none of these translated sexual hygiene guides did the translator attribute the divine source of the knowledge to a Confucian or Chinese God. In his opening to *Laws and Mysteries*, Lauw suggested that different religions in fact shared the same source of divinity: "[This] lesson or knowledge is given by Alam, a creature that is also called God or in foreign languages simply Natuur, Nature, Natur. People who have religion name the creature: Allah, in Malay and Arab, etc., or God, as called by the Dutch." In *What a Woman Has to Know*, the anonymous translators, who called themselves "knowledgeable people," chose a text that opened with the claim, "Marriage is the principal of all the duties of creatures." To fulfill their marital duties, people needed sexual hygiene knowledge, which were both "measures given by the power of Nature" and "public knowledge gifted by God."[49] Gouw Peng Liang, in the opening chapter of *The Life of Husband and Wife*, attributed to "the power of nature, the connection between the bodies (of the husband and wife)," and reasoned that it was nature's "way to increase the count of humans in the world."[50]

These translator-reformers were clearly aware of the novelty and sensitivity of discussing sex and sexual organs in the printed word for their Malay-reading audience. *Laws and Mysteries* carried illustrations of the male and female sexual organs, and medical diagrams of nude men and women. Consistent with the sexual hygiene literature, all three carried extensive discussions on sex and menstruation, sexually transmitted diseases, the ideal frequency and timing of sex with one's spouse, and the harms of masturbation for the young. The fact that the first two guides appeared under pseudonyms and anonymously was an indication that the translators considered the subject controversial. The translators of *Laws and Mysteries* warned: "Children who have not reached majority should not be given the book to read. But a parent must feel it his/her responsibility, to put the book in the hands of his/her mature son, so that he will not remain in the dark about the secrets and dangers of the law of love."

By their choice of text, the translators emphasized the curbing of sexual desire within a monogamous love marriage as a moral duty. In *Laws and Mysteries*,

Lauw framed his collation of sexual hygiene advice with the medieval Jewish philosopher Maimonides's concept of the "law of love." This was a concept he gleaned from a French Jewish text, from which he also appropriated the title of his work.[51] Love is interpreted here as an omnipresent force that animates and connects all living beings. It operates according to strict laws, whose transgression would bring about disaster—namely, syphilis.[52] Lauw went so far as to burnish his advice with the marriage and sex laws laid down in the Judaic Talmud, including strict monogamy and separate sleeping arrangements during the wife's menstruation.[53]

Gouw Peng Liang's marriage guide had a less severe God but a stern father figure dispensing the moral disciplinary message. Giving the sexual hygiene literature a Confucian twist, Gouw highlighted how sex was not to be pursued for pleasure but for the sake of procuring an heir to the lineage. It would be going against the wishes of Nature, Gouw warned, to "seek pleasure without knowledge [M: *keruan*], for the primary goal of sex [M: *sabadan*] is to procure descendants."[54] In fact, all three guides failed to mention contraception, although it was a key element in the contemporary Euro-American sexual hygiene movement. The notion that sex could be had for pleasure without the need for procreation appeared alien to these translator-reformers. Gouw paid particular attention to the urban youth:

> There are surely many ways to satisfy one's lust [M: *napsoe*] in the big cities, so that even people who have very fresh bodies, either men or women, are unable to follow the [prescribed] path. Moreover, in big cities, people interact with many others. The looks of one person becomes more attractive from one to another. The affairs of pleasure are so many that one's lust expands by not a little. Even more so one has to be able to control one's lust. That is because everyone has to fight his/her predatory [M: *memburu*] lust from young. This is especially [true] for those who have less strong bodies. You will need to take care of yourself.[55]

He saved his most emotion-laden words, however, for the final chapter, "Advice from a good father to his newly married son." For this transitional generation, parents like Gouw were prepared to grant their children free-choice marriage, although not without a healthy dose of parental advice. A woman would "become your wife not only because your parents agreed. . . . She is the wife of your own choice and she has such good qualities that cannot be weighed."[56] No longer should sex outside of marriage be tolerated. In fact, even sex within marriage should be moderated for one's healthy being: "A young newly married husband can give in excessively to pleasure, until he quickly loses his strength. Such a marriage cannot be said to be a good one.... No part of the body is hurt more from excessive pleasure, than the brain, where one's most noble strengths are stored."[57] The son whose wife was pregnant was advised to "sleep separately,... control your lust,.... [and] stay loyal to her by not visiting prostitutes."[58] Gouw's hypothetical father went so far as to threaten personal condemnation if the son would abuse his marital sexual compact: "I will hate you, if you forget your duty and become disloyal to your wife. Later on, you will be cursed with that poison (syphillis) which you will have bought at such a high price and with such disaster, when you infect your wife, who had done nothing wrong to you."[59]

Over the course of the 1910s and 1920s, more and more Dutch-educated young Chinese would have had access to the original sex hygiene manuals in Dutch. But the overwhelming majority of the Chinese in Java, even the Dutch educated, would have been equally if not more comfortable with the Malay translations. Collectively, these sexual hygiene manuals presented a radically new notion of sex, marriage, and moral duty to Malay readers in colonial urban Java. The reformers tried to ground free-choice marriage in God or Nature-prescribed duties of self-restraint, sexual fidelity to one's spouse, hygienic sexual practices, and procreation. These manuals presented sex and marriage as stark moral choices between pleasure and duty, with Nature-prescribed diseases and disasters as the consequence for missteps. What they left unsaid—the moral and emotional bond that undergirded marital sex—would become the central theme of Sino-Malay literature throughout the late colonial period.

These mystically inclined sexual hygiene manuals prefigured in tentative ways the advent of more clinical and socially oriented ways of discoursing about sexuality, morality, and race in the 1930s. Although the Chinese were never in the position to change the course of the colonial state's racial policy, medically educated creoles would serve as intermediaries, disseminators, and disputers of eugenics-tinged policies and opinions. It was not until the mid-1930s that some Dutch-educated Chinese were in a position to not only adapt and mystify but also speak back to colonial sexuality knowledge production. Among others, Dr. Loe Ping Kian, based at the charity hospital Jang Seng Ie in Batavia, would be at the center of a network of socially concerned medical doctors and intelligentsia who contributed to late colonial discourse on sexuality through research on sexually transmitted diseases and fertility among Chinese and Indonesian women.[60] Loe was one of the main collaborators with Kwee Yat Nio on *Maandblad istri* (M: Women's monthly), which aimed to educate married women in domestic science, sexuality, and motherhood in the late 1930s.[61] Loe's doctoral dissertation, published in 1941, would use social scientific research to dispel the colonial myth that syphilis was more common among Chinese and Indonesian women.[62]

The modern creole Chinese subject was discursively born in Java with the THHK's announcement of a moral reform project addressed to "all Chinese" within the reach of their publishing network. The moral subject, I have shown, was modeled in important ways on the Christian and Enlightenment split between reason and affect, the latter element of which was to be disciplined by both religion and scientific knowledge about sexuality. Marriage, with its rites modernized toward equality between the two genders, and sex within marriage, with its social meaning tethered to one's duty to God and reproducing the male lineage, were two basic ways a new morally "Chinese" subject was reinterpreted at the turn of the twentieth century. Let us now turn to how affect or the discourse of love itself became a racialized and nationalistic trope for the remaking of Chinese identity.

6

LOVE, DESIRE, AND RACE

Chapter 5 showed how a Chinese moral subject was born through Confucian reformers' appropriation of Christian morals and Western sexuality. This chapter examines how that moral subjectivity became racialized and popularized through the medium of the love story. Print was central to this process. In 1903, Chinese moral discourse assumed a new form when a new literary genre—the local-themed love story—emerged and in subsequent years flooded the print market. Although only a handful of these stories were written initially, about fifty creole Chinese writers, all male, would pour forth a torrent of more than a hundred love stories between 1911 and 1923. According to Claudine Salmon—the foremost scholar of Sino-Malay literature in Indonesia—they were "realist novels arising . . . from a local news item reported in the press, or professing to be based on events from real life."[1] Between moral commentary and social reportage, a racialized Chinese subjectivity was born.

In the initial philosophical-religious phase, reformers had imagined "desire" as something best dealt with alongside reformed marriage and subject to the modern science of reproduction. In its turn to romance, reformers set the male desire free to explore the racial and class terrain of late colonial Indies society, only to subject the ego to a discourse of moral restraint. Toggling between the social and the fictional, this chapter traces the formation of a desiring Chinese moral subject to three moments in the late colonial period. First, in a "racializing" moment of birth (1903–17), writers experimented with the Western binary approach to sexual love (M: *cinta-birahi*) in a series of lust caution stories. Safely pursued outside the context of Confucian marriage, the stories centered on

Chinese men's attraction to native women, at the same time as they turned native concubinage into a moral problem. Second, in a "spiritual" turn, authors appropriated the Christian concept of redemptive love in the 1910s by secularizing their translations and adaptations of Alexandre Dumas fils's *Camille* with a modern Confucian spiritual twist. Third, in a "bourgeois cultural" moment of closure, "love" and love marriages became the ideal not only for the super-wealthy Chinese but also for the rising middle classes between the 1910s and 1930s. This closure, a final section shows, normalized for the male bourgeois imagination Western romantic practices while retaining women's "purity" at the core of what defined Chineseness.

Lust Caution: Native Concubines, Race, and Love

The first stories the Chinese published of themselves in a colonial Java setting were their love stories with native women. Between 1903 and 1911, out of the first nine local-themed stories, six were about Chinese men's sexual love relationship with native women. Written at a time when colonial anxiety about interracial intimacy was on the rise, these novels, written by Dutch-educated Chinese authors, were framed explicitly as lust caution moral tales to warn their readers against sexual excess. The philandering ways of the recently deposed Chinese officers (and their sons), along with their "immoral" native lovers, served as negative role models for a new Chinese reading public. Read as social texts, these stories presented to their readers for the first time an emotional road map for navigating the moral structure of desire as a Chinese male ego in colonial society. A closer reading shows that they set forth an ideology of emotional self-determination in love, at the expense of the age-old parents-arranged Confucian marriage.

The nyai was always more a European than a Chinese settler problem. The Dutch colonial will to regulate sexuality did not extend beyond the European group. Although steadily on the decline since the mid-nineteenth century, in its last quarter, between 25 and 50 percent of all European men in Java still cohabited with native "housekeepers."[2] At the turn of the century, the *Encyclopaedie van Netherlandsch-Indië* defined the nyai as "the housekeeper and concubine [D: *bijzit*] of a European."[3] From that decade onward, Christian missionary and feminist voices in the Indies began to openly deplore the phenomenon. These critics saw the phenomenon as a disguised form of prostitution, with one pamphlet calling such women "incorrigible slaves of lust."[4] In 1913, Governor-General Idenburg announced the gradual elimination of concubinage among

Europeans and native Christians in the colonial army, while removing restrictions that only permitted marriage between soldiers and women of "irreproachable conduct."[5] With more European men marrying their Asian concubines, marriages between European men and Asian women rose from 15 percent in 1905 to a peak of 27.5 percent of all European marriages in 1927.[6]

Before the passing of the monogamous marriage law for Chinese in 1919, the Dutch hardly pried into the private sexual lives of their Chinese subjects, although individual officials may have frowned on the polygamous practices of some Chinese. As I show in chapter 7, the Chinese treatment of native concubines as "female slaves" was raised in the debates leading to the passing of the Mixed Marriages Act (1898). But the official position, until 1919, was to allow adat to prevail in the personal lives of Asian subjects. Unlike European civil servants or salaried soldiers, the colonial state had little hold over the private conduct of a population mostly engaged in trade. The Dutch were only forced to take a stand when the Chinese disputed among themselves over the inheritance rights of nyai-born sons. Between 1913 and 1915, three cases of Chinese primary-wife-born children challenging the right of their nyai-born half siblings to inherit from their Chinese father reached the Indies Supreme Court.[7] Reflecting the puritanical concerns of the time, the court, in adjudicating the Surabaya case, appointed a panel of three experts to determine "when, according to Indies-Chinese legal concepts in Surabaya, . . . sexual intercourse between a Chinese and a Javanese woman [is] considered illicit [D: *ongeoorloofd*]"[8]

The panel's brief report represents the furthest the colonial state went in reaching an official legal-ethnographic understanding of the Indies Chinese relationship to concubinage in Java. How it formed the adat legal opinion was as important as its actual content. At this juncture, the colonial state proved to be more pragmatic than judgmental about their Chinese subjects' sexual lives. Among the sinology-trained Dutch official, the Dutch notary, and the Chinese member of the local probate court, the court gave the greatest weight to the notary, the local-born Mens Fiers Smeding (1862–1923), who had the longest local experience and most nuanced opinion. Smeding noted that the Chinese in Surabaya considered sexual relations with native women illicit if they were "temporary and clandestine," both before and in the midst of marriage. However, two other types of extramarital cohabitation were not considered illicit. First, it was acceptable if the poorer Chinese, who could not afford a Chinese wife, cohabited with a Javanese woman. Despite not going through marital ceremonies, the local Chinese and native headmen were informed, and these relations were "almost always enduring." Second, the keeping of *bini muda* (M: younger wife) was legitimate if the sojourner's wife remained in China, or if the local wife remained childless. It was acceptable for these men to take Javanese women as secondary wives (D: *bijvrouwen*) to bear sons for their families.⁹ Having said that, he added that "there will always be . . . the young and the licentious among the Chinese, who could not leave the pretty woman undisturbed and who pursued liaisons one after, or at the same time as, another."¹⁰

The Dutch-educated and reform-minded Chinese writers responded with their moralizing lust caution stories. As introduced in chapter 5, these early recipients of Dutch education were involved in the contemporary pan-Java Confucian renewal movement. Their stories had titles that piqued the curiosity of the potential reader, with the attendant moral lessons to be learned explicitly laid out. Gouw Peng Liang's *A Story That Really Happened on the Island of Java of an Affair of the Landlord and Opium Revenue Farmer of Benawan Residency Named Lo Fen Koei* (1903) directly addressed its audience: "Readers remember! Whoever digs a hole for another who is not evil [M: *berdosa*] will most certainly end up in the hole himself, just as we have seen happen in this story."¹¹ The anonymously written *Story of Njonja Lim Pat Nio: A Story That Is Very Good (for You) and Really Happened on the Land of Babakan in the Batavia Region* (1909) featured a cover page announcing it to be "an example for anyone who gives in to carnal desire [M: *hawa nafsoe*] and inappropriate courtship [M: *pengadoean jang tiada sah*]."¹²

The novels featured the Chinese elites of Dutch colonial indirect rule not so much for political criticism but as relatable and representative Chinese characters for moral pedagogy. All male protagonists in these novels invariably belonged to the *hartawan* elite—the class of merchants who controlled the opium revenue farms, owned private land with feudal rights, and were appointed as Kapitans. The Malay neologism hartawan, a combination of property (M: *harta*) and aristocracy (M: *bangsawan*), was likely coined in this period to refer derogatorily to this class of aristocrats-by-wealth. Under indirect rule, Kapitan leaders themselves embodied what it meant to be Chinese on Java. If these novels portrayed them as morally corrupt, they were critical at a time when the heyday of indirect rule had clearly already passed. At the turn of the century, the opium revenue farm had been replaced by a government monopoly, while the Kapitan system of administration took another decade to be phased out.¹³ What appears to be polemical attacks against the Kapitans or their son(s) did not so much contribute to indirect rule's demise as create the myth that their downfall was due to their own moral corruption. The genre had to latch on to the old emblem of patriarchal Chineseness to pronounce its corruption, if only to clear the way for a new Chinese moral subject to emerge.

These old emblems of Chineseness were misled by their excessive lust (M: *birahi*), not only in a sinful way but in a criminal way. Their criminality ensured that their sins would be punished in this rather than the afterworld. Where money could not purchase them their objects of lust, they bribed their way to obtain their objects of desire through murder or abduction. Gouw Peng Liang's male protagonist was a young and wealthy philanderer, who abused his authority as landlord, and plotted murders with his native assistant (M: *joeragan*) to abduct beautiful young Chinese women living on his land to be his concubines (M: *bini moeda*).[14] In *Story of Njonja Lim Pat Nio*, the male protagonist was "a big Chinese hartawan named Khouw Tek Kan who was already advanced in age, and despite that, is still very lustful for young women. He loves pleasure very much, and does not really need to work on his land."[15] Tjoa Boe Sing's *Story of Lim Tjin Sioe, or A Victim of a Love Relationship That Really Happened in the Banger Residency in the Year 1886* (1911) was about the son of a Kapitan, "who was famous for being the wealthiest, such that [his] wealth and rank ... enabled [him] to live in the most respectable standard in accord with his status."[16] A serial womanizer, Liem built his clubhouse, a *soehian*, where "several pretty young girls, who can be called, 'the roses of Probolinggo,'" were kept and guarded by Arinten—a nyai of a European man.

The prominence of native women (in contrast to the Chinese wife's or concubine's absence) as casual lovers spoke to the unequal racial division of sexual labor on contemporary Java. Beginning in 1870, the new plantation economy, extension of railway lines, and factories brought more foreign and working men to the cities. Brothels began to spring up near railway stations across urban Java during this period, most likely drawing their sex workers from impoverished families in the surrounding villages.[17] The early nyai stories show some facets of this unequal division of sexual labor between the Chinese and native Indonesians. In the *Story of Njonja Lim Pat Nio*, the protagonist Khouw was already married to a young and capable Chinese wife, although the main plot revolved around his pursuit of Amina, the beautiful daughter of a tenant on his land. *Story of Lim Tjin Sioe* depicted its young male protagonist relying on an older nyai to procure pretty young girls from the surrounding region for his pleasure house in the coastal town of Probolinggo in eastern Java.

In these novels, the language of desire remained formulaic in the Malay literary tradition, if its subject had ventured into the realm of the real. In Malay poetic verses (*syairs*), "birds, fishes, insects, flowers and fruits act and talk like human beings ... [and are] based on real incidents ... of human romances."[18] As early as 1865, a certain Tan Kittjoan of Batavia wrote and published one such syair.[19] By the 1880s, these verses were circulating in romanized script in Batavia, Semarang, and Surabaya, "to be used by those who wanted to impress their beloved or their superiors or were in need of a string of words to create excitement [M: *bimbang*] or lust [M: *nafsoe birahi*]."[20] In the pleasure house depicted in *Story of Lim Tjin Sioe*, courtesans sang and danced to *pantun*, a freer form of poetry, to entertain their guests.[21] In these novels, not unlike how it was done in the poetry, authors used formulaic descriptions of the native woman's beauty to introduce the central theme of men's desire. Retained in this new prose of desire were the poetic comparisons of beauty with fruits that whetted the appetite:

Of Nyai Amina in *Tjerita Njonja Lim Pat Nio*: "Her body is svelte and supple [M: *denok montok*], her face round, complexion yellow like the langsat fruit, she has dashing eyebrows, beautiful eyes, such that there is no surprise, whoever gets to see Amina, nobody does not go mad over that child, as a result of lust [M: *birahi*]."[22]

Of Si Manisee in *Tjerita Lim Tjien Sioe*: "This child of the Haji, is a young lady who just turned seventeen, the features of her face are beautiful, her complexion which is yellowish white [M: *putih kuning*] is delicious to behold, her body very slim, while the sharp rays from her eyes are balanced by the drooping redness [M: *merah gandul*] of her lips, where when she laughs makes her sweet, and capable of capturing the heart of any young man."[23]

Of Si Alimah in *Tjerita Njai Alimah*: "Surely Si Alimah is so pretty that her face resembles that of an angel from heaven, her face is round and sweet, always smiling, her eyes are like those of a perched peacock, her brows look like they were painted on a drawing, her forehead is high, her flat nose rises to a sharp end, her lips are like a Javanese lute split into two, her neck is like the stem of a rose moving in the wind, . . . her waist is slim like wayang puppet figures. . . . The color of her complexion is yellow like a fresh langsat fruit."[24]

In fact, as social texts, fiction also allowed these authors to experiment with desirous egos unencumbered by their parents' authority. One study of Gouw's *Lo Fen Koei* notes that the "novella places little emphasis on ties of kinship."[25] This was the pattern across the nyai genre of Chinese lust caution tales. The authors designed plots for the male protagonists to become autonomous actors in colonial society who could direct their own amorous careers. Oey Tambah, the famous Don Juan figure of Batavia, could engage in his amorous and criminal pursuits only after the death of his father and his inheritance of the latter's wealth. Lim Tjin Sioe was the renegade son who was "very different from his two brothers." From a young age, "he had mixed with those who were born rich [M: *kaum perojalan*] and was very good at spending wastefully."[26] In Lim's case, although his Kapitan father was mentioned at the beginning, the latter was not central to the rest of the plot. The drama of the moral struggle with love and desire was meant to be played out between the male ego himself and his beloved nyai within colonial society.

These early love stories can be read as romantic projections of their authors, who knew of but were denied the chance to pursue love marriage at the turn of the twentieth century. Despite their explicit moral framing, it is doubtful that moral instruction was the only or even the most important aim of the novels' authors. As writers of commercial products, the authors were clearly conscious that it was the love, desire, courtship and intimacy, rather than the moral injunctions, that sold the novels. If the intention was to tantalize so as to moralize, consuming the tantalizing while ignoring the morals might well have been the unintended effect among readers. In any case, these new novels introduced for the first time descriptive prose depicting scenes of physical attraction, flirtation, and intimacy in the local setting and in everyday language—all useful for young men and women venturing out on their first experiments with courtship. An early instance of such a contemporary romantic is Tio Tek Hong (b. 1877).[27] In his memoirs, he described how the Confucian match-made marriage "conflicted with [his] conscience" (M: *bertentangan dengan hati-nurani*): "Two years after stopping school, in 1896, my mother married me with a girl from Sukabumi. Actually, I had fallen in love with a girl, a sister of a friend, but Mother did not agree because the girl's mother was, according to her, very fussy [M: *cerewet*]. Although I debated with Mother as hard as I could [M: *sekeras-kerasnya*], in the end I was forced to submit. I was not allowed to get to know this girl, chosen by Mother, beforehand. That was how an ancient practice like the forced marriage [M: *perkawinan paksaan*] usually worked."[28]

Where parents did appear, they served as foils alongside tradition, against which the male protagonists' quest for love revolted. In an important departure within the genre, Sie Hian Ling's *Story of "Yang Soen Sia": A Story That Really Happened in Central Java* (1908) started a new trend by setting up the nyai as an object of love and refuge from onerous parent-arranged marriages. Set in Magelang in Central Java, the author built his plot around a love triangle between the sons of a Chinese Kapitan (Yang Soen), an opium revenue farmer (Kim Bie), and their common affection for Nyai Wasti. Both men were fugitives from their family-arranged marriages. Yang Soen had a dutiful Chinese wife whom he detested and eventually killed at the behest of Nyai Wasti. Kept by Yang Soen, the nyai, however, really loved Kim Bie, who could not be more committed because he was busy with his parents-arranged Chinese wedding. Yang Soen "did not like *njonja* Sien Nio when his father Kapitein Lauw Sek Ting wanted to marry the young girl to him, but because Chinese adat dictates that it should be so, whether he liked it or not, [he] had to follow his father's order."[29]

It was in this turn to Chinese adat that *gundik*—the derogatory term for kept women as opposed to the more respectable nyai—first came into view. In this story, the "immorality" of lust for native women was played out more explicitly within the colonial hierarchy of sexual desires. It was "only after the death of [Yang Soen's] father . . . that he dared to keep a mistress [*goendik*] of the native race named Wasti."[30] Wasti had in fact been "kept by a European man as a nyai" before she "gradually turned to perform[ing] immoral deeds... after being courted by several young playboys [M: *mata krandjang*] of the Chinese race."[31] The nyai was moral in her relationship with the European until the Chinese playboys corrupted her. Like all nyai stories, the ending had to be a tragic one for the cautionary effect to take hold. Yang Soen died, and his *gundik* neither married nor lived happily in love with either of her suitors. "Remember that this story is an example for men who are so into [M: *medus*] women's affairs that they die and leave behind a bad name."[32]

In *Tambahsia* (1915), the tension in the lust caution genre between the moral Confucian marriage and immoral love for native women reached a turning point when the latter was given full reign over the former.[33] In this retelling of the legendary story of Oeij Hap Ho, alias Tambah, the anonymous author picked the familiar plot of a philandering hartawan to deride Chinese adat, Confucian marriage, and the Chinese Kapitans in one fell swoop, while giving the male protagonist the full literary license to indulge in his interethnic sexual love, like a Don Juan of colonial Batavia.[34] The precise line between fact and fiction is no longer clear, but the author clearly made a polemical point about the outdatedness of Chinese adat and the Kapitans without having to name them as such. He was clearly on the side of Tambah and his family, who were forced to move from Pekalongan to Batavia after they were allegedly ostracized by the Chinese there for allowing a daughter (Tambah's elder sister) to marry a native aristocrat, with whom she was in love.[35] Devoted to building his pleasure house (Hk: *soehian*) at Ancol, on the outskirts of Batavia, Tambah attracted "Chinese and Dutch ladies" and "mostly the concubines of the respectable folks, who, because they had been sweet-talked to and under the influence of money,... became so tempted that they went crazy over Tambahsia."[36]

In a creative twist to the tale, the author gave his mid-nineteenth-century Tambah the freedom young Chinese men craved but even in 1915 did not enjoy in deciding their own marriage. He most likely fabricated this episode to draw his young readers into the plot.[37] At seventeen years of age, Tambah searched for his own bride by "walking around the city on foot, wanting to peep at the most beautiful daughters of the noble and rich, to make his wife."[38] He saw none. Rather than go through a matchmaker, he insisted on examining any potential bride himself, and thereby antagonized the entire noble and rich class, making it "very hard... to obtain a wife."[39] He eventually married a pretty daughter of the poor Siem family of Pasar Senen, to whom he had paid 1000 guilders for a face examination before settling for the match.[40]

Tambahsia celebrated the love for the nyai, even if it was told in the morally conservative framing of the lust caution tale. Tambah was the first Chinese male character in the genre to attain an awareness of love as a self-conscious moral restraint against one's lustful desires. He had a Chinese wife and three concubines—one Chinese and two native. It was with the court dancer Mas Ayu Goendjing, his second native concubine, that he fell deeply in love. They met in the Pekalongan court for his nephew's circumcision ceremony. In the presence of his elder sister, Tambah did not dare reveal his desire for Mas Ayu because "it would embarrass his sister . . . [who would be] very disappointed if a noble and rich person from Batavia came to Pekalongan and liked an immoral [M: *hina*] woman and dancer who was loved by many people."[41] It was the only moment in the entire story when Tambah showed any restraint. It was one deliberately crafted by the author:

> His sister's words made Tambahsia hold back his lust [M: *napsu birahi*] for this dancer, but the more he looked, the greater the feeling of love [M: *kecintaan*] accumulated in his heart. Aduh! Her body was slim, and her arms, which were very supple, stretched out straight as she flung her sash.
>
> Tambah's hand itched momentarily, raised, wanting to pinch Mas Ayu Goendjing's cheek, being made of such refined complexion, but he immediately constrained his intention [M: *niat*], because gathered in that district hall were many *priyayi* [Javanese aristocrats].[42]

Lust when constrained is made to serve love. With the connivance of his *priyayi* brother-in-law, Tambah was able to rendezvous with Mas Ayu at a separate locale, where they exchanged their love vows. In Mas Ayu, the love relationship was also expressed in opposition to another form of lust—money. Other women always asked Tambah for more money. "Never was there a Javanese girl like this one, who turned down his gift of 1000 guilders, hence making Tambahsia love her even more, because he can now be sure, that this fine woman loves him with all her heart."[43]

The creole Chinese lust caution stories tried to morally restrain men's extramarital desire for the racial other if ironically, by telling local-themed interethnic love stories. The men who wrote and read these stories were limited by their own social experience of love, desire, and marriage. They had encountered how Europeans courted in school, in public, and, most frequently, in novels, but the social experience they could draw from was of philandering wealthy Chinese men and their native lovers. These novels exposed the creole reading public to the social forms of courtship and love, while appearing to morally affirm the Confucian marriage. Later on, they quietly took on the contemporary theme of courtship and love as the modern answer to traditional Chinese adat marriages, while remaining under the cover of the lust caution genre. These lust caution moral tales prepared the ground for the late 1910s, when writers opened the floodgate for a full-fledged conflict between Chinese adat and love marriage. In the intervening years, it was with a French romance that the Chinese sentimentalized the question of wealth, morality, and the spirit over the quest for love.

Confucianizing the Love of Lady Camille for Colonial Java

Between the immoral nyai love stories of the 1900s and the endogamous romances of the 1920s, an important shift in the ethno-structure of feeling occurred among the urban Chinese of Java. During the 1910s, love was no longer the preserve of the hartawan. The urban middle class, especially young school-going men and women, began to fall in love in school and go on dates behind the backs of their parents. The story of Alexandre Dumas fils's *La Dame aux Camélias* (1848) (henceforth *Lady Camille*) was particularly popular during the decade, with a translation and an adaption of the novel appearing in 1917 and 1918, respectively. Through a close reading of these two texts, I show how two authors appropriated a discourse of romantic love and companionate marriage while making them safe for bourgeois Confucian morality.

In 1906, a fourteen-year-old Tjan Kim Bie had an emotional epiphany when he first encountered *Lady Camille* either in Dutch or French on a train ride from Surabaya to Semarang. "In my thoughts," he recounted twelve years later, when he translated the novel, "I felt a secret force [M: *tenaga-resia*] order me to choose just that book and not others." "Impulsive, as young people generally are," he explained, "I had followed the wish [M: *kehendaknja*] of my heart, and bought that story book about a lady with her flower."[44] He then sat transfixed, reading throughout the journey, with his "heart so strongly attracted by the story of Marguerite's self-effacing [M: *jang meloepaken diri sendiri*] love." So engrossed that he missed the Semarang station, it was only when the train conductor alerted him at the terminal station in Solo that he realized "his two eyes had filled with tears." Without being aware of it, he "had felt Marguerite's sadness—the result of her act of sacrificing herself."[45]

This text had a special hold on the imagination of the Chinese of Java.[46] Throughout the late colonial period, they produced two translations and three adaptations of *Lady Camille*. Phoa Tjoen Hoay apparently translated and serialized the novel for *Li Po*, the Confucian journal based in Sukabumi (West Java), in 1907.[47] Ten years later, Thio Tjin Boen's *Sie Tjaij Kim (Nona Kim)* adapted Dumas's characters to make it a Chinese love story set in contemporary colonial society.[48] Thio flexibly adapted most of Dumas's plot and text verbatim, without attributing the source, and even claimed on the title page that the story "really happened in Bandung."[49] A year later, Tjan Kim Bie, by then the chief editor of the Confucianist periodical *Tjhoen Tjhioe* of Surabaya, would retranslate the novel into Sino-Malay for a Batavia publisher under the title *Marguerite Gauthier atawa Satoe pertjinta'an jang soetji dari satoe prampoewan latjoer* (Marguerite Gauthier, or pure love from an immoral woman).[50] Two other adaptations into plays were published, most likely in the 1920s, in East Java.[51] My close reading will focus on Thio's 1917 adaptation and Tjan's 1918 translation.

By the mid-1910s, the formulaic discourse and conception of love and lust in nyai love stories were no longer adequate for the rapidly changing romantic lives of the young. The anthropologist James Siegel observes that gendered expectations of women in this period were complicated by wealth considerations in two ways. In the traditional mode, parents arranging marriages with money considerations in mind made those matches suspect to the young, while in the new mode, lovers who married for money were thought to be inauthentic.[52] Women in this transitional mode of marriage "had to be at once not a prostitute but a wife and also the object of desire. . . . [She] had to be modernized, [and] she had to be the object of desire in a context in which who one was was defined by one's relation to [men's] desire." Based on his study of emblematic texts in the Chinese adat love story genre, to which I will turn in the next section, Siegel's argument that the Chinese were "blind" to modernity's demand that such "desire . . . be tamed" is problematic when read alongside Thio's and Tjan's Confucianist solution to Lady Camille's moral conundrum.[53]

In *Lady Camille*, the creole Chinese authors found a female protagonist who could play all the objectifying roles the bourgeois man desired of woman in this transitional phase. As a Parisian courtesan, Marguerite Gauthier offered the young Chinese a model for what an ideal modern female lover could be like: exchanging love letters, verbalizing her desires and emotions, going on dates at the opera and in the shops, being physically intimate with her lover, and, of course, being calculative about costs. The novel played on Marguerite's liminal role as a prostitute who not only fell in love with a young bourgeois man but was reformed enough by his love to settle for an alternative life of peaceful domesticity. The embrace of *Lady Camille* signaled a shift of authorial preoccupation with the male ego of the hartawan to focusing on that of the average bourgeois man on the street. One critic of the original novel notes that "the reality underlying the romantic and erotic story is economic."[54] Armand Duval, the male protagonist, is not wealthy enough to stop Marguerite from having to entertain other patrons to keep up with her own bourgeois lifestyle. As prostitute, lover, wife-to-be, and betrayer, *Lady Camille* gave its bourgeois readers the full range of emotional exposure that the creole Chinese male ego desired in the 1910s.

Marguerite did not only satisfy male desires, but she did so *while* speaking back at the end of the day to educate her lover and save the patriarchal order. The plot must have attracted the Chinese through the patriarchal moral solution it provided for the aforementioned triangulating conundrum young Chinese men faced at the time: At the behest of her lover's father, Marguerite gives up her own happiness to advance his social standing and honor the filial duty to family. This play on sexuality, class, and morality had particular appeal to Chinese middle-class readers of the 1910s and 1920s in urban Java. Tjan Kim Bie's addition of the subtitle "pure love from an immoral woman" demonstrates the appeal of such liminal love to him and his readers.

By removing Dumas's Christian framing of "love," both Thio and Tjan rendered it a secular or Confucian ethic in service of patriarchy. In Dumas's writing, two particular Christian concepts—devotion and redemption—served to undergird the romantic love between the protagonists. Both were left out in the translations. In the original novel, when Marguerite asks Armand to name the wish he had to be with her every night, he called it "devotion," after the Catholic practice of expressing love and fidelity to God or saints through ritual. This she took as a sign that he was "in love with [her]."[55] Both Thio and Tjan removed the line that referenced "devotion" while retaining Marguerite's reference of that wish to "love."[56] The key to the plot's climactic event—Marguerite's redemption by self-sacrifice for Armand—was an allegory of Christ's love and death for humanity. Historian Lynn Pan, in her study of the novel's reception in China, argues that "everyone could relate to a story of passion, sacrifice and expiation, but *La Dame's* underlying theme of redemption through *love* is not one that would speak to many Chinese."[57] It was the same with the Chinese of Java. Thio simply omitted these key lines of Marguerite's dialogue with Armand's father: "Do you believe that I love your son... with a love that does not come from self-interest?... Do you believe that I have made this love the hope, dream and redemption of my life?" Tjan retained this last line but substituted "hope, dream and redemption" with "forgiveness" (M: *pengampoenan*).[58]

Yet the moral authority of the Chinese patriarchy in colonial society was ultimately limited. Thio's creative adaptation of *Lady Camille* into a love story set in contemporary Bandung offered an additional commentary on the place of the Chinese within the intersecting relations of class, race, and sex in contemporary colonial society. If the bourgeois male protagonist in Paris was a trainee lawyer, Thio cast a Chinese shop manager as his hero for Bandung.[59] Equally important was the choice of Bandung, which, as the so-called Paris of Java, provided the consumerist mise-en-scène for the modern love story, with the cinema standing in for the opera, and the department-store-filled Braga Street for the Champs-Élysées. Otherwise known for his nyai love stories, Thio, in this instance, reserved the role of the prostitute-lover for a Chinese *nona* (M: unmarried lady), Sie Tjiai Kim. But Nona Kim's sexual history served as a metonymy of the Chinese condition in relation to the colonial civilizing project. Her current patrons may all be well-to-do Chinese men, but she was formerly a kept woman of a local Dutch official, from whom she learned to conduct herself like a European lady.

There was another limit to what the Confucianizing framing devices could achieve. After all, the bulk of Dumas's novel was about two young people courting, sharing their feelings about each other with one another, and working their way toward a love marriage between companionate partners. As a social text, this segment would have had the greatest novelty and relevance to contemporary youth—the social act of a young man and a young woman conserving and acting intimately as equals. In a clear departure from the racially subordinated nyai in the earlier genre, Marguerite, precisely because she was a prostitute, spoke with conviction about how money complicated one's choice of the ideal companionate lover: "Because," Marguerite continued, "you were the only person who ever made me feel instantly that I could think and speak freely.... Naturally, we don't have friends. We have selfish lovers who spend their fortunes not on us, as they say, but on their own vanity."[60] Both Thio and Tjan struggled (though in interestingly different ways) to find suitable terms for "speak freely" and the "vanity" that comes from bought affection. Between the two, Thio's translation was closer to the meaning of the original text. For Thio, speaking freely meant having no "secrets," a trope widely used to refer to young people dating in defiance of their parents. In an important departure from the lust caution warning, this novel makes the distinction clear regarding affections that are purchased with friendship-based companionate love. Thio made sure he added "to satisfy their lust" to his translation of "vanity" as "pride": "I know furthermore that you are the one person with whom I don't have to keep any secrets.... For sure, we don't have friends, we only have lovers, whose only need is themselves and who throw away money not to make themselves proud, but to satisfy their lust [M: *napsoe*].[61] Tjan, as editor of a Confucian journal, embellished the intentionality of friendship with the enlightened Confucian values of clarity, sincerity, and purity. For him, to speak freely meant to speak with enlightened clarity. True friendship, especially the type headed for love marriage, had to be based on sincerity rather than pleasure: "Furthermore, I had thought that you are the only person with whom I can speak with clarity [M: *teroes terang*].... I don't have any real sincere [M: *toeloes*] friends. My lovers don't care about loving me, they only love themselves and wish to obtain more pleasure [M: *kesenangan*] for their own heart."[62] If Thio was confident that his reader could understand companionate love once it was contrasted with purchased lust, the

Confucianist Tjan made sure to specify that that friendship had to be sincere and pure. Tjan's text is littered with liberal embellishments of these two attributes. For instance, where Marguerite had simply declared in the original that she yearned to "make you into the man I had longed for," Tjan, besides translating it as "you can give me what I lack so much," hastened to specify that "that is love, sincere and pure."[63]

If the nyai stories had opened up the moral questions of sexual love in the realm of interracial relationships, from *Lady Camille* onward the morality of love relationships would be explored predominantly among Chinese characters in Sino-Malay literature. The adaptation and translation of *La Dame aux Camélias* in 1917 and 1918 took place alongside a sudden eruption of social commentary, principally through dime novels, on the clash of cultures between Western forms of courtship and love, and Chinese adat. The imposition of new burdens of male desire on modern women, on both the money and sexual fronts, as theorized by Siegel, was real. But the gossipy dime novels circulated alongside more serious works by established authors like Thio Tjin Boen, or authors with established reformist credentials like Tjan Kim Bie. They signaled that for the more progressive and younger opinion leaders, courtship, romance, and some intimacy were beginning to be accepted, even as they tried to tame the bourgeois male egos circulating in the cities with Confucianized love stories, such as that of Marguerite Gauthier.

Creolizing Love as Bourgeois Chinese Morality

By 1938, Oey Beng Liong, a recent graduate of Dutch schools, could declare, in a speech given in Dutch, that the "period of free marriage choice" had arrived, with "love, appreciation for each other's feelings, [and] learning to know each other's character . . . becom[ing] the ideal of the youth." He qualified the statement, however, with the observation that "the free marriage choice is being practiced more among the higher strata [D: *hoogere lagen*] of our Indies-Chinese Society . . . than among the lower classes and the undeveloped."[64] Between 1917 and the mid-1930s, the freedom to date and determine their own marriage partners became an established norm among the educated middle- and upper-class Chinese. As young men and women demanded the freedom to socialize, an intergenerational struggle unfolded over the question of Chinese morality and souls. By the mid-1930s, this struggle over the souls of the youth was resolved in popular culture (novels) and manuals that creolized "love" (*tjinta*) as moral, while condemning excessive desire (*birahi*) as un-Chinese.

New sensibilities toward love and marriage were planted in the hearts and minds of young Chinese girls and boys, who began to attend modern schools in large numbers in the 1910s. The children of the wealthiest Chinese elite, like their Javanese aristocratic counterparts, had been admitted to Dutch schools since the 1870s. While the Chinese medium THHK schools had had a head start on mass education in 1900, by the 1910s and 1920s, Dutch medium schools, which were further segregated into European and Chinese (D: Hollandsch-Chineesche Scholen, or HCS) streams, became the school of choice for the local-born *peranakan*.[65] A small minority enrolled in the elitist European stream, which, culminating in the Hoogere Burgerschool (HBS), prepared students for universities in the metropole. Chinese enrollment in the HCS across the Dutch East Indies increased from 2,697 in 1910 to 9,741 in 1920, plateauing in the 22,000s in the 1930s (22,400 in 1930 and 22,818 in 1940).[66] Some graduates from HCS entered one of the vocational schools, while others either worked as clerks and cashiers for Dutch firms or went into trade, like their parents. By 1940, there were eight girls (10,149) for every ten boys (12,669) in the Dutch language-stream Chinese schools. Chinese language-stream schools were not far behind.[67]

The first sparks of adolescent romance were lit furtively in these co-educational schools, which brought Chinese girls, formerly cloistered at home, out into the open. Parents gave their sons bicycles and thus more freedom of movement about town. Throughout the late colonial period, many a relationship must have been initiated by boys spying on girls, then sending them secret letters from their bicycles. In Malang, Kwee Thiam Tjing (1900–1974), who attended the European Primary School and the MULO Higher Primary School (D: Meer Uitgebreide Lagere School) and referred to 1915–20 as the period of his youth, would call it the "traditional era" (M: *zaman kuno*). "There was no such thing among the youth around the 1920s," he recalled fifty years later, "as any talk about 'girlfriends' or 'boyfriends.' Young man or woman, anyone would feel embarrassed even if they were to just walk together."[68] Yet Kwee remembers a "group of more or less twelve boys, they cycled every morning and stopped below that famous window" of a missionary girls' school at Tjelakat.[69] There was little open contact between boys and girls, but according to Kwee, secret relationships began to be formed: "Although the way we led our lives as male and female students from the same school always had the appearance of being split into separate groups, there were 'romantic' [M: *asmara*] relationships. It was just that we were not out in the open as they are now. We, the boys, have our own 'meisje' [D: girl], and among the female students, they definitely had their special male friends. . . . It was not out in the public, but everyone in fact knew who laid claim to 'meisje' A and B was 'meijse' to whom."[70] In early 1922, Teddy Kan Hway An was seventeen when he wrote in his diary about timing his journey to the King William

III High School in Batavia so as to "run into [Betty Tan] at Kramat, and then from the bridge by [Pasar] Senin and Prapatan, cycle so long as possible next to the *sado* [M: two-wheeled horse carriage] and talk to her, so attracted am I to that beautiful child."[71]

Despite these early experiments in courtship, Chinese parents, even Dutch-educated ones, were wary of giving their children the freedom to select their own spouses. Chinese hartawan parents began to give their children some leeway to have boy-girl interactions within the elitist HBS and their own social circles. Parents might consult their children about their preferences, but into the 1920s, the children of the hartawan elite continued to have their marriages arranged, or at least chosen from within circles preapproved by their parents. In April 1922, Teddy Kan went to a wedding party at Molenvliet, where he kept an eye out for Betty. "It is well-known," he noted in his diary, "that mothers take their daughters on such occasions 'to the marriage market,' as they call it."[72] As Steve Haryono's study of creole Chinese genealogies show, the descendants of nineteenth-century Chinese officers continued to marry within hartawan circles into the twentieth century.[73] Teddy's father, Kan Hok Hoei (alias H. H. Kan)—who, as a member of the Volksraad and president of the Chung Hua Hwie, became the political face of the pro-Dutch Chinese—continued to arrange marriages for his HBS-educated children in the 1920s. When the marriage of an elder sister failed and ended in divorce, Teddy remarked, "Voila! The fault of imposing marriages! Who is to blame!"[74]

Teddy's experience illustrate how parents were beginning to accommodate their children's preferences. His own choice of Betty Tan, who was of an equally well-established if slightly less well-off family, was a safe one. His parents most likely approved of this match, for they helped to create opportunities for their social interaction. They went on board the same ship to the Netherlands and studied in Leiden at the same time.[75] When she was forced to cut short her Leiden sojourn (July 1922–April 1924), Teddy suspected that she was summoned home to marry a rich groom. "I shouldn't ask you why, Betty!" cried Teddy into his diary, "I would never be able to give you all that wealth, that you, luxurious woman, have need for!"[76] In March 1925, Betty married another HBS schoolmate, Kwee Zwan Ho, the son of a sugar planter of Cheribon, who had proposed marriage twice before she finally agreed. Teddy's diary shows that Betty, even if she did like him, never communicated directed with him. They neither corresponded nor dated when they lived in close proximity in Leiden. Even if Betty had chosen him over Kwee Zwan Ho, it would not have been based on love and mutual understanding either.[77] Still, it was remarkable that parents were beginning to let their children have some say over their own marriage.

Betty's reticence in the face of her suitors was emblematic of what Chinese society expected of young women (and men) who were beginning to find their own matches. Young women might secretly maintain a correspondence with a male suitor, but the latter was expected to propose marriage before they could meet and go on dates. Published in the early 1920s in Batavia, the manual *Templates for Love Letters* sought to address the anxiety of young men who were "not so good at writing attractive love letters, so that his marriage proposals are always rejected by the lady involved."[78] The typical scenario outlined by the author revealed the gendered bourgeois expectations of men and women maintaining relationships through secret correspondence. In the eleven letters exchanged that preceded their first physical meeting, a man had to first declare his desire (M: *napsoe*), demonstrate his stable employment status (preferably a bookkeeper for a European *toko*), send an engagement ring, and send his mother to propose marriage. On the woman's part, she reciprocated her interest, declared her virginity (M: *soetji*), promised to be a hardworking wife, and let it be known that she "will not be disgraced as a flirtatious girl who dares to engage in a secret love affair [M: *pertjintahan resia*]." It was only after their parents approved the match that they were able to go on their first date in public.[79]

Race, Love, and Women's Purity

From around 1917, a new ethno-moral gender boundary formed through the didactic fictional discourse of sexual love, which served to counter what was perceived as excessive Westernization among the elite Chinese. Claudine Salmon has noted that in the novels of this time, "girls above all seem to earn reproach for the damaging effects of their education in this domain [of marriage], namely the liberties they take with established customs."[80] Elizabeth Chandra has gone on to detail how the specter of Dutch-educated Asian women's "financial independence, fame, [and] sexual liberation," and young Chinese women's exposure to the public eye in particular, triggered the rise of the femme fatale genre, in whose plot the female protagonist always dies in tragedy, as a form of "male retribution."[81] While patriarchal retribution was no doubt one of the key tropes, my close reading of the exemplary love stories of this period shows that men tried to creolize romance within the Chinese imaginary at the same time as they drew an imagined moral boundary around women's "purity" (read virginity).

A more misogynistic attack against the "Westernized" daughters of the hartawan elite was discernible in an early wave of moral scandal exposés in 1918 and 1919. While the shaming of the hartawan elite was a familiar subject, previous writers limited themselves to the philandering elite themselves or their young scions. In 1918, there was a sudden turn not only to publicizing the scandalous love affairs of hartawan daughters but to framing them as alien to Chinese morals. Local scandals were nothing new, but these writers—some with personal grudges—seized on isolated incidents of elopement and premarital pregnancy to make broader cultural claims that approached a Java-wide moral panic about Dutch-educated Chinese women's sexuality. One of the more famous titles, which recently received a reprint for its heritage value, is *The Secret of Bandung, or A Love Affair That Clashed with the Customs of the Chinese Race: A Story That Really Happened and Ended in Bandung in the Year 1917*.[82] These realist "male retributive" moral tales, to borrow Chandra's term, spread across major cities in Java (and Sumatra): Bogor (1918), Surabaya (1919), Palembang (1919), and Kediri (1924).[83]

A more enduring genre of didactic love stories normalized contemporary experiments in courtship and love marriage but continued to make moralizing distinctions between Western and Chinese behavior and sentiments. These novels shifted the principal subject from love scandals to the trials and tribulations of courtship. In so doing, they did not so much reject love marriage but try to appropriate its discourse and practice through a set of "Chinese" morals, centered on the behavior of young men and women. While the hartawan elite remained the main characters, middle-class actors, often as victims, began to enter the love-story plots. Three such works between 1917 and 1919 started a genre of didactic love stories that endured into the 1920s and 1930s.

Lim Kim Lip's *Boenga Raya, or Two Kinds of Pleasure* (Batavia, 1918) revealed an acceptance of love marriage with qualifications.[84] As a realist writing that showcased contemporary practices, Lim retained the trope of the philandering hartawan, whose confusion of "two kinds of pleasure," sex and love, made them unfit for love marriage without first undergoing some moral lesson. Written in 1916–17 by a Bandung Chinese, the novel went into a second edition in Batavia in 1918. Set in the British Straits Settlements (Singapore, Malacca, and Penang), the themes explored were entirely those of the Chinese of Java. Tan Hin Jan, a young Chinese hartawan, has been in love with and secretly engaged to Lee Sin Nio, a girl of a moderately wealthy family, for four years. Although they exchanged rings of their own accord, Lee is anxious when Tan is slow to initiate a marriage proposal through his parents. Her worries are not unfounded. A Chinese hartawan from Siam is vacationing in Penang and Malacca when he chances upon the beautiful Lee Sin Nio. He sends his mother to propose but is turned down by Lee, whose mother she consults before giving an answer. The Siam Chinese hartawan, whose desire cannot be restrained, conspires to abduct Lee but is stopped just in time.

Although Tan Hin Jan and Lee Sin Nio finally marry, marriage itself brings no happiness when the hartawan does not stay sexually loyal to his wife. On a business trip to Singapore with his father, Tan Hin Jan falls for a Shanghainese courtesan at the opera and is so taken with his new love that he refuses to return to his Malacca family. It is only when his father demonstrates, through a ruse, that the prostitute is after his money and not love that he learns his lesson. The story "served as advice for all men and women, who, with love and whatever [other] hopes in their hearts, must remember this saying: the polite speech may accomplish more than a stern face, but it is the truthful [M: *djoejoer*] heart that works like the clear mirror."[85]

The Story of What Young Ladies Did in Secret (1919) constructed the ideal woman, who was modern and bound for marriage but still retained a Chinese moral interiority.[86] The cast of characters in this story socialize in the cosmopolitan colonial milieu in Batavia: Dutch schools, dance parties hosted by an Indo-European woman, the Komedie theater, and shopping on the streets. Like authors before him, the pseudonymous Nemo chose as a negative role model Lim Gim Tek, a well-mannered but philandering Dutch-educated son of a hartawan. Thio He-Kiauw, the female protagonist, is from an average bourgeois family. Her father, a cashier for an insurance firm, sends Thio to a Dutch school, but he cannot afford to give her the servants or the piano and dance lessons that would enable her to lead a more polished life, like that of her friends.[87] Commenting on the class distinction, one of Lim Gim Tek's friends notes that "He-Kiauw is such a pretty and learned girl that although she is no hartawan, she will be a woman beyond reproach as your wife."[88] Unlike her female friends, she would rather stay at home to care for her sick mother and younger sibling than go out with her friends. This class-based distinction from the hartawan is central to her retention of a moral purity distinct from European-ness: "The preference for pleasure and mingling definitely became the habit of young people who embrace Western culture/civility [M: *kesopanan*]. But He-Kiauw's morally pure [M: *soetjie*] character was neither formed by her surroundings, nor by her European education, but by the education of her mother."[89]

The author made Chinese women's "purity" (read virginity) stand for the ethno-moral contrast between Chinese and European culture. The scions of Chinese hartawan transgressed racial-sexual boundaries when they built their own pleasure house, where native and European women served them. Young Dutch-educated Chinese women risked losing their moral "purity" (M: *kesoetjian*) when they were exposed to Western cultural habits, such as dating, and seduced into premarital sex with their boyfriends. Thio He-Kiauw's parents thought that her suitor, the Dutch-educated young scion of a Chinese hartawan, was a good match, for besides his wealth, he was well-educated, had good manners, and had a knowledge of business. It is not clear how the story ends, but the author early on sets up the male protagonist as immoral opposite Thio He-Kiauw. She is pure in thoughts, he wanton; she is responsible and hardworking, he pleasure-seeking; she inherited her mother's cultured personality, he, "despite being very well-educated, has neither decent behavior nor firm thoughts."[90]

Perhaps no better novel than *An Obstructed Match* (1917) came to represent the Chinese creolization of courtship and love marriage.[91] For Tjoe Bou San, then editor of the diasporic nationalist *Sin Po* and best known for leading a campaign to oppose Dutch-Indies nationality, it was the unequal access to Dutch culture rather than the culture itself that obstructed the youth from happy love marriages.[92] To him, the conflict over culture was generational, between parents and children, whereas youth attitudes and access to courtship and love were determined by class differences. Tjoe (writing as Hauw San Liang) set up a love triangle among the male protagonist Giok-kim, an upright *warunghouder* (shopkeeper); his antagonist, an HBS-attending hartawan scion; and their love interest, Kiok-lan, a girl from a humble family who attended the lower tier HCS. Kiok-lan's mother is saved from an illness by Giok-kim. In recognition of his kindheartedness, the mother arranges a marriage between her savior and her daughter. Giok-kim, the open-minded shopkeeper, discovers that he is in love with the girl, but he respects and even financially supports her wish to complete her education at the HCS. His openness to women's education sows the seeds for the failure of his arranged marriage. Kiok-lan falls in love with her classmate's HBS-attending elder brother, who courts her but then falls in love with another HBS-educated hartawan girl, introduced by his parents.

The novel takes a similar polemical stance against Western culture's influence on Chinese girls, but only from the perspective of Kiok-lan's mother: "From this day onwards, you don't need to go to school anymore. I don't like that you are mixing with others. The more you learn, the less good a person you become, and the more you pick up ugly customs [M: *peradatan*]. There [in school] you mimic Dutch adat, by looking for love behind your parent's back. Sigh, Kiok-lan, you will be damned for your mistakes."[93] The deeper tension is one of class between the HBS-educated bourgeois and the average shopkeeper petit bourgeois. The shopkeeper and the girl from humble origins both become victims of hartawan interests and imperatives. Kiok-lan's mother is in fact the only voice against Dutch culture in the novel. The youth love and suffer knowingly and without repent for their unrequited love. Unlike most other dime novels of the period, Tjoe Bou San made no explicit moral lesson for his readers except for this meditation on what he called the "mysterious forces" behind love: "What do I mean by finding a match? It is said that people who are separated by thousands of miles may meet and be ensnared. That is not wrong, but it is not only that. The two people—a man and a woman—must feel bound to each other. They must not only be able to live together, but must also feel bound together in the soul. That, that is what called a match."[94]

The greater thrust of love stories in the 1920s and 1930s was in the Chinese creolizing direction set forth by Tjoe Bou San. The misogynistic strain—women who dated and loved died for their scandalous sins—remained an important device, but the more prominent and popular writers wrote progressive stories of petit bourgeois men breaking down barriers of traditional customs to set up monogamous Chinese families founded on love. While conceding that "some writers run the risk of depicting characters in their novels who stand up to the established order," Salmon argues that the general tone of these stories remained patriarchal.[95] But that "established [gender] order" of social permissiveness toward fostering native nyai and Chinese concubines was surely if slowly disintegrating over the 1920s as younger generations of school-going Chinese embraced monogamous love marriages as a mark of modernity.

In *The Loan Eng* (1922), described by Nio Joe Lan as "a gem within the field of Chinese-Indonesian literature," Tjoe Bou San takes a tougher stance against Dutch culture than in his earlier love story.[96] Here he features a young Lorenz Yo Kim Sioe, raised by a Dutch stepfather and Chinese mother in the Indies and educated in the Netherlands, as the archvillain. In a twist to the colonial critique of traditional Chinese marriage, it is the Dutch-raised Lorenz Yo who aspires to foster a concubine and marry for money rather than love. Rejected in a marriage proposal made to Loan Eng's uncle and guardian, he plots to elope with the beautiful Loan Eng for her potential inheritance of a huge estate. In contrast to the previous novel, Tjoe represents his Chinese characters as progressive for the early 1900s—Loan Eng's uncle-guardian consults her before her arranged marriage, and her eventual groom does not mind her past. In this way, the hybrid form of love marriage is projected backward in time and assimilated as always and already Chinese, while its Western roots are denied.

This pattern of creolizing "love" as a bourgeois pattern of change internal to the Chinese themselves rather than imposed on them by the Dutch is evident in the category of Chinese Indonesian literature Nio Joe Lan classified as "romantic." Spanning the period 1914 to 1935, Nio chose ten stories to showcase the "development of the romantic" in the literature, which "reflected the circumstances and dreams (M: *idam-idam*) of the *peranakan* Chinese before the Pacific War."[97] These novels, which included the two by Tjoe Boe San, featured the romantic trials and tribulations of self-made bourgeois Chinese men rather than the elitist hartawan. They mostly ended with happily (and monogamously) married Chinese couples, after struggles with some aspect(s) of Chinese tradition or practice.

Oen Tong Tjoan's *Waves of the World* (undated) made Confucian filial piety the ends of a romantic competition between a good (adopted) and a bad son. A wealthy man adopts a son and a daughter from different families and arranges for them to marry. His own ill-disciplined biological son, attracted to the girl, finds a reason to evict his foster brother and thus foils the marriage. Later on, the bad son, who fails to take advantage of his foster sister, evicts her after he tires of her. She meets her former fiancé by chance in his own shop, falls in love with him, and marries him. They take their foster father into their newly formed family after he loses everything in a fire.[98]

Conflict with wealth and status-conscious parents over marriage decisions was one of the most common themes dramatized in these novels. How parents' preferences for hartawan over petit bourgeois groom-suitors were resolved in the stories demonstrates particular authors' position on the salience of class difference in Chinese marriages. Tjoe Bou San is pessimistic in *An Obstructed Match*, where the young hartawan falls for another wealthy girl recommended by his parents, leaving the two petit bourgeois protagonists' love unrequited. In Tan Boen Kim's *Gan Liang Boen, or A Scary Night!* (1924), love marriage can transcend class boundaries only when a Dutch-educated woman's bad but wealthy husband dies in an accident, leaving her free to remarry her own preferred petit bourgeois man. In Ong Ping Lok's *Just for One* (1927), class conflict is resolved in a comic fashion when a shabbily dressed trekker, with whom a wealthy girl falls in love, has his marriage proposal rejected, only to be re-embraced when his own mother turns up to reveal their millionaire background.[99]

Sisters' competition for the affection of the same man reflected another variant of youths' conflicts with their parents over marriage decisions. This theme fed off a pattern in traditional *peranakan* Chinese marriages where it was common for parents to arrange multiple marriages between two families, often hatched between the mother's brother or the brother's sister. In *Gan Liang Boen*, the hartawan whom Gan Liang Boen's two Dutch-educated daughters fall in love with is their mother's elder brother's son, Tjoe Kim Han. Tjoe, however, is but an ordinary shopkeeper. Although Gan's daughters are given the freedom to attend dance parties, "on the matter of marriage, [their] parents [do] not give [them] the permission to choose their own husband."[100] The parents arrange for their daughters to marry two young hartawans. The younger sister's love will only be realized after her husband dies in a car crash and she marries Tjoe Kim Han.[101] In this creolized Chinese form, petit bourgeois love eventually prevails over the traditional arranged marriage *and* the protagonist's Dutch-educated competitors.

A final creolizing romantic theme was to de-sinicize the practice of taking concubines. In Ong Ping Lok's *Song from Seven Heavens* (1931), good petit bourgeois men protect young women from traditionally minded and Western-educated Chinese men, who want to keep them as concubines.[102] The heroine, Kho Gwat-hoei, is the daughter of a hartawan heir who eschews wealth to avoid a fight over inheritance with his brother. Born wealthy but now impoverished, Gwat-hoei becomes susceptible to the immoral desires of an elder Chinese man (tradition) and John Tan (Westernized Chinese). The former plans to keep her as a concubine, whereas the latter, after her looks and wealth, abducts a native woman as nyai even as he is trying to court Gwat-hoei to be his wife. But she has already fallen in love with a neighbor, Thio Ing-tiong, who cares for her father and her without knowing their real hartawan identity. This hardworking young man, also known for his filial feelings for his mother, is able to foil John's kidnapping plot and marry Gwat-hoei in the end.

By the mid-1930s, this creolized Chinese monogamous love ethic had become a petit bourgeois moral norm. Mrs. Tjoa Hin Hoei, née Kwee Yat Nio, the editor of the Sino-Malay *Maandblad istri*, a women's monthly, noted in an article advocating Chinese religious marriage customs that "parents have awoken to the fact they can no longer exercise authority over children's marriage in the twentieth century." They now "simply let their children choose [their spouses], while remaining as advisers only."[103] Kwee argued that "marriage is holy, not only in the eyes of law, but also in a spiritual [M: *rohani*] way." While the youth were free to date and choose their own spouses, praying to God and ancestors in Confucian marriage ceremonies made it a "holy marriage." Displaying a similar attitude as her male peers, Kwee warned that only those "couples who ran away from parents, young girls who have been defiled or whose morals have been destroyed, . . . marr[ied] at the Civil Registry quietly without ceremonies." She decried that "moral law" (D: *wet moral*), a term she retained in Dutch, "among the young today, whether in their social interactions or in marriage have sunk far too low!"

This chapter traced the birth and transformation of a moral discourse of sexual love among the Chinese of Java to three moments of discursive change in their popular imagination and everyday intimate practices. At its birth, the new moral discourse of sexual love identified native women as both the cause and exploited object of Chinese male desire. In its turn to the spiritual, writers creolized sexual love by Confucianizing the Christian discourse of moral sin to the Chinese context of colonial Java. The transformation was complete when between parents and youth, love was yoked onto Chinese marriage, while sex and desire was de-sinicized as backward and Western. Let us now turn to how the Chinese responded to colonial marriage and birth registration law reforms in the midst of these moral projects of self-renewal.

Part 4
LEGALIZING DESCENT, RACIALIZING PATRILINY

Part 4 discusses how the creole Chinese patriliny became entangled with colonial legal reforms for the Chinese in Java and the wider Dutch East Indies. Chapter 7 looks at the creole Chinese response to the introduction of a Chinese monogamous marriage law, while chapter 8 examines the impact of colonial birth registration. It shows that the Dutch approach to colonial law was, at its base, a racial one. The colonial state used the difference of private law (family law) as a justification for the racialized legal apartheid between Europeans and Asians. The Chinese, in a way, became both a political pawn (between the white ruling elite and the Muslim indigenous majority) and a liberal experiment for reforms to the colonial racial-legal project when a monogamous marriage law was imposed on them with no consultation in 1919. As a result, despite early bottom-up experiments with courtship and self-determined marriages, the Chinese were slow to warm up to the idea of consensual marriage and civil law marriage registration. Birth registration, on the other hand, provided them with the opportunity to officially pass on the father's patrilineal name. The Chinese in Java embraced birth registration and subscribed, consciously or unconsciously, to the assumptions colonial civil law made about race and paternity.

7

THE CIVILIZING GIFT OF MONOGAMY

On 15 April 1916, the jurist-cum-law reformer Pieter H. Fromberg, speaking to Chinese students from the Dutch East Indies gathered in Amsterdam, announced that the impending family law reforms would "ennoble Indies-Chinese family life and elevate the civilizational standard [D: *beschavingspeil*)] of Indies-Chinese society."[1] The new laws, which would go into force on Java on 1 May 1919, applied the previously exempted family law portions of the Dutch Civil Code onto the empire's Chinese subjects. Nowhere else among the Chinese overseas in colonized Asia, or even in the modernizing Republican homeland, was a monogamy law in force during the 1910s and 1920s. Republican China passed its modern monogamous marriage law in 1931 in a form that continued, as critics pointed out, to make concessions to the rights of existing concubines. Closer to Java, the British rulers of the Straits Settlements (Singapore, Malacca, and Penang), offered their Chinese subjects a civil marriage law in 1926, only to be robustly turned down in the consultation stages of the legislative process.[2] Across the British Empire, the full embrace of monogamy and equality for women almost always took place after the Westernized Asian elite of the colonies took over the reins of government. Among the British colonies with significant Chinese populations, it took a populist government in Singapore to adopt a monogamous marriage law in 1961, in contrast to colonial Hong Kong's belated move in 1971.[3] From a purely legislative standpoint, Fromberg was not wrong to tout this reform as the Dutch Empire's early gift of civilization to its Indies Chinese subjects.

Studies of Chinese family law reform in colonial Indonesia have until now focused on international politics and its ramifications for colonial racial-legal structures. This chapter examines how the Dutch and the Chinese of Java negotiated the gender aspects of this civilizing discourse of Europeanized family law between the 1890s and the 1920s. Liberal colonial jurists like Fromberg presented gender equality in general, or monogamous marriage in particular, as a gift of civilization. Yet outside of a small sliver of metropole-educated young Indies Chinese, the concept of family law reform as a civilizing project was received with moral ambivalence by the leading voices of the creole Chinese community in Java. After a brief and heated debate with a young Indies Chinese feminist, the patriarchal reformist leaders proceeded to redefine Chineseness in the realm of customary rites in a bid to counter the civilizational claims of the colonial state. Enforced with little consultation in 1919, the concept of civil law marriage remained peripheral to the cultural lives of the creole Chinese of Java.

Civilizing the Indies Chinese: A Gift of Monogamy

The offer of Europeanized family law as a civilizing gift to the Chinese was a pawn the Dutch tossed out too late in their attempt to salvage imperialism and its built-in racializing hierarchy.[4] Internationally, the Dutch racializing structure of legal apartheid came increasingly under siege as Asian nations, beginning with Japan in 1899, began to argue for jurisdictional rights equal to those of Europeans in Dutch colonial territories after they proved capable of adopting European forms of family law.[5] Among the Dutch ruling elite, liberal reformers like Fromberg, Governor-General J. P. van Limburg Stirum, and their allies pressed for legal unification under one civil code as a step toward phasing out racial classification and the dualist legal system altogether. Having granted Japanese visitors "European" racial-legal status in 1899, the colonial state painted itself into an even smaller corner in the Indies Staatsregeling (D: Constitution) commission of 1906, when it erected "national" family law as the criterion for determining whether its Asian subjects could qualify as "European" or had to remain "Native." It was according to this warped colonial logic that even with its own enactment of a Europeanized family law for the Chinese in 1919, the Indies Chinese remained "Native" in their racial status, as determined by the family law of a "national" homeland many had left behind for generations. However, a colonial shift away from liberal reformism in the 1920s doomed the larger legal unification project to failure, leaving the Indies Chinese subject category in racial limbo between homeland-oriented nationalism and localized civic loyalty.

Colonial anxiety about the Chinese subjects' sexual practices did not escalate into a public moral panic. As various scholars have shown, Dutch colonial moves to address Chinese social needs tended to be reactionary either to China's nationalist outreach to the diaspora or to demands from local Chinese settlers themselves. Two colonial concessions to pan-Chinese nationalism made family law reform even more urgent. In 1908, the government finally gave in to local Chinese demands for Dutch schools. A year later, preempting Qing China's passing of a *jus sanguinis* nationality law, the Dutch signed a dual-nationality treaty with the Chinese to prevent their overseas consulates from meddling in local Chinese matters.[6] Dutch moves in the 1910s to reform Chinese family law on Java must be seen in the context of late Qing and early Republican Chinese efforts to modernize the state's law codes and judiciary system. The late Qing and early Republican adoption of a preliminary draft civil law code gave the liberal colonial jurists the opportunity to push through their long-held reform agenda: a monogamous marriage law as a civilizing gift to the Chinese of Java.

Chapter 4 discussed how colonial reform efforts surrounding the property rights of Chinese women had created "legal certainty" for trade as its aim for much of the nineteenth century. At the turn of the century, colonial reformism took a moralist turn. The burgeoning Dutch language press on Java, and ideas of liberal reformism originating from the metropole, cemented colonial public opinion around what C. Th. van Deventer coined the Netherlands' "debt of honor" to develop the Indies in return for decades of exploitation. One area targeted by liberal reformers was the official tolerance of native concubinage among European men. It was estimated that more than half of all European men living in the Indies kept local women as servants-cum-concubines.[7] Not only did concubinage contradict Christian principles, but the abandoned mixed-race European children, especially those fathered by colonial soldiers, contributed to as many as one in three European paupers at the turn of the twentieth century.[8] Reformers encouraged these men to form more stable families, while urging the government to outlaw concubinage altogether. The patriarchal Mixed Marriages Act of 1898 removed the legal hindrance that required Asian brides to be assimilated before marriage with European men.[9] Even then, marriages between European men and Asian women rose from only one in ten to one in three between 1900 and 1925. Despite decades of public criticism, it was only in 1919 that Governor-General J. P. van Limburg Stirum officially prohibited European and Native Christian soldiers from maintaining concubines in the army barracks.[10]

This moralist impetus spilled over into the ongoing jurists' interest in reforming the legal status of the Chinese subject. Around 1898, I. A. Nederburgh, a member of the Court of Justice in Batavia and initiator of the Mixed Marriages Act, launched a critique of his colleague's traditionalist approach to Chinese legal reform in the colony.[11] At the peak of liberal reformism (1900–1920) in the Indies, Nederburgh was the preeminent advocate for legal unification of all European and Asian subjects under the civil code. He championed the development of the Asian subject's legal conscience (D: *rechtsbewustzijn*) as a means of assimilation into the European rule of law.[12] For Nederburgh, the Chinese presented a different set of challenges to the colonial civilizing project on two fronts. First, ongoing efforts by colonial jurists to uphold and "restore the Chinese *patria potestas*" according to "the law of China" were misplaced. For instance, Pieter H. Fromberg's draft of Chinese family law code for Java, completed in 1897, recognized polygamy and ruled out the notion of marriage consent from bride and groom. To Nederburgh, this was "out of touch with the local legal conscience, and with the impulse of the local needs and desires of the Chinese."[13] Some of the localized Chinese settlers, he argued, had moved away from the patriarchal moral standards of their homeland. They should be encouraged to move toward a European rather than a Chinese legal conscience.

Second, the recognition of traditional Chinese family law set a morally harmful example for the other population groups the Dutch were trying to improve. While Fromberg's draft code had a "philosophical basis for concubinage"—the Chinese zeal for sons to perpetuate the ancestral worshipping lineage—this often turned women into "a vessel for pleasure [D: *werktuig tot zingenot*]." Permitting Chinese polygamy would contradict international law "when they are unwilling to be subject to the public order of the land, on whose hospitality they are dependent as foreigners."[14] It effectively enslaved native women, tempted childless European men with the same vice, and threatened the mixed-race Indies Europeans to moral degeneration:

> The Chinese, who understands so well the art of taking the native into his power, finds therefore in Indië ample room to procure for himself exquisite vessels and does not name them *dzi-ngè*, as the Chinese concubine is called, but "*loe-pi*," in other words "female slave." So the foreigners come both with and to make money, and acquire everything, demoralize our people and to make them half-slaves....
>
> One imagines that the European whose marriages are not blessed with offspring... would perhaps succumb to the temptation when the condition existed for him to beget an offspring through a second wife....
>
> A large part of the European population of Indië are surrounded... more by Easterners than Westerners. Should we needlessly leave Indies Europeans to degeneration by our complete indifference to demonstrate to foreigners the main principles of law, which deprive them of the support for their already wavering esteem?[15]

Nederburgh's associationist argument prevailed. Reviewing the debate among the jurists, Governor-General Idenburg found "no objection of overriding nature to declare the entire personal law for Europeans on the Chinese."[16] By 1904, the reformist tide had clearly turned against the earlier orientalist mode of colonial jurisprudence, but it did not lead immediately to a monogamous Indies Chinese marriage law. It took another external stimulus—the drafting of preliminary civil codes by China—to stir the Dutch into action.

In March and April 1912, the Republican government in Beijing had declared the late Qing state's criminal code, including its civil law chapters, to be provisionally in use. "These new laws," warned Henri Borel, then the adviser for Chinese affairs in Surabaya, almost immediately "would only recognize monogamous marriage."[17] The Batavia-based adviser for Japanese and Chinese affairs, B. A. J. van Wettum, translated the relevant new provisional Chinese Republican civil code for the Justice Department.[18] In response, in January 1913, Governor-General Idenburg requested that the Department of Justice draft statutes for a civil registry and private legal status for the Chinese in the Indies.

B. A. J. van Wettum's translation showed that "the draft cannot be spoken of as a strict monogamy in the western sense."[19] No doubt the code had expressly banned bigamy.[20] But J. W. C. Cordes, the director of the Justice Department, thought the code still "recognize[d] . . . the institute of secondary wives [C: *bijvrouwen*], even if it painstakingly avoids mentioning her." This it did by recognizing for inheritance "three sorts of sons, namely the primary wife's sons, the secondary wife's sons and natural sons."[21] The greatest advancement was in the area of divorce. The terms for divorce had become more equal between the sexes. But the stipulation that family affairs be run by a family council—or, more precisely, a lineage council—and the prevention of estate division in the lifetime of one's parents indicated to Cordes that the Chinese still upheld "the concept of the family being the unit of society and of property belonging to it." For these reasons, he thought the code was "in many ways below the pale of civilization (D: *beschaving*) achieved by the Chinese who had settled here from generation to generation."[22]

To meet China's progress to a supposedly semicivilized state, Cordes proposed a monogamous marriage law that tolerated promiscuity. A full "transition to [the Dutch] legal system in this respect would have been too great." In early 1914, the Justice Department drafted a civil law code for the Chinese that included the monogamy clause (Art. 27) but absolved the husband from conjugal sexual fidelity.[23] Adultery would not be a crime for the Chinese. In other words, bigamy would have been illegal, but concubinage or other sexual liaisons outside marriage were not forbidden for men.[24] In effect, this code would not have departed much from the sexual morality tolerated under Chinese adat law, as discussed in the previous section.

In The Hague, Pieter H. Fromberg, the retired jurist and expert on Chinese family law, disagreed. Between September and December 1915, Fromberg sent six lengthy notes in reply to the minister of colonies' queries about the draft code. The first note opened with three principal reasons why and how Dutch family law in general, and a full-fledged monogamy marriage law in particular, ought to be applied to the Chinese in the Indies. First, the Chinese community in the Indies were "self-emancipating in a Western orientation." This point was underscored by the fact that more and more Chinese litigants were using Dutch civil law categories to disinherit children born by concubines.[25] Second, there was no legal foundation for a watered-down version of civil law. Third, it was an important step for the eventual unification of unequal colonial laws for all subjects.[26]

Of the two major exemptions—concubinage and adoption—the draft, in recognition of the Confucian desire for a male heir, recommended that only the latter should be permitted. The colonial state should no longer give in to the conservative elements in Indies Chinese society. A monogamy that tolerated concubinage "tarnished" (D: *ontsieren*) the civil law by "implying that a married Chinese man was not duty-bound to marital fidelity." Conjugal fidelity should be restored and all euphemistic references to permissible extramarital relations in the draft code removed.[27] If the "monogamy principle can be accepted unadulterated," the lawgiver would "exercise a moral influence and be in harmony with the (Indies-)Chinese political movement, which aims for elevation and association."[28]

Would the Chinese men, who already had concubine(s) before the passing of the law, asked the minister of colonies, be liable for adultery?[29] The answer was yes, although the state was unlikely to receive many such charges. Fromberg pointed out that since the adultery law (Art. 256) in the Native Criminal Code punished men who "fostered a concubine [M: *gundik*] in the same house as the married wife," the onus was on the wife to sue her husband. In existing cases of Chinese concubinage, the cohabitation of man, wife, and concubine already "presume(s) that the major wife tolerates the concubine, or at least is at peace with her presence, so that no lawsuit will be filed from her side, even if art. 256 were applied."[30] Application of Article 256 had a "more ostensible than real import." In any case, if the latest Dutch criminal law developments were to be applied to the Indies, "the threat of legal penalty for adultery would in fact lose its import."[31]

One consequence of applying the adultery law to all concubinage sexual relations was the uncertain legal status of children born to them. To be fair to men already living with secondary wives or concubines, they would have three hundred days after the passing of the law to legally acknowledge children conceived before the passing of the law. All children born to secondary wives and concubines after the three hundred days would count as children born from adultery. Along with children sprung from incestuous relationships, they would be denied any opportunity to be legally acknowledged by their fathers. These special transitory provisions (D: *overgangsbepalingen*) for already existing secondary wives and concubines were included in the law that eventually passed in 1917.

The colonial government adopted Fromberg's advice for adopting a stricter monogamy for the Indies Chinese over an earlier version that was monogamy in name but perpetuated polygamy in practice. The design of the Chinese monogamous marriage in Staatsblad 1917 no. 129: Regulation of the Private Legal Status of the Chinese was essentially the result of Fromberg's contribution to the colonial lawmaking process. In leaning on Fromberg's counsel, the government counted not only on his Chinese legal expertise but on his contacts with the Chinese community in Java and his analysis of their changing attitudes to colonial racial policy, international politics, and familial and gender norms. Crucially, Fromberg claimed that the Department of Justice "did not consult the leaders of the Indies-Chinese society" while drafting the 1914 code.[32] How then did Fromberg justify his push for a strictly monogamous marriage law, and how did the Chinese in Java react to these impending changes to their family law when the new law was announced in 1917?

Advocating Women's Equality: The Patriarchal Pushback

The retired Pieter H. Fromberg was not an armchair advocate of reform. He wrote pamphlets addressing the public in both the metropole and the colony about the urgent need to recognize the social movement of the Chinese of Java, and for the colonial government to pursue a more progressive reform agenda with the community.[33] He cultivated a following in Amsterdam and The Hague among sojourning Chinese students from the Indies, and he made another trip to Java to collect evidence for his proposed policy changes. His advocacy of more equal rights for Chinese women in the colony found ready and enthusiastic adherents among Dutch-educated Chinese students from Java. One of them, Caroline Tan Souw Lien, would serve very briefly as the public voice of that campaign. A brief and fiery exchange between Tan and her detractors back in Java in 1913 and 1914 revealed the depth of creole Confucian patriarchal resistance to the concepts of the individual's autonomy and gender equality in marriage matters.

Besides his role as legal adviser to the colonial state, Fromberg publicly championed the goal of Java's Chinese movement to achieve parity of status with Europeans in the Indies. His best-known pamphlet, *The Chinese Movement in Java* (1911), explained to the Dutch public the colonial government's past mistreatment of the Chinese and argued for granting them equal legal status with Europeans.[34] The pamphlet could not have appeared in a more opportune year—

that of the fall of dynastic China and the founding of the first Chinese republic. Fromberg's pro–Indies Chinese political advocacy was most likely calculated to win over the Dutch-educated Chinese elite to a liberal multiracial colonial associationist policy. In the same year, Indies-born Chinese students formed Chung Hwa Hui in the Netherlands—a student political body representing the interests of the Chinese in the Dutch Indies.

From Amsterdam, Fromberg and Caroline Tan would launch their feminist critique against the patriarchal practices of the Chinese of Java, becoming the first keynote lecturers for Chung Hwa Hui's annual meeting in 1912 and 1913. In his 1912 lecture, Fromberg praised the Chinese of Java for having achieved great strides in modernizing education but identified the subordination of women and superstitious beliefs in geomancy as the two "shadows . . . not in agreement with . . . the modern strive towards the reception of Western culture."[35] On the question of Chinese women's status, Fromberg shared his experience as codifier of the aborted Chinese private law code of 1897. Previously, "if the lawgiver in the Indies had to deal with primitive or half-civilized situations, for example with polygamy or concubinage, . . . he will just leave its regulation to adat." Yet "as a civilized lawgiver," he now had to proceed "from the principle of monogamy," which not only consisted of the exclusive union of a man and a woman but also "required the free consent of the prospective spouses." Without this free consent, the woman "would be subordinated to a situation bordering on slavery, in case she was coupled with a man for whom she felt no affection."[36] Fromberg related how back in 1892, the "civilized Chinese" of Batavia, Semarang, and Surabaya protested against a draft of Indies Chinese marriage law, which would have required the prospective spouses' consent. Back then, they had argued that "marriage is not a volition of the bride and groom, but a submission to the will of the parents."[37]

Caroline Tan belonged to a small elite group of what historian Didi Kwartanada calls the "Female Nobility" (M: Bangsawan Perempoean) of colonial Java society at the turn of the twentieth century. Through a liberal education and the acquisition of Western-style feminine skills and hobbies, these young Dutch-educated Chinese women—like Kartini, their Javanese aristocratic counterpart—were groomed to become the enlightened wives of Java's Asian male elites. By the 1910s, the first Indies Chinese girls were sent to the colonial metropole for higher education. A daughter of the Chinese Kapitan of Bangkalan (Madura), Caroline Tan Souw Lien received her middle school education in the Netherlands during the 1910s and became the first Indonesian woman to graduate with a law degree, receiving it from the University of Utrecht in 1923.[38] It was in the Netherlands, and most likely under the influence of Pieter Fromberg, that she first enunciated her critical feminist discourse against Indies Chinese society.

A year after listening to Fromberg, Tan, in her maiden public speech, framed her feminism as a moral invective against the oppression of women by patriarchal Indies Chinese customs. She likened the parent who arranged marriages for the daughter, and especially the husband who received the wife, to "the tyrant." Marriage for girls at a young age was "moral murder." And the "cruel customary law" of secluding young girls from the public gaze should be abandoned. The condition of Chinese women was so drastic that it was "high time the government deal[t] with it." Her call for the "moral uplifting" of the Chinese woman met with "loud applause" from Chung Hwa Hui members.

Her talk borrowed heavily from Fromberg's juristic assessments of Chinese women's civil law rights in the Indies, but she trained her polemic against their perceived oppressors. While Fromberg saw the arranged marriage as "bordering on slavery," Caroline likened it, especially the marriage of very young brides, to "moral murder." In traditional Chinese marriage, she argued that the husband served as the "master" and "tyrant" of his wife. She called for absolute equality between Chinese men and women. In concrete terms, she demanded (1) increased access to education for Chinese girls in the Indies, (2) equal inheritance rights between daughters and sons, and (3) an end to female segregation from society upon reaching puberty. In short, the Dutch newspapers reported, she wanted "the Chinese girls [to] be brought up like her white sisters, so that not only can her soul resonate deeply with the learning of sweet Western musical notes, but also so that the tones learned can be paired with her own to full harmonious accord with the Eastern music of the future."[39] A truncated version of Tan's speech was carried on the front page of two Dutch newspapers: the liberal broadsheet *Algemeen Handelsblad* and *Haagsche Courant*. Back in the Indies, it was carried a month later in *Het nieuws van den dag voor Nederlandsch-Indië* under the title "Young China in The Hague."[40] The Dutch in both the metropole and the colony were clearly impressed with the rise of this new Dutch-educated and gender-conscious young Chinese.

In contrast to the Dutch press, the Sino-Malay press in Java translated her speech in full and rebutted her criticism head-on.[41] The Surabaya weekly *Bok Tok* version revealed the more precise list of the ills and evils of the Indies Chinese parents and husbands mentioned in her speech. Not mentioned in the Dutch reports was her critique of Chinese men's sexual infidelity and the practice of polygamy under the rubric of the husband's tyranny. While it was true, she argued, that the young man likewise had no choice in an arranged marriage, after marriage he became "unhindered to do as he wished ... without the wife having any power to counter or limit that desire.... Nothing stops him from setting up a harem, [or] why not a pleasure quarters [Hk: *soehian*], however unjust it may be to his wife, who is only his female slave. This man is only afraid of one person, his own Papa, but considering that his father does likewise . . . , [he] is often silenced by this reply, "What now? Whenever you don't like the wife I found for you, can't you just take a wife number two outside?"[42] The Malay translation of her speech also showed a more severe diatribe against traditional Chinese customs. Castigating parents for limiting the education of their daughters in fear of their development and independence, she argued against blind adherence (M: *buta toeli*) to ancient customs (M: *adat kuno*). Have some of these "immoral (M: *lacoer*) regulations," she asked, become "hereditary over a few generations—a legacy that cannot be changed?"[43]

Besides Surabaya's *Bok Tok*, the nationalistic Batavia-based *Sin Po* waded into the polemical debate. In refuting both Tan's depiction of the Chinese patriarchy and her calls for gender equality in all aspects of social life, the male *peranakan* opinion leaders rallied around a racially defined notion of love, marriage, and adat in their assertion of an authentic space for patriarchal self-determination. Kwee Tek Hoay, then of *Sin Po*, presented a realist rejoinder to what he saw as an elitist and naive call for reform. Writing under the pseudonym K. Buitenzorg, he pointed out that Tan's gender-equal ideas were only applicable to the richest 5 percent of the Indies Chinese, or the members of the Netherlands-based Chung Hwa Hui in particular, and were "completely unthinkable or utopian" for the remaining 95 percent who "belong to the poorer class." While Tan acknowledged the existence of a class divide, she held her ground by pointing out the "bitterly few" girls among the steadily expanding numbers of Chinese receiving an education on Java.[44]

A more sustained effort to engage and fend off Tan's feminist views emerged on the pages of *Bok Tok* in Surabaya. Begun in October 1913 by a group of modern educated Confucian reformers, the editors of *Bok Tok* tried to marry popular social science with their search for racial (M: *bangsa*) and Confucian authenticity.[45] "Bok Tok," literally the Chinese bronze bell, stood here for knowledge and manners (M: *ilmoe peladjaran dan toto kromo*), as cited from a line in the Analects the group interpreted as "God will send the Prophet Confucius to be the messenger of knowledge and manners for the world."[46] Politically, it looked to the nationalistic line of *Sin Po* in "defending the Chinese [race], [so as] not to be looked down on, at a time when many were courting equal status with Europeans."[47] *Bok Tok*'s pages displayed a keen interest in applying scientific knowledge to reform Indies Chinese family life. Sex and marriage were a constant feature. The third issue introduced a female Japanese doctor's book, most likely a eugenicist text, that advocated smaller age gaps between married couples and warned against marriage with close kin and people with irreputable blood descent.[48] In "Papa and Mama," the author TTL declared reproduction to be a duty to one's parents and nation (M: *bangsa*), and those who did not reproduce to be unfilial (M: *tidak bakti*, Hk: *Poet Hao*).⁴⁹ Although more than a month late, *Bok Tok* carried a full transcript of Tan's talk in its tenth issue, paired with three articles to refute her feminist advocacy.

For two months, the writers at *Bok Tok* debated and launched polemical attacks against Tan's speech. Although participants in the debate agreed that parents should continue to arrange marriages for their children, the consensus soon broke down over the question of how far Dutch colonial education and legal reform should be allowed to intervene in Chinese family life. The editors dismissed Tan's feminist critique as a proxy for the European civilizing mission. "Miss C. V. Tan has no other aim," wrote the chief editor Kwee Kang Tik, "but to pull her race [M: *bangsa*] towards embracing European style customs [M: *atoeran*]." In particular, Kwee doubted that free social interaction between boys and girls, as advocated by Tan, would lead to love (M: *katjintaan*) marriages. Instead, the European penchant for the public display of affection, he argued, would "only give rise to lust." Tan was too young "to experience how great and pure the love in the heart of our race was, on the matter of marriage between a wife and the husband." European learning was "only for the increase of knowledge, and NOT for its . . . turning into fundamentals or roots that are pure."⁵⁰

The young Kwee Hing Tjiat defended Chinese marital rules and rituals as a domain to be reformed not by European but by ancient Chinese ethical norms.⁵¹ Traditional Chinese family laws (M: *atoeran*) were eternal, he argued, not only because they originated from Confucius but by the fact of their survival among the Chinese, the longest continuous civilization, as compared with the ancient Romans, Greeks, and Carthaginians. This proved, for Kwee, that "current Chinese marriage customs are sufficiently perfect [M: *sempoerna*]." What was needed was not so much any change in the marriage laws but the "inculcation of morals [M: *kesopanan*] in the husband . . . through the holy books of the early prophet."⁵² It was this love (M: *katjinta'an*) that was the foundation of Chinese family life. Addressing Tan in direct speech, Kwee pointed out that "the survival [of Chinese culture] in this world had already been threatened by competition [with European culture (D/M: *cultuur*)] yet here you are trying to introduce that culture into Chinese households, which, fortunately until now has managed to remain sacred (M: *soetji*)."

A more nuanced and less polemicized rejoinder was included in the same issue. The mixed sentiments of Tan Siok Tjwan, the private secretary of a "big" Surabaya lawyer, was probably reflective of Indies Chinese who were appreciative of their Dutch colonial education and less nationalistic than their peers. Tan's sentiments most likely captured how the average educated Indies Chinese father reacted to Caroline Tan's feminist pleas: "While reading the report, I felt quite strange [M: *aneh*] in my thoughts [M: *pikiran*]. One moment I wanted to laugh, and the next I was like a crying man, and yet another moment my goosebumps were all standing. In short, the state of my mind [D: *gemoedstoestand*; M: *pembrasahan hati*) fluctuated between Heaven and Hell. Having been put very much at ease after reading two passages, I felt like a soaring kite in the wind, the next moment a part of the speech made me fearful and sad, as though I was peering into a broad and dangerous ravine."[53] Unlike the two polemical Kwees, Tan Siok Tjwan did not reject Caroline Tan's critique out of hand but instead pleaded for a more gradualist approach to Chinese marital reforms. "A caged bird," he argued, "cannot be immediately set free."[54] "We cannot make our own nature and character those practices we imitate from Europeans."[55] For Tan Siok Tjwan, parents should themselves have enjoyed a Western upbringing before they could legitimately be expected to bring up their children as "European." Otherwise, as had happened with several extremely well-educated Indies Chinese girls, they might "go astray" (M: *njasar*). But like the two Kwees, he objected to some of the excesses of Caroline Tan's critique, particularly her suggestion that fathers encouraged sons to take concubines. "How can I remain silent and join in the applause," he asked, "when parents are insulted in such an important organization?"

Tan Siok Tjwan went so far as to call for legislation to forestall many of the marital problems faced by the Chinese in the Indies. "The law [D: *wet*] must be made," he argued, "to give our marriages the rules [M: *atoeran*] that the white race already have, so that the husband cannot do as he pleases."[56] Legislation would address marital problems among Chinese couples he had most likely encountered personally in his legal work. These included the husband's resort to violence, disparity in wealth on either side, the shrewish wife, and disparity in educational levels.

While Tan Siok Tjwan was prepared to concede husband and wife relations to the regulation of colonial civil law, he wanted parents to remain the "sovereigns [M: *pembesar negri*; D: *souverain*] who hold all laws in their hands" over their children. Unlike the Confucian reformer nationalists, Tan thought that the "laws" the parents held would not so much be Chinese as European. In "the foundations of upbringing and education," he argued that there were two kinds of knowledge in the development of a person—learned knowledge (M: *ilmoe peladjaran*; D: *wetenschap*) and spiritual knowledge (M: *ilmoe berboedi*; D: *geestelijke ontwikkeling*). One cannot count on "learned knowledge" to make a child a perfect person. Children's upbringing belonged to the spiritual realm, where they would be nurtured by the natural instincts of a mother and the moral example of their parents' lives. The parents in turn relied on "classical models," which "form the basis of a free/civil person's and government's life" (M: *penghidoepan orang merdika dan pemerentah*; D: *grondbeginselen van burgerlijk en staatkundig leven*). Where did one look for these classical models? "Just as the Bible was the classic of the Christians," he argued that "now, in this age, Europe is considered the classic model of the Japanese and Chinese races."[57]

In December 1913, Tan Siok Tjwan stood out for his call for reforms to Chinese family law in the Indies on the basis of equal rights between man and woman. On "the emancipation of the Chinese race," he argued that the state of Chinese familial relations "is the cause of our race remaining at the bottom of the stairs of freedom and finding it so hard to ascend it."[58] As the patriarchal nationalist attacks against Caroline Tan mounted, Tan Siok Tjwan, the advocate of gradualist Europeanization of familial norms, became her only ally and defender in the Sino-Malay public sphere. He likened the attacks against her to the "watering hot water [and also carbolic acid] on a flower [Miss Caroline Tan] that is beginning to blossom and has yet to have time to show us her fragrance."

The continuing Chinese patriarchal attacks revealed anxieties over the loss of control over Chinese womenfolk. In a rebuttal against Tan Siok Tjwan, Tjioe Tik Lien argued that Caroline Tan had "crossed the line" with her "demand for equal rights" (M: *hak sama rata*) because "it would be difficult for people to understand where [such demands might] end." It was unthinkable for Tjioe that men's freedom to go watch a "gentlemen's show" in the cinema might be extended to women. On the proposed reforms to Chinese marriage law, he pointed to the age-old custom among the poorer Chinese, who "only report to their Wardmaster or Lieutenant of their race with a pair of red candles without buying [applying for] the marriage certificate, yet between husband and wife, they have held firmly on to the loyalty they owe each other." Tjioe did not see why the emancipation of the Chinese had to be linked to family law reform: "If by the word 'emancipation' [M: *kamerdika'an*] is intended the emancipation of the race [M: *bangsa*], I cannot see how it has anything to do with the matter of marriage, and if the emancipation of the husband-and-wife relationship is what is intended, then all the more I cannot agree that equal rights, whose meaning is vast, should immediately be granted to women."[59] Instead, Tjioe counseled against any "careless" changes to Chinese customs (M: *adat-istiadat*). The consequences, which "can already be seen in the last one or two years, are having our girls—too many it can be said—enter shops wearing dresses that reveal their naked arms and [becoming] no longer shy to let others hear their melodious laughter." The final straw that would "turn everything upside down" was if "marriage certificates . . . had to be written like a contract," which would give women the rights to say, "True, you may be my legal [M: *sah*] husband, but you must fall under my influence; you cannot order me anytime to do anything to which I don't agree."[60]

Pressures to assimilate European gender norms also triggered racial anxiety over the loss of Chinese women to European society. Real life tragedies of Dutch-educated Chinese girls' relationships with European men were sensationalized as cautionary tales against love marriage. The chief editor Kwee Kang Tik himself related a story of the Surabaya major Tan Sing Tan's Dutch-educated daughter, Tan Kiam Nio, being swindled of her inheritance by a Dutch soldier to whom she was engaged.[61] Even Tan Siok Tjwan, who eventually came out for women's rights, drew a clear line between emancipating Chinese women and freeing them to cross the racial boundary. His short story, "Long Live the Emancipation (of Chinese women)!" caricatured a Leiden-educated "Miss Progress" (M/Hk: *Majoe Nio*) against the virtuous housewife "Miss Conservative" (M/Hk: *Kolot Nio*) in a dialogue, which ended with the former departing at ten o'clock in the evening for the Dutch district controller's house.[62]

The pushback from the Sino-Malay press stood for three kinds of Chinese patriarchal responses to the Dutch conception of gender equality as a civilizational gift. Kwee Hing Tjiat's reaction against Caroline Tan's auto-critique of Chinese traditions was emblematic of a male-chauvinistic conception of a new diasporic Chinese identity on Java. Its attempt to justify patriarchy from the classical texts might have persuaded the more ardent among the followers of the Confucian religion, but it is hard to imagine such an argument enjoying any wider appeal. Tan Siok Tjwan's more self-reflective and moderate stance, admitting the ills of traditions while counseling gradualist change, was probably the most representative educated opinion among the *peranakans*. As Kwee Tek Hoay's and his daughter's championing of a moderate feminism later in the 1920s and 1930s would confirm, he would have agreed with Tan's gradualist approach. At this early stage in 1913, his remark was in a way prescient. His prediction that only the top 5 to 10 percent of the Chinese of Java could afford to care about the advancement of women was largely borne out by the fate of Dutch efforts at family law reform.

Limited Consultation, Ambivalent Reception

If monogamy was meant to be a civilizing gift, the Chinese reception of the law made it seem more like an imposition than a reward. In one of Fromberg's answers to the minister of colonies' queries, polygamy, being the "hobby of the wealthy, c[ould] create no opposition from a political viewpoint" when it was abolished.[63] There would in fact be no opposition to the new family law in part because the majority of the Chinese themselves were not aware of the legal reforms until the eleventh hour. For a law that governed the intimate lives of a group of its subjects, it was surprising how little consultation and public education went into the law's design and its eventual enactment in May 1919.

The Department of Justice approached the impending reforms as a question of introducing a new marriage registry rather than a new conception of marriage altogether. Contacted in the latter months of 1913, the government most likely informed the leaders that the new family law would be revised along the lines of the Chinese republic's provisional civil code and would include a local civil registry. As the department's initial draft code indicated, there were no plans to impose monogamy until Fromberg's intervention in the last months of 1915. According to Nio Joe Lan's history of Tiong Hoa Hwee Koan (THHK)—the pan-Java Chinese reformist association—its executive committee held an Extraordinary Meeting, in the presence of Major Khouw Kim An, to discuss the question of a civil registry for the Chinese on 31 October 1913. The meeting approved the new "rules for making permits for marriage, divorce, birth and death, which the Resident of Batavia had specified in his order dated 29 September 1913," and "left the matter to the Kong Koan [Chinese Council] to handle if changes had to be made later on."[64] The reformist THHK most likely judged any change to be more of an administrative nature than a legal-moral one. Van Wettum's translation and publication of the Chinese republic's provisional civil code in 1914 would have given the leaders the impression that the colonial state intended to follow the new laws of their diasporic homeland.

It is telling that when Sino-Malay newspapers translated Republican China's provisional civil code via Dutch into Malay, they highlighted its effects on legal administration and inheritance rather than marriage. For the more radical and nationalist *Sin Po*, which had a mass readership, it was the occasion to remind its audience of the legal uncertainty caused by the Dutch court's "sometimes ma[king] judgments referring to the Qing Code, and other times to Indies-Chinese law."[65] The more conservative *Perniagaan*, known as the paper of the old elite (D: *Majoorspartij*), lamented "the absence of firm regulations over the inheritance rights of Indies-Chinese . . . [and of] a civil registry."[66] Translated and serialized in the newspaper in March and April 1914, the editors did not comment on the provisional code's ban on bigamy (Art. 1335) or its requirement of legal consent from bride and groom (Art. 1341).[67]

On 15 April 1916, Fromberg announced to the Chung Hwa Hui annual meeting in Amsterdam the full extent and meaning of the impending new Chinese private law code. His lecture, "The Indies-Chinese Family and the Legislation," marked the first time a Dutch official explained to any member of the Indies Chinese public the rationale behind the new law. Besides the administrative question of legal certainty, one of its major goals was to "bring the position of the Indies Chinese woman up to date with demands of the time and . . . promote the dissolution of outdated circumstances." He cited traditions such as the match-made marriage, double standards for sexual fidelity, and the unequal conditions for divorce between husband and wife as "the reprehensible of the old," which had to give way to the "better of the new." In their place, the new marriage law would institute "free choice and affection" between the spouses, mutually bonding fidelity, and the equal conditions for divorce.[68]

To the young Indies Chinese studying in the Netherlands, Fromberg entrusted the task of defending and spreading the feminist values of the new law. He expected that "many conservative Chinese will regard with less favor a legislation that takes the woman to be an equal being with the man."[69] He reminded them of the conservative backlash Caroline Tan faced after her 1912 lecture on the same theme. For the Dutch-educated elite, this law promised to bring the Chinese to the same legal standing as Europeans in the colony. Above all, the law would emancipate the 1,013 Chinese girls who had enrolled in the Dutch Chinese elementary schools in 1913 from the oppressive practices of the Chinese. "They would become women," said Fromberg, "who will be entitled to a civilized legislation, which protects her dignity and self-worth."[70]

In contrast, the law was passed with hardly any effort at public education in Java. The Indies Chinese public was essentially left on its own to interpret and publicize their newly imposed Dutch-style family law. On 26 April 1917, a month after the publication of the law, *Sin Po* introduced it in a brief article, "Privaatrecht bagi orang Tionghoa" (Private law for the Chinese) with little fanfare.[71] The report was a summary of the statutory law with neither elaboration nor commentary on how it might change the family life of the Chinese in the colony. However, the editor did "feel the need to translate a few important articles from the Civil Code of the Dutch Indies which had been applied to the Chinese," namely the section "On marriage" and another on "The rights and duties of husband and wife." It was here that the principle of monogamy, Article 27 of the Dutch Civil Code, most likely first appeared to the readers of *Sin Po*: "A man can only have a wife and a woman a husband." To remind readers of the consequences of contravening it, the editor included the law of adultery in the Native Criminal Code in parentheses: "Any man who fosters a mistress [M: *goendik*] in his own house . . . , who is clearly in the wrong and is sued by his wife, will be punished with a fine of 50 to 100 rupees."[72]

Phoa Tjoen Hoay's translation-cum-commentary of the Dutch-reformed Chinese family law was revealing of the older reformist elite's moral ambivalence toward their new legal status. One of two sons of a Bogor Chinese Kapitan, Phoa's extended family had been at the forefront of Java's Chinese movement since the turn of the century.[73] Both he and his elder brother were professional journalists and writers who served for a time as editors of *Perniagaan*. During the 1910s, the junior Phoa developed a career out of translating law codes for the *peranakan* Chinese from Dutch into Malay: the commercial code (1912), bankruptcy law

(1913?), the local court ordinance (1914), and the Chinese private legal status code (1919).[74] His translation and guide to the law *Privaatrecht dan burgerlijke-stand boeat bangsa Tiong Hoa* (Private law and civil registry for the Chinese nation) appeared in April 1919, a month before it came into force. As news editor, interpreter of laws, and reformer, Phoa could not have been unaware of the limited colonial efforts at consultation in the latter half of 1913. As suggested previously, Chinese community leaders had most likely thought the Dutch would pass a local civil registry to enforce the Chinese republic's provisional family law code. As someone familiar with Dutch Indies law and attuned to how the Chinese operated under it, his critical remarks about the colonial mode of legislation are worth noting:

> There is one question I would like to record here: "Should not the government, when these laws were still in their planning stages, have also heard the thoughts of the Chinese nation [M: *bangsa*], especially when those laws have been specially made for that nation? If not, why did the government not do it? Sure, it *cannot be denied* that these changes bring a lot of *good* to the Chinese nation, but it can only be just [M: *adil*] if the thoughts of that nation were heard *before* the laws were implemented. So what now? I am afraid now that these published laws will be implemented . . . it will cause much difficulty to government officials, sooner than I will finish the other things I want to say!"[75] (emphasis in the original)

Phoa could not deny the *good* civilizing intent of a Dutch reformer and friend like Pieter H. Fromberg, who tried to put the Chinese in the Indies on an equal legal footing as Europeans. Yet without consultation, legislation to change how the Chinese ran their families could not have been a *just* way of government. Phoa tried his best to mitigate the sudden legal changes by being at the same time thorough in his translation of the entire code and selective in his interpretation of what his readers needed to know. As he explained, "I only translate whatever is there (in the law), but I am free [M: *merdika*] to give further clarifications to the reader, so that people who read my translation will obtain all the necessary certainty."[76]

The *Perniagaan* group clearly did not grasp the feminist intent of the law despite devoting more attention to it. Instead of explaining what constituted a civil marriage, as *Sin Po* did, Phoa treated the new laws as additional administrative burdens. To begin with, he translated "civil and commercial law" as "rights of residents and traders" (M: *Hak penduduk dan saudagar*). Phoa saw no equivalent for the concept of "civil" (D: *burgerlijk*), which signified for the Dutch the abstract and universal values associated with the citizen and civilization.[77] By translating and commenting on the statutes verbatim, he mired himself in the technicalities of how the state adapted civil law for the Chinese without actually touching on the civil law itself. Hence, the most important Dutch family law chapters were supposedly subsumed under the all-encompassing line, "On the Chinese will be applied 1. The Civil Code for the Netherlands Indië, with the following exceptions." Phoa himself confessed that "many Chinese will find it difficult having to refer back and forth between translations of the [new statutes] ... and the Civil Code."[78]

Instead of rights and duties that bound two individuals together and to the state, Phoa saw it rather as a series of legal prohibitions that restricted mostly the male ego. "People are confused," he noted, "particularly by the legal clauses on matters surrounding marriage." To explain the new marriage laws, he appended an eleven-page guide (M: *penoendjoek jalan*) at the end of his book, consisting mostly of a list of "Prohibitions on Men." In this way, the laws of monogamy and of marital consent were presented as taboos on men rather than the mutually binding rights and duties of husbands and wives:

> After a man has been legally married once, he is forbidden to marry another woman, if his legal wife is still alive and has not been legally divorced from him. This clause is set down in article 27 of the Civil Code.
>
> After 1 May 1919, a man may no longer marry by forcing a woman to be his legal wife, without that woman's approval. Article 28 of the Civil Code stipulates that a man and a woman may only become husband and wife when they indicate their own consent. If a man tries to marry a woman without her agreeing to take him as her husband, when they sign their papers before the official of the Civil Registry, she may insist on saying that she herself did not like to be his wife, and with the official of the Civil Registry refusing to confirm it, that marriage will fail.[79]

Even the lone voice of approval was couched with qualifications. Two months after the law came into force, a self-styled Tionghoadjin (Hk: Chinese) refuted a Bandung Chinese call to boycott the Civil Registry as part of the broader move to reject Dutch subject status. Published in the Semarang Dutch newspaper *De Locomotief*, the writer noted that "a good number of people" among the Chinese now subscribed to the "more luminous ideas ... and strive for freedom." He was of the opinion that "if one asked the local born Chinese [M: *Pranakan*], both man and woman, if they agreed with the Civil Registry, they would all reply in the affirmative, except for the outdated and stupid people." These outmoded Chinese, he noted, were opposed to the prohibition of keeping more than one wife and for inheritance provisions for wives and daughters. He attributed Chinese apprehensions with the new Civil Registry to poor communications. "If the government wants to know feelings of the Chinese," he urged, "it is best to do a survey of all Chinese, for only then can one say for sure how many are for and how many against it."[80]

The surprise and patriarchal bias with which the creole Chinese community of Java greeted and translated the "Chinese private law" the Dutch gifted them spoke to their ambivalence about becoming civilized like the Europeans through marriage law reform. To the Dutch, the new laws were meant to protect the new generation of Chinese women, who were beginning to graduate from Dutch colonial schools in the 1910s and would do so in greater numbers in the coming years. For liberal reformers like Fromberg, they also held the promise of unifying the diverse races of the Indies under one uniform civil code.

Reforming Communal Rites, Hybridizing Civil Rights

Until the end of formal colonial rule in 1942, the Chinese of Java remained ambivalent about the Dutch attempt to turn marriage into a rights-based bond protected by the state. Across the island, only a small proportion of Chinese marriages were solemnized at the new Chinese Civil Registry (D: Chineesche Burgerlijke Stand). Even then, parents exploited a loophole in the law to incorporate the civil solemnization ceremony into Confucian marriage rites. Although marriage registration rates rose moderately in the last two decades of colonial rule, the parent-, ancestor-, and Confucian Heaven–centered marriage rites remained central to the Chinese marriages.

The notion that a marriage was only legitimate when the bride and groom authenticated their wishes before a civil servant remained alien to many Chinese. The centerpiece of the Dutch solemnization ceremony involved posing in "public" (D: *in- het openbaar voorgehouden*) the following question to bride and bridegroom: "Do you take each other as husband and wife, and in so doing assume all the duties bound to marriage by Law, while remaining faithful for the rest of your lives?" Translated into Malay, the language in which solemnization was held for the Chinese, the question read more like this: "Would you like to be husband and wife, and be loyal to fulfilling all duties stipulated in the laws for husband and wife? [M: . . . soeka djadi suami-isteri dan akan setia memnuhi segala kewadjiban-kewadjiban, jang dibebankan oleh undang-undang kepada suami-istri.]"[81] In 1922, a Chinese parent explained to a Dutch journalist that the civil ceremony contained "offensive and shocking things," which were "highly hurtful to the true Chinese." When the civil registry "official asks the woman:

whether she desires [D: *begeert*] that man ..., [it] makes the woman, the witnesses, and the whole family horribly '*maloe*' [M: shameful]." According to the writer and his informant, it was "clear idiocy that a Chinese woman would 'want' something." A "properly brought up Chinese woman is not so obscene and coarse." She followed the wishes of her parents.[82]

Until the end of Dutch colonial rule in 1942, very few Chinese families saw the need to go through the civil solemnization ceremony at the Chinese Civil Registry. In the twenty or so years of its existence, registration rarely exceeded 120 couples a year in the three regional capital cities (Batavia, Semarang, and Surabaya). Comparing marriage rates (number of marriages per 1,000 in population) among the Chinese across cities and between the Chinese and Europeans yield more interesting results. The population figures in tables 7.1 and 7.2 are based on the 1930 census and the demographer Peter Boomgaard's estimates.[83] Chinese and European civil law marriage numbers are taken from the registries themselves.[84]

As shown in the two tables, the marriage rates for Chinese were 7 to 9 percent (Batavia), 11 to 14 percent (Semarang), and 12 to 22 percent (Surabaya) of those

TABLE 7.1. Average annual marriages registered in the Chinese Civil Registry of Java, and marriage (registration) rate among the Chinese of Batavia, Semarang, and Surabaya, 1920–1940

YEARS	BATAVIA (POPULATION)	MARRIAGE RATE (MR) (MARRIAGES/1,000)	SEMARANG (POPULATION)	MR	SURABAYA (POPULATION)	MR
1919–21	88 (116,928)	0.75	115 (39,966)	2.88	99 (36,079)	2.75
1929–31	100 (149,225)	0.67	90 (40,651)	2.21	89 (39,276)	2.28
1938–40	156 (171,608?)	0.9	90 (41,057?)	2.20	190 (41,043?)	4.63

TABLE 7.2. Marriages and marriage rate for Europeans in Batavia, Semarang, and Surabaya (1920–1940)

YEAR	BATAVIA (POPULATION)	MR	SEMARANG (POPULATION)	MR	SURABAYA (POPULATION)	MR
1920	302 (36,912)	8.16	? (14,835)	?	265 (21,065)	12.6
1930–31	346 (38,048)	9.11	348 (17,686)	19.3	555 (29,776)	18.5
1940	491 (38,629?)	12.6	289 (19,366?)	15.2	?	?

of their European counterparts' in the three cities. Clearly, the much lower Chinese figures were more reflective of the community's alienation from the concept of civil law marriage than of their actual marriage rate. Assuming that both groups practiced universal marriage, these figures suggest that only between 7 and 22 percent of Chinese registered their marriages with the colonial government, while the remainder, between 78 and 93 percent, went through customary marriages without registering with the authorities as they were required by law to do after 1919.

Even among the minority who did solemnize their marriages with the authorities, there was a tendency (in the early years at least) for the Chinese to incorporate the civil ceremony into the final Confucian marriage rites. In the first seven months of its implementation in Batavia (May to December 1919), only sixteen out of thirty-nine registered marriages were solemnized in the physical office of the Civil Registry. The remainder, close to six in ten, opted to hold the solemnization in the houses of the parents on either side or a close relative. They were able to remove the civil ceremony to a private setting by "a declaration [usually] from the bride, which showed that she was prevented by sickness from appearing in the building, where the deeds of the Civil Registry were made, for the solemnizing of this marriage."[85] The exposure of the bride to the "public" was clearly too far a step even for those who saw the benefits of civil marriage registration. Interestingly, reflecting the bilateral kinship pattern of the creole Chinese, the private solemnization ceremonies were evenly split between those held on the bride's side (12) and those held on the groom's side (13).

The Chinese ambivalence toward the new marriage law became apparent in its barely repressible absence from the agenda of a general congress of Confucian Associations to "determine the rites of marriage, funeral, worship and everyday customs" in 1924. Charles Coppel has described the formation of Khong Khauw Tjong Hwee, the centralized body for local chapters of Confucian Associations (Khong Khauw Hwee), as the culmination of a "second wave of the Confucian movement in Java."[86] Less often noted is how the second wave of Confucian revivalism in the 1920s was in fact a response to "Chinese people who were for adat becoming Westernized" [M: *pro-adat ka-Baratan*].[87] Attended on 25–26 September 1924 in Bandung by about one hundred representatives from THHK committees, Confucian Associations, and other Chinese societies across Java, the president of the congress, Poey Kok Gwan, defined its goal as "improving on and adapting with the flow of time our nation's customary institutions [M: *peradatan*], which in the Indies as far as is known, has not changed."[88] Despite the recent application of Dutch family law to the Chinese of Java, the relationship of Chinese customs to colonial law was curiously left out of the conference's agenda. Yet the conference attendees' anxieties about encroaching

Dutch or Western cultural norms could not have been more obvious. In speaking of marriage rites reforms, Poey referenced the Javanese principalities as role models: "For until today, the Sunan of Solo and the Sultan of Djogja prioritize the marital rules of their own nation, such that despite having lived for a long time in Europe, and having obtained the education of the Europeans, a prince always practices the rules and dons the attire of his nation. Even his hair, which had been cut short during his stay in Europe, was lengthened with a long wig, while the rules and customs of the Javanese nation were adhered to in their timeless fashion [M: *dipegang kekal*]."[89]

The succinct way the attendees cruised through the question of marriage rites reform suggests that they did not perceive the general structure of the Six Rites of marriage to be under threat. What was disputed, and subjected to a vote, was the appropriate attire of the bride and groom, and the appropriate modes of obeisance they ought to adopt before their guests, parents, and the Almighty Heavens. For all the talk about "timeless fashion," the overwhelming majority of attendees voted for modern attire for both bride ("Shanghai dress") and groom (M: *labaar hitam*), while only 5 percent stood for "traditional" (M: *koeno*) wear. There was a greater diversity of views on whether the bride and groom should kneel, bow, or simply greet each other with joined hands in front of guests, parents, and the Heavens, but a clear consensus did emerge. Regarding the most self-lowering act of kneeling, 80 percent thought it was appropriate for the Heavens, 60 percent for the parents, and none for the other guests. Again, defying the president's call for timeless traditions, 85 percent requested that traditional customs (M: *atoeran koeno*)—such as decorating the bridal chamber with the eight Taoist trigrams (Hk: *Patkwa*) to ward off evil spirits and rice bushels (M: *gantang*) to symbolize fertility—be abolished.[90]

The 1924 congress on marriage rites did not comment on the new marriage law. But the organizers did ensure that the subsequent publication of their ritual reform recommendations came appended with excerpts of rules from the Chinese Civil Registry where necessary. Introducing the new 1919 law to his readers, the author Lie Tjoei Khai (pseudonym: Tjoekat Liang) rehearsed a familiar grievance but with a new sense of irony: "The Government did not consult the Chinese beforehand on all aspects of these applicable laws. While the laws applied to the Chinese were a kind of justice that once promulgated could not be criticized [M: *dikeloearkan dengan berdasar atas kaadilan jang tida boleh dibanta lagi*], the application of the Civil Registry on the Chinese definitely made the majority in the community unhappy and harbor reservations because it is precisely on this that the Chinese maintained general illusions [M: *angan-angan*]."[91] This illusion, Lie went on to note, lay in how the Chinese "valued sons as continuators of the descent line such that whoever, even if they were dutiful [M: *berbakti*] to their parents, if they did not have male descendants, they would be seen as unfilial [Hk: *poethauw*]."⁹² Lie understood that the new law would encroach on some imperatives of the Chinese patriliny, especially in its equalization of the share of inheritance between sons and daughters, "but since the Civil Registry had already been applied on the Chinese . . . let us not create anymore fuss."⁹³

As a manual for performing reformed rites and navigating the new Civil Registry laws, Lie's publication prescribed a creolized template of moral ambivalence for Chinese living in the midst of the Dutch colonial civilizing project. Its structure was more telling than its content. The appropriate rites took precedence over law. It was important that the latter be kept separate and introduced to the reader as an unjust imposition. Lie's interpretation of the new Chinese family law status in Java turned the civilizing project on its head by stripping the civil code of its loftier language, while he guided his readers to navigate colonial legality as a series of bureaucratic hurdles one had to learn in order to negotiate from birth and marriage to death. For instance, nowhere in his sections on marriage law did he translate or mention that "to enter into a marriage, the voluntary consent of the prospective spouses is required."⁹⁴ Instead, he chose to translate Article 71, which listed the seven kinds of documents (birth certificates, elders' written approval, and so on) the bride and groom needed to submit to the Civil Registry to apply for marriage. And he explained how applicants could make an oath instead if they did not have these documents. Only in the final paragraph of a short two-page section did he mention, with characteristic ambivalence, the monogamous character of civil law marriage: "On the notion that a husband can only marry one wife and conversely a wife is permitted to marry only one husband, that cannot be expressed in clearer terms here [M: . . . *itoelah di sini boleh troesa diseboetken lebi djelas lagi.*)"⁹⁵

Understanding the Chinese reluctance to register their marriages, Lie warned of how the new law jeopardized the reproduction of the patriliny: "A marriage that occurred after 1 May 1919 and was not legitimized [M: *disahken*] at the Civil Registry officers' office would be considered an illegitimate, and if a child were born, that child would not be able to assume the lineage name [M: *nama toeroenan*; Hk: *she*] of the father, except if the birth mother herself informed the Civil Registry official in person, that she was happy [M: *dengan ridlah hati*] to give that child to her husband."⁹⁶ To be fair, Lie did give significant attention to the new provisions for divorce and how either party had to approach lawyers to apply to the Courts of Justice for it.⁹⁷ But it was also clear that he placed greater attention on adapting the interests of the patriliny to the law than on the rights of the individual before the law. This was evident from how he went to great lengths to discuss the procedures for adoption—a Dutch concession to the Chinese religious zeal for a male heir—and inheritance.⁹⁸

The stalling of the greater liberal reformist civil law unification project in the 1920s did not help to alleviate the ambivalence the Chinese of Java felt toward the Dutch civilizing project. A year after the application of the entire civil code to the Chinese of Java, the Dutch Parliament formulated an amendment to Art. 109 of the colonial constitution, which enlarged the definition of "European" to "everyone who *in his country of origin* was subjected to a family and marriage law 'mainly' based on the same principles as had been adopted in Dutch law."[99] The irony could not have been made clearer to the creole Chinese, who had been gifted civilized Dutch family law in Java but remained bound in their sub-European racial status to their country of origin. In 1925, the inclusion of this family-law racial criterion into the new Indies constitution added Siam and Turkey, which had adopted civil law and negotiated treaties of friendship and commerce with the Netherlands, to the ranks of the "Europeans."[100] Then, in 1931, China itself completed its legal modernization project and began to place pressure on the Dutch to classify Chinese as "Europeans." As historian Cess Fasseur has shown, throughout the 1920s and 1930s, Dutch colonial jurists continued to recommend the abolition of the racial classification clause in their formal committee-based proposals, although neither the jurists nor, more importantly, the entire political elite could muster the will to deliver an end to the legal apartheid of whites and Asians in the colony. To do so, Fasseur argues, "would have required quite another colonial mentality."[101]

This chapter emphasizes how the Chinese of Java stood out from their compatriots elsewhere in the diaspora or in the homeland by their early adoption of a modern monogamous family law. But they were also a pawn in the racialized international politics of colonial lawmaking. I showed how the patriarchal reformers reacted to the civilizing legal discourse of gender equality with a sense of moral ambivalence. In practice, only about one in ten Chinese married under the new civil law in the final two decades of Dutch colonial rule. From the creolized Confucian point of view, law was seen as a bureaucratic hindrance rather than a sign of civilizational progress. This was not only because the Dutch failed ultimately to elevate the Chinese of Java to European racial status, as some liberal reformers had promised since the turn of the twentieth century. There was a long-running tradition of practicing Six Rites marriage on Java. In the 1920s, the creole Chinese themselves tried to counter the Dutch civilizing project with their own determination of cultural continuity and modernity. A new creole Chinese identity was no doubt forged through these Dutch Chinese determinations and counter-determinations of gender, family, and civilization, but how did they transform intimate Chinese-native race relations on the ground?

8
REGISTERING BIRTHS, RACIALIZING ILLEGITIMACY

Along with monogamy, family law reform introduced compulsory birth registration for the Chinese in Java as of May 1919. Chinese fathers, whose duty under civil law it was to pass on their family name and give the child a personal name, did not avoid the birth registry the way they shunned marriage solemnization. This chapter demonstrates how customary Chinese notions of patrilineal descent overlapped with new civil law categories of illegitimacy to fortify the sense of a racial boundary between Chinese and Indonesians in late colonial and early postcolonial Java. Birth registration strengthened the Chinese patrilineal notion of race, even if most Chinese continued to have unregistered customary marriages. Beginning to accumulate concomitantly within these registries were records of "illegitimate" mixed-race children born to Indonesian mothers that the Chinese continued to exclude, by Confucian custom, from ritual marriage. Racial difference was experienced through morally judgmental views on extramarital sexuality, as colonial reformers and a younger generation of Dutch-educated Indonesians came to see enduring extramarital relationships between less wealthy and polygamous Chinese men as immoral.

Birth Registries and a New Patrilineal Racial Border

Claudine Salmon has traced the building of ancestral and funeral halls in colonial cities on Java to the 1860s.[1] At the turn of the twentieth century, most creole Chinese maintained some form of rudimentary practice of the ancestral cult, in which perhaps one or two generations of forebears were worshipped on an altar at home. The contemporary rise of Confucian cultural nationalism prompted wealthier families to compile their genealogies and build ancestral halls. In May 1919, the advent of colonial Chinese birth registration gave the practice of patrilineal naming a further legal basis. Private genealogies and public registries strengthened a racially Chinese sense of patrilineal descent, creating through the colonial rule of paternity a new affective racial border between Chinese and Indonesians.

The Chinese patrilineal ancestral cult in Java sat awkwardly atop what had, since the first waves of immigration and intermarriage in the eighteenth century, developed into creole patterns of bilateral kinship. One of the few seriously conducted social surveys of religious practice in rural areas with Chinese enclaves was carried out in Tangerang in 1955, and it showed that 92 percent of household heads engaged in some form of ancestor worship over the course of the year.[2] These heads of households were just as likely to be worshipping their father's as their mother's patrilineal ancestors. More generally, the bilateral kinship practices of the creole Chinese contrasts with their patrilineal antecedents in China. These changes were evident in the form of the prevalence among the creoles of ambilocal (vs. patrilocal) marriage residence, and the non-distinction (vs. clear distinction) of the father's and mother's relatives in kinship appellations. William Skinner traces this adaptation of kinship to intermarriage with the bilateral indigenous groups and the widely practiced creole pattern of business succession through the selection of competent sons-in-law.[3]

Among the wealthier and more powerful elite, the building of ancestral halls and compilation of genealogies became popular after the turn of the twentieth century. For families with Dutch-appointed Chinese officers, it became almost obligatory to devote a section of the house, if not an entire building (or shophouse), to be the ancestral hall—or what the creoles call in Malay ash houses (M: *rumah abu*). The famous ancestral halls of the Han, Tjoa, and The families of Surabaya are the best-known examples.[4] That the genealogical memories of these Chinese officers remain alive to this day is amply demonstrated by family historian Steve Haryono's ability to reconstruct complex familial alliances of the mid-nineteenth century forward (but no earlier) from his vast collection of privately maintained genealogies.[5] I have shown in my own work how the Thung brothers of West Java founded a localized lineage organization, complete with *rumah abu* and a genealogy connected to an Ur-ancestor in Fujian, as they rose up the commercial and political hierarchy of colonial society after 1900.[6] Ancestor worship and the more serious act of compiling genealogies kept the Chinese pattern of patrilineal naming alive on Java.

The advent of the colonial Chinese birth registry in May 1919 gave the Chinese an official place to authenticate the names they gave their descendants. Given how they had shunned marriage registration, one might expect the Chinese to do likewise with birth registration. But in fact, they embraced it. Tjoekat Liang, in his aforementioned 1924 Confucian guide to the Civil Registry, did not have to qualify his choice of words when he reported that "the father of the new-born is the person responsible for informing the Civil Registry official about the birth."[7] Obtaining official recognition of a newborn's name and patrilineal connection with the parents was not as alien a bureaucratic process as swearing an oath of marital fidelity to a colonial official. Neither infant nor mother was required to be present. It was the civic duty of the father, attested by two other witnesses, to declare the child's given name, date and time of birth, the mother's name, and the couple's marital status within three days of birth. One reason Chinese fathers embraced this new civic duty was the colonial recognition of their patrilineal naming system. The Dutch, unlike their Indonesian successors half a century later, were not interested in assimilating Chinese names.[8] Neither were they compelled to do it by public health authorities. The fact that almost all births were recorded "in the house of the applicant" serves to highlight the father's voluntarism in complying with his new civil duty.

Table 8.1 suggests close to universal registration of births among the Chinese of Java. The actual registered birth figures (row *a*) were very close to the expected birth rate of Chinese women of childbearing age (row *c*).[9] The latter is an estimate I calculated by multiplying the number of women of childbearing age (15–49 years old; see row *b*) with the estimated birth rhythm of Chinese women (3 births in 10 years), as determined by one contemporary Chinese study of reproductive health in Batavia.[10]

This close-to-universal registration of births in racially segregated colonial registries unwittingly created a bureaucratic means for the state to trace and track Chinese racial subjects. The sociologist Ariel Heryanto has argued that

TABLE 8.1. Close correspondence between birth registration and expected birth rate of Chinese women

		BATAVIA	SEMARANG	SURABAYA
a	Total number of births registered a year around 1930	2,406	847	995
b	Married women aged 15–49 in 1930 census	7,100	3,470	2,434
c	Expected births in 1930 (row *b* × birth rhythm of 3 in 10 years)	2,364	1,156	811

postindependence Indonesia continued the colonial "practice of Othering the ethnic Chinese" as "non-native . . . in order to assert an identity of Self (the so-called *pribumi*, or 'native') in a binary opposition."[11] Less often noted is how the ability of the colonial or postindependence state to officially identify anyone, especially those with an Indonesian-sounding name, as Chinese was also built on this relatively mundane assemblage of the father's voluntary act of birth registration, which only began in earnest in the 1920s.

Birth registration, which followed civil law's rule of paternity, created a new racial border between Chinese and Indonesians by fortifying the existing Chinese patrilineal exclusion of non-Chinese from customary marriage. Colonial law introduced the concept of illegitimate descent, which did not at first translate easily, but did come to be associated with children born of native mothers. Civil law ranked children at birth by their parents' marital status. Married parents had "legal" children, while the unmarried had "natural" children. A child born "natural" could either be "legalized" if the parents married later on or be "recognized" by the father with the mother's consent. A "naturally recognized" (D: *natuurlijke erkende*) child was entitled to one-third the share of the "legal" child's inheritance.[12] Tjoekat Liang, in distilling the birth registration law into a summary three-page instruction, failed to mention any of these distinctions.[13] Phoa Tjoen Hoay, in his translation of the new law (discussed in chapter 7), revealed a fundamental misunderstanding of its intention to discriminate against the illegitimate. His translation of "legal" as "legitimate" (M: *sah*) and "legalized" as "recognized" (M: *diakoe*) were accurate enough, but his interpretation of "natural" as "pure-bred" (M: *sedjati*) mistakenly romanticized a legal category meant for punishing sexual infidelity. "The pure-bred child is authentically conceived [M: *tulen*] but accidentally born to parents who have yet to marry. This means that s/he came into being in a free love affair [M: *pertjintaan merdika*] between her/his parents."[14]

The paternity rule of descent in civil law itself was race neutral, but the Dutch had amended it to favor European fathers against native concubine-mothers when it was applied to the Indies in 1848. Article 284 stipulated that the father's recognition of the natural child "annulled . . . the civil relations (between mother and child) derived from natural descent . . . when the mother belongs to the Native or therewith equated population group."[15] Historian Reggie Baay notes that while the law protected the rights of mixed-race children to maintenance by their European fathers, it also removed any legal means of redress for the abandoned and unmarried native mothers.[16] The same unequal relationship was now extended to Chinese fathers.

In practice, the distinction between "legal" and "natural" children did not seem to matter to the majority of the Chinese. From admittedly small random samples I took from the main registries in Batavia and Semarang, I found that roughly one-third of children were registered as born to "unmarried" parents: 32 percent in Batavia (1934–35 and 1938–39) and 34 percent in Semarang (1939).[17] If these estimates are near the mark, they translate to about 900 and 300 cases of illegitimate births (row *b* in table 8.2), out of which 200 and 100 were subsequently legally recognized in Batavia and Semarang, respectively. In other words, only about 2 in 9 (18%–20%) or 1 in 3 (36%) children born out of wedlock were legally recognized by their parents (row *e* in table 8.2). The great proportion of children born out of wedlock in the 1930s was most likely a result of a stricter enforcement of civil law marriage, which would have excluded those who underwent customary marriages after May 1919. These customarily married Chinese parents, who had avoided civil marriage to begin with, would not be unduly worried about their children being classified as "natural" and hence "illegitimate."

TABLE 8.2. Numbers and proportions of total births that were illegitimate, and numbers and proportions of illegitimate children who were naturally recognized by Chinese and native Indonesian mothers (and Chinese fathers) in the Chinese Civil Registries of Batavia, Semarang, and Surabaya

		BATAVIA		SEMARANG	
		1934–35	1938–39	1926	1939
a.	Actual total births registered	2,805	3,217	801	916
b.	Estimated number of illegitimate births according to (%) figure derived for random sampling	898 (32%)	1,037 (32%)	N/A	311 (34%)
c.	"Natural" children recognized by Chinese mothers	160	172	163	69
d.	"Natural" children recognized by native mothers (% of total births)	18 (0.6)	13 (0.4)	59 (7.4)	42 (4.5)
e.	Percentage of natural children legally recognized (c + d) / a	20.0%	17.8%	N/A	35.7%

		SURABAYA		
		1924	1933	1939
f.	Total births (excluded native mothers)	954	1,093	1,635
g.	"Natural" children recognized by Chinese mothers	12	7	37
h.	"Natural" children recognized by native mothers (% of total)	48 (5)	50 (4.6)	58 (3.5)
i.	Percentage of naturally recognized children (g + h) / (f + g + h)	6.0%	5.0%	5.5%

Surabaya presents an interesting contrast. I do not have estimates of the proportion of illegitimate births for the city. The very low rate of legal recognition by Chinese mothers (and fathers) suggests that those who were customarily married but classified as "unmarried" under civil law were not concerned with questions of legitimacy for their children in the eyes of colonial law. As noted in chapter 7, the city had a relatively higher rate of civil marriage registration among the Chinese. Those few Chinese mothers who had their illegitimate children registered (row *g* in table 8.2) belonged to the minority group for whom marriage registration had become the norm. A greater proportion of these Chinese mothers were literate and hence educated.[18]

In all three cities, *all* children born of Indonesian mothers were illegitimate. The number of Chinese fathers who legally recognized their children born of native mothers was close to negligible in Batavia, but this group formed a not insignificant minority in the other two cities. In fact, the size of this group is likely to be more significant than previously thought. For estimates, scholars have mostly turned to the 1930 census, which "counted indigenous women, who were drawn to the Chinese population by marriage with a Chinese."[19] Census surveys, answered by heads of households themselves, returned 1 native among 100 wives of Chinese households in West Java (Batavia), and 2.6 among 100 in the rest of Java (Central: Semarang; Eastern: Surabaya).[20] In rows *d* and *h* of table 8.2, I show that the actual proportion of indigenous mothers of Chinese children might have been as high as 3.5 to 7.4 percent in Central and Eastern Java, as indicated by the number of native mothers indirectly registered through their "naturally recognized" children in Semarang and Surabaya.[21]

The institution of birth registries after 1919 formalized the Confucian pattern of patrilineal naming the creolized Chinese had been practicing in their private lives. Yet it also unwittingly created a new racial hierarchy of legitimate and illegitimate children among those born of Chinese and Indonesian mothers. Who were these Chinese fathers and Indonesian mothers? How did the Dutch and society from both sides of the ethnic divide perceive such relationships? And how did perceptions change after Indonesian independence?

Native Mothers: From Nyai to *Gundik*

Chinese men who legally recognized their children by native mothers might have wanted those quasi-marital ties to endure, but the intensifying colonial civilizing mission and the rise of mass nationalism in Java made such relationships increasingly suspect in the eyes of colonial jurists and Indonesian intellectual leaders of all ethnicities. Dutch, Chinese, and Indonesian reformers began to frown on such nonmarital relationships between Chinese men and their nyai at the turn of the twentieth century. On the Indonesian side, this would culminate in the mid-1950s with a local government-led moral panic campaign on Java to end Chinese men's fostering of *gundik* (M: mistresses). Across the twentieth century, the unmarried partner of Chinese men became an "immoral" feminine figure writ large that helped define the patriarchal ethno-nationalism of reformed and refined men on all sides.

I compiled seventy-eight cases of legal recognition from Batavia (1932), Semarang (1926), and Surabaya (1933), categorizing the Chinese fathers by class and sub-ethnicity. Individuals in the middle class were found in sectors where they either were merchants or worked in European firms, for the government, or as craftsmen "on [their] own account," whereas the working class were in wage labor or less autonomous jobs.[22] Across the three cities, working-class men outnumbered the middle class but only at a 6:4 ratio. Table 8.3 shows the class status, occupation, average age of the Chinese father and Indonesian mother, and their average age difference.

Compared to customary or civil law marriage with Chinese women, Chinese men settled down with their Indonesian partners relatively late—in their mid- to late thirties. This legal recognition procedure was an indication of both

TABLE 8.3. The class status, occupation, and average age of the Chinese father, the average age of the Indonesian mother, and their average age difference

	BATAVIA (1932)	SEMARANG (1926)	SURABAYA (1933)
Middle-class Chinese fathers & Indonesian mothers	2 typesetters, 1 cashier, 1 merchants, 1 goldsmith 1 *mandur* (foreman) Total: 6 Average age: Chinese father: 32.7 Indonesian mother: 23.2 Difference: 9.5 years	6 merchants, 1 banker, 1 baker, 1 carpenter Total: 9 Average age: Chinese father: 37.3 Indonesian mother: 22.6 Difference: 14.7 years	10 merchants, 3 carpenters, 2 shoemakers, 1 barber, 1 newspaper employee, 1 hardware storeowner Total: 18 Average age: Chinese father: 33.6 Indonesian mother: 28.5 Difference: 5.1 years
Working-class Chinese fathers & Indonesian mothers	3 daily-wage earners, 3 vendors, 2 shopkeepers 1 transport worker, 1 trader's assistant Total: 10 Average age: Chinese father: 36.8 Indonesian mother: 26.6 Difference: 10.2 years	5 trader's assistants, 1 small trader, 1 daily-wage earner Total: 7 Average age: Chinese father: 33.9 Indonesian mother: 22.6 Difference: 11.3 years	9 unemployed, 5 peddlers, 5 small traders, 3 coolies, 2 itinerant noodle hawkers, 2 trader's assistants, 1 snack seller, 1 shopkeeper Total: 28 Average age: Chinese father: 38.1 Indonesian mother: 28.9 Difference: 9.2 years

parties' entry into a more enduring form of partnership. Since any prior birth was not recorded, it is possible that the parents' ages at first birth were lower, but most likely not by much—with the exception of Surabaya—given the already relatively young ages of those mothers (in the low twenties). Chinese men who registered their mixed race children did so at an older age than their peers who chose (or had the means) to marry. For comparison's sake, I use data from the 1930 Batavia Chinese Civil Registry, which recorded 109 marriages, of which 81 were entered into by first-timers (see table 8.4).[23] Despite the registry's lack of popularity among the Chinese masses, the data becomes particularly illuminating when controlled for class and sub-ethnic distinctions. Middle-class men generally married in their late twenties, with a five- to six-year age gap between groom and bride. Working-class immigrants who were less well connected in local kinship networks generally had to delay their marriage, if they could afford a Chinese bride at all.[24]

Stable relationships with Indonesian women were thus formed on the margins of the Chinese marriage market, especially among immigrant working-class men in their thirties. Birth registration was an occasion for the Indonesian mother to appear before the Chinese father's friends and relatives, if they had not already met. Witnesses to such birth registrations came mostly from the father's side, occasionally from neither side, but never from the Indonesian mother's side—a reflection of the broader colonial patriarchal norm of women crossing-over in interethnic marriages. Since the Indonesian mother had to be present to consent to the child's registration out of wedlock, fathers who were prepared to show up with family and friends as witness(es) can be presumed to be open about the relationship. Many witnesses were clearly family, based on their similar family and given names.[25] In my tabulation, I have included less obviously related same-surname witnesses, since they tend to be of a more senior age and might possibly be elder cousins or uncles.

Friends, particularly people sharing the same trades and occupations, were also popular as witnesses, especially for immigrants with few local relatives. When the carpenter Tan Sia Hiem registered his five-year-old son by Roeminah

TABLE 8.4. Average age at first marriage by birthplace of groom and by class among the Chinese of Batavia in 1930

	MIDDLE CLASS (57)			WORKING CLASS (24)		
	GROOM	BRIDE	DIFFERENCE	GROOM	BRIDE	DIFFERENCE
Local-born grooms: 70	27.2 (50)	22.5	4.7	24.0 (20)	20.6	3.4
China-born grooms: 11	29.0 (7)	23.1	5.9	34.3 (4)	19.5	14.8

in February 1933, the fact that he invited two other carpenters, Jan Thoe and Tan Hay, to be his witnesses would have made it an occasion within the carpenters' guild of Surabaya.[26] Conversely, there were also cases in which fathers brought no witnesses as required by law. In Batavia, for instance, it was not uncommon for bourgeois *peranakan* men to show up with their Indonesian partners and have registry clerks stand in as witnesses. On 11 February 1932, the twenty-three-year-old merchant Khouw Ke Siang registered his six-month-old son by the seventeen-year-old Simoena, with the clerks Benjamin and Masto as their witnesses. Class played no significant role, but immigrant fathers tended to treat the legal recognition of their children with Indonesian women more seriously than did their creole counterparts. Distinguishing those who brought friends or family to their civil registry from those who did not, immigrant fathers were more likely than their creole counterparts to treat birth registration as a form of de facto "marriage" ceremony (see table 8.5).

Who were the Indonesian mothers? By the early 1930s, the use of "nyai" as an appellation connoting respect for the unmarried Indonesian partners of Chinese men had become rare. In my sample of seventy-eight unmarried Indonesian mothers, there was only one referenced as "nyai." Nyai-hood by this point was associated with the Dutch colonial social milieu. On 30 March 1932, Roem was thirty-six years old when she gave consent to Tjeng Kong Boen, forty-seven, a cashier for the Netherlands Indies Railway Company in Batavia, to recognize their eleven-year-old daughter, Certi Nio.[27] Roem was the only literate Indonesian woman among all seventy-eight cases. The signature, "Roem," revealed an unsteady hand. The word "Njai" appeared next to her name in the registry officer's handwriting, indicating that it was a term of respect accorded her by the official, although it was also likely earned through her relationship with a state employee.

More importantly, by the 1930s, the nyai figure itself had become morally problematic in colonial society, as the state had put an end to its toleration of

TABLE 8.5. Estimated de facto "marriage" rates of immigrant vs. creole fathers who legally recognized their children by Indonesian mothers

	IMMIGRANT OR CREOLE ACCORDING TO WHETHER FATHERS SIGNED THEIR NAMES IN CHINESE OR ROMANIZED FORM	
	CHINESE—IMMIGRANT (MARRIAGE RATE)	ROMANIZED—PERANAKAN (MARRIAGE RATE)
Batavia (1932)	2 of 4 (50%)	5 of 10 (50%)
Semarang (1926)	4 of 5 (80%)	6 of 10 (60%)
Surabaya (1933)	20 of 25 (80%)	11 of 20 (55%)
	26 of 34 (76%)	22 of 40 (55%)

Source: Bijregister van geboorten [Supplementary registries of birth] cited in this section.

barrack concubinage and encouraged European men to marry their concubines. Marriage became the moral standard against which men's sexual relationships were judged. It was in this context that reform-minded colonial jurists made futile attempts to retrospectively impose a more stringent definition of the legitimate descent for children born to "minor wives" (M: *bini modea*; D: *bijvrouw*) *before* May 1919. In 1922, Pieter Fromberg, in an open critique of the transitionary legal situation, went so far as to argue that all children "born outside of marriage are considered illegal [D: *onwettige*] regardless of whether they are born of the minor wife or of a clandestine woman [D: clandestine woman; M: prostitute/mistress (*soendal*)]."[28] His view was only partially accepted. In its final 1924 version, the transitory law "considered ... children, born to the minor wives [D: *bijvrouwen*] of their father and openly treated as children by the latter, ... *legal* children, if the relationship between the father and the minor wife existed before the [1919] ordinance."[29] In that event, the courts, ignoring the need to identify descent from the "minor wife," stuck to the existing practice of recognizing as legal all children "openly treated" by their Chinese fathers as such. According to R. D. Kollewijn, a professor at the Batavia Law School (Rechtshogeschool), the Supreme Court had "very wrongly, in an unthinking instant, let slip by recognizing old Chinese legal family relations under the new legislation without recourse to the transitory law." Judges were put in an impossible position, Kollewijn pointed out, because the law made no distinction in "explicit words" between the minor wife's children and those "born out of a 'loose' woman."[30] In other words, between a *bini moeda* and a *soendal* or *goendik*.

Anecdotal evidence suggests that older Chinese men ignored the new monogamous law and continued to take *bini moeda* after May 1919. The Kediri-born (East Java) and Dutch-educated Anna Tan Sian Nio (b. 1912) recounts in her memoirs that in 1922, her mother, after having undergone thirteen difficult pregnancies, "arranged to 'give' Kasminah, then aged 15, to [her] father to gratify his sexual needs." Her father, a third-generation local-born Chinese and a wealthy sugar miller, was at the time forty-two. Kasminah had just started working for Anna's grandmother as a cook's assistant when she was spotted and assessed by Anna's mother as a "young, attractive and healthy" woman. Becoming the "mistress" of one of the wealthiest men in town, and with servants of her own, Kasminah was "envied by many other indigenous people." She gave birth to "three children [b. 1923, 1931, 1943], of whom all were adopted by [Anna's] parents as full members of the Tan family."[31]

Extrapolating from their age profiles, no more than perhaps a handful of the registered Indonesian mothers in the birth registries were, like Kasminah, taken as previously unmarried bini moeda *after* the man had married a Chinese wife. There were only three women in Semarang (1926) and one in Batavia (1932), all in the eighteen-to-twenty-year-old range, when they gave birth to the children of relatively wealthy Chinese men in the mid- to late thirties.[32] As I have laid out in table 8.3, Indonesian women were on average between twenty-two and twenty-six years old in Batavia and Semarang, and between twenty-eight and twenty-nine in Surabaya when they bore children for their Chinese partners. If we can assume that most were bearing children with these Chinese men for the first time, then the majority were likely to have been divorcées.[33] Take Nyai Roem, for example. In 1921, she was twenty-five years old when she bore Certi Nio with the then thirty-six-year-old Kong Boen. Hildred Geertz observed that among young women in urban East Java, "most have been married—at least briefly—by the time they are sixteen or seventeen."[34] This observation is supported by the three women who brought their divorce papers with them to the birth registry in Surabaya: Sahilah, 22, had been divorced for two years; Rohaja, 25, for six; and Kartining, 30, for eight.[35] Their age at divorce (20, 19, and 22, respectively) suggests a pattern of five to seven years in their first (or second) Muslim marriage(s) before they settled with their Chinese partners two to seven years afterward. That some brought along their divorce papers reveals the quasi-marital character of these birth registration ceremonies.[36]

During the late colonial era, Indonesian sentiments toward these illicit relationships appear to have been muted as long as the women were not taken as previously unmarried brides. When an adat law survey in West Java in the early 1930s inquired about the local customs surrounding children born outside wedlock, local Indonesian officials first replied that "there was no adat law on giving birth outside wedlock," and then went on to explain how fathers, village chiefs, penghulus, and district (D: *regency*) officials arranged emergency (M: *darurat*) marriages for girls who were pregnant before marriage. In a passing mention of a childbirth from an Indonesian woman's relationship with a Chinese man, there was no apparent sanction or moral opprobrium attached to the act. "In the Ciparay desa [M: village], Bandung regency, a widow ever gave birth to a child outside of wedlock. It was publicly known that the child belonged to an assistant in the Chinese toko."[37]

In cohabitation relationships, especially those with working-class Chinese men, respect for the Indonesian mother was gained over time as their familial relationship endured. Of the five couples whose birth registration occurred only years afterward, four consisted of Chinese men of more humble means. Birth registration of "natural children" presumed extramarital relationships between the parents, but the men had most likely remained monogamous over the years. On 29 November 1933, Nie Bales, who was thirty-eight years old, accompanied forty-four-year-old Tjoa Tiong Hok, a small trader, to the Civil Registry office in Surabaya to recognize their eighteen-year-old son, Djie Hwie.[38] As a more senior woman who had raised a grown-up son, she was accorded the feminine appellation of respect "Nie" in Javanese by the registry officials, as must have been the case in daily life. The other Indonesia mothers, who were not necessarily younger but had younger children, were not accorded that term of respect when addressed.[39]

The relatively stable pattern of interethnic relationships among the poorer Chinese fathers was reflected in the previously mentioned social survey of Tangerang—the only place on Java where the Chinese were predominantly rural and their social gap with native Indonesians relatively smaller. In 1955, it was found that "approximately half of the family heads (53% indigenous, 46% Chinese) said they would have no objection if their son wanted to marry a girl of the other ethnic group, while a fifth to a quarter said they would strongly object to such a marriage (20% of indigenous and 24% of the Chinese)."[40] About a quarter of family heads on both sides already had relatives from the other group, and they were disproportionately more open-minded about interethnic marriages.

However enduring these quasi-marital relationships turned out to be, the younger generation of bourgeois Indonesians of all ethnic origins did come to view them as unbecoming and even offensive. Witnessing her father take a "mistress" made Tan Sian Nio "avoi[d] marriage because [she] was afraid [her] future husband . . . would do the same." She was "deep down . . . offended how this practice made females less equal than males."[41] In the postindependence 1950s, Gouw Giok Siong, a student of Dutch professors of comparative law in Jakarta, lamented in his doctoral study of the Mixed Marriages Act that the rate of Chinese intermarriages with Indonesians lagged far behind that of Europeans. "The process of caste lines breaking down between Europeans and Indonesians," he argued, "cannot be seen in the caste relation between the Chinese and Indonesian. Looking at social reality at this moment, it can be said that precisely to the contrary, the caste restrictions are becoming thicker."[42] Limiting his definition of marriage to those registered with the authorities, Gouw completely ignored other customary forms of Sino-Indonesian relationships.[43] At around the same time, Mely G. Tan, a budding scholar trained in the University of Indonesia's Sinology Department and guided in her fieldwork by the American sociologist William G. Skinner, observed that in considering young men's marriage proposals, "mothers . . . object to [those] who are known to have more or less permanent extra-legal relations, especially when there are children involved. This situation," she elaborates, "not infrequently occurs with young men employed on the estates around Sukabumi [in West Java], where they have the opportunity to live with a Sundanese girl."[44] Writing his history of *Chinese-Indonesian Literature* in the mid-1950s, Nio Joe Lan swapped all references to the concubine or *bini moeda* in the novels to gundik in his literary history.[45]

Postindependence Indonesia confronted illicit Sino-Javanese relationships in two ways. First, the civil law route to marriage was severely constricted as Muslim activists in government moved to end intermarriage between European men and Indonesian women. Under the Mixed Marriages Act (1898), Indonesian women had to obtain the approval of the local penghulu before they could marry European men. By the racially and religiously conceived notions of colonial law, the bride would turn "European" following her husband's legal status and thereby stop being classified as "Native" and, by extension, Muslim. When a new Ministry of Religion was formed in 1946—a year after the declaration of independence—one of its first acts was to pass through parliament a law "requiring that all Muslims register their marriages and divorces with the ministry's local office." As John R. Bowen points out, this set in motion a conflict between Islamic and civil law definitions of marriage, especially in the 1970s, when the government-drafted Marriage Law (1974) was passed.[46] In fact, penghulus began to deny women their appeals to marry European or Christian men the moment Indonesians assumed control of Jakarta in 1949–50. In a mass resolution sent to the head of state and members of parliament, a mosque gathering of five thousand people in Tanah Abang (Jakarta) called for the abolition of the colonial-era law. They claimed that it "conflicted with the law and teachings of Islam . . . [and] causes people to feel apathetic about struggling for development."[47] These objections from Muslim activists and the Ministry of Religion were overruled in court, but tensions between civil law and Muslim definitions of marriage have remained in place ever since. Given the Chinese avoidance of civil law marriage, however, this push to constrict civil law's jurisprudence over Muslim women's marriage with non-Muslim mostly Christian men might not at first glance have affected existing Sino-Indonesian relationships.

A more radical move targeting illicit sexual relations between Chinese men and Indonesian women came from local governments in Central and East Java in the mid-1950s. In 1954, the local representative councils of Banyumas (East Java) and Surakarta (Central Java) appointed members for the "eradication of the mistress-keeping" (M: *pemberontakan pergundikan*) in general and among the Chinese in particular.[48] According to the campaign's advocates, "The keeping of gundik or the living as husband and wife outside of marriage leads to a decline in the standard of morals [M: *tata* susila], lowers the status of women, complicates the question of descent and inheritance, and also disrupts order." More specific to the Chinese, the local council legislator noted that there was "at present no difference between a gundik married [M: *dikahwin*] before or after 1 May 1919; they should not be allowed to marry anymore." The legislator must have been aware of the durability of such relationships when describing them as being "married" (*dikahwin*), but the label for such a woman remained "gundik."

The legislator then went on to explain the procedures for legalizing these children by marriage, while omitting to mention the possibility of recognizing them outside marriage, as was then customary among the Chinese. The urgent need for legislative action from Jakarta and policy measures in the localities was stressed by the fact that "the fostering of gundik or illegal [sexual] relationships is now flourishing [M: *meradjalela*]."

By the 1950s, Indonesian opinion in general had turned against the age-old colonial-Chinese male-settler practice of forming durable and often monogamous nonmarital relationships with local women. The mid-1950s localized campaigns against illicit interethnic sexual relations did not culminate in any legal reforms that furthered women's rights. Opposition by Islamic parties and attempts by President Sukarno himself to undergo a second marriage stalled Indonesian feminist efforts to pass a uniform monogamous marriage law in 1957–59.[49] A unified marriage law would only be passed in 1974.

A Sentimentalist Auto-critique of the Chinese Patriliny

No other creole Chinese text expresses the ambiguity Chinese men felt toward the nyai better than the religious reformer Kwee Tek Hoay's *Boenga roos dari Tjikembang* (*The Rose of Cikembang*) (1927). As mentioned previously, by the late 1920s and early 1930s, the fostering of nyai had become a rare phenomenon among Chinese men on Java. Those who still cohabited with Indonesian women tended to be either working-class immigrants on the periphery of the endogamous marriage market or, if they were local born, less well-educated or more advanced in age. It was at the point of the nyai's disappearance and socio-moral marginalization that Kwee wrote *The Rose*—a love story about *the failures of* Chinese patriliny and patriliny's redemption by two third-generation nyai-descended women on Java. As the most popular love story of its time, the novel reflected a sentimentalist self-critique of the excesses of the Chinese patriliny in Java (see figure 8.1).

Born in Buitenzorg (West Java) in the 1880s to parents who were shopkeepers, Kwee left his classical Chinese school early to work in the shop and later grew to become "one of the most creative figures in twentieth century Indonesia." In his multifaceted adult life, Kwee combined in one person the multiple careers of a "businessman, newspaper contributor, editor and publisher, polemicist and social critic, historian, visionary, lecturer on theosophy and mysticism, novelist, poet, and playwright."[50] Besides his obvious contributions to Chinese Indonesian literature, he is remembered today for founding the Tridharma—the

FIGURE 8.1. Front cover of Kwee Tek Hoay's *Boenga roos dari Tjikembang*, published by Panorama in 1930.

"Peranakan version of the Chinese three-in-one redemptive society"—in the 1930s by combining Confucianism, Buddhism, and Daoism as an alternative to the iconoclastic Confucianists of the earlier decades.[51] As Prasenjit Duara notes, the moral transcendence project that Kwee pursued attempted to spiritually interiorize the syncretic religious practices of the *peranakan* Chinese that also borrowed from Islamic and Javanese beliefs. "To the extent that the transcendence he advocated was dialogically related to the variety of [Indonesian] faiths and practices," Duara argues that "Kwee's Tridharma could not homogenize Chineseness," although it did prepare the creole Chinese in Java "for a nationalist society by delineating the inner self that could adapt to it."[52]

There was in fact a sentimentalist gender dimension to Kwee's syncretic construction of a Chinese Indonesian spiritual identity. His commitment to gender issues was clear. In late colonial Java, the two most prominent creole Chinese journals that devoted space to women's causes—*Panorama* and *Maanblad istri*—were run successively by Kwee and his daughter, Mrs. Tjoa Hin Hoei, née Kwee Yat Nio.[53] Neither Kwee nor his daughter were feminists advocating for women's right to vote or for women to be equals with their male peers in the workplace, as some of their contemporary peers in Indonesia were. Rather, they were champions of Chinese women being educated mothers, equipped with domestic science and a progressive syncretic Chinese religion-based morality.[54] No other work by Kwee Tek Hoay captured the gendered imagination of the creole Chinese of Java as *The Rose of Cikembang* did. The story was first composed for the vernacular Malay opera Bangsawan and then serialized on the pages of *Panorama* in 1927. Its popularity among the Chinese ensured that it would be republished multiple times (1930, 1963, 2001, and 2013), made into one of Indonesia's first talkies (1931), and reproduced twice more in the 1970s.[55] Written as it was in the moral pedagogical mode, what was it that Kwee was trying to teach, and what explains its longevity to this day?

While following important elements of its moral pedagogical framing, Kwee set the Chinese nyai story plot on its head by casting native women not so much as objects of lust but as subjects of wifely and motherly love, and agents of moral change in Chinese men. By opening with a verse conveying the moral of the story, he was following a well-worn tradition, although it was immediately clear that his was going to be a different moral: "When you are feeling extremely fearful, Consider the one whose fortunes are ill-destined, Watch your actions, so that you yourself, Do not become the cause of another's suffering."[56] While other writers had warned their readers against potential harm to the self in one's desire for the ethno-sexual Other, Kwee made the potential harm to the Other the reason for reflection on one's lustful intent. The critic Nio Joe Lan was wrong to call it a tragedy.[57] The nyai antagonist does indeed die, but unlike in other Sino-

Malay nyai stories, the male protagonist does not die or end up in jail for his lust. He, along with his male ascendant and descendant, is saved in that ultimate form of Chinese happy ending: a temporal and spiritual-ancestral family reunion at a wedding ceremony.

In the story, the protagonist Ay Cheng removes himself from the city after failing to win any Chinese bride in the modern game of love marriage. As a competent manager of a Chinese tea plantation in Bogor, he lives happily in love with Nyai Marsiti, his housekeeper and concubine. Keng Jim, the plantation owner, offers to marry his daughter to Ay Cheng, but Ay Cheng is reluctant. The plantation owner pays Marsiti to leave Ay Cheng, but she leaves on her own accord so that he may have a good Chinese marriage. Thinking that he is abandoned, Ay Cheng agrees to the marriage proposal and grows to love his boss's daughter over time. They give birth to a daughter, Lily. At seventeen, Lily falls in love with Bian Kun, a young American-educated creole Chinese man. Two weeks before their marriage, however, Lily is struck by an illness and dies. Bian Kun channels his love for Lily toward China, the motherland, to which he decides to devote his service and life. While convalescing in the mountains, he meets Rosminah—an exact replica of Lily. It turns out that Marsiti was pregnant when she left Ay Cheng and died soon after giving birth, but not before leaving word with a trusted friend to not raise Rosminah as a Muslim. Bian Kun teaches her Chinese and sinicizes her name to Meigui [C: Rose], and she replaces Lily just in time for the scheduled wedding. At the Confucian marriage ceremony, the couple kneel before Ay Cheng, his Chinese wife, and Marsiti's portrait, while the latter's spirit quietly makes an entrance. They do not bother to solemnize or register their marriage. It is further revealed that Marsiti herself was an illegitimate daughter of the plantation owner by his nyai. Happily married, Bian Kun foregoes his wish to go to China and stays in Java to run his father-in-law's plantation.

At first reading, Kwee's story sentimentally reified the patrilineal colonial Chinese boundaries of race on Java, confirming for his readers the age-old colonial and Chinese exclusion of native women from parents-arranged Confucian marriage. Yet it was not so much love and marriage as love and failed patrilineal descent that was at the center of his plot. It was rare for love stories to stretch over three generations. Kwee presented the transition from arranged to love marriage as something that occurred over two generations, with some tension only in Ay Cheng's time. On descent, his attitude was Chinese assimilationist. The plot revolved around the "loss" of Roos to native Indonesian society, and her recovery to Chinese society through a process of sinicization, which included a name change from Rosminah/Roos to Meigui. His arrangement for Roos to be raised among Muslim Indonesians but as a non-Muslim was necessary for fiction but highly unlikely in reality.

Embedded within the plot, I argue, was a pedagogy of love that sought to reform the patriarchal and patrilineal racial bias of the Chinese. If descent through the father's line was not challenged, Ay Cheng (and male actors in general) would be repeatedly punished for his (their) racially discriminatory treatment of his (their) nyai. Kwee was at pains to show his readers that despite the cultural hurdle to marriage, romantic love between the Chinese man and his nyai was real, and equal if not prior to his love for the Chinese wife. It had to be Ay Cheng's wife who insisted that he not forget his love. "If you did not have that sort of heart and simply forgot that good nyai because you had now married someone of your own race, I must say that you would not be worthy of being my husband."[58] Furthermore, from a transgenerational point of view, it was Ay Cheng and his father-in-law's abandonment of their nyai for Chinese marriages that gave rise to the subsequent confusion of identities and the related familial tragedies. As is made clearer in the genealogical chart (see figure 8.2), both Keng Jim and his son-in-law, Ay Cheng, failed to pass down their family name despite the wealth they had accumulated in their lifetimes.

The genealogical chart reveals a pattern of Chinese patrilineal identity Kwee dramatized as a sentimentalist form of critique—Chinese male egos were isolated

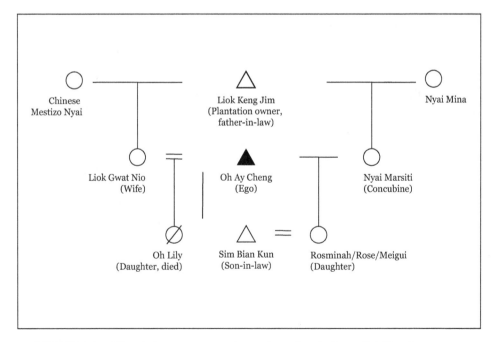

FIGURE 8.2. Kin relations among major protagonists in Kwee Tek Hoay's *Bunga roos dari Cikembang* (1927).

and alienated. Neither Keng Jim nor Ay Cheng had any sons. Furthermore, they committed the same wrong of raising one daughter as Chinese while abandoning another to be raised by the neglected nyai as native. The three successive plantation owners, Liok Keng Jim, Oh Ay Cheng, and Sim Bian Kun, all failed to pass the property down the male line. From Liok to Oh to Sim, the plantation was in fact handed down through the daughters to sons-in-law bearing different family names. More importantly, the family reunion, while occurring in a Chinese familial setting, turned out to be rooted in Java rather than China. If Marsiti still had to die like the other nyai antagonists, she did return for the grand family reunion, albeit in the context of a syncretic blend of Chinese and Javanese beliefs in the ancestral cult and spirits. At the scene of Bian Kun and Meigui's wedding, Marsiti's "spirit [was] standing there," next to her portrait, "in a brilliant glow, watching over all with a sweet smile that contained boundless compassion and love for her daughter, son-in-law, husband, sister, and everyone who paid homage to her."[59]

Kwee's text compelled his creole Chinese readers to countenance the forgotten fact of their common descent from native mothers and the inherent injustice embedded in Confucian patrilineal endogamy. The novel did not challenge the colonial-Chinese assimilationist tendency of interethnic relationships, although it did shine light on the politics of flexible racial identities for creole Chinese on the whole. If there was any lineage dynamics at work, it was the women who connected families over time through motherly descent—something Chinese patrilineality could not bring itself to recognize.

This chapter showed that the modern creole Chinese concept of patriliny became closely entangled with civil law notions of paternity and legitimacy. Civil law in and of itself was race neutral, but in the context of Dutch colonial legal apartheid in Indonesia, segregated civil law registries themselves became the everyday-life legal manifestation of the constitutional classification of humans into "Europeans" and "Natives." Birth registration was popular among the Chinese, but their customary exclusion of native women from Confucian ritual marriage condemned native mothers to the separate "illegitimate" category. When Indonesians took over these Chinese birth registries in 1949, the category of the illegitimate and of the native mother became obviously and awkwardly synonymous. Despite some attempt at moral self-critique, the unequal pattern of interethnic sexual relationships ended only in the 1950s and 1960s at the intervention of local governments. In the conclusion, I will discuss how the creole Chinese patriliny emerged from another period of cultural transformation under Indonesia's assimilationist name-changing policy from the 1960s to the 1980s.

CONCLUSION

To be Chinese in colonial Indonesia meant being born to a Chinese father and being known by one's patrilineal family name. Leveraging on the niche they occupied in the commercial sphere, male settlers formed temporary relationships with slave and local women. A new settler society was formed the moment they made children according to the patrilineally endogamous rules of marriage they brought from China. This book has shown how a settler patriliny manipulated women, children, property, and ideas about modernity and desire in collaboration and contestation with the colonial state to remain a stranger minority in their adopted homeland. It told the stories, wherever possible, of girls and women who were intimately connected with but excluded from either patrilineal privilege or Chineseness altogether. This history of inclusionary and exclusionary familial manipulations was replicated wherever the Chinese settled overseas, especially in nineteenth-century colonial Southeast Asia, but with varying outcomes in terms of the local society's gendered ethnic norms.

Wherever Chinese patrilinies took root, the Chinese overseas managed racial difference primarily as a set of endogamous rules that excluded native women from Confucian ritual or legal marriage but not from concubinage or various other sorts of temporary intimate relationships. To date, most histories of Chinese overseas have treated the "absorption" of native women and their mestizo children *descriptively* as a passing, if culturally significant, phase in the reproduction of early Chinese settler societies. By unpacking class and legal-moral constructions of and contestations over womanhood, this book has shown that gender itself remained an unstable category over which men determined ethnic boundaries in colonial society. Until the 1850s, women could and did move more easily across racial lines.[1] That also meant, however, that gender as a category was central to how men conceptualized racial difference on the ground and, more abstractly, in colonial law.

Historicizing the native concubines and Chinese wives, this book has shown that notions of Chinese man- and womanhood, and especially the latter, were ideological constructs whose class content and cultural meaning fluctuated over time. Although the transplanted Chinese patriliny was maintained by male Kapitan leaders, with legal authority conferred by colonial law, women, from the slave-turned-nyai to Chinese concubines and wives, crafted a creolized feminine agency out of what was essentially a pragmatic Confucian patriarchy. In the nineteenth century, "Chinese" wives had surprisingly expansive rights to divorce in urban colonial Java. For instance, although polygamy was recognized for the Chinese, the Kapitans readily granted divorces to wives who had sued on account of their husband's preference for the concubine. From around the 1820s onward, creole women themselves became active players in the Confucian marriage market, taking over the role of marriage go-between from men and, among the wealthier elites, arranging marriage alliances through making matches and writing wills that reinforced patrilineal interests.

Many have argued that it was the emergence of diasporic Chinese nationalism around 1900 that deepened ethnic divisions.[2] However, this book has shown that processes of sinicization can be traced to the 1850s to a more rigid interpretation of Chineseness, ironically not by the Chinese settlers (or migrants) themselves but by sinology-trained colonial officials. Creole Chinese women bore the brunt of this colonial sinicization when they lost, in the 1890s, their preexisting right to hold and transact properties under their own names once they were married. It was, however, the Dutch colonial push to reform Asian marriage laws in the 1910s and, more ominously, to turn women's status in marriage law into a civilizational justification for colonial racial hierarchy that triggered a self-racializing patriarchal response from the Chinese of Java. The establishment of separate civil registers for the Chinese in 1919 laid the legal basis for racial management by both the colonial and the Indonesian states for more than eighty years, until separate legal ethnic markers were removed for the Chinese in Indonesia in 2006.

In the final analysis, however, race trumped law. This book has shown that race was imagined and constructed by the creole Chinese themselves in the formation of a new patriarchal Confucian religion and in viscerally emotional and moralizing terms through mass-market love stories. In the 1910s and 1920s, patriarchal reformers and writers shaped a new imagined community by framing morally Other-ing stories around the emancipated Chinese girl and the illicit native concubine. This new Chinese identity was ultimately ambivalent about the racializing and civil law–based Dutch reformist efforts. Betraying its own patriarchal and patrilineal tendencies, the Chinese avoided civil law's marriage registration process but made sure they registered their children's births. The colonial legal sanction they sought for the next generation's succession of the father's family name unwittingly made possible the perpetuation of race management via the civil registers in postcolonial Indonesia.

Colonial Southeast Asian Chinese Comparisons

This book has retraced processes of gender formation in and alongside colonial law in Dutch Java, which it argues accentuated the patrilineal identity of Chinese settlers and kept them as aliens with intimate connections to the local community. To what extent was the Chinese settler patriliny reproduced in such intimate yet at the same time alienating ways elsewhere among Chinese communities in colonial Southeast Asia? What has been the experience of women elsewhere in the region, both native and creole Chinese, in the reproduction of and struggle against the patriliny? I begin by comparing the Chinese of Dutch Java with the Chinese of the British Straits Settlements, followed by semicolonial Thailand (Bangkok) and the Philippines.

A similar Chinese settler patriliny developed in the Straits Settlements despite a drastically different British approach to family law. In the Straits Settlements, there was neither a Kapitan to manage marriage registries nor a racially segregating approach to law. Still, Confucian ritual marriage prevailed among the wealthier Chinese even without the legal bureaucratization of Kapitan-managed Confucian rites marriage and divorce. The British designated no "Chinese" authority in charge of religious or communal affairs.[3] In the Straits Settlements, patrilineal clan and speech-group association leaders emerged organically among the wealthier merchants in the 1830s and 1840s, centered around temple-based ancestral and deity worship.[4] Without the mitigation of a Confucianized form of "Islamic law" divorce, the domestication and sinicization of mestizo women must have happened earlier than they had in Java, most likely in the 1830s and 1840s. It did not help the women, of course, that the urban indigenous Muslim population was smaller, but in terms of legal norms, British policy was not that different from its Dutch counterpart—the preexisting Islamic *kathi* (judge) system (penghulu on Java) was endorsed and supported by both colonial authorities.

An important distinction between the two Peranakan Chinese communities, then, was the fact that the nyai was absent from the lived domestic experience of the Straits Settlements Chinese for much of the nineteenth century. In Java, the nyai served as the liminal ethno-moral border between the Chinese and much bigger indigenous communities up to the 1850s and remained a socially significant phenomenon on the fringe of Chinese communities as late as the 1910s, if not the 1950s. She was at once domestic servant, sexual companion, temporary wife, and enduring mother for the male Chinese settler and their mestizo children. Although she could never become Chinese in the same way that Asian nyai became nominally "European" after they converted to Christianity for marriage, quasi-kinship relations did develop across emergent colonial racial boundaries. In the Straits Settlements, the nyai phenomenon probably began to die out with the British abolition of slavery in the 1810s. Within the emerging Straits Settlements Chinese bourgeois household, she was replaced as domestic servant by (Hainanese) houseboys after the 1850s and, in the 1910s, by the adult (Cantonese) *amah*, sworn to a lifetime of service in celibacy, and the *mui-tsai*, who was married off by her owner when she came of age and vulnerable to sexual exploitation both during and after her period of service.[5] Without this element of sexual contact or quasi-kinship ties through concubinage or live-in domestic service, the Chinese in the Straits Settlements were much less "intimate" with the indigenous population as compared with their peers in Java. The plural society was more absolutely plural in the Straits Settlements than in Java.

In the Straits Settlements, family law reform was thus more easily containable within colonial categories of race, but it turned out to be more difficult to implement partly because of this. As I have shown in chapter 7, the Dutch were pressured into reforming Chinese family law in Java out of fear that legal changes in China would entitle their Chinese subjects to European legal status. The political stakes of marriage law reform were not as high for the British, as under English law, subjects of all races were already formally equal from the moment London granted the colony Charters of Justice in 1807 (Penang) and 1826 (Malacca and Singapore). Granting the Chinese a monogamous marriage law would not have upset the racial hierarchy in the colonial legal system as it threatened to do in the Dutch Indies. The British hence did not have to machinate behind closed doors. They appointed English-educated Chinese men and women in the Straits Settlements to a committee of inquiry to ascertain if the community wanted marriage law reform in 1926. The almost universal rejection of this call for reform by patrilineal clan representatives delayed the legislation of monogamy in the Straits Settlements for close to four decades. Yet as I have shown in chapters 7 and 8, the Dutch colonial "victory" was also pyrrhic. The take-up rate for Chinese marriage registration did not exceed 15 percent in urban Java throughout the 1920s and 1930s. This comparison reveals that the capacity for colonial legal reforms to change social gender norms was ultimately very limited. In truth, creole Chinese women only became more autonomous from the 1970s onward, when education and employment became more acceptable.

In the Philippines, the Spanish policy of converting all its subjects to Catholicism appears at first glance to have removed the fundamental cause of marital inequality within and across ethnic lines. In theory, the Chinese patriline ceases when ancestral worship ends. Monogamy in civil law has its roots in Christianity. Unlike the Dutch, the Spanish colonial state actively encouraged interethnic unions by compelling the Chinese settler to convert to Catholicism in order to marry. On a purely legal basis, then, the native (*indio*) wife-mother in Manila enjoyed higher status than her nyai counterpart in urban Java. Yet in fact the overwhelming majority of interethnic relationships between migrant Chinese men and local women went unregistered and were in effect not unlike the interethnic concubinage relations found in the Dutch Indies.[6] Richard Chu's revisionist study of Chinese families and hybrid identities shows that patrilineal norms, previously thought to have disappeared with the first mestizo generation, survived in at least the first if not the second mestizo generation during the final decades of the nineteenth century.

Catholicism did make a difference in twentieth-century gender-inflected identity politics. Unlike the Peranakan Chinese of the Dutch Indies or British Malaya, the middle-class Chinese mestizos, as Catholics, were bound by their religion to be monogamous. The Americans, who took over as imperial masters in 1902, did not have to civilize their newly acquired Chinese subjects with marriage law reform. Many early twentieth-century Filipino nationalist mestizos (and *indios*) who collaborated with the Americans were descended from Chinese mestizos. To them, the polygamous habits of newer Chinese migrants became one of the ways for the new nationalists to differentiate themselves as civilized "Filipinos" against the uncivilized "chinos" or "sinkehs." Thus, Catholicism (and its strictures on marriage) did ultimately serve to bond the Chinese mestizo more closely to *indio* society, while it drove an ethno-moral wedge between them and new Chinese migrants.

Like in the Philippines, the male Chinese settlers and their *lukjin* (Chinese mestizo) descendants were absorbed into the middle- and upper-class urban milieu in nineteenth-century Bangkok. The Siamese Thai, however, were polygynous like the Chinese, although as Buddhists they were not necessarily patrilineal. Despite these differences with the Philippines, Chinese settler patriliny's encounter with Thai society, as Skinner has shown, at first followed a similar path.[7] Patrilineal ancestral worship stopped after three or four generations. In the southern provinces more than in Bangkok, it appears that a patrilineal identity survived among the culturally hybrid Sino-Thai elite Khaw family.[8] We know too little about the native and mestizo Chinese wives of *lukjin* men in Bangkok in the mid- to late-nineteenth century to make any purposive comparison with the nyai and the nyonya.

As the only noncolonized nation in Southeast Asia, Siam passed its monogamous Family Registration Act in 1935 to meet the civilizational norms of the West. Tamara Loos shows that the Thai ruling aristocratic elite struggled to let go of their virile notions of masculinity, even as they strived to join the "family of (civilized) nations" by introducing a monogamous marriage law.[9] Like in the Dutch Indies, the passing of the law did not equalize gender relations within marriage, when registration rates remained low for all Thai citizens as late as the 1980s.[10] The law apparently had little effect on elite Thai men's adherence to a masculine cult of virility. The similarity of ethno-gender norms between the Thai and the Chinese meant that it did not become fodder for identity politics. New Chinese migrants were ostracized by other administrative legal means throughout the twentieth century. Chinese, *lukjin*, and Thai men were united in the sexual privileges they assumed over women. Bao Jiemin's ethnography of Chinese and Sino-Thai society in Bangkok from the 1990s shows that some second-generation Sino-Thai men continued to practice polygyny out of the patrilineal desire for sons while also embracing Thai notions of virile masculinity.[11]

Becoming Indonesian

Dutch colonial rule accentuated the patriliny-inflected racial identity of the Chinese settlers in Indonesia. Patrilineality in turn became a point of contention between the postcolonial nation-state and its alienated minority. We know more about the Chinese response to Indonesia's restrictive nationality laws than to its assimilationist cultural policies.

Indonesia was restrictive in its naturalization terms for "alien" residents. Only third-generation settlers—that is, local-born residents of parents who were also local born—qualified.[12] Both the revolutionary Sukarno (1945–65) and authoritarian Suharto governments (1965–97) encouraged the Chinese to adopt localized indigenous names so as to "assimilate" themselves with the Indonesian masses. The colonial-era Chinese Civil Registry unexpectedly served as an everyday political arena for the Chinese to authenticate their claims to be naturalized, assimilated, and in some cases indigenized. Yet despite all these efforts at performing and displaying "Indonesian-ness," the postcolonial state's maintenance of separate civil registration for the Chinese made it impossible for them to escape discriminatory treatment as an "alien" group.

The vicissitudes of Indonesia's naturalization policy for its Chinese minority have received much scholarly attention. The broad outline of that policy has been summarized as follows. Although the anticolonial revolutionary government at first conferred citizenship to all local-born residents, once the nation assumed sovereign control of the state, citizenship terms were changed in the mid-1950s so that only second-generation jus soli residents qualified, and they had to actively apply to receive Indonesian citizenship.[13] Much scholarly attention has focused on estimating the varied Chinese response to these naturalization routes. As Leo Suryadinata notes, the numbers continue to be disputed, and any estimates should be treated only as rough indicators of political identity. According to the official figures, between 1965 and 1971, out of an estimated 3 million resident Chinese across the archipelagic nation, the number of citizens of Chinese descent grew from 1.5 to 2 million, while the number of "alien" Chinese who did not take up or failed to qualify for citizenship remained consistent at around 1 to 1.1 million.[14] For Java, where the creolized group was larger and a creole-initiated assimilationist movement was launched, its naturalization rate was most likely significantly higher than the 50 to 67 percent national figure, perhaps between 80 and 90 percent.

Those who naturalized faced after 1965 an assimilationist regime bent on desinicizing what was seen as an exclusivist and privileged "alien" minority. Charles Coppel has shown that the local-born Chinese themselves were split into two groups. The leftist integrationists argued for the Chinese to be accepted as one of the diverse nation's recognized ethnic group, while right-leaning assimilationists wanted them to merge and "disappear" as a separate group. Coppel traces the origins of the assimilationist movement to army-linked Catholic Party Chinese intellectuals, who launched their manifesto in March 1960. The integrationists at first had a wider following, but the assimilationist agenda would come to the fore after the failed communist coup of 1965 triggered widespread political repression. Despite its purportedly voluntary nature, mass killings of people associated the communist party, and recurring hostile policies targeting the Chinese meant that name changing took place in a climate of coercion. On 29 May 1966, for instance, pro-assimilation Chinese leaders and the military assembled and gave Sukabumi's Chinese population three days to reregister new Indonesian names in a mass ceremony.[15] In December 1968, the Ministry of Justice announced that about 60 percent of the Chinese Indonesian population in the province of Semarang (Central Java) had changed their names.[16]

The pro-assimilation call did not in fact stop at name changing but went further to promote intermarriage. Advocates pointed out that it was a Chinese sense of racial superiority that prevented closer ties with Indonesians. As early as 1954, Thung Liang Lee, a retired prewar politician, had called for a "change of heart" among the creole Chinese, for them to "realize . . . Indonesia [as] the country of our mothers, our grandmothers, great-grandmothers and great-great-grandmothers."[17] Despite the proximity of their language and psychology, he lamented that "there were few intermarriages" between the Chinese and indigenous groups, and that some had "succumbed to the Dutch view of regarding the Indonesians as a somewhat inferior race." He then turned to precolonial history for lessons on how Chinese settlers assimilated completely with the native population before Dutch divide and rule. In 1960, Ong Hok Ham, a historian and prolific champion of assimilation, declared that the Indonesian goal of "Bhinneka Tunggal Ika" (M: Unity in Diversity) meant unity of the ethnic majority and minority "until the distinction [between the two] disappears." Assimilation was the only route to unity, for it ensured that the "exclusivity of the minority will disappear, and that the two become closer with rising numbers of mixed marriages."[18] In his call for name changing, Ong, like Thung, turned to history to show how before Dutch colonization, Chinese settlers were absorbed into the Javanese aristocracy and thereby assumed Javanese names.[19]

Ironically, the legacy of the colonial paternity rule of descent prevented the Chinese from forging their father's family name. Ong Hok Ham himself admitted that it was a "pity the laws originating from the colonial era, which divided residents into three groups legal statuses, i.e. Adat, European and Foreign Asiatic, were still partially in place."[20] Article Six of the Netherlands Indies Civil Code, as Ong pointed out, forbade anyone from changing their last name without the approval of the governor-general. This made it easy to distinguish a person with a family name as "Chinese" in comparison with most Javanese, who went by single given names. Aside from the law, both the government and pro-assimilation activists also recognized that some Chinese might wish to retain their "clan" identity in their new names. The Minister of Social Affairs, Muljadi Djojomartono, himself had proposed that those surnamed "Tan" or "Ong" might choose to be renamed "Tanojo" or "Onggowasito."[21] Without overtly contradicting the minister, Ong counseled against such a move, as transliterated names "often did not have meaning, because they are nothing but a sequence of sounds, whereas in the East the meaning of names are important."[22]

It was in this context of alternatingly forceful and subtle coercion that name changing for most Chinese, at least in the early years, panned out as a way to hide one's ethnic identity or patrilineal name from public view, rather than as a voluntary embrace of Indonesian culture. A study of high school students' names, sampled from a predominantly Christian and Chinese Indonesian private school in Jakarta in the 1990s, found that fifty-six out of one hundred students retained family names, and thirty-seven of those family names were "distinctively Chinese Indonesian," like Tanojo (Tan), Salim (Lim), or Wijaya (Wee).[23]

Yet patrilineal identity is also an intrinsic part of the practice of the ancestral cult. My study elsewhere of the Thung line of Bogor shows that for a localized Chinese lineage group, collectively changing the family name could involve complex adjustments to their genealogical self-understanding and orientation toward the local mystical landscape.[24] Legally registered as a nonprofit society in 1906, the Kioe Seng Tong lineage group of Bogor had regular meetings at its ancestral hall, and a mutual aid fund for all descendants of its nine fraternal founders. For the third generation Thung line, who helmed the lineage group in the 1950s and 1960s, changing the family name was as much about hiding one's Chinese patrilineal name as reconnecting with "lost" Indonesian kin from their maternal ancestors.

During the Suharto era, whether or not their new (family) names were sincerely adopted, the state retained means and ways to mark citizens as "Chinese" and thus aliens. Many post-Suharto-era studies show that grievances accumulated not so much from name changing itself but from the persistence of covert forms of state-endorsed discrimination, such as unofficial racial quotas (in higher education, civil service, and so on), even after they had complied with the state's assimilationist demands. Tim Lindsey shows that Internal Affairs and Justice Ministry administrative laws in 1966 and 1975 that "purport[ted] to abolish the colonial racial groupings" in fact merely instructed government agencies to remove the overt use of "European" or "Chinese" labels, while retaining those same colonial statutes that instituted separate civil registries for Europeans, Chinese, Christian Indonesians, and those of mixed marriages.[25] To be registered by one's father at the Chinese Civil Registry was enough proof of one's alienness, regardless of the authenticity of the name one carried.

The removal of these overt measures of racial labeling and discrimination after the end of Suharto's authoritarian rule in 1998 has not brought about any mass revival of Chinese patrilineal identity. Despite some minor exceptions, the overwhelming majority of ethnic Chinese Indonesians have retained their assimilated names. Their mass conversion to Christianity at the height of authoritarian repression during the 1960s and 1970s may have reduced the impulse, derived from ancestral worship, to carry on the patrilineal name. For those who hold on dearly to their Chinese ancestry, it is more likely that they are still biding their time, and doing so while hiding their patrilineal identity within their assimilated Indonesian names. As memories of racialized violence and overt discrimination against the "alien" Chinese minority fade with time, and as Indonesian civil society matures, there may come a time when commemorating one's immigrant ancestry will cease to be a matter of everyday ethnic politics.

Appendix

A NOTE ON DIVORCE CASES AND PATTERNS (CHINESE COUNCIL OF BATAVIA)

This note provides a more technical explanation for how I derived the three bar graphs in chapter 3. The divorce cases I study in that chapter are assembled from the minutes of the proceedings of the Chinese Council of Batavia from the 1820s to the 1890s. There were 738 divorce cases, 549 of which were filed by women (189 by men). In the chapter, I present the statistics and patterns by decade. Readers should take note that the data on the number of divorce cases per year during each decade are averages, accurate down to monthly numbers. As table A.1 shows, the minutes that have survived are most complete in the 1850s and 1860s (116 and 113 months, respectively, out of 120 months per decade), and least so in the 1830s and 1880s (27 and 24 months). The annual averages based on these figures are thus most accurate in the former case, and least so in the latter.

The numbers of marriages per year were calculated from the Batavia Chinese Marriage Registry. A version of the marriage registration has been published in 2010.[1] I calculated my marriage numbers from an Excel spreadsheet of the same registry, compiled and held by Chen Menghong, editor and archivist at the Kong Koan Archives in the Leiden University Library. I thank Menghong for sharing the data with me. The crude divorce rate (figure 3.2) was calculated by dividing average number of divorce cases per year with the same figure for marriages. The proportion of divorce proceedings initiated by wives (figure 3.3) should be self-explanatory.

How I read and categorized the causes for divorce and their corresponding trends in figure 3.4 requires more explanation. When I first started trying to analyze the divorce trials back in 2011–12, I had two initial reactions. First, I was

APPENDIX

TABLE A.1. Completeness of Batavia Chinese Council minutes and the number of divorce cases filed per year by husbands and wives

	MONTHS ON RECORD	IN YEARS	TOTAL CASES	CASES/YR	MARRIAGES/YR	WIFE-INITIATED	HUSBAND-INITIATED
1820s	32	2.67	25	9.4	159.3	15	10
1830s	27	2.25	42	18.7	197.3	29	13
1840s	74	6.17	104	16.9	238.2	73	31
1850s	116	9.67	212	21.9	200.1	157	55
1860s	113	9.42	192	20.4	154.9	152	40
1870s	79	6.58	115	17.5	182.2	91	24
1880s	24	2	11	5.5	150.2	7	4
1890s	96	8	37	4.8	112.8	25	12
Total	561	N/A	738	N/A	N/A	549	189

surprised by the high rates of pleas filed by women. Some reading of the literature, both historical and contemporary, quickly disabused me of the idea that this was a unique gendered pattern. The high rates of divorce in Southeast Asia may be particular to the region, but the literature on divorce elsewhere demonstrates that wherever the legal facility of divorce is available, it is a universal truth that women are far more likely to be the initiators of divorce proceedings than men. Marriages could fail for all kinds of reasons, but men generally tend to be less willing than women to confront the facts and move on.

Second, the highly personal accounts of the women's (and men's) pleas led me to the initial conclusion that no two marital tragedies were the same. Every marriage that failed seemed to fail for reasons unique to the parties concerned. This led me, somewhat foolhardily in hindsight, to read and transcribe all 738 cases. Some obvious patterns did emerge. I then proceeded to code each case according to the way the concerned party framed her or his plea. It turned out that the five causes women most frequently cited in their divorce pleas were desertion, abuse (physical or verbal), jealousy of the concubine (or other women), eviction, and tensions with in-laws (particularly mothers-in-law). As I explain in chapter 3, women often cited more than one of these reasons in their pleas. While they complained most regularly about being deserted by their husbands, the desertion was often triggered by another source of tension.

In the interest of length, I have limited my analysis in this book to the way that women filed their divorce pleas and what these patterns say about women's moral agency with respect to the creole Chinese patriarchy. The raw coded data, which may run up to thirty or forty pages, has not been published due to space constraints. Readers who have questions about my methodology can approach me by email.

Notes

ABBREVIATIONS

The following abbreviations are used in the notes:

AMK: Archief Ministerie van Koloniën (Archives of the Ministry of Colonies)
ANRI: Arsip Nasional Republik Indonesia (National Archives, Republic of Indonesia)
BP: Boedelpapieren (Probate Papers)
FHL: Family History Library (Salt Lake City)
HRNI: *Het regt van Nederlandsch-Indië* (The law of the Netherlands India)
ITR: *Indisch weekblad van het recht* (Indies weekly law journal)
NA: Nationaal Archief (National Archives, the Netherlands)
WBK: Arsip Wees-en Boedelkamer (Archives of the Orphans and Probate Council)

INTRODUCTION

1. See chapter 6 in this volume.
2. Kwee, *The Rose of Cikembang*, 6–7.
3. I analyze this text more fully in the final section of chapter 8.
4. McClintock, *Imperial Leather*; Stoler, *Carnal Knowledge and Imperial Power*.
5. See, for instance, Wallerstein, *Modern World-System*.
6. Fanon, *Black Skin, White Masks*, 62.
7. Stoler, *Carnal Knowledge*.
8. Andaya, *Flaming Womb*, 104–33.
9. Khan, *Sovereign Women in a Muslim Kingdom*.
10. Hoadley, "Javanese, Peranakan, and Chinese Elites in Cirebon, 503–51; Cushman, *Family and State*.
11. Andaya, "From Temporary Wife to Prostitute."
12. Stoler, *Race and the Education of Desire*; Stoler, *Carnal Knowledge and Imperial Power*; Ghosh, *Sex and the Family in Colonial India*; Firpo, *Uprooted*.
13. Loos, "Transnational Histories of Sexualities in Asia," 1315.
14. Loos, *Subject Siam*.
15. Furnivall, *Colonial Policy and Practice*, 304. See also discussion in Davidson, "Study of Political Ethnicity in Southeast Asia," 210.
16. For more on *kabya*, see Ikeya, *Refiguring Women*, 120–42; on *peranakan* as a hybrid category deployed by the indigenous polities on Java, see Hoadley, "Javanese, Peranakan, and Chinese Elites in Cirebon; on *lukjin*, see Skinner, *Chinese Society in Thailand*, 126–34; on *minh hương*, see Wheeler, "Interests, Institutions and Identity."
17. Ikeya, *Refiguring Women*, 120–42.
18. Ho, *Graves of Tarim*, 152–87.
19. Simmel, "The Stranger," 403. I thank Robert Cribb for pointing out that Simmel theorized his "stranger" always from the viewpoint of the local, not the diaspora.
20. See Hsu, *Under the Ancestors' Shadow*; Freedman, *Chinese Lineage and Society*.

21. Skinner, *Chinese Society in Thailand*, 128. This was in part because "there was in Siam no racial barrier to complete assimilation. Differences in physical appearance between Thai and Chinese [were] not marked." "Fourth-generation Chinese were unheard of," he continued, "not because Chinese had not been settled and rearing families for at least four generations, but because all great-grandchildren of Chinese immigrants had merged with Thai society." Skinner, "Chinese Assimilation and Thai Politics," 237. For a still-developing critique of the Cold War–oriented politics of Skinner's social science intervention, see Eaksittipong, "Textualizing the 'Chinese of Thailand.'"

22. Sangren, *Chinese Sociologics*, 190–91
23. Spivak, "Can the Subaltern Speak?"
24. Kelly, *Politics of Virtue*.
25. Toer, *Chinese in Indonesia*.
26. Hui, *Strangers at Home*.
27. Reid, *History of Southeast Asia*, 188–95.
28. Reid, "Flows and Seepages," 40.

29. *Verslag van het beheer en den staat der oost-indische bezittingen* over 1857 [Report over the governance of the state of East Indian possessions for 1857, henceforth, *Koloniaal Verslag*]. Netherlands: Second Chamber, 1860. Appendix no. 2, 4. Note that these numbers did not include more than fifty-eight thousand children counted among the Chinese.

30. "Bijlage A: Statistieke betreffende de bevolking van de Nederlandsch-Indie over 1883" [Appendix A: Statistics on the population of the Netherlands Indies for 1883] in *Kolonial Verslag van 1885: Nederlandsch Oost-Indie*. [Colonial Report of 1885: Netherlands East Indies] Netherlands: Second Chamber, 1886. Children were no longer being distinguished, so these numbers almost certainly overestimated the number of immigrant men.

31. The Java numbers contrast with those of the British Straits Settlements, where labor migrants absorbed port cities (Singapore, Melaka, and Penang) and *babas* (traders and businessmen) numbered only 45,000 to 50,000, accounting for 9 to 10 percent of the total Chinese population in the 1890s. See Skinner, "Creolized Chinese Societies," 58.

32. Unlike the more accurate figures provided by the 1930 census, this is an estimate Skinner made based on the assumption that women in China did not migrate and that there were equal numbers of local born men as the number of women reported. See Skinner, "Creolized Chinese Societies," 56.

33. Departement van Economische Zaken (Nederlandsch-Indië), *Volkstelling 1930*, pt. 7, 22.

34. Although Charles Coppel did not frame it as such, his monograph shows the aftermath of how the *peranakans* and their assimilationist politics prevailed over a more China-oriented political identity. Coppel, *Indonesian Chinese in Crisis*.

35. For how a creole Chinese intellectual labels his creole subjects as *babas*, see Loe, "Sociale ellende en geboortebeperking."

36. Blussé, *Strange Company*; Skinner, "Creolized Chinese Societies"; Carey, "Changing Javanese Perceptions"; Kwee, *Political Economy of Java's Northeast Coast*; Rush, *Opium to Java*; Chen, *De Chinese gemeenschap van Batavia*; Claver, *Dutch Commerce and Chinese Merchants in Java*; Lohanda, *The Kapitan Cina of Batavia*.

37. Williams, *Overseas Chinese Nationalism*; Lohanda, *Growing*; Suryadinata, *Peranakan Chinese Politics in Java*; Coppel, *Indonesian Chinese in Crisis*; Claudine Salmon, *Literature in Malay by the Chinese of Indonesia*; Myra Sidharta, *100 tahun Kwee Tek Hoay*; Chan, "Chinese Women's Emancipation as Reflected in Two Peranakan Journals"; Tjiook-Liem, *De rechtspositie der Chinezen in Nederlands-Indië*; Chandra, "Blossoming Dahlia";

Chandra, "Women and Modernity"; Sai, "Mandarin Lessons"; Kwartanada, "Bangsawan Prampoewan"; Zhou, *Migration in the Time of Revolution*; Hoogervorst, "What Kind of Language Was 'Chinese Malay' in Late-Colonial Java?"

38. Blussé and Chen, *Archives of the Kong Koan of Batavia*, 2.

39. See Blussé and Wu, *Gongan bu*.

40. "2. Minutes of Council Meetings," Archive of the Kong Koan of Batavia, Leiden University Library.

1. *NYAI* LIMINALITY

1. Skinner, "Creolized Chinese Societies." I belatedly came across a similar history of creole Chinese womanhood in Southeast Asian port cities in Peter Lee's pathbreaking fashion history of the creole Chinese. Lee relies on a larger corpus of primary sources to make a broader argument about creole women across the region's port cities. My account is more focused on Batavia and class- and race-inflected tensions. See P. Lee, *Sarong Kebaya*, 80–103.

2. Andaya, "From Temporary Wife to Prostitute," 27.

3. These and other population figures are taken from Raben, "Batavia and Colombo," 91, 93.

4. Abeyesekere, "Slaves in Batavia," 288.

5. Taylor, *Social World of Batavia*, 70–71; Abeyesekere, "Slaves in Batavia," 310.

6. See Reid, "'Closed' and 'Open' Slave Systems."

7. Abeyasekere, "Slaves in Batavia," 300.

8. In the Chinese Council minutes of the late eighteenth century, the Chinese used wen as their unit of currency. This refers to the standard silver Dutch East India Company coin, which was worth 2 guilders May See Blussé and Wu, *Gong an bu* 1:372n6. I have converted all money values in wen to guilders. Slave girls were transacted for 200–500 guilders, but mostly within the 200–250 range. See "2. Minutes of Council Meetings or *Gong-an Bu* 公案簿," Archive of the Kong Koan of Batavia (吧城公館) (ubl209): "2. Minutes of Council Meetings or *Gong-an Bu* 公案簿," 18 Mar. 1789, 5 May 1790, 19 Dec. 1790, 12 Aug. 1789, Digital Collections, Leiden University (hereafter cited as Chinese Council Minutes).

9. For the respective cases in that sequence, see Chinese Council Minutes, 21 Nov. 1787, 5 July 1788, 29 Dec. 1790, 14 Apr. 1790.

10. A newly arrived carpenter's apprentice earned 62.50 guilders in his first year of work. See Chinese Council Minutes, 7 July 1790.

11. Chinese Council Minutes, 21 July 1790.

12. Chinese Council Minutes, 27 Sept. 1790.

13. Chinese Council Minutes, 5 May 1790.

14. Chinese Council Minutes, 1 Apr. 1789.

15. Chinese Council Minutes, 14 Apr. 1790.

16. Chinese Council Minutes, 5 May 1790.

17. Jones, *Wives, Slaves, and Concubines*.

18. Chinese Council Minutes, 28 Apr. 1790.

19. Vickers, *Bali: A Paradise Created*, 34.

20. "Njai," in van der Lith and Snelleman, *Encyclopaedie van Nederlandsch-Indië*, 30.

21. Chinese Council Minutes, 14 Apr. 1790. For more examples, see Jones, *Wives, Slaves and Concubines*, chaps. 4 and 5.

22. Chinese Council Minutes, 19 Nov. 1788, 27 June 1789.

23. Chinese Council Minutes, 8 Dec. 1790.

24. She was later sued for owing wages to the dyer. See Chinese Council Minutes, 27 Aug. 1788.

25. See the relevant cases in Chinese Council Minutes: Nyai Jo Hang, 7 Dec. 1788; Nyai Kong Hwie, 14 Jan. 1789; Nyai Liem Tim Tjwie, 25 Nov. 1789; Nyai Po Sengkong, 19 Dec. 1787; Nyai Tjia Hoe, 19 Nov. 1788; Nyai Lik Koe, 26 Nov. 1788.

26. See the relevant cases in Chinese Council Minutes: Nyai Liem Tjek, 20 Aug. 1788; Nyai Lo Tjek, 12 Nov. 1788; Nyai Jo Tjeng, 5 May 1790; Nyai Fong Kwie, 23 June 1790; Nyai Tan Jong, 22 Dec. 1790; Nyai Tai Kim, 22 Dec. 1790.

27. Chinese Council Minutes, 27 May 1825.

28. On his appointment as lieutenant, he founded Beng Sing Su Ie (C: Mingcheng Shuyuan)—the first Confucian classics school in Southeast Asia. See Blussé and Nie, *Chinese Annals of Batavia*, 178–79.

29. Mann, "Grooming a Daughter for Marriage," 205.

30. Chen, *De Chinese gemeenschap*, 6–8.

31. The quotation is from the annals kept by the Chinese in Batavia. In fact, he was also a bad merchant. Oeij served briefly as secretary before being promoted to Kapitan in the Chinese Council in 1750. His leadership of the Chinese in Batavia ended in 1755, when he was imprisoned for five years for unpaid debt he'd incurred. Upon his release in 1761, he returned to China with a son. See Blussé and Nie, *Chinese Annals of Batavia*, 157, 159.

32. Article 16 in Chineesch Regt. [Chinese Law], cited in "Bijdragen tot de kennis van de wetten en instellingen der Chinezen in Nederlandsch Indië."

33. "Marriage Registry, Batavia Chinese Council, 1772–1919," Leiden University Library. I thank Chen Menghong for sharing this database with me.

34. *Staatsblad van Nederlandsch-Indië* [Statutory law of the Netherlands India], no. 46, 1828. These are executive statutory laws passed by the governor-general of the Chinese Council.

35. Van der Chijs, *Nederlandsch-Indisch Plakaatboek, 1602–1811*, vol. 8, *1765–1775*, 142 (25 July 1766 entry).

36. Blussé, "One Hundred Weddings and Many More Funerals a Year."

37. Blussé, "One Hundred Weddings," 19, 25.

38. Kapitan Tjoa Toenko and assembled officers' reply to the aldermen court, Chinese Council, Batavia, 4 Aug. 1788. See Chinese Council Minutes, 13 Aug. 1788.

39. Chen, "Between the Chinese Tradition and Dutch Colonial System," 64.

40. Men were listed as matchmakers for 439 out of 882 marriages. "Marriage Registry, Batavia Chinese Council, 1772–1919."

41. They were between a Tan groom and a Liem bride, and a Tjam and an Oeij. See Chinese Council Minutes for the respective cases on 16 Nov. 1784 and 2 May 1790. For the case of his son, see Chinese Council Minutes, 16 Nov. 1790.

42. Chinese Council Minutes, 5 May 1790. The dispute was in fact over who had custody of the bride. The nyai had to dissolve the proposal once she learned that her husband's surviving brother, who had custody over her daughter, disapproved of the match.

43. I use "mestizo" and "mestiza" to refer to the descendants of mixed unions.

44. Progress through the Six Rites only stalled when Tey refused to proceed with picking an auspicious wedding date by claiming that he had lost hold of his daughter's horoscope. Chinese Council Minutes, 19 Aug. 1789.

45. "Marriage Registry, Batavia Chinese Council, 1772–1919."

46. Chinese Council Minutes, 18 July 1856.

47. Taylor, *Social World of Batavia*, 155.

48. Skinner, "Creolized Chinese Societies in Southeast Asia," 52.

49. Skinner, "Creolized Chinese Societies," 53n6.

50. Chinese Council Minutes, 1 Aug. 1834.

51. Chinese Council Minutes, 12 May 1848.

52. Chinese Council Minutes, 31 May 1850

53. The compensation amounted to three-quarters of a house in Batavia and 750 silver guilders. Chinese Council Minutes, 31 May 1850.

54. Chinese Council Minutes, 1 Aug. 1834.

55. Chinese Council Minutes, 1 Aug. 1834.

56. Chinese Council Minutes, 12 May 1848.

57. See the case of Sim A-Tjwee. Before he went on a trading run with junk owner and relative Siem Lak, he left his nyai and daughter Sim Kwienio in Siem Lak's household under the care of the wife, Souw Lai Nio. Such boarding often came with obligations for the nyai and children to work for the *nyonya* boss. Souw Lai Nio, the nyonya head of this male-absentee household, had three young nyonya under her charge. When they were caught running away to a Eurasian Dutchman's household, they claimed they had been worked too hard on sewing and embroidery and were often abused. See Chinese Council Minutes, 28 June 1824. During the nineteenth century, "Baba" and "Nyonya" were the honorific forms of address for local born men and women of foreign origins across the Malay-speaking island Southeast Asian world. By the late nineteenth century, the terms were used, especially in the British Straits Settlements, interchangeably with "Peranakan" to refer to the local born and acculturated Chinese. See Tan, *The Baba of Melaka*, 11–18.

58. Tan Ngim handed his two daughters either to his nephew Tan Tjiang To or to his good friend Jo Ie. Tan Ngim's nyonya wife remarried a native man. See Chinese Council Minutes, 25 Mar. 1789.

59. Chinese Council Minutes, 27 May 1825.

60. Chinese Council Minutes, 8 June 1849.

61. Chinese Council Minutes, 8 June 1849.

62. "Begrip van vaderlijke magt onder de Chinezen."

63. "Begrip," 30–31.

2. BOURGEOIS MANHOOD AND RACIAL BOUNDARIES

1. Unlike in Christianity, sex is not a moral sin for the Chinese and has no theological significance beyond the prescriptions in the Confucian classics for men to produce patrilineal male heirs for ancestral worship.

2. Claver and Lindbald, "Going Bankrupt?," esp. 141–42.

3. In the 1790s, all officers in Batavia were already signing their names in Latinized form, although half still appended the Chinese versions. In the following Chinese century, the Chinese signatures would completely disappear. See Chinese Council Minutes, 16 June 1790, 25 June 1824, and all minutes henceforth.

4. Albrecht, "Het schoolonderwijs onder de Chineezen op Java."

5. He obtained an entry-level prefectural degree (Xiucai) in China and returned to Surabaya to teach in his birth city. Albrecht, "Het schoollonderwijs," 229. See also Salmon and Lombard, "Confucianisme et esprit de réforme dans les communautés Chinoises d'Insulinde."

6. Albrecht, "Het schoollonderwijs," 240.

7. Govaars-Tjia, *Dutch Colonial Education*, appendix A.

8. Projecting the age structure of local-born Chinese in Java from the 1930 census backward, there would have been just over half the male population—60,000 in the 1880s and 70,000 in the 1890s—falling within the age range of birth to nineteen years. If we conservatively take a further half of these youths to be of school-going age, we see that 3,211 boys out of 30,000 in the 1880s and upwards of 5,000 out of 35,000 in the 1890s were being tutored in the classics in Confucian schools. But if we assume three years to be the average length of Confucian schooling, the numbers will be two to three times as

large. For the age structure of local-born Chinese, see Departement van Landbouw, Nijverheid en Handel, *Volkstelling 1930*, 7:53–54. Chinese male population figures in Java were 120,653 in 1883 and 139,045 in 1894. See *Kolonial verslagen* 1885 and 1895.

9. Albrecht, "Het schoolonderwijs," 239.

10. "Collection of Correspondence, 1874," manuscript no. 156, Go Sian Lok Collection, Leiden University Library.

11. Albrecht, "Het schoolonderwijs," 237.

12. Chinese Council Minutes, 24 July 1869.

13. Chinese Council Minutes, 24 July 1869.

14. Rush, *Opium to Java*, 92–95.

15. Haryono, *Perkawinan strategis*.

16. *Tambahsia*, chap. 4.

17. *Tambahsia*, 33–34.

18. *Koloniale verslagen*, 1873, appendix 4, "Beroepen en bedrijven uitgeoefend door Inlanders en Vreemde Oosterlingen" [Occupations and enterprises run by Natives and Foreign Asiatics], 14–17.

19. De Waal, *Onze Indische Financien*, 170–89.

20. *Koloniale verslagen*, 1875, appendix 4, 14–17.

21. These prices were revealed when betrothal agreements broke down and disputes were brought to the Chinese Council for resolution. "Proposal gift of ƒ90 in Tso Kim Sei v. Jap Tjoen Hien," Chinese Council Minutes, 20 Aug. 1824; "Proposal gift of ƒ60 followed by 100 guilders in Lo Teng Sieu v. Tjeng Hoa," Chinese Council Minutes, 9 Dec. 1825; "Remarrying widow asking for 100 guilders in Tio Twie v. Liem Jin Nio," Chinese Council Minutes, 25 June 1826; "Initial proposal gift of 50 guilders in Oei A Kioe v. He A Moa," Chinese Council Minutes, 14 Jan. 1849; "Gift to bride of 75 guilders in Oei Tan Nio v. Tsie Ping Lien," Chinese Council Minutes, 21 Nov. 1862; "Tjing Sing Goan promised to pay a 100 guilders bridal gift after being caught eloping with the unmarried Tio Ting Nio in Tio A Djoen v. Tjing Sing Goan," Chinese Council Minutes, 9 Mar. 1866. The time required for a craftsman to save for his marriage gifts is calculated by taking ƒ150 to be the average expenses and dividing it by between ƒ2 and ƒ.080 of wages per day.

22. See the case of Oei Lo v. Lie A Jo, Chinese Council Minutes, 25 Aug. 1826.

23. Tan Kim Nio v. Tjia King Lai, Chinese Council Minutes, 26 Feb. 1868.

24. Oei A Kioe v. Ho A Moa, in Chinese Council Minutes, 14 Jan. 1849.

25. According to government surveys in the 1850s, coolies in public civil works in the Batavia region earned between 30 and 50 cents, whereas craftsmen like bricklayers and carpenters earned between 80 cents and 2 guilders a day. Based on this estimate, the upper end of annual incomes of coolies was roughly 150 guilders, compared to 600 guilders for craftsmen. See Dros, *Wages: 1820–1940*, 52.

26. Staatsblad 1828, no. 46, art. 63.

27. Sutherland, *Making of a Bureaucratic Elite*, 20.

28. Chinese genealogies usually record no more than the family name of the primary wife. The councils did not register secondary wives.

29. Chen, *Chinese Gemeenschap van Batavia*, 15–16.

30. Chinese Council Minutes, 20 May 1853.

31. The Boen Liang, "Riwajatnja familie Tjoa di Soerabaja" [The Story of the Tjoa Family of Surabaya], in *Mata Hari*, 1 Aug. 1934. English translation in box 5, folder 27, William Skinner Papers, Cornell University Library.

32. Kan, "Personal Data Tjoe-Hong Lie (1846–1896)."

33. Mahameru, *Oei Tiong Ham*, 26–27.

34. *Uitkomsten der in de maand November 1920 gehouden volkstelling*, 124.
35. Tio Ie Soei, *Lie Kimhok, 1853–1912*, 14.
36. Tio, *Lie Kimhok*, 23, 35.
37. Tio, *Lie Kimhok*, 44.
38. Tio, *Lie Kimhok*, 45–46.
39. These were unpublished and discovered after his death in 1912. See Tio, *Lie Kimhok*, 95–99.
40. Lie, *Orang Prampoewan*.
41. Lie, *Orang Prampoewan*, 1–4.
42. Sidharta, "Making of the Indonesian Chinese Woman," 62.
43. Chen, "Between the Chinese Tradition and Dutch Colonial System," 62. She retains the Chinese *sui*, which counts a newborn as one, and adds one *sui* on every subsequent Lunar New Year. I have subtracted one *sui* from her figures.
44. Palmier, *Social Status and Power in Java*, 120.
45. Geertz, *Javanese Family*, 119. In contrast, Tony Reid argues that only aristocratic elites married their daughters before or immediately after the first menstruation, whereas the Javanese commoner delayed their daughters' marriage to between the ages of fifteen and twenty-one. See Reid, *Southeast Asia in the Age of Commerce*, 1:153.
46. Chen, "Between the Chinese Tradition and Dutch Colonial System," 62.
47. Palmier, *Social Status*, 121.
48. From an 1837 European observation cited in Reid, *Southeast Asia in the Age of Commerce*, 1:153.
49. Chinese Council Minutes, 30 May 1856.
50. Chinese Council Minutes, 2 May 1834.
51. Chinese Council Minutes, 12–13 Nov. 1847.
52. Chinese Council Minutes, 9 Mar. 1849.
53. Chinese Council Minutes, 9 Mar. 1866.
54. Chinese Council Minutes, 9 Mar. 1849.
55. Chinese Council Minutes, 9 Mar. 1866.
56. Chinese Council Minutes, 29 Dec. 1848, 19 July 1850, 8 Feb. 1871, 7 Dec. 1875, 21 June 1889.
57. Chinese Council Minutes, 8 Feb. 1871.
58. Chinese Council Minutes, 29 Dec. 1848, 7 Dec. 1875.
59. Chinese Council Minutes, 7 Dec. 1875.
60. These were cited in de Waal, *Onze Indische Financien*, 172.
61. Staatsblad van Nederlandsch-Indië [Statutory Laws of the Netherlands India] 1837, no. 37.
62. "In the interest of agriculture and industry, or of the revenue farms and public works, regional chiefs are authorized to permit foreign orientals to settle in places where no wards are designated for them, until [such permission] is withdrawn." Staatsblad 1866, no. 56, art. 3.
63. Tio Ie Soei, *Lie Kimhok*, 16.
64. Chinese Council Minutes, 4 May 1827.
65. Chinese Council Minutes, 20 Oct. 1790.
66. E. Jones, *Wives, Slaves, and Concubines*, 97–98.
67. Chinese Council Minutes, 18 Feb. 1789.
68. Chinese Council Minutes, 21 Oct. 1789.
69. Chinese Council Minutes, 18 July 1851.
70. Chinese Council Minutes, 30 July 1790.
71. Chinese Council Minutes, 20 Oct. 1790.

72. Her husband, a gambling addict, had pawned away her clothes and sent her packing to her parents. According to Hau Nio, after eight months at home, her mother "could no longer tolerate" her and had her evicted.
73. Chinese Council Minutes, 1 May 1846.
74. Chinese Council Minutes, 25 June 1847.
75. Chinese Council Minutes, 24 Mar. 1826.
76. Chinese Council Minutes, 9 Mar. 1849.
77. Chinese Council Minutes, 9 May 1845.
78. Chinese Council Minutes, 9 May 1845.
79. Lie Djan Nio eloped with Ko Sia but was not caned. See Chinese Council Minutes, 29 Oct. 1788. For the extent to which Chinese authority might settle disputes within the community in the Company era, see Raben, "Batavia and Colombo," 202–3.
80. Chinese Council Minutes, 30 July 1790.
81. Chinese Council Minutes, 20 Oct. 1790.
82. Chinese Council Minutes, 29 Oct. 1788.
83. Chinese Council Minutes, 21 Oct. 1789.
84. Ravensbergen, "Courtrooms of Conflict," 130.
85. Chinese Council Minutes, 9 Mar. 1849.
86. Chinese Council Minutes, 4 Mar. 1834.
87. Chinese Council Minutes, 1 May 1846.
88. Chinese Council Minutes, 1 May 1846.
89. Chinese Council Minutes, 25 June 1847.
90. Chinese Council Minutes, 9 May 1845.
91. Chinese Council Minutes, 4 May 1827.

3. DIVORCE AND WOMEN'S AGENCY

1. See the appendix for more technical details about how I coded these cases for analysis.
2. Maurice Freedman studied the Chinese of Singapore for the period 1946–51. From 1948 to 1951, he notes that between 500 and 1,000 family disputes were handled by the colonial Department of Social Welfare, out of which between 75 and 143 divorces were granted—what must have been a very small proportion of total Chinese marriages per year. No study was made of who inititiated the plea for dissolution. Freedman suggests that the majority of divorces were filed by secondary wives. This was very different from the situation in nineteenth-century Java, where secondary wives went unregistered and did not appear in any of the divorce pleas. See Freedman, *Chinese Family and Marriage in Singapore*, 176–89.
3. Chü, *Law and Society in Traditional China*, 118.
4. Theiss, *Disgraceful Matters*, esp. 65–81.
5. Djamour, *Malay Kinship and Marriage in Singapore*, 110–17; Geertz, *Javanese Family*, 69–73.
6. Raffles, *History of Java*, 320.
7. Raffles, *History of Java*, 318.
8. Yahaya, *Fluid Jurisdictions*, 35.
9. Pijper, *Studiën over de geschiedenis van de Islam in Indonesia*, 68–73.
10. Pijper, *Studiën*, 68–70.
11. The two secretaries would have sat in the two chairs in front of the table. When in session, they were most likely placed behind the table but still facing each other.
12. Chinese Council Minutes, 2 July 1874.
13. Chinese Council Minutes, 1 Oct. 1874. The assistant resident's letter was copied here.

14. Chinese Council Minutes, 16 Oct. 1874.

15. Djamour researched the Singapore Muslim marriage registry since 1921. It showed that half of marriages consistently ended in divorce. Her comparative registry data from elsewhere in Malaya and Java, although capturing only the trends in the 1940s, revealed similar patterns of divorce rates, ranging from 40 to 60 percent. Djamour, *Malay Kinship and Marriage in Singapore*, 117, 134–40. For Pare, a secondary town in East Java, the divorce rate fluctuated between 45 and 73 percent from the 1920s to the 1950s, although for one decade (1930s), it was 16.4 percent. See Geertz, *Javanese Family*, 69.

16. See the appendix for my tabulation of divorce records. These figures need to be qualified in three ways. First, marriage registration was nowhere near universal, even at its peak in the mid-nineteenth century. Second, since the 1880s, there was clearly a decline in the perceived authority of both the Chinese officers and the colonial state to sanction marriages, as the rate of marriage registration fell even as the population continued to grow. Marriages registered per year declined from a peak of 182 in the 1870s, to 150 in the 1880s, to 112 in the 1890s, while the Chinese population in Batavia grew from 52,416 in 1870, to 73,224 in 1880, to 78,925 in 1890, to 89,064 in 1900. Boomgaard and Gooszen, *Population Trends*, 127, 135.

Third, the figures for the 1880s are problematic and should probably be discounted as an aberration. Council minutes survived for only two of the ten years and were less methodically kept compared to previous decades.

17. The actual figures must be higher, since legal marriages were limited to the middle class. For these figures, I assume universal marriage among the adult Chinese population of Batavia for the years 1857 and 1864, whose population figures are from the annual *Koloniale Rapport*. The annual reports stopped counting children after the 1860s.

18. Civil law divorce was first made available in England in 1857. The divorce rate grew from 0.92 to 1.93 per 100,000 married population between 1857 and 1909. For the United States, the rates were 47 (1887) and 86 (1909) per 100,000. See Savage, "Operation of the 1857 Divorce Act, 1860–1910," 104. For Shanghai, refer to Bernhardt 1994, 301n1, cited in Mann, *Gender and Sexuality in Modern Chinese History*, 75.

19. See the appendix in this volume.

20. See Kuo, *Intolerable Cruelty*.

21. Geertz, *Javanese Family*, 79.

22. Statistics recorded only for the 1870s. See Gooszen, "Marriage Market for Chinese Girls in Batavia."

23. Chinese Council Minutes, 27 Nov. 1873.

24. Chinese Council Minutes, 25 June 1847.

25. Chinese Council Minutes, 21 Feb. 1868.

26. See figures for "coolies" in Dros, *Wages: 1820–1940*, 50–61.

27. The sole reference to rental price mentioned ƒ5 per month for a kampong house. See Chinese Council Minutes, 27 Nov. 1873.

28. Chinese Council Minutes, 21 Jan. 1859.

29. Chinese Council Minutes, 19 Dec. 1845.

30. Chinese Council Minutes, 22 July 1864.

31. See Chinese Council Minutes, 17 Dec. 1847, 7 Dec. 1849.

32. Chinese Council Minutes, 9 July 1858.

33. Chinese Council Minutes, 9 July 1858. The Sieuw Nio had complained that her husband Ong Hai Goan did not rent a house and only paid her half a gulden a month. Ong Hai Goan acknowledged, "I am poor. I work as a coolie, for which I am paid ƒ10 a month. I pay her half a gulden a week, which is hardly enough to keep us fed, not to mention pay for rent."

34. For the working-class men, see the cases of a temple administrator, a duck farm worker, an extremely poor man, and an unemployed man in Chinese Council Minutes, 17 Dec. 1847; 10 Oct. 1855; 26 June 1862; and 27 May 1864, respectively. For wealthier men, usually traders, see Chinese Council Minutes, 29 Jan. 1847; 1 Aug. 1855; 31 Oct. 1856; 30 Dec. 1859; and 11 Jan. 1860.

35. Chinese Council Minutes, 17 Dec. 1847.

36. See twenty-three cases in Chinese Council Minutes, 5 Sept. 1845; 29 Jan. 1847; 17 Dec. 1847; 30 Mar. 1849; 12 Oct. 1849; 23 June 1853; 19 Jan. 1855; 8 Jan. 1855; 10 Oct. 1855; 4 Aug. 1854; 19 Jan. 1855; 24 Feb. 1857; 11 Nov. 1858; 30 Dec. 1859; 26 June 1863; 9 July 1858; 20 Apr. 1860; 11 Mar. 1864; 15 July 1864; 21 Jan. 1870; 19 Apr. 1872; 14 Nov. 1873; and 27 Nov. 1873.

37. Chinese Council Minutes, 12 Oct. 1849.

38. This figure is based on declarations made by 92 out of the 135 divorce applicants, who mentioned the duration of abandonment by their husbands.

39. Chinese Council Minutes, 30 Jan. 1851 and 15 Jan. 1852. Kong Hor refused to accept the verdict. The case was then sent to the resident, who followed the officers' advice to approve the divorce.

40. Chinese Council Minutes, 11 Mar. 1864.

41. Chinese Council Minutes, 11 Mar. 1864.

42. See, for instance, the cases in Chinese Council Minutes, 6 Aug. 1894, and 27 Aug. 1894.

43. Chinese Council Minutes, 31 Oct. 1856.

44. Chinese Council Minutes, 30 Oct. 1869.

45. Chinese Council Minutes, 29 June 1876.

46. Chinese Council Minutes, 19 June 1891.

47. Chinese Council Minutes, 27 Aug. 1894.

48. Chinese Council Minutes, 13 June 1843.

49. Chinese Council Minutes, 30 Aug. 1872.

50. Chinese Council Minutes, 19 Apr. 1844; 9 July 1852; 7 Oct. 1859; 16 Dec. 1863; and 10 Aug. 1876.

51. Chinese Council Minutes, 19 Dec. 1845; 7 Mar. 1856; and 26 June 1863.

52. Chinese Council Minutes, 16 Dec. 1863; 4 Nov. 1864; 3 Feb. 1871; 28 Dec. 1871; 19 Apr. 1872; and 30 Dec. 1873.

53. Chinese Council Minutes, 18 Dec. 1846; 26 Mar. 1858; 11 Nov. 1858; 7 Oct. 1859; 26 June 1863; 16 Dec. 1863; 16 Sept. 1863; 7 Oct. 1859; and 28 Sept. 1894.

54. Chinese Council Minutes, 18 Dec. 1846.

55. Chinese Council Minutes, 25 Apr. 1856; 22 July 1864; 23 Mar. 1870; and 14 Oct. 1872. The other two cases involved the more conventional men who left to seek work and never returned. See Chinese Council Minutes, 20 May 1864 and 14 Nov. 1873.

56. Chinese Council Minutes, 23 Mar. 1870.

57. Chinese Council Minutes, 25 Apr. 1856; 22 July 1864; and 14 Oct. 1872.

58. Chinese Council Minutes, 14 Nov. 1873.

59. Respectively, the cases appeared in this order: Chinese Council Minutes, 22 Dec. 1857; 7 Oct. 1859; 5 Jan. 1866; 28 Dec. 1871; and 27 Aug. 1894.

60. Freedman, *Chinese Family and Marriage in Singapore*, 57.

61. Reid, *Southeast Asia in the Age of Commerce*, 1:146.

62. Reid, *Age of Commerce*, 1:151.

63. Reid, *Age of Commerce*, 1:147.

64. See cases in Chinese Council Minutes, 15 Dec. 1843; 5 June 1846; 2 Apr. 1847; 17 Dec. 1847; 7 Dec. 1849; 8 Dec. 1854; 25 Apr. 1856; 15 Jan. 1857; 15 Apr. 1859; 12 Feb. 1859; 20 Apr. 1860; 18 May 1860; and 26 Mar. 1870.

65. Chinese Council Minutes, 14 Nov. 1862.
66. Chinese Council Minutes, 23 Mar. 1860.
67. Chinese Council Minutes, 16 Sept. 1863.
68. Chinese Council Minutes, 15 Jan. 1857.
69. Chinese Council Minutes, 17 Dec. 1847.
70. Hsieh, *Concubinage and Servitude in Late Imperial China*, 41–94.
71. Theiss, *Disgraceful Matters*, 65–81.
72. Only two of the native concubines (from the 1840s–1850s) were accorded the "nyai" appellation. Chinese Council Minutes, 2 Sept. 1846 and 4 June 1852. For the properly recognized native concubines, they were most likely referred to either as nyai or perhaps even as *bini muda*, a term also used to refer to Chinese concubines.
73. Chinese Council Minutes, 14 Nov. 1845.
74. Hsieh, *Concubinage and Servitude*, 18.
75. Chinese Council Minutes, 9 Feb. 1846.
76. Chinese Council Minutes, 15 May 1851.
77. Chinese Council Minutes, 6 July 1849.
78. Chinese Council Minutes, 24 May 1844; 6 July 1849; 23 Apr. 1852; 31 Mar. 1854; 27 July 1860; and 17 Mar. 1865.
79. Chinese Council Minutes, 17 Mar. 1865.
80. Chinese Council Minutes, 31 Mar. 1854 and 21 Nov. 1862.
81. Chinese Council Minutes, 21 Nov. 1862.
82. Chinese Council Minutes, 24 May 1844.
83. Chinese Council Minutes, 15 May 1851.
84. Chinese Council Minutes, 21 Nov. 1862.
85. For the cases involving native concubines co-residing at home, see Chinese Council Minutes, 15 Dec. 1843; 2 Sept. 1846; 12 May 1848; 23 Apr. 1852; 4 June 1852; 29 Dec. 1854; 21 Apr. 1863; 11 Oct. 1867; 19 Jan. 1870; 17 Nov. 1871; and 5 June 1896. For the cases involving those living outside the home, see Chinese Council Minutes, 29 Dec. 1847; 10 Sept. 1852; 12 May 1865; 11 Oct. 1867; and 26 Feb. 1868.
86. Chinese Council Minutes, 15 Dec. 1843.
87. Chinese Council Minutes, 20 Apr. 1860.
88. Chinese Council Minutes, 11 Oct. 1867.
89. Chinese Council Minutes, 2 Sept. 1846. The concubine was addressed elsewhere as "Second Nyai."
90. Chinese Council Minutes, 17 Nov. 1871.
91. De Sturler, appendix, 135, cited in Josh Stenberg, *Minority Stages: Sino-Indonesian Performance and Public Display* (Honolulu: University of Hawai'i Press, 2019), 25.
92. Stenberg, *Minority Stages*, 25.
93. Chinese Council Minutes, 18 May 1847.
94. Chinese Council Minutes, 30 Dec. 1864.
95. Chinese Council Minutes, 24 Sept. 1858.
96. Chinese Council Minutes, 30 Dec. 1864.
97. Chinese Council Minutes, 4 Nov. 1864
98. Chinese Council Minutes, 16 Sept. 1863.
99. Chinese Council Minutes, 17 Mar. 1862.

4. WOMEN'S WEALTH AND MATRIARCHAL STRATEGIES

1. Skinner, "Creolized Chinese Societies in Southeast Asia," 62–63.
2. Goody, *Development of the Family and Marriage in Europe*, 225–27.
3. Skinner, "Creolized Chinese Societies in Southeast Asia," 62–63.

4. Wolf, *Women and the Family in Rural Taiwan*, 33. I thank Shelly Chan for this reference and for introducing me to the concept of the uterine family.

5. Chinese Council Minutes, 7 June 1861.

6. Chinese Council Minutes, 22 Feb. 1865.

7. "Oeij Kioksoei (1861-6)," Boedelpapieren (hereafter BP) 5411, Arsip Wees- en Boedelkamer, 1819-1937, Arsip Nasional Republik Indonesia, Jakarta (hereafter WBK, ANRI).

8. By the time he died on 13 Dec. 1871, one son and one daughter had attained majority. His testament (30 June 1863) can be found in "Tan Tjoeijseeng (1872-7)," BP 2719, WBK, ANRI.

9. See "Lim Thiang Seng" BP 5414, WBK, ANRI.

10. "The Tjoen Sek," BP 7698, WBK, ANRI.

11. Van der Chijs, "Aansprakelijkheid eener Chinesche vrouw voor de schulden van haren echtgenoot," 130-32.

12. Staatsblad 1855, no. 79, art. 2.

13. Chinese Council Minutes, 14 July 1848.

14. Chinese Council Minutes, 22 Nov. 1850. These cases had been referred to the Chinese Council by the landraad.

15. Chinese Council Minutes, 16 Sept. 1863.

16. See cases in Chinese Council Minutes, 1864 and 1869-70. For these years, loans were mainly in the $f1,000$–$f4,000$ range, with a minority in the $f4000$–$f10,000$ range. For more on this community credit association, see Chen, *De Chinese gemeenschap*, 117-21.

17. Chinese Council Minutes, 2 Aug. 1869.

18. Chinese Council Minutes, 11 Nov. 1864.

19. Tjiook-Liem, *De rechtspositie der Chinezen*, 155.

20. "Tan Ahoen (1875)," BP 2757, WBK, ANRI. For other merchants who died in debt, left nothing for their widows, and only had daughters and no sons, see "Tjiam Yoeseng (1876)," BP 6432, WBK, ANRI; "Tan Gioktat (1854-6)," BP 2584, WBK, ANRI.

21. "Tan Ginko (1854-1866)," BP 900, WBK, ANRI.

22. Unfortunately, with a few exceptions, the archivists at the Arsip Nasional Republik Indonesia have not been able to find most of the female probate files listed in the catalog. My analysis is thus limited to the following twelve cases heard at the Chinese Council. See Chinese Council Minutes, 19 Apr. 1844; 21 Apr. 1848; 8 June 1849; 6 July 1849; 26 Apr. 1850; 18 Oct. 1850; 22 Nov. 1850; 17 Dec. 1852; 18 Jan. 1856; 24 Aug. 1860; 17 Mar. 1862; and 10 July 1862.

23. This exception in fact reinforces the general rule. In this case, Lie Soen Nio had been abandoned by her husband for eighteen years. She left the house she bought with lottery winnings to her sister. The husband sued to recover the property but was denied by the officers for he "no longer followed Chinese customs, when he lived with his concubine in Padang, abandoning his wife to suffer alone in Batavia." Chinese Council Minutes, 10 July 1862.

24. Chinese Council Minutes, 8 June 1869.

25. For an authoritative, if dense, reconstruction of the legislative and jurisprudential twists and turns of Dutch Indies Chinese family and nationality law, see Tjiook-Liem, *De rechtspositie der Chinezen*.

26. Sharafi, *Law and Identity in Colonial South Asia*, 138.

27. Claver and Thomas, "Going Bankrupt?," 140.

28. NHM Factorij to Wichers, 9 July 1847, inv. 2.10.02, 621; MR 17 July 1857, no. 30, Archief Ministerie van Koloniën 1850-1900, Nationaal Archief (hereafter AMK, NA).

29. NHM Factorij to Wichers, 9 July 1847.

30. See *Burgerlijk Wetboek voor Nederlandsch-Indië*, title 6, bk. 1 (Persons); *Wetboek van Koophandel voor Nederlandsch-Indië*, art. 866.

31. NHM Factorij to Wichers, 9 July 1847.

32. Staatsblad 1855, no. 79, chap. 2, art. 2.

33. Kuiper, "Early Dutch Sinologists," 11–13.

34. The Dutch sinologists brought their Chinese mandarin tutors—imperial provincial examination graduates—to the Indies to serve as personal secretaries throughout their translation and advisory careers. See the biographies of the sinologists in Kuiper, "Early Dutch Sinologists," 828–945.

35. Mulock Houwer (director of justice) to governor-general, 26 Sept. 1896, in Fromberg, "Nieuwe regeling van den privaatrechte-lijken toestand der Chineezen," 129.

36. Tjiook-Liem, *De rechtspositie der Chinezen*, 218.

37. Under the governorship of Reijner de Klerk (1777–80), the secretary of the alderman's court Pieter Haksteen compiled a compendium of Chinese law for the use of Dutch colonial courts. This was still circulating and sometimes cited in the nineteenth century. In 1849, it was republished as "Chineesch regt" in *Het regt van Nederlandsch-Indië* (hereafter *HRNI*), vol. 2 (1849), 311–47.

38. College van Boedelmeesteren in Batavia to Wichers, Batavia, 29 Sept. 1847, inv. 2.10.02, 621; MR 17 July 1857, no. 30, AMK, NA.

39. See also Kuiper, *Early Dutch Sinologists*, 538–47.

40. "Wettelijke bepalingen omtrent de huwelijken in China en beschrijving der daartoe gebruikelijke plegtigheden," *HRNI*, vol. 20 (1862), 394–408, citation from 394. He would later become the first professor of sinology at Leiden University (1877–1902).

41. "Wettelijke bepalingen," 405.

42. G. Schlegel, "Chineesch regt: Iets over Chinesche testamenten, donatiën en erfopvolging," *HRNI*, vol. 20 (1862), 372.

43. "Berigten van deskundigen" [D: Reports from the experts], *Indisch weekblad van het recht* (hereafter *IWR*), no. 142 (1866).

44. "Berigten van deskundigen," *IWR*, no. 154 (1866).

45. He was asked to review if "according to inheritance laws valid in China, children inherited without distinction of sex from their father and if so by what proportions." See W. P. Groeneveldt, Lie Hoet Seng, and Lie A-Lim, "Rapport van deskundigen" [D: Experts' reports] (24 Sept. 1877), in "The Pitnio ca. the Tianseng en the Wantjiang," *HRNI*, vol. 30 (1878), 384–94.

46. Groeneveldt, Lie & Lie, "Rapport van deskundigen," 388–89.

47. Groeneveldt to Minister van Kolonien, March 6, 1877, inv. 2.10.02, 3000; MR 16 June 1877, no. 44, AMK, NA.

48. P. Meeter, "De regtstoestand der Chineesche vrouw" [The legal status of the Chinese woman], *HRNI*, vol. 32 (1879), 345–73, citation from 371.

49. Meeter, "De regtstoestand," 349.

50. The draft law was published some thirty years later in Fromberg, "Nieuwe regeling van den privaatrechte-lijken toestand der Chineezen."

51. Fromberg, "Nieuwe regeling," 221.

52. Fromberg, "Nieuwe regeling," 221–22.

53. Fromberg, "Nieuwe regeling," 221–22.

54. Fromberg, "Nieuwe regeling," 222.

55. "Tan Paginio ca. Lim Eng Tjay," *IWR*, no. 1222 (1886).

56. Faber, *Het familie- en erfrecht der Chineezen in Nederlandsch-Indië*, 36–37.

57. For Van Heeckeren's career in Java, see Post, "Profitable Partnerships." For his position on Chinese law in Java, see Van Heeckeren, *Beschouwingen over het voor Chineezen op Java geldende recht*.

58. "Tan Pa Ginio ca. Liem Tiang Keng," *IWR*, no. 1464 (1891).
59. "Tan Pa Ginio ca. Liem Tiang Keng," *IWR*, no. 1464 (1891).
60. "Tan Pa Ginio ca. Liem Tiang Keng," *HRNI*, vol. 58 (1892).
61. In 1876, he researched the legislative history of the 1855 Staatsblad no. 79 to show that the legislators had proposed to include an extra clause to guarantee the married woman's freedom to contract, although this would not be included in the final version of the law. Trip, "Vraagpunten, mededeelingen en bermerkingen van verschillenden aard, betreffende Nederlandsch-Indisch regt," *HRNI*, vol. 27 (1876), 65–96, esp. 88–89.
62. "Tan Pa Ginio ca. Liem Tiang Keng," *IWR*, no. 1464 (1891).
63. Goody, *Development of the Family*, 225–27.
64. Haryono, *Perkawinan strategis*, 80.
65. See *Soerabaijasch handelsblad*, 22 July 1882; *De locomotief: Samarangsch handels- en advertentie-blad*, 7 June 1888.
66. As nephew and son-in-law, Oeij Tjiang Piauw was in a way an agent for Oeij Gin Nio. For instance, in July 1864, when there was a dispute over the inheritance of Ong Boen Seng's elder brother (by the primary wife), Kapitan Ong Boen Hien, Oeij Gin Nio did not trust her own younger son but sent instead Oeij Tjiang Piauw to present her testimony before the Chinese Council. Chinese Council Minutes, 1 July 1864.
67. Oeij Tjiang Piauw to Collegie van Boedelmeesteren, 28 Feb. 1881, 20 Aug. 1881, BP 1746: Ong Boen Seng, WBK, ANRI.
68. Oeij Tjiang Piauw to Collegie van Boedelmeesteren, 20 Aug. 1881, BP 1746: Ong Boen Seng, WBK, ANRI.
69. The estate had been awarded to Boen Seng's two sons born by two secondary wives. There was no indication that the three wives of Boen Seng were going to contest the estate among themselves. The probate court most likely instigated Boen Seng's primary wife to claim the estate for her two daughters to the exclusion of his sons by two secondary wives, in accordance with Dutch policy to apply Dutch inheritance law in intestacy cases. In the trial, Kapitan Oeij testified in favor of both of Boen Seng's sons. See BP 1746: Ong Boen Seng, WBK, ANRI, and "Lim Kwie Nio etc. ca. Ong Doortje Nio, College van Boedelmeesteren" (Landraad Batavia, October 17, December 19, 1881), *HRNI*, vol. 40 (1883), 229–41.
70. The probate court was first informed by a son-in-law of Ong Kwie Nio. See Kapitan Liem Tjiong Hien to College van Boedelmeesteren in Batavia, August 7, 1883, BP 1746: Ong Boen Seng, WBK, ANRI.
71. P. Meeter saw how "the management of their legacies by the probate courts . . . [was] a thorn in the eye" and how marriages were arranged for "barely adult" children so that they might immediately assume legal adulthood and prevent probate intervention. See Meeter, "De regtstoestand," 369.
72. Lie Pektat to College van Boedelmeesteren, 22 May 1884, BP 7262: Ong Boen Seng, WBK, ANRI.
73. Note on Kapitan Lim Tjong Hien's letter to College van Boedelmeesteren, 7 Aug. 1883, BP 1746: Ong Boen Seng WBK, ANRI.
74. BP 1746: Ong Boen Seng, WBK, ANRI; "Ong Kwi Nio ca. De Weeskamer te Batavia," *IWR*, no. 1236 (1887).
75. At the time of the loan, Ong Boen Seng had already mortgaged five-sixths (f515,000) the total value of the lands he had inherited from his father. Shortly thereafter, he stood as a guarantor for Thung Siong Kie, Chinese lieutenant of Buitenzorg, for two consignments of goods (most likely opium) worth f112,648 from the Batavia-based Scottish firm Maclaine Watson and Co. Had Thung defaulted, Ong Boen Seng, as surety, would have gone bankrupt. The fictitious mortgage gave his sister about a one-half share claim to his total debt (entire estate).

76. "Ong Kwi Nio ca. De Weeskamer," 42.
77. "Weeskamer te Batavia ca. Ong Kwee Nio" (Supreme Court, October 10, 1889), *HRNI*, vol. 53 (1889), 403–21, quote on 420.
78. "Weeskamer te Batavia ca. Ong Kwee Nio," 419.
79. "Ong Kwie Nio en Oeij Gen Nio, 1899," BP 4240, WBK, ANRI.
80. Interview with Sioe Yao Kan, 26 June 2016. See also S. Y. Kan, "Kan Keng Tjong en Jo Heng Nio," Kan Han Tan Chinees Indische Peranakan Families, updated May 2022, www.kanhantan.nl/13kan_keng_tjong.html.
81. In 1887, Jo Heng Nio was on record as the third largest Chinese landowner. Jo Heng Nio's lands were worth ƒ1.3 million compared with Khouw Oen Djioe's ƒ4.1 million and Lie Tjoe Hong's ƒ1.7 million. See *Handboek voor cultuur- en handelsondernemingen in Nederlandsch-Indië*. Measured by their taxable (which was often also the resale) value—the *verpondingswaarde*—Chinese owned consistently more than half of all private lands.
82. For Kan Keng Tiong's succession plan, see "Jo Heng Nio, Kan Tjeng Sie en Kan Tjeng Soen ca. Lim Kong Koen, Lim Mok Gie en Lim Mok Soen," *IWR*, no. 697 (1876).
83. *De Sumatra post*, 12 Dec. 1900, 5.
84. *Java-bode*, 30 Oct. 1954.

5. CONFUCIANISM, MARRIAGE, AND SEXUALITY

1. Williams, *Overseas Chinese Nationalism*; Skinner, "Creolized Chinese Societies in Southeast Asia."
2. Coppel, "From Christian Mission to Confucian Religion."
3. Coppel, "From Christian Mission to Confucian Religion," 306.
4. "Soerat kiriman kapada sekalian bangsa Tjina, terkirim oleh lid-lid pengoeroes dari pakoempoelan 'Tiong Hoa Hwe Koan' di Batavia (1900)" [M: A letter to all among the Chinese race, sent by the managing committee members of the group "Tiong Hoa Hwe Koan" in Batavia], reproduced in Nio, *Riwajat 40 Taon dari Tiong Hoa Hwe Koan*, appendix A, 201–3.
5. "Soerat kiriman kapada sekalian bangsa Tjina," 201. These are the four neo-Confucian classics. The latter two books refer to parts 1 and 2 of the *Analects*.
6. "Soerat kiriman kapada sekalian bangsa Tjina," 201.
7. The Dutch translation was by Keijzer (*De heilige boeken der Chinezen, of de vier klassieke boeken van Confucius en Mencius*). Sutrisno, "Moral Is Political," 196–97.
8. Lie, *Hikayat Khonghoetjoe*, 87; Keijzer, *De heilige boeken der Chinezen*, lx.
9. Echols and Shadily, *Kamus Indonesia Inggris*, 91.
10. Liu, "Creolised Confucianism," 166. I find Liu's claim that the pair "developed a synthesized interpretation of Christianity, pantheism, and Arabic and Sinitic concepts and religious vocabulary under the label of Confucianism" to have gone too far. The only sign of Arabic is in the use of "Allah" to translate to "God," an appropriation long established by Christian missionaries in the region, not by the Chinese themselves.
11. Yoe Tjai Siang, "Thian To," in *Kitab Tai Hak—Tiong Iong*, by Tan Ging Tiong and Yoe Tjai Siang, 107–8.
12. "Soerat kiriman kapada sekalian bangsa Tjina," 202. The other mission was the creation of schools devoted to the Chinese language and modern forms of knowledge.
13. Williams, *Overseas Chinese Nationalism*, 59–60. To make this claim, Williams cites Kwee, *Origins of the Modern Chinese Movement in Indonesia*. The sinicizing tendency was evident in the reformers' recommendation for ending the practice of "filing the teeth," which was seen to be a "thing for the native race," and "readying the bride" with herbs for ingestion and body-scrubbing, which was deemed "bad for . . . health." See Kwee, *Origins*, 48–52. See also Skinner, "Creolized Chinese Societies in Southeast Asia," esp. 85–93.

14. Young, *Het huwelijk en de wetgeving hierop in China*, 4.

15. Both Dutch and Malay versions were published by Albrecht & Rusche of Batavia in 1894.

16. As for the Chinese in the Indies, whether they were "European" or "Native" depended on the "assessment of the general state of civilization in their country, not the religion of each individual . . . , but *the religion of the majority of natives in the country.*" This refers to China and not the Indies (emphasis in the original). Faber, *Het familie- en erfrecht der Chineezen in Nederlandsch-Indië*, 23.

17. Most likely in tandem with their rites reform project, both men collaborated in the translation into Malay of the *Classic of Filial Piety* (*Hauw King*) in 1901. Unfortunately, this translation has not survived. It was reported in the second issue of *Li Po* in 1901. See Coppel, "Origins of Confucianism as an Organized Religion in Java," note 29.

18. Ahmat Adam, *Vernacular Press and the Emergence of Modern Indonesian Consciousness*, 76.

19. In 1904, branches were formed with Batavia's approval in Malang, Pemalang, Pasuruan, Pekalongan, Bogor, Jombang, Bandung, Tangerang, Cianjur, and Solo on Java, and even Kuala Lumpur in British Malaya. The movement reached its peak in 1905-7, when new branches were organized in Tanah-Abang, Indramayu, Palembang (Sumatra), Purbolinggo, Serang, Banjermasin (Borneo), Muntok (Bangka), Sukaraja, Sumedang, Cilacap, Purwokerto, and Belinyu (Bangka). See Nio, *Riwajat 40 Taon dari Tiong Hoa Hwee Koan*, 147-68.

20. "Reproduction of the work of the Commission to rule on the celebration of marriage in the THHK building (28.10.1906)," reproduced in Nio, *Riwajat 40 Taon dari THHK*, appendix D, 208, no. 4-5.

21. "Reproduction of the work of the Commission," no. 3.

22. Kwee Tek Hoay, *Origins of the Modern Chinese Movement in Indonesia*, 56.

23. Williams, *Overseas Chinese Nationalism*, 59.

24. Kwee Tek Hoay, *Origins*, 57.

25. Nio, *Riwajat 40 Taon dari THHK*, 124.

26. Nio, *Riwajat*, 131.

27. See the first entry for 1912 in "Marriage Registry, Batavia Chinese Council, 1772-1919," Leiden University Library. It is likely that more parents were choosing to arrange their children's marriage personally than rely on the go-between.

28. Anderson, *Imagined Communities*. For Indonesia, see Ahmat Adam, *Vernacular Press*.

29. Reyes, *Love, Passion and Patriotism*.

30. Ahmat Adam, *Vernacular Press*, 22-25, 31-33.

31. In 1886, Tjoa Tjoan Lok, from the wealthy and politically connected Tjoa family in Surabaya, took over *Bintang Timur*, renamed it *Bintang Surabaya*, and turned it into a Chinese-oriented newspaper in the Indies. Some Chinese takeovers or new ventures were transient; Sie Hian Ling's *Tamboor Melayoe* (founded 1888) in Semarang, Lie Kim Hok's *Pembrita Betawi* (f. 1886-87), and Yap Goan Ho's *Sinar Terang* (f. 1888) and *Chabar Berdagang* (1894) in Batavia did not last more than a year before they closed or were resold. Oeij Tjai Hin's *Bintang Barat* (f. 1893) and the Sie Hian Ling-edited *Bintang Semarang* (f. early 1900s) lasted longer. See Ahmat Adam, *Vernacular Press*, 67-69.

32. Ahmat Adam, *Vernacular Press*, 44-45.

33. Adam, *Vernacular Press*, 75.

34. Adam, *Vernacular Press*, 75-77.

35. See their biographies in Salmon, *Literature in Malay by the Chinese of Indonesia*, 147-372.

36. Salmon, *Literature in Malay*, 300.

37. Salmon, *Literature in Malay*, 310–11. Tan never received formal education. As a bank clerk, he would have known some Dutch. But his journalism, political speech-giving, and fiction writing were self-taught.
38. For Kwee Hing Tjiat, see Salmon, *Literature in Malay*, 201. Hauw has no entry in Salmon's annotated bibliography.
39. This was before his better-known stint at the helm of *Sin Po* from 1919 to 1925. Salmon, *Literature in Malay*, 360–61.
40. Salmon, *Literature in Malay*, 331–32.
41. Its wide circulation must have been the cause of an attack on such lewd advertisements.
42. *Java-bode*, 30 Sept. 1895.
43. Butatuli and Hemeling, *Boekoe Wet dan Rasia tentang Perhoeboengan antara Prampoean dan Lelaki atawa pengatahoean hal bagi Kamanoesiaan*).
44. A self-made son of Batavia, Lauw was single-handedly brought up by his widowed mother, who had to do needlework to raise him. He attended a private Dutch primary school and worked for a while for the previously mentioned Van Dorp, the printer-publisher of the newspaper *Java-bode* and importer of the Dutch sexual hygiene literature from the Netherlands. I made this conjecture based on his exposure to *Java-bode* and Van Dorp and the fact that he was one of the most prolific translators from Dutch to Malay in the early 1910s. The Indo-European play he translated into Malay (*Karina-Adinda*) was also published in the same year (1913). For his biography, see Salmon, *Literature in Malay*, 223–24. Hemeling might have been his journalist wife Lie On Moy (1884–?). See Salmon, *Literature in Malay*, 233.
45. *Orang perempoean haroes tahoe: boeat goenanja siapa jang ingin djadi beroentoeng, senang dan sehat* (original title in Malay). Place, publisher, and year of publication unknown. According to its place in the genre and the style of the publication, I estimate that it was published around 1916.
46. Gouw, *Penghidoepan laki-istri* (original title in Malay).
47. Gouw, *Perniaga'an Prempoean dan anak-anak Prempoeana* (original title in Malay).
48. For purity crusades in Europe, see Clark, *Desire*, 142–61.
49. Gouw, *Penghidoepan laki-istri*, 8, 10.
50. Gouw, *Penghidoepan laki-istri*, 1.
51. Lauw took "Laws" from the original Hebrew title of the work, whereas the French translated version only retained "Mysteries." See Weill, *Les Mystères de l'amour*, 7.
52. Butatuli and Hemeling, *Wet dan Rasia*, 5–6.
53. Butatuli and Hemeling, *Wet dan Rasia*, 39.
54. Gouw, *Penghidoepan laki-istri*, 44.
55. Gouw, *Penghidoepan laki-istri*, 45.
56. Gouw, *Penghidoepan laki-istri*, 102.
57. Gouw, *Penghidoepan laki-istri*, 103.
58. Gouw, *Penghidoepan laki-istri*, 107.
59. Gouw, *Penghidoepan laki-istri*, 107.
60. See for instance Loe, "Sociale ellende en geboortebeperking."
61. See his foreword in the inaugural issue of *Maandblad istri*, no. 1 (1935): 1.
62. Loe, "Syphilis en zwangerschap bij Chineesche en Indonesische vrouwen."

6. LOVE, DESIRE, AND RACE

1. Salmon, *Literature in Malay by the Chinese of Indonesia*, 32–36.
2. Ming, "Barracks-Concubinage in the Indies," 52. Baay has the higher estimate, see *De njai*, 62.

3. Van der Lith and Snelleman, *Encyclopaedie van Nederlandsch-Indië*, 30. Besides indigenous Javanese, Sundanese, or Betawi women, a significant minority were Chinese and Japanese. As the housekeeper of a European, she was socially distinct from other Asian women. It became customary for the nyai "to exchange her colored or indigo kebaya for a white one and to wear slippers, the clothing symbolizing her new status and passage from the Indonesian to the halfway world of a bachelor-centered Indies society." See Taylor, *Social World of Batavia*, 147. In July 1858, a Chinese man sued his nyonya for divorce when he "saw her go out with two to three other nyai in a horse carriage, with a completely different [European] dressing style." See Chinese Council Minutes, 9 July 1858.

4. Cited in Ming, "Barracks-Concubinage in the Indies," 89.

5. Ming, "Barracks-Concubinage," 87.

6. Marle, "De groep der Europeanen in Nederlands-Indië, 322.

7. All three nyai-born Chinese sons were successful in defending their rights by demonstrating their fathers' public recognition, recognition by the surviving family in ancestral worshipping rites, or their parents' enduring relationship. See 1) "Oeij Kian Aij en Oeij Kian Tek ca. Weeskamer te Batavia, Ong Kek Nio," *HRNI*, vol. 100 (1913), 455–62; "Lie Tian Laij en Lie Tian Yoe ca. Weeskamer te Batavia (Lie Tian Hoei) (HooggerechtsHof van Nederlandsch-Indië, 24 June 1915)," *ITR*, no. 105 (1915): 278–93; "Tjoa Tjwan Bo ca. Tjoa Sien Tjing," *HRNI*, vol. 103 (1015), 346–59.

8. "Tjoa Tjwan Bo ca. Tjoa Sien Tjing," 358.

9. "Tjoa Tjwan Bo ca. Tjoa Sien Tjing," 358.

10. "Tjoa Tjwan Bo ca. Tjoa Sien Tjing," 358–59.

11. Gouw, *Tjerita jang betoel soeda kedjadian di Poelo Djawa*. (Original title in Malay.) Adapted from a news item, serialized in the same newspaper (*Bintang Betawi*) in April–May 1903, and finally published as a book that same year, the author, Gouw Peng Liang, was an assistant to the paper's editor. See Worsley, "Gouw Peng Liang's Novella, *Lo Fen Koei*," *Archipel* 68, no. 1 (2004): 87.

12. Go, *Tjerita Njonja Lim Pat Nio*, cover page. (Original title in Malay.)

13. Rush, *Opium to Java*, 217–41.

14. Gouw, *Tjerita jang betoel soeda kedjadian di Poelo Djawa*.

15. Go, *Tjerita Njonja Lim Pat Nio*, 4.

16. Tjoa, *Tjerita Lim Tjin Sioe*, 22. (Original title in Malay.)

17. Jones, Sulistyaningsih, and Hall, "Prostitution in Indonesia," 2–8.

18. Overbeck, "Malay Animal and Flower Shaers," 108–9.

19. Tan Kittjoan, *Saier mengimpie dan Saier boeroeng*, 29, 40. His *Syair mengimpie*, for instance, most likely represented a Chinese man's encounter with a girl of mixed origins (M: *moeda bastarie*) (11) and his attempt to court and keep her as a concubine: "My lady the best soother of pains / My love for you is exceedingly remarkable / If I don't keep [M: *piara*] you as my girl / In suffering, I will die; . . . My rose in the garden of the Dutch / Your flowers are blooming so beautifully / Desire [M: *Birahie*] fills my chest / because the devil entered to seduce me."

20. Maier, *We Are Playing Relatives*, 139.

21. Tjoa, *Tjerita Lim Tjin Sioe*, 13.

22. Go, *Tjerita Njonja Lim Pat Nio*, 11.

23. Tjoa, *Tjerita Lim Tjin Sioe*, 25

24. Oei, *Tjerita Njai Alimah*, 4–5.

25. Worsley, "Gouw Peng Liang's Novella, *Lo Fen Koei*," 255.

26. Tjoa, *Tjerita Lim Tjin Sioe*, 23.

27. Although not a writer himself, Tio belonged to the same Dutch-educated middle-class cosmopolitan milieu as many of the reformers. Attending a Dutch elementary school for ten years (1884–94) before the turn of the twentieth century, he opened a gramo-

phone records store in Pasar Baru, printed postcards of Batavia for tourists, and went hunting with Dutch friends.

28. Tio Tek Hong, *Keadaan Jakarta Tempo Doeloe*, 18–19.
29. Sie, *Tjerita "Yang Soen Sia,"* 11.
30. Sie, *Tjerita "Yang Soen Sia,"* 12.
31. Sie, *Tjerita "Yang Soen Sia,"* 17.
32. Sie, *Tjerita "Yang Soen Sia,"* 70.
33. *Tambahsia*. Although anonymously authored, it was most likely written by Thio Tjin Boen, who became well-known for his interethnic love stories. Thio, who was born in Pekalongan, which he used as the setting for his novels, had earlier authored a biography of the protagonist's father. See his *Cerita Oey Se*.
34. The murderous exploits of Oeij Hap Ho, alias Tambah, eventually led to his execution by the Dutch authorities in 1856. His legend lived on half a century later. In Dutch, "Dierlijke lusten," *Preanger-bode*, 29 Aug. 1900. In his telling, Tambah himself rejected all associations with the officers, for he "was not so stupid to become slave to the public, and to be in charge of the work of the Kong Koan." *Tambahsia*, 27.
35. *Tambahsia*, 15–18.
36. *Tambahsia*, 28.
37. According to Oeij Hap Ho's marriage certificate at the Batavia Chinese Council, he married with the approval of a paternal uncle and through a matchmaker. See his certificate dated 21 Nov. 1847 in the Kongkoan archives.
38. *Tambahsia*, 21.
39. *Tambahsia*, 22.
40. In a snub against the Kapitan elites, he obtained the Dutch resident's approval to stage a big monthlong Chinese wedding, which closed off an entire street in the Chinese quarter. He managed to override Major Tan Eng Goan's opposition by appealing directly to the assistant resident. *Tambahsia*, 33–34.
41. *Tambahsia*, 41.
42. *Tambahsia*, 41.
43. *Tambahsia*, 53.
44. Dumas, *La Dame aux camélias*, 3.
45. Dumas, *La Dame*, 3–4.
46. Lynn Pan points out that for contemporary China, where this story was likewise extremely popular, "in one respect, Marguerite could have been a Chinese character: at their most idealized, courtesans were glamorously romantic figures in Chinese life and lore, celebrated and adored by men of letters, especially by those who thought themselves men of taste and feeling." See Pan, *When True Love Came to China*, 91.
47. See Salmon, *Literature in Malay by the Chinese of Indonesia*, 529. Unfortunately, *Li Po* has not survived in any library or archive. For a paper regularly engaged in polemical debate with the Dutch Reformed Church, it would have been interesting to analyze Phoa's and the paper's Confucian moral stance on the issues of love marriage, premarital courtship, and sex raised in the novel.
48. Thio, *Sie Tjaij Kim*.
49. It was Claudine Salmon who first pointed out that the text was actually a liberal translational adaption of *Lady Camille*. See Salmon, *Literature in Malay by the Chinese of Indonesia*, 337.
50. Dumas, *Marguerite Gauthier*.
51. Two other undated adaptations were most likely published later on in the 1920s: Pouw Kioe An's play *Sedap malem* [Delicious night] and Terang Bulan's *Kecintaan dan penghidoepan* [Love and life], published in Gresik, East Java. See Salmon, *Literature in Malay by the Chinese of Indonesia*, 337, 529.

52. Siegel, *Fetish, Recognition, Revolution*, 115–33, esp. 117–18.
53. Siegel, *Fetish*, 119.
54. Hughes-Hallett, "The Beautiful Corpse," 97.
55. Dumas, *Lady of the Camellias*, 69.
56. Dumas, *Marguerite Gauthier*, 110; Thio, *Sie Tjaij Kim*, 78.
57. Pan, *When True Love Came to China*, 91.
58. See Thio, *Sie Tjaij Kim*, 221; Dumas, *Marguerite Gauthier*, 319. In religious scenes that cannot be avoided, such as when the priest administers the last rites to Marguerite, Tjan made it clear that they belonged to the religion of another nation. In this case, he explained in a footnote, "Christians of the Catholic group, to which most French belong, have the custom of confessing to a priest all sins [M: *dosa*] and wrongs they have committed in their lives, nearing death. This custom originates from the view that no one can enter Heaven before his soul [M: *batin*] was cleansed" (340).
59. Thio left untranslated two paragraphs on Armand's career and familial background. See Dumas, *Lady of the Camellias*, 119–20; Thio, *Sie Tjaij Kim*, 137. He mentioned very briefly in Kim Koan's voice, "My own shop was managed well because I held on to tough and correct rules, so that my employees did not dare to play the fool with me" (138–39).
60. Dumas, *Lady of the Camellias*, 116–17.
61. Thio, *Sie Tjaij Kim*, 132–33.
62. Dumas, *Marguerite Gauthier*, 192.
63. Dumas, *Lady of the Camellias*, 117; Dumas, *Marguerite Gauthier*, 194.
64. Oey Beng Liong, "Vrije huwelijkskeuze" [D: Free marriage choice], *Sin Po Wekelijksche Editie*, June 4, 1938, 27–28.
65. I base this comment on the observation by Nio Joe Lan, a Dutch-educated writer who wrote the authoritative history of the THHK schools in 1940. Nio wrote in 1934 that the THHK schools were no longer of social importance. The Chinese language stream was most likely surpassed in enrollment during the 1920s, although not by much. In 1934, it still had twelve thousand students on Java alone. See Govaars-Tjia, *Dutch Colonial Education*, 111.
66. Groeneboer, *Weg tot het Westen*, 486–87, cited in Govaars-Tija, *Dutch Colonial Education*, appendix D, 257.
67. A survey of Batavia's Chinese schools in 1940 found seven girls (1529) for every ten boys (2243) enrolled. See Govaars-Tjia, *Dutch Colonial Education*, 256, 262.
68. Kwee Thiam Tjing, *Menjadi Tjamboek Berdoeri*, 59.
69. Kwee, *Menjadi Tjamboek Berdoeri*, 60.
70. Kwee, *Menjadi Tjamboek Berdoeri*, 59.
71. Diary entry for Jan./Feb. 1922, *Dagboek Teddy Kan Hay An*, 3, www.kanhantan.nl/familiedocumenten/11teddy_kan_hay_an/dagboek_teddy_kan_hay_an.pdf.
72. Diary entry for April 1922, *Dagboek Teddy Kan Hay An*, 5.
73. Haryono, *Perkawinan strategis*.
74. Diary entry for December 1927, *Dagboek Teddy Kan Hay An*, 42.
75. They were also seated next to each other at his send-off party.
76. Diary entry for April 1924, *Dagboek Teddy Kan Hay An*, 14.
77. See also Post and Thio, *Kwee Family of Ciledug*, 45.
78. Kwee Seng Tjoan, *Model soerat soerat pertjintahan*, 1–2. It is also written for "young people when they turn adults, and become like a ship without a rudder, whenever they are not lucky enough to obtain another's love." Using these templates, the writer assured, "the lady will immediately be tamed (M: *djadi djinek*) and agree to marry the young man."
79. Kwee, *Model soerat soerat pertjintahan*, 3–24, quote on 17.
80. Salmon, *Literature in Malay by the Chinese of Indonesia*, 37.
81. Chandra, "Women and Modernity," 170–71.

82. Chabanneau, *Rasia Bandoeng atawa satu percinta-an yang melanggar peradatan bangsa Tiong Hoa*.

83. Phoa, *Tjhik Tjhik Boeng Nona Kampoeng atawa Rasianja Bogor Ngapoeng*; Sin, *Tjerita rasia-Soerabaja*; Yong, *Peroentoengan jang mengandoeng ratjoen atawa kesenangan membawa kasedian*.

84. Mimi, *Boenga Rajah atawa doea roepa kasenangan!*

85. Mimi, *Boenga Rajah*, 116.

86. Nemo, *Boekoe tjerita nona-nona dalem roesia*.

87. Nemo, *Boekoe tjerita nona-nona*, 54.

88. Nemo, *Boekoe tjerita nona-nona*, 55.

89. Nemo, *Boekoe tjerita nona-nona*, 29.

90. Nemo, *Boekoe tjerita nona-nona*, 58–59. The ending is unknown because in the only extant copy, the latter half of the book is missing.

91. Hauw, *Satoe djodo jang terhalang*.

92. For Tjoe's role in publicly leading the campaign to oppose compulsory service in the colonial militia (D: *Indies Weerbaar*) between 1916 and 1920, see Suryadinata, *Peranakan Chinese Politics in Java 1917–1942*, 34–38.

93. Hauw, *Satoe djodo jang terhalang*, 141.

94. Hauw, *Satoe djodo jang terhalang*, 160.

95. "Men who abandon their wives, take second wives and keep nyai are hardly criticized, whereas the slightest misdemeanor on the part of a woman is blown out of all proportion." Salmon, *Literature in Malay by the Chinese of Indonesia*, 57.

96. Hauw, *The Loan Eng*; Nio, *Sastera Indonesia-Tionghoa*, 30, 55; quote on 55.

97. Nio, *Sastera Indonesia-Tionghoa*, 73.

98. I base my analysis on Nio Joe Lan's summaries of their plots. Nio's account is mostly descriptive.

99. Ong Ping Lok, *Tjoema boeat satoe*.

100. Tan Boen Kim, *Gan Liang Boen*, 27.

101. See also Liem, *Manoesia*.

102. See synopsis in Nio, *Sastera Indonesia-Tionghoa*, 66–71.

103. *Maandblad istri*, September 1935, no. 1.

7. THE CIVILIZING GIFT OF MONOGAMY

1. Fromberg, "De Indo-Chineesche familie en de wetgeving," 584.

2. Hooker, "English Law and the Invention of Chinese Personal Law in Singapore and Malaysia."

3. Lewis, "Requiem for Chinese Customary Law in Hong Kong."

4. Fasseur, "Cornerstone and Stumbling Block"; Wertheim, "Political Status of the Chinese in Pre-war Netherlands Indies."

5. See Tjiook-Liem, "Feiten en ficties bij het ontstaan van de Japannerwet." In the heyday of high empires, European nations, especially civil law states like France and the Netherlands, ranked others by "a standard of civilization" based largely on the status of their domestic law. Japan was the first Asian nation to meet the standard of civilization in 1899, when it adopted a German-inspired civil code. These reforms ended European extraterritorial legal privileges in Japan and forced countries like the Netherlands to redesignate Japanese in the East Indies as "Europeans" in the colony's dualist legal system. See Becker Lorca, *Mestizo International Law*.

6. Williams, *Overseas Chinese Nationalism*, 165–6.

7. Ming, "Barracks-Concubinage in the Indies," esp. 55.

8. Baay, *De njai*, 163.

9. The previous 1848 legal hindrance was designed to discourage interracial unions. Note that its immediate context was the reformers' concern over the rising incidence of Eurasian women living in concubinage with Asian men. The patriarchal principle was meant to deter European women from marrying Asian men. See Stoler, "Sexual Affronts and Racial Frontiers."

10. Baay, *De njai*, 96–97, 173.

11. See Nederburgh, *Wetgeving voor Nederlandsch-Indië*.

12. Nederburgh, "Het Indisch-Chineezen recht der toekomst," 169.

13. Nederburgh, "Het Indisch Chineezen-Recht," 190.

14. Nederburgh, "Het Indisch Chineezen-Recht," 61.

15. Nederburgh, "Het Indisch Chineezen-Recht," 61–63.

16. Raad van Nederlandsch-Indië to Gov.-Gen, 8 Apr. 1904, 1900–1963, inv. 2.10.36.04, 276; MR 25 Oct. 1904, no. 11, AMK, NA. Citing Nederburgh's recommendations, the state council recommended that the only exemptions to be made were the provisions for adoptions and for the recognition of Chinese corporations (*kongsi*). The Chinese eventually benefited the most through a slew of associationist policies ranging from the provision of Dutch schools (1908), to the removal of residential and travel restrictions (1910s), to family law reform (1917–9). For education, see Govaars-Tjia, *Dutch Colonial Education*. For political representation, see Lohanda, *Growing Pains*.

17. Borel communicated his concern to the Department of Justice on 16 April 1912. Enclosed in 1901–1953, Openbare Verbalen, inv. 2.10.36.04, 991, Min. van Koloniën bundle, 19 Dec. 1912, AMK, NA.

18. Van Wettum, "Family- and Inheritance Law."

19. *Ontwerp eener regeling van den privaatrechtelijken toestand der Chineezen in Nederlandsch-Indië* [Draft of a regulation of the private legal status of the Chinese in Netherlands-Indië] (hereafter *Ontwerp Cordes/Heijman*), Batavia, 28 Mar. 1914, 2. Enclosed in 1900–63, Openbare Verbalen, inv. 2.10.36.04, 1487; MR 15 Dec. 1915, no. 13, AMK, NA.

20. See Van Wettum, "Family- and Inheritance Law," art. 1335.

21. *Ontwerp Cordes/Heijman*, 8.

22. *Ontwerp Cordes/Heijman*, 7–8.

23. In contrast, legislators in 1930s Republican China refused to deal with the longstanding practice of concubinage under the purview of bigamy law. They eventually compromised with the feminist lobby by treating concubinage under adultery law. See Tran, "Concubines under Modern Chinese Law," chap. 2.

24. This was done by amending Dutch civil law provisions on the rights and duties of spouses. See *Ontwerp Cordes/Heijman*: Where European "spouses are mutually indebted to each other for trust, help and sustenance" (art. 103), the same mutual obligations applied, "except where with regard to the Chinese adultery is understood to mean" (1914, art. 1[e]). "It is not forbidden for the married man to have a carnal union [*vleeschelijke gemeenschap*] with an unmarried woman." The same latitude however was not extended to the married Chinese woman. Adultery for Chinese was amended to refer only to the woman's breach of sexual fidelity (art. 1[g]).

25. While the new code was being drafted between 1913 and 1915, three such cases reached the Indies Supreme Court. See *HRNI*, vol. 100 (1913), 455–61; *HRNI*, vol. 103 (1915), 347–59; *ITR* no. 105 (1915): 278–93.

26. Pieter H. Fromberg, "Nota I," 15–16, in inv. 2.10.36.04, 1487; MR 15 Dec. 1915, no. 13, AMK, NA. This meant the deletion of articles 1e, g, h, I, j, k, l, and n.

27. Fromberg, "Nota I," 15–16.

28. Fromberg, "Nota I," 15–16.

29. Fromberg, "Nota I," section A1 memorandum, Ministry of Colonies.

30. Fromberg, "Nota VI," 2 Dec. 1915, inv. 2.10.36.04, 1487; MR 15 Dec. 1915, no. 13, AMK, NA.

31. Fromberg, "Nota VI," 2 Dec. 1915.

32. Fromberg, "Nota III," 3-4, 11 Oct. 1915, inv. 2.10.36.04, 1487; MR 15 Dec. 1915, no. 13, AMK, NA.

33. After serving twenty-five years in the colonial legal service, Fromberg spent the remainder of his life (1908-24) championing the causes of the Indies Chinese in particular and of all emergent Indonesian nationalist groups more generally in the removal of all racially discriminating laws in the Dutch colony. Based in The Hague, he wrote for colonial journals and lectured among the Indies Chinese students in the Netherlands. He returned to the Indies twice (1913 and 1921-23) as a private citizen, when he surveyed Indonesian nationalist leaders and pushed for legal unification of the different ethnic groups.

34. Fromberg, *De Chineesche beweging op Java*.

35. It must have been no accident that the Chung Hwa Hui convention on 20 October 1913 was occasioned by the appointment of "seven Dutch gentlemen . . . to assist it in all areas and as a supervisory commission to keep a close watch in the course of events." These seven gentlemen included, among others, the former governor-general of the Netherlands Indies, J. B. van Heutsz; retired officials in the Indies Chinese Affairs Department, H. N. Stuart and B. Hoetink; and the former counselor in the Indies Supreme Court and drafter of the 1897 Chinese private law code, P. H. Fromberg. Politically aware of their extraction from the Chinese Bangsawan stratum in Indies society, the newly appointed Dutch advisers reminded the "Indies Chinese students studying in the Netherlands of their isolation from the masses, and consequently, alienation from their racial compatriots." To reconnect these students with their compatriots, the colonial government pledged subsidies for a newly created Chung Hwa Hui scholarship (D: *studiefonds*) for "talented but poor young people of Chinese descent to continue their studies." One of the first contributors to the scholarship fund was Caroline Tan's father, Tan Thwan Soen, Chinese Kapitan of Bangkalan in Madura. Caroline's feminism cannot be read apart from her familial wealth and connections with the colonial state. See *Algemeen handelsblad*, 21 Oct. 1913.

36. Fromberg, "Voorheen en thans," 501.

37. Fromberg, "Voorheen en thans," 502.

38. Kwartanada, "Bangsawan prampoewan," 446.

39. *Algemeen handelsblad*, 21 Oct. 1913

40. *Algemeen handelsblad*, 21 Oct. 1913; *Haagsche Courant*, 23 Oct. 1913; *Het nieuws van den dag voor Nederlandsch-Indië*, 19 Nov. 1913.

41. *Pewarta Soerabaya*, 21 Nov. 1913, cited in Tan Siok Tjwan, "Educatie Prampoean Tionghoa," *Bok Tok*, no. 10, 6 Dec. 1913.

42. Tan, "Educatie Prampoen Tionghoa."

43. Tan, "Educatie Prampoen Tionghoa."

44. *Sin Po*, 26 Nov. 1913. Cited in Caroline Tan, "Het Chineesche Meisje," in *Bataviasche nieuwsblad*, 1 Apr. 1914. Unfortunately, I have not been able to locate any of *Sin Po*'s 1913 issues. Kwee Tek Hoay's identity was revealed in *Bok Tok*, no. 20, 14 Feb. 1914. Hauw Tek Kong, the editor of *Sin Po*, accused Caroline of "secretly arming the woman with a weapon (intellectual development) to fight her husband."

45. They cited the Dutch social science journal *Wetenschappelijke bladen* as a role model.

46. *Bok Tok*, no. 1, 4 Oct. 1913.

47. *Bok Tok*, no. 1, 4 Oct. 1913.

48. *Bok Tok*, no. 3. 18 Oct. 1913.

49. *Bok Tok*, no. 7, 15 Nov. 1913.

50. *Bok Tok*, no. 10, 6 Dec. 1913.

51. At twenty-two years old, he would in time take over the chief editorship of *Bok Tok*, its successor *Tjhoen Tjhioe*, and then *Sin Po* in Batavia.
52. *Bok Tok*, no. 10, 6 Dec. 1913. His occupation was described in *Bok Tok*, no. 17, 24 Jan. 1914.
53. "With one hand patting the left chest and the other holding the head, I continued to read the speech from the report. Amazing, how very amazing! There were many highly learned Chinese nationals gathered for that meeting, none of whom failed to applaud to show their agreement with what lady C. Tan said."
54. *Bok Tok*, no. 10, 6 Dec. 1913.
55. *Bok Tok*, no. 10, 6 Dec. 1913.
56. *Bok Tok*, no. 10, 6 Dec. 1913.
57. Tan Siok Tjwan, "Dasarnja Pemlihara'an dan peladjaran" [Basis of parental care and education], *Bok Tok*, no. 11, 13 Dec. 1913.
58. Cited in Tjioe Tik Lien, "Anti-hak sama rata" [Anti-Equal Rights], *Bok Tok* 3, no. 1 (Jan. 1914).
59. Tjioe, "Anti-hak sama rata."
60. Tjioe, "Anti-hak sama rata."
61. Kwee Kang Tik, "Satoe tjonto kawin katjinta-an" [An example of love marriage], *Bok Tok*, no. 11, 13 Dec. 1913.
62. Tan Siok Tjwan, "Leve de emancipatie! Hidoeplah kemerdika'an (prampoean Tionghwa)" [Long live emancipation! Love live freedom (Chinese women)], *Bok Tok*, no. 12, 20 Dec. 1913.
63. Fromberg, "Nota I," 9.
64. Nio, *Riwajat 40 Taon dari THHK*, 131.
65. Cited in Fromberg, "Nota III," 2.
66. *Perniagaan*, 23, 25, 30, and 31 Mar. 1914; and 1 and 2 Apr. 1914.
67. Van Wettum, *Hak familie dan hak poesaka*.
68. Fromberg, "De Indo-Chineesche familie en de wetgeving," 576–77.
69. Fromberg, "De Indo-Chineesche familie," 587.
70. Fromberg, "De Indo-Chineesche familie," 579.
71. *Sin Po*, 26 Apr. 1917.
72. *Wetboek van Strafregt voor Inlanders in Nederlandsch-Indië*, art. 256.
73. His paternal elder uncle, Phoa Keng Hek, was one of the two founders of the Confucian revivalist organization—the Tiong Hoa Hwee Koan—responsible for the creation of a pan-Java network of modern Chinese schools from 1901 forward. See "Phoa Keng Hek," in Salmon, *Literature in Malay by the Chinese of Indonesia*, 290.
74. Phoa, *Wetboek tentang oeroesan perniagaän*; Phoa, *Landgerecht*. See page 4 for his translation of bankruptcy law.
75. Phoa, *Privaatrecht*, 97–98.
76. Phoa, *Privaatrecht*, 84–85.
77. Phoa, *Privaatrecht*, 4–5.
78. Phoa, *Privaatrecht*, 103. In fact, it might not have been easy to get hold of a translated Dutch Civil Code. The Malay translation I have found dates to 1900. See *Burgerlijk Wetboek, Kitab dari hak-haknja*. The only other attempt appears to have been made by Indonesians after they gained independence (1949), and only in 1961.
79. Phoa, *Privaatrecht*, 103–4. He also provided a list of prohibitions on women, which occupied only one out of the eleven pages.
80. *De Locomotief*, 6 July 1919.
81. Cited from entry in 1951 Chinese marriage register for Jakarta. See Family History Library (Salt Lake City) (henceforth, FHL): file 1997758, item 2, "Jakarta, Perkawinan Cina 1951–5."

82. *Het nieuws van den dag voor Nederlandsch-Indië*, 2 May 1922.

83. Population figures are from Boomgaard and Gooszen, *Population Trends*, 135; and Departement van Landbouw, Nijverheid en Handel, *Volkstelling 1930*, 7:7, 11, for Surabaya's 1930 figure. No official population count for the year 1940 is available to me. For Batavia, I calculated a 15 percent growth rate between 1930 and 1940 to arrive at 171,608. This represents half the rate (30%) at which the Chinese population grew between 1920 and 1930. Immigration from Europe and China was drastically reduced with the onset of the Great Depression in 1930. Using the same formula as Batavia, I calculated a 1 percent growth rate for Semarang between 1930 and 1940 to arrive at 41,057. Likewise, the growth for Surabaya being 9 percent between 1920 and 1930, I estimated a 4.5 percent growth in the next decade to get 41,043. The population figures for Europeans are referenced from Boomgaard and Gooszen, *Population Trends*, 133. As I did for the Chinese, I calculated a growth rate of 1.5 percent for Europeans in Batavia between 1930 and 1940 to arrive at 38,629, and a 9.5 percent growth for Semarang over this decade to yield 19.366.

84. For Chinese civil marriage registry figures for Batavia, see FHL: files 1357784, item 13 (1919); 1357784, item 14 (1930–32); and 1357784, item 18 (1940). For Semarang, see FHL: files 1357862, item 12 (1919); 1357862, items 13–17 (1921); 1357863, items 7 and 8 (1930); and 1357863, item 36 (1940). For Surabaya, see FHL: files 1474353, 8214150, items 2–8 (1919–43). There is one caveat: I have calculated these numbers based on the final registration number for that particular year. The actual number of marriages is slightly lower than what is cited here, since divorce registrations were included in the running tally. To give an example, out of the 109 cases registered in the Batavia Chinese Marriage and Divorce Registry in 1930, 93 were marriages registered in Batavia, and 16 were divorces registered across the Indies, out of which 5 were of Batavia residents. In this example, divorces were less than 5 percent of total cases in each locality. The same caveat stands for my European figures. For European marriage numbers for Batavia, see FHL: files 1208810, item 6 (1920); 1208811, item 5 (1930); and 1357938, item 6 (1940). For Semarang, see FHL: files 8214134, 1357781 (1931), and 1357782, 8214134 (1940). For Surabaya, see FHL: files 1474349, 8117301, item 3 (1920), and 1474350, item 4 (1930). Unless divorce rates are seriously divergent among Chinese and European, my comparison of relative marriage registration rates should stand.

85. See, for instance, entry no. 8, 27 Aug. 1919, FHL: file 1357784, item 13.

86. Coppel, "Origins of Confucianism as an Organized Religion," 272.

87. Liang, *Perobahan besar tentang adat istiadat bangsa*, 3.

88. Opening speech of President Poey Kok Gwan, cited in Liang, *Perobahan besar*, 5.

89. Liang, *Perobahan besar*, 6

90. Liang, *Perobahan besar*, 7.

91. Liang, *Perobahan besar*, 48–49 (emphasis in original).

92. Liang, *Perobahan besar*, 49.

93. Liang, *Perobahan besar*, 49.

94. Book I, chap. 4, art. 28, Dutch Indies Civil Code.

95. Liang, *Perobahan besar*, 60.

96. Liang, *Perobahan besar*, 52.

97. Liang, *Perobahan besar*, 70–76.

98. Liang, *Perobahan besar*, 61–69, 76–81.

99. Emphasis in the original. Fasseur, "Cornerstone and Stumbling Block," 40. This amendment went into effect in 1925.

100. Indies Staatsregeling, art. 163.

101. Fasseur, "Cornerstone and Stumbling Block," 54.

8. REGISTERING BIRTHS, RACIALIZING ILLEGITIMACY

1. Salmon, "Ancestral Halls, Funeral Associations, and Attempts at Resinicization."
2. G. William Skinner, "Results of a Social Survey in Kabupaten Tangerang," unpublished manuscript, n.d., box 5, folder 1, G. William Skinner Papers, #14-27-2778, Division of Rare and Manuscript Collections, Cornell University Library (henceforth Skinner Papers).
3. Skinner, "Chinese Kinship Change in Java," unpublished manuscript, n.d., box 7, folder 36, Skinner Papers, #14-27-2778.
4. Salmon, "Ancestral Halls, Funeral Associations, and Attempts at Resinicization."
5. Haryono, *Perkahwinan strategis*.
6. Seng, "Fujianese Pioneers and Javanese Kings."
7. Liang, *Perobahan besar*, 51.
8. The new law even made a concession to let the Chinese cite their family before their personal names. The Dutch and Chinese also shared naming systems that were patrilineal in contrast with the singular or patronymic naming patterns in ethnic Javanese and Malay Indonesian traditions. See Staatsblad 1917, no. 130, art. 14. Those who obtained "European" legal status did abbreviate and inverse their family and personal names to conform to Dutch practice. Elite Chinese public figures like Kan Hok Hoei and Phoa Tjoen Hoey began to appear in public as H. H. Kan and Th. H. Phoa. Wealthy and powerful as they were, the average Chinese referred to these elites as *belanda staatsblad* (M/D: statutory Dutch)—a reference to how their European status had to be declared by statute, or *belanda anderhalve pop* (M/D: f1.50 Dutch puppet)—for the application fee they paid to become "European." The Dutch-educated Kwee Thiam Tjing makes fun of Phoa's naming in Kwee Thiam Tjing, *Menjadi Tjamboek Berdoeri*, 64–65.
9. I have taken the numbers for Batavia from 1929. See Batavia, "Hoofdregister van geboorte, Chinezen" [Main register of birth, Chinese], 1929, item 6, film 1357822, Chinese Civil Registry Records, Indonesia, Family History Library (henceforth FHL). The numbers for Semarang are an average of 1926 (801) and 1933 (893) figures. See Semarang's main registers of Chinese births, 1926, items 14–16, film 1357811; and 1933, items 1–2, film 1357825, FHL. Surabaya's numbers are arrived at from an average of 1932 (897) and 1933 (1,093) figures. See Surabaya's registers of Chinese birth, 1932, items 1–2; and 1933, items 4–5, film 1208847, FHL.
10. The census counted women in four age brackets: 0–14, 15–19, 20–49, and 50+. I have added the second and third groups here. See Departement van Landbouw, Nijverheid en Handel, *Volkstelling 1930*, 2:256, 258, 262. The birth rhythm was calculated from a sample size of 742 Chinese female patients who were subjected to a meticulous interview of their reproductive biographies at Batavia's Chinese hospital Jang Seng Ie. See Loe, "Sociale Ellende en geboortebeperking," 117–18.
11. Heryanto, "Ethnic Identities."
12. Netherlands Indies Civil Code, art. 863.
13. Liang, *Perobahan besar*, 51–53.
14. Phoa, *Wetboek tentang oeroesan perniagaän jang berlakoe dalam Hindia Ollanda*, 76–77. In interpreting these categories of descent to his readers, he most likely had the youth who were experimenting with courtship in mind. The more important intention of the law to prohibit a married man from developing a full relationship with a "natural" child born out of wedlock did not occur to him.
15. This was originally article 354. Amended by Staatsblad 1896, no. 108. See also Baay, *De njai*, 83.
16. Baay, *De njai*, 101–2.

17. These samples were taken from the main registers. For Batavia, 1933, item 6, film 1208832; 1938, items 1–3, film 1357822. For Semarang, 1933, items 1–2, 6, 18; 1934, items 10–12, 16–7; 1935, item 25, film 1357825, FHL.

18. They could sign their names, and almost all in romanized form. Among the eleven Chinese mothers in Semarang who naturally recognized their children in 1934, mostly without the fathers present, eight were literate, and all eight signed their names in romanized form. See Semarang, Bijregister van geboorten (Chineezen), 1934 [Supplementary registry of births (Chinese)], item 14, film 1357825, FHL. For Surabaya, seven of the fourteen Chinese mothers were literate, and six of them signed their names in romanized form (one in Chinese form) for the years 1933 and 1934. See Surabaya's supplementary registries, items 3 and 6, film 1208847, FHL.

19. Departement van Landbouw, Nijverheid en Handel, *Volkstelling 1930*, 2:93.

20. Elsewhere in the census report, it was clarified that native mothers were most likely undercounted, whereas "a number of children of Chinese fathers by Native women, with whom they are not legally married, but were—following the old notions—reported as Chinese children to the counters." In the end, the census made no distinction between Indonesia wives and mothers. Departement van Landbouw, Nijverheid en Handel, *Volkstelling 1930*, 2:56, 93.

21. The numbers for outside the cities were most likely even higher.

22. See the respective Bijregister van geboorten (Chinezen) for Batavia, 1932, item 11, film 1208843; Semarang, 1926, items 17–8, film 1357811; Surabaya, 1933, item 3, film 1208847, FHL. For a similar "occupational division" of the "Javanese population working outside the agricultural sector" in 1905, see Dros, *Wages: 1820–1940*, 22.

23. Batavia, Register tot huwelijken en echtscheidingen [Register for marriages and divorces], 1930, item 14, film 1357784, FHL.

24. Remarkably, for those who could, their brides—75 percent of whom were local born—were the youngest of the lot.

25. For instance, when Lie Soei Liong registered his son by Saira in January 1932, Lie Soei Lin, who was seven years his elder, was clearly a relation.

26. Bijregister van geboorten (Chinezen), Surabaya, 1933, item 9, film 1208847.3, FHL.

27. Bijregister van geboorten (Chinezen), Batavia, 1932, item 9, film 1208843.11, FHL.

28. Fromberg, "De nieuwe Chineezenwetgeving," 335.

29. Staatsblad 1924, no. 557. If the father dies before the child comes of age, "these children will come by law under the guardianship of their carnal [D: *vleeschelijke*] mother." Between its original 1917 and final 1924 versions, the Justice Department amended the wording in the statute from "concubine" (D: *bijzit*, 1917, 1918) in the original law and its first amendment, to the mother who had "undergone a legal secondary marriage [D: *wettig nevenhuwelijk*]" (1921), before settling on "minor wives" (D: *bijvrouwen*, 1924). Staatsblad 1924, no. 557.

30. Kollewijn, "Nieuwe Arresten van Het HoogGerechtshof over Chinees Familierecht," 14.

31. Pearson, *Bittersweet*, 39–40.

32. They averaged 19.5 years old when they bore children for their relatively wealthy (three merchants and a goldsmith) Chinese partners. The four men averaged 35.5 years old.

33. The conclusion holds even if subtracted, say, two years to account for those who might be returning to register their second or even third children.

34. Geertz, *Javanese Family*, 119 and 56.

35. See Surabaya, Bijregister van geboorten (Chinezen), Surabaya, 1933, item 9, film 1208847.3, FHL.

36. Staatsblad 1858, no. 158, art. 7, para. 3.

37. Supomo, *Hukum perdata Adat Djawa barat*, 3.

38. Surabaya, Bijregister van geboorten (Chinezen), Surabaya, 1933, item 9, film 1208847.3, FHL.

39. Surabaya, Bijregister van geboorten (Chinezen), Surabaya, 1933, item 9, film 1208847.3, FHL. Ramena (31) raised three Chinese children (aged 13, 10, and 8), whom she and Oey Kim Liang (37), a trader's assistant, recognized on 8 Nov. 1932 in Batavia. She would have been with Oey Kim Liang since she was eighteen. Marpoeah (37) and Soepiahtie (25), mothers of six- and seven-year-old daughters, had partners who were unemployed and a trader's assistant.

40. Skinner, "Results of a social survey in Kabupaten Tangerang," Skinner Papers, 9–10.

41. Pearson, *Bittersweet*, 41.

42. Gouw Giok Siong, "Segi-Segi hukum Peraturan Perkawinan Tjampuran," 38.

43. Comparing the marriage registry records of "Europeans" and "Chinese" in Jakarta, Gouw expressed concern that while European Indonesian (including Chinese women) mixed marriages had risen from about 10 percent of total European marriages before the war to around 20 percent in 1950, the same figure for the Chinese rose from zero in 1930, to less than 1 percent in 1940, to a peak of 3 percent in 1949, before falling back to less than 1 percent in 1953. See Gouw, "Segi-Segi," 38.

44. M. Tan, *Chinese of Sukabumi*, 81.

45. See, for instance, Nio, *Sastera Indonesia-Tionghoa*, 57, 68.

46. Bowen, *Islam, Law and Equality in Indonesia*, 75–81, 178.

47. "Resolusi Ummat Islam Djakarta mengenai Perkawinan jang dilarang Agama Islam, 14 Sept. 1952," in Gouw, "Segi-Segi," 248.

48. *Keng Po*, 18 Sept. 1954; also cited in Gouw, "Segi-Segi," 269.

49. Blackburn, *Women and the State in Modern Indonesia*.

50. Fowler, introduction, xxiv–xxv.

51. Duara, *Crisis of Global Modernity*, 218.

52. Duara, *Crisis of Global Modernity*, 221.

53. Chan, "Chinese Women's Emancipation as Reflected in Two Peranakan Journals." *Panorama* was a journal the editors sold as something "that must be read by people who like to think and care about questions of elevated significance [M: soeal-soeal jang tinggi]." Administration of Panorama, "Have you already subscribed to the journal *Panorama*?," in Kwee Tek Hoay, *Boenga roos dari Tjikembang*, front material.

54. Chan, "Chinese Women's Emancipation."

55. See Fowler, introduction, vii. The most recent Bahasa edition is collected in *Kesastraan Melayu Tionghoa dan kebangsaan Indonesia*.

56. I have translated this from the third edition of the novel: Kwee Tek Hoay, *Bunga roos dari Tjikembang: Tjerita Roman Sedih Dan Girang* [The soul ripens in tears], 3rd ed. (Surakata: Swastika, 1963), 3. This verse has been left out of the English version translated by Fowler. Elsewhere I quote from Fowler's translation.

57. Nio Joe Lan classified it as a "tragic" story with "mystical" characteristics. See Nio, *Sastera Indonesia-Tionghoa*, 77–78, 108.

58. Kwee Tek Hoay, *The Rose of Cikembang*.

59. Kwee, *The Rose of Cikembang*, 99.

CONCLUSION

1. Taylor, *Social World of Batavia*.

2. The most sociologically sophisticated remains Skinner, "Creole Chinese Societies in Southeast Asia."

NOTES TO PAGES 190–197

3. The closest the British came in Singapore was in their appointment of between two and four Chinese to the European-dominant Grand Jury from the 1850s to 1873. The Grand Jury was made up of (23–30) unofficial (European) men of good standing. They were appointed to serve as prosecutors, but they also sometimes publicized common grievances against the government. See Y. K. Lee, "Grand Jury of Singapore."

4. Lim How Seng, "Social Structure and Bang Interactions"; Yen Ching Hwang, "Early Chinese Clan Organizations in Singapore and Malaya." Only much later on, in the early twentieth century, did they begin to register marriages.

5. Lowrie, *Masters and Servants*.

6. Chu, *Chinese and Chinese Mestizos of Manila*.

7. Skinner, *Chinese Society in Thailand*, 126–134.

8. Cushman, *Family and State*.

9. Loos, *Subject Siam*, 1–28.

10. Across Thailand, apparently only 55 percent of women between fifteen and forty-nine years old registered their marriages. See Bao, *Marital Acts*, 80.

11. Bao, *Marital Acts*, 41–43, 80–81.

12. Applicants also had to formally renounce China's unilaterally declared citizenship, even if that was largely symbolic. Suryadinata, *Pribumi Indonesians, the Chinese Minority and China*, 115. By the late 1950s in neighboring Singapore and Malaysia, citizenship was, in effect, offered to all postwar residents.

13. Willmott, *National Status of the Chinese in Indonesia*.

14. Suryadinata, *Pribumi Indonesians*, 122–24.

15. Coppel, *Indonesian Chinese in Crisis*, 82–85.

16. This contrasts with only 230,000 out of Indonesia's three million name changes by Chinese across Indonesia in August 1969. These statistics are cited in Suryadinata, *Pribumi Indonesians*, 148, and 263–64n73.

17. Thung, "Unreality of Chinese Nationalism in Indonesia." A London-educated creole Chinese, who in his heyday in the 1930s published books on Chinese history and served the Republican and Manchukuo Chinese governments in ministerial roles, Thung Liang Lee was a marginal figure on the postwar Indonesian political scene.

18. Ong Hok Ham, "Asimilasi dan manifesto politik," 4.

19. Ong Hok Ham, "Tentang nama-nama warganegara Indonesia keturunan Tionghoa," 41.

20. Ong Hok Ham, "Soal nama-nama warganegara Indonesia ggolongan Peranakan (II)," 15.

21. Mentioned in Ong, "Tentang nama-nama," 41.

22. Ong, "Soal nama-nama," 15.

23. Bailey and Lie, "Politics of Names among Chinese Indonesians in Java," 27. See also Kwee, "Many Implications of Name Change for Indonesian-Born Chinese."

24. See Seng, "Fujianese Pioneers and Javanese Kings."

25. Lindsey, "Reconstituting the Ethnic Chinese in Post-Soeharto Indonesia," 45–46.

APPENDIX

1. Wu, Nie, and Xie, *Yajiada Hua ren hun yin*.

Bibliography

ARCHIVAL SOURCES

Indonesia

Arsip Nasional Republik Indonesia, Jakarta
  Arsip Wees- en Boedelkamer, 1819–1937
    Boedelpapieren

The Netherlands

Leiden University Library
  "Marriage Registry, Batavia Chinese Council, 1772–1919" (Excel database compiled by Chen Menghong)
  Digital Collections, Archive of the Kong Koan of Batavia (吧城公館) (ubl209)
  Go Sian Lok Collection
Nationaal Archief (NA), The Hague
  Archief Ministerie van Koloniën, 1850–1900

United States of America

Cornell University Library, Ithaca
  G. William Skinner Papers, Division of Rare and Manuscript Collections
Family History Library (FHL), Salt Lake City
  Chinese Civil Registry Records, Indonesia (microfilm)

CONTEMPORARY SOURCES IN DUTCH

Albrecht, J. E. "Het schoolonderwijs onder de Chineezen op Java." In *Tijdschrift voor Indische taal-, land- en volkenkunde* [School education among the Chinese of Java], edited by J. E. Albrecht and K. L. Van Schouwenburg, 25:225–41. Batavia, W. Bruining, 1879.

"Algemeen Handelsblad." *Nieuwe Amsterdamsche Courant en Algemeen Handelsblad.*

"Begrip van vaderlijke magt onder de Chinezen" [The concept of paternal power among the Chinese]. *Het regt van Nederlandsch-Indië*, no. 2 (1849): 25–31.

"Bijdragen tot de kennis van de wetten en instellingen der Chinezen in Nederlandsch Indië" [Contributions to the knowledge of laws and customs of the Chinese in Netherlands India]. *Tijdschrift voor Nederlandsch Indië* 15, no. 1 (1853): 241–55.

Burgerlijk Wetboek, Kitab dari hak-haknja, permistian-permistiannja dan pembikinan perdjandjian-perdjandian roepa-roepa satoe pada lajin boewat orang Olanda dan siapa-siapa jang di bersama-samaken pada orang Olanda di dalem Tanah Hindia Nederland [Civil Code, Book of Rights, on obligations and the making of agreements between one and others for the Dutch and whoever is equated with the Dutch in the land of the Netherlands Indiës]. 2nd ed. Batawi: Albrecht, 1900.

Burgerlijk Wetboek voor Nederlandsch-Indië. Amsterdam: Müller, 1846.

De Locomotief: Samarangsch Handels- en Advertentie-Blad [Semarang Commercial and Advertising Paper]

Departement van Landbouw, Nijverheid en Handel. *Volkstelling 1930*. Vol. 2, *Inheemsche bevolking van Midden-Java en de Vorstenlanden* [Native population in Middle Java and the Native States of Java]. Batavia: Landsdrukkerij, 1934.

———. *Volkstelling 1930*. Vol. 7, *Chineezen en andere vreemde Oosterlingen in Nederlandsch-Indie* [Chinese and other non-indigenous orientals in the Netherlands Indies]. Batavia: Landsdrukkerij, 1936.

De Sturler, W. L. Appendix to *Over de verledenen en tegenwoordigen toestand van het eiland Java* [Regarding the past and present condition of the island of Java], by Eduard Selberg. Translated by W. L. de Stuler. Groningen: Omkens, 1841.

De Waal, E. *Onze Indische Financien: Nieuwe Reeks Aanteekeningen*. Vol. 1. 'S-Gravenhage: Martinus Nijhoff, 1876.

Faber, Godfried von. *Het familie- en erfrecht der Chineezen in Nederlandsch-Indië* [The family and inheritance rights of the Chinese in the Netherlands Indies]. Leiden: Eduard IJdo, 1895.

Fromberg, Pieter Hendrik. *De Chineesche beweging op Java*. Amsterdam: Elsevier, 1911.

———. "De Indo-Chineesche familie en de wetgeving: Lezing gehouden voor Chung Hwa Hui te Amsterdam op den 15den April 1916." In *Verspreide geschriften*, edited by Chung Hwa Hui, 567–84. Leiden: Leidsche Uitgeversmaatschappij, 1926.

———. "De nieuwe Chineezenwetgeving (transitoir recht and het 'wettig Nevenhuwelijk')." In *Indisch tijdschrift van het recht: Orgaan der Nederlandsch-Indische Juristen-Vereeniging*. Vol. 117. Batavia: Papyrus, 1922.

———. "Nieuwe regeling van den privaatrechte-lijken toestand der Chineezen, ontworpen op last der Regeering van Ned.-Indië." In *Verspreide geschriften*, edited by Chung Hwa Hui, 129–307. Leiden: Leidsche Uitgeversmaatschappij, 1926.

———. *Verspreide geschriften*. Edited by Chung Hwa Hui. Leiden: Leidsche Uitgeversmaatschappij, 1926.

———. "Voorheen en thans (Lezing voor 'Chung Hwa Hui,' 28 Dec. 1912)." In *Verspreide geschriften*, edited by Chung Hwa Hui, 491–510. Leiden: Leidsche Uitgeversmaatschappij, 1926.

Handboek voor cultuur- en handelsondernemingen in Nederlandsch-Indië. Vol. 1. Amsterdam: J. H. De Bussy, 1888.

Indisch Tijdfschrit van het Recht [Indies Review of Law]

Java-Bode—Nieuws, Handels—en Advertentieblad voor Nederlandsch-Indië [Java Messenger—News, Commerce and Advertisement Paper for Netherlands India]

Keijzer, Salomo, trans. *De heilige boeken der Chinezen, of de vier klassieke boeken van Confucius en Mencius (Khoeng-tseu en Meng-tseu)* [The holy books of the Chinese, or the four classical books of Confucius and Mencius (Khoeng-tseu en Meng-tseu)]. Haarlem: J.J. van Brederode, 1862.

Kollewijn, R. D. "Nieuwe Arresten van Het HoogGerechtshof over Chinees Familierecht." In *Indisch Tijdschrift van Het Recht: Orgaan Der Nederlandsch-Indische Juristen-Vereeniging*. Vol. 135, 1932.

Koloniaal verslag . . . Nederlandsch-Indië.. Aangelegenheden behoorende tot den werkkring van het Departement van Landbouw; Mijnwezen. . . . [Colonial report . . . (on) Netherlands India . . . (on) Matters Pertaining to the Work of the Departments of Agriculture, Mines . . . s-Gravenhage: Algemeene Landsdrukkerij, 1850–1907, 1907–1919.

Loe Ping Kian. "Sociale ellende en geboortebeperking" [Social misery and birth control]. In *Ons nageslacht: Orgaan van de Eugenetische Vereeniging in Nederlandsch-Indië* 7 (July 1934): 107–25.

———. "Syphilis en zwangerschap bij Chineesche en Indonesische vrouwen en de behandeling van syphilitische Chineesche en Indonesische vrouwen tijdens de zwanger-

schap als prophylaxis van congenitale syphilis." Medical College at Batavia, Keng Po, 1941.
Nederburgh, I. A., "Het Indisch-Chineezen recht der toekomst" [The Indies-Chinese law of the future]. In *Wet en Adat; bladen gewijd in het algemeen aan het recht en aanverwante onderwerpen, in het bizonder aan Indische rechtsbelangen*, edited by I. A. Nederburgh. Batavia: G. Kolff, 1896.
———. *Wetgeving voor Nederlandsch-Indië I: Rangschikking, benoeming, ontslag, ... Der N. Indische Rechterlijke Ambtenaren (Staatsblad 1901, No. 201). II: Gemengde Huwelijken, Vervolg (Staatsblad 1901, No. 348)*. Weltevreden: Visser, 1902.
Paulus, Jozlas, D. G. Stibbe, and Simon de Graaff. *Encyclopaedie van Nederlandsch-Indië*. Pt. 2. The Hague: E. J. Brill, 1899.
Preanger-Bode [Preanger Paper]
Schlegel, G. "Chineesch regt: Iets over Chinesche testamenten, donatiën en erfopvolging." *Het regt van Nedernlandsch-Indië* 20 (1862): 369–74.
Soerabaijasch Handelsblad [Surabaya Commercial Paper]
Staatsblad van Nederlandsch-Indië [Statutory Laws of Netherlands India]. s'Gravenhage / Weltevreden: A. D. Schinkel / Landsdrukkerij, 1827–1922.
Uitkomsten der in de maand November 1920 Gehouden Volkstelling [Results of census held in the month of November 1920]. Batavia: Ruygrok, 1922.
Van der Chijs, J. A., ed. "Aansprakelijkheid eener Chinesche Vvouw voor de schulden van haren echtgenoot, May 23, 1766." In *Nederlandsch-Indisch plakaatboek*, Vol. 9, *New Statutes of Batavia*. Batavia: Landsdrukerij, 1891.
———. *Nederlandsch-Indisch plakaatboek, 1602–1811* [Book of Dutch East Indies edicts]. 17 vols. Batavia: Landsdrukerij, 1885–1910.
Van der Lith, P. A., and Joh. F. Snelleman. *Encyclopaedie van Nederlandsch-Indië*. Pt. 3. The Hague: E. J. Brill, 1902.
Van Heeckeren, C. W. *Beschouwingen over het voor Chineezen op Java geldende recht*. Semarang: Van Dorp, 1901.
Van Wettum, B. A. J., trans. "The Family- and Inheritance Law in the Newly Drafted Chinese Civil Code." *Het regt in Nederlandsch-Indië: Regtskundig Tijdschrift*, 102 (1914): 105–50.
Weill, Alexandre. *Les Mystères de l'amour: Philosophie et hygiène*. Paris: Amyot, 1868.
Wetboek van Koophandel voor Nederlandsch-Indië. Amsterdam: Müller, 1846.
Wetboek van Strafregt voor Inlanders in Nederlandsch-Indië [Criminal Code for Natives in the Netherlands India]. Batavia: Landsdrukerij, 1872.
Young, J. W. *Het huwelijk en de wetgeving hierop in China* [Marriage and its legislation in China]. Batavia: Albrecht & Rusche, 1894.

CONTEMPORARY SOURCES IN INDONESIAN/SINO-MALAY

Brightson, H. Sair. *"Resia-Kedirie" atawa "Kedjatoehan Tangan Allah."* Kediri: Boedi-Karjo, 1924.
Butatuli and Hemeling [pseud.]. *Boekoe Wet dan Rasia tentang Perhoeboengan antara Prampoean dan Lelaki atawa pengatahoean hal bagi Kamanoesiaan*. Batavia: Drukk. Tjiong Koen Bie, 1913.
Chabanneau. *Rasia Bandoeng atawa satu percinta-an yang melanggar peradatan bangsa Tiong Hoa: Satu cerita yang benar terjadi di Kota Bandung dan berakhir pada tahon 1917*. Edited by Ridwan Hutagalung. Bandung: Ultimus, 2016. Originally published in 1918.
Dumas, Alexandre, fils. *Marguerite Gauthier, atawa Satoe pertjinta'an jang soetji dari satoe prampoewan latjoer*. Translated by Tjan Kim Bie. Batavia: Tjiong Koen Bie, 1918. Originally published as *La Dame aux Camélias* (Brussels: Alphonse Lebègue, 1848).

Echols, John, and Hassan Shadily. *Kamus Indonesia Inggris*. [English-Indonesian dictionary]. 3rd ed. Jakarta: Gramedia, 1997.
Go, Kok Liang. *Tjerita Njonja Lim Pat Nio: Swatoe tjerita jang amat bagoes jang betoel soeda kadjadian di tanah Babakan bilangan Betawie*. Batavia: Kho Tjeng Bie, 1909.
Gouw Peng Liang. *Penghidoepan laki-istri*. Weltevreden: Favoriet, n.d., ca. 1918.
———. *Perniaga'an Prempoean dan anak-anak Prempoean: Satoe nasehat Aken Tjega perkara Djina*. Weltevreden, Favioriet, 1919.
———. *Tjerita jang betoel soeda kedjadian di Poelo Djawa dari halnja satoe toean tana dan pachter opium di Residentie Benawan bernama Lo Fen Koei*. Batavia: Goan Hong, 1903.
Hauw San Liang [Tjoe Bou San]. *The Loan Eng*. Batavia: Sin Po, 1922.
———. *Satoe djodo jang terhalang*. Batavia: Lie Tek Long, 1917.
Kwee Seng Tjoan. *Model soerat soerat pertjintahan*. Batavia: Kwee Seng Tjoan, 1920.
Kwee Tek Hoay. *Boenga roos dari Tjikembang*. 2nd ed. Batavia: Panorama, 1930.
———. *Bunga roos dari Tjikembang: Tjerita roman sedih dan girang* [The Soul Ripens in Tears]. 3rd ed. Surakata: Swastika, 1963.
Liang Tjoekat [Lie Tjoei Khai]. *Perobahan besar tentang adat istiadat bangsa Tionghoa jang soeda dipoetoeskan dalam Congres "Khong Kauw Hwe"* [. . .]. Semarang: Lie Ping An, 1924.
Lie Kim Hok. *Hikayat Khonghoetjoe* [Biography of Confucius]. Batavia: G. Kolff, 1897.
———. *Orang Prampoewan*. Batavia: Karsseboom, 1889.
Liem Khing Hoo. *Manoesia*. Sourabaya: Hahn, 1930.
Mahameru, Eidelweis. *Oei Tiong Ham: Raja Gula, orang terkaya dari Semarang* [Oei Tiong Ham: Sugar King, the richest man of Semarang]. Jakarta: Hi-Fest, 2011.
Mimi [Lim Kim Lip]. *Boenga Rajah atawa doea roepa kasenangan!* Batavia: Drukkerij Lie Tek Long, 1918.
Nemo [pseud.]. *Boekoe tjerita nona-nona dalem roesia: Soeatoe tjerita jang soenggoe bagoes, heran serta menarik hati. Baik dibatja oleh orang-orang prempoean dan lelaki kaoem moeda djaman sekarang*. Batavia: Toko & Drukkerij Lie Tek Long, 1919.
Nio Joe Lan. *Riwajat 40 Taon dari Tiong Hoa Hwe Koan—Batavia (1900–1939)*. Batavia: Tiong Hoa Hwe Koan, 1940.
———. *Sastera Indonesia-Tionghoa*. Djakarta: Gunung Agung, 1962.
Oei Soei Tiong. *Tjerita Njai Alimah: Jaitoe satoe tjerita jang amat endah dan loetjoe, jang betoel soeda kedjadian di Djawa Timoer* [Story of Njai Alimah: A very beautiful and funny story that really happened in East Java]. Batavia: Kho Tjeng Bie, 1915.
Ong Hok Ham. "Asimilasi dan manifesto politik." *Star Weekly*, no. 744, 2 April 1960.
———. "Soal nama-nama warganegara Indonesia golongan Peranakan (II)." *Star Weekly*, no. 737, 13 February 1960.
———. "Tentang nama-nama warganegara Indonesia keturunan Tionghoa." *Star Weekly*, no. 736, 6 February 1960.
Ong Ping Lok. *Tjoema boeat satoe*. Soerabaia: Tan's Drukkery, 1927.
Phoa T. H., Jr. [Phoa Tjoen Hoay]. *Landgerecht: Salinan atoerannja dan djoega salinan dari lain-lain wet jang berhoeboeng pada ini hal*. Batavia: Tjiong Koen Bie, 1914.
———. *Privaatrecht dan burgerlijke-stand boeat bangsa Tiong hoa ia'ni Staatsblad Hindia Ollanda taon 1917, No. 129 en 130. Keadaan oendang-oendang bangsa Timoer Asing. Dalem Pengidoepannja sebagi pendoedoek dari dan Soedagar di Hindia Ollanda moelai berlakoe 1 Mei 1919*. Batavia: Tjiong Koen Bie Electr. Drukkerij, 1919.
———. *Tjhik Tjhik Boeng Nona Kampoeng atawa Rasianja Bogor Ngapoeng: Satoe tjerita di bilangan Buitenzorg jang oetaraken koetoekan berhoeboeng dengan pertjintaan antara orang Tiong Hoa jang sama nama toeroenannja* [M: Tjhik? Tjhik? village

girl's curse or Bogor's secret spreads: A story that happened in Buitenzorg demonstrating the curse on Chinese who have a love affair but share the same family name]. Bogor: Drukkerij Thetenghoeij, 1918.

———. *Wetboek tentang oeroesan perniagaän jang berlakoe dalam Hindia Ollanda*. Batavia: Tjiong Koen Bie, 1911.

Sie Hian Ling. *Tjerita "Yang Soen Sia": Soewatoe tjerita jang bener telah kedjadian di Djawa Tengah*. Solo: Sie Dhian Ho, 1908.

Sin Gan Peng. *Tjerita rasia-Soerabaja: atawa Katjentilannja satoe gadis hartawan jang dapet didikan adat Europa* [Story of Surabaya's secret: or the haughtiness of a very wealthy girl, who was educated in European customs]. Grissee: Boekhandel Pek Pang Ing, 1919.

Supomo. *Hukum perdata Adat Djawa barat*. Translated by Nani Soewondo (into Indonesian). Jakarta: Penerbit Djambatan, 1967.

Tambahsia: Suwatu cerita yang betul sudah kejadian di Betawi antara tahun 1851–1856 [Tambahsia: A story that really happened in Batavia during the years 1851–1856]. Semarang: N.V. Hap Sing Kong Sie, 1915.

Tan Boen Kim. *Gan Liang Boen atawa Malem jang serem!!* [Gan Liang Boen, or A Scary Night!]. Batavia: Lie Tek Long, 1924.

Tan Ging Tiong and Yoe Tjai Siang. *Kitab Tai Hak–Tiong Iong: Disalin dalem bahasa Melajoe*. Soekaboemi: Soekaboemische Snelpersdrukkerij, 1900.

Tan Kittjoan. *Saier mengimpie dan Saier boeroeng*. [Verse of dreams and Verse of birds]. Batawie: W. Ogilvie, 1865.

The Boen Liang. "Riwajatnja familie Tjoa di Soerabaja" [The Story of the Tjoa Family of Surabaya]. *Mata Hari*, 1 Aug. 1934.

Thio Tjin Boen, *Cerita Oey Se, yaitu satu cerita yang amat endah dan lucu yang betul sudah kejadian di Jawa Tengah*. [Story of Oey Se, being a very beautiful and funny story that really happened in Central Java]. Publisher unknown, 1903.

———. *Sie Tjaij Kim (Nona Kim), Atawa saorang prampoean jang bertobat: soeatoe tjerita jang betoel kedjadian di Bandoeng*. Batavia: Lie Tek Long, 1917.

Tio Ie Soei. *Lie Kimhok, 1853–1912*. Bandung: Good Luck, 1958.

Tio Tek Hong. *Keadaan Jakarta Tempo Doeloe: Sebuah Kenangan, 1882–1959*. Jakarta: Masup Jakarta, 2006.

Tjoa Boe Sing. *Tjerita Lim Tjin Sioe Atau Korban dari satoe katjinta'an jang sasoenggoenja soedah terdjadi di Residentie Banger pada taoen 1886* [Story of Lim Tjin Sioe, or Tragedy from a romance that really happened in the Banger residency in the year 1886]. Batavia: Oeij Tjajj Hin, 1911.

Van Wettum, B. A. J. *Hak familie dan hak poesaka di Burgerlijk Wetboek baroe di Tiongkok*. Batavia: Hoa Siang In Kiok, 1914.

Yong, Pat Kwah. *Peroentoengan jang mengandoeng ratjoen atawa kesenangan membawa kasedian: Satoe tjerita jang betoel telah kedjadian di afdeeling Djember* [A happiness that contains poison, or pleasure that brings sadness: A story that really happened in the Jember district]. Grissee: Boekhandel Pek Pang Ing, 1919.

BOOKS AND ARTICLES

Abdullah, Taufik. *Indonesia: Towards Democracy*. Singapore: Institute of Southeast Asian Studies, 2009.

Abeyasekere, Susan. "Slaves in Batavia: Insights from a Slave Register." In *Slavery, Bondage, and Dependency in Southeast Asia*, edited by Anthony Reid and Jennifer Brewster, 286–314. New York: St. Martin's Press, 1983.

Adam, Ahmat. *The Vernacular Press and the Emergence of Modern Indonesian Consciousness (1855–1913)*. Ithaca, NY: Southeast Asia Program, Cornell University, 1995.
Adam, Asvi Warman. "The Chinese in the Collective Memory of the Indonesian Nation." *Kyoto Review of Southeast Asia, Nations and Other Stories*, no. 3 (March 2003). https://kyotoreview.org/issue-3-nations-and-stories/the-chinese-in-the-collective-memory-of-the-indonesian-nation/.
Aguilar, Filomeno V., "Citizenship, Inheritance, and the Indigenizing of 'Orang Chinese' in Indonesia." In *Positions: East Asia Cultures Critique* 9, no. 3 (2001): 501–33.
Andaya, Barbara Watson. *The Flaming Womb: Repositioning Women in Early Modern Southeast Asia*. Honolulu: University of Hawai'i Press, 2006.
———. "From Temporary Wife to Prostitute: Sexuality and Economic Change in Early Modern Southeast Asia." *Journal of Women's History* 9, no. 4 (1998): 11–34. https://doi.org/10.1353/jowh.2010.0225.
Anderson, Benedict. *Imagined Communities: Reflections on the Origin and Spread of Nationalism*. London: Verso books, 2006.
Atsushi, Ota. *Changes of Regime and Social Dynamics in West Java: Society, State, and the Outer World of Banten, 1750–1830*. Boston: Brill, 2006.
Baay, Reggie. *De njai: Het concubinaat in Nederlands-Indië*. Amsterdam: Athenaeum-Polak & Van Gennep, 2008.
Bailey, Benjamin, and Sunny Lie. "The Politics of Names among Chinese Indonesians in Java: The Politics of Names among Chinese Indonesians." *Journal of Linguistic Anthropology* 23, no. 1 (2013): 21–40. https://doi.org/10.1111/jola.12003.
Bao Jiemin, *Marital Acts: Gender, Sexuality, and Identity among the Chinese Thai Diaspora*. Honolulu: University of Hawai'i Press, 2005.
Becker Lorca, Arnulf. *Mestizo International Law: A Global Intellectual History, 1842–1933*. Cambridge: Cambridge University Press, 2014. https://doi.org/10.1017/CBO9781139015424.
Blackburn, Susan. *Women and the State in Modern Indonesia*. Cambridge: Cambridge University Press, 2004. https://doi.org/10.1017/CBO9780511492198.
Blussé, Leonard. "One Hundred Weddings and Many More Funerals a Year: Chinese Civil Society in Batavia at the End of the Eighteenth Century." In *The Archives of the Kong Koan of Batavia*, edited by Leonard Blussé and Chen Menghong, 8–28. Leiden: Brill, 2003.
———. *Strange Company: Chinese Settlers, Mestizo Women and the Dutch in VOC Batavia*. Dordrecht, Netherlands: Foris, 1986.
Blussé, Leonard, and Chen Menghong, eds. *The Archives of the Kong Koan of Batavia*. Leiden: Brill, 2003.
Blussé, Leonard, and Nie Dening, eds. *The Chinese Annals of Batavia, the "Kai Ba Lidai Shiji" and Other Stories (1610–1795)*. Leiden: Brill, 2018.
Blussé, Leonard, and Wu Fengbin. *Gong an bu, Bacheng huaren Gongguan Dangan Congshu* [Minutes of the Board Meetings of the Chinese Council]. Vol. 1. Xiamen: Xiamen University Press, 2002.
Bocquet-Siek, Margaret. "The Peranakan Chinese Woman at a Crossroad." In *Women's Work and Women's Roles: Economics and Everyday Life in Indonesia, Malaysia, and Singapore*, edited by Lenore Manderson and Margaret Bocquet-Siek, 31–52. Canberra: Australian National University, 1983.
Boomgaard, Peter, and A. J. Gooszen. *Population Trends, 1795–1942*. Vol. 11. *Changing Economy in Indonesia: A Selection of Statistical Source Material from the Early 19th Century Up to 1940*. Amsterdam: Royal Tropical Institute, 1991.

Bowen, John Richard. *Islam, Law and Equality in Indonesia: An Anthropology of Public Reasoning.* Cambridge: Cambridge University Press, 2003. https://doi.org/10.1017/CBO9780511615122.

Carey, Peter. "Changing Javanese Perceptions of the Chinese Communities in Central Java, 1755-1825." *Indonesia* (Ithaca), no. 37 (1984): 1-47. https://doi.org/10.2307/3350933.

Chan, Faye Yik-Wei. "Chinese Women's Emancipation as Reflected in Two Peranakan Journals, (c. 1927-1942)." *Archipel*, no. 49 (1995): 45-62.

Chandra, Elizabeth. "Blossoming Dahlia: Chinese Women Novelists in Colonial Indonesia." *Southeast Asian Studies* 4, no. 3 (2015): 533-64.

———. "Women and Modernity: Reading the Femme Fatale in Early Twentieth-Century Indies Novels." *Indonesia* 92 (2011): 157-82.

Chatterjee, Partha. *The Nation and Its Fragments: Colonial and Postcolonial Histories.* Princeton, NJ: Princeton University Press, 1993.

Chen Menghong. "Between the Chinese Tradition and Dutch Colonial System: Chinese Marriages in Batavia in the Nineteenth Century." In *The Archives of the Kong Koan of Batavia*, edited by Leonard Blussé and Chen Menghong, 59-68. Leiden: Brill, 2003.

———. *De Chinese gemeenschap van Batavia, 1843-1865: Een onderzoek naar Het Kong Koan-Archief.* Amsterdam University Press, 2011.

Chu, Richard T. *Chinese and Chinese Mestizos of Manila: Family, Identity, and Culture, 1870-1925.* Leiden: Brill, 2010.

Chü, Tung-tsu. *Law and Society in Traditional China.* Westport, CT: Hyperion Press, 1980.

Clark, Anna. *Desire: A History of European Sexuality.* New York: Routledge, 2008.

Claver, Alexander. *Dutch Commerce and Chinese Merchants in Java: Colonial Relationships in Trade and Finance, 1800-1942.* Leiden: Brill, 2014. https://doi.org/10.1163/j.ctt1w8h115.

Claver, Alexander, and Thomas J. Lindbald. "Going Bankrupt? Business Failure in Colonial Indonesia, c. 1870-1940." *Economics and Finance in Indonesia* 57, no. 2 (2009): 139-57.

Coppel, Charles A. "From Christian Mission to Confucian Religion: The Nederlandsche Zendingsvereeniging and the Chinese of West Java, 1870-1910." In *Studying Ethnic Chinese in Indonesia*, 291-312. Singapore: Society of Asian Studies, 2002.

———. *Indonesian Chinese in Crisis.* New York: Oxford University Press, 1983.

———. "The Origins of Confucianism as an Organized Religion in Java, 1900-1923." *Journal of Southeast Asian Studies* 12, no. 1 (1981): 179-96. https://doi.org/10.1017/S0022463400005063.

Cushman, Jennifer Wayne. *Family and State: The Formation of a Sino-Thai Tin-Mining Dynasty, 1797-1932.* Singapore: Oxford University Press, 1991.

Davidson, Jamie S. "The Study of Political Ethnicity in Southeast Asia." In *Southeast Asia in Political Science: Theory, Region, and Qualitative Analysis,* edited by Erik Kuhonta, Dan Slater, and Tuong Vu, 199-227. Stanford, CA: Stanford University Press, 2008.

De, Rohit. "Mumtaz Bibi's Broken Heart: The Many Lives of the Dissolution of Muslim Marriages Act." In *The Indian Economic and Social History Review* 46, no. 1 (2009): 105-30. https://doi.org/10.1177/001946460804600106.

Djamour, Judith. *Malay Kinship and Marriage in Singapore.* 1st reprint with corrections. London: Athlone Press, 1965.

Dros, Nico. *Wages: 1820–1940*. Vol. 13. *Changing Economy in Indonesia: A Selection of Statistical Source Material from the Early 19th Century Up to 1940*. Amsterdam: Royal Tropical Institute, 1992.

Duara, Prasenjit. *The Crisis of Global Modernity: Asian Traditions and a Sustainable Future*. Cambridge: Cambridge University Press, 2015.

Dumas, Alexandre, fils. *La Dame aux camélias*. Brussels: Alphonse Lebègue, 1848.

———. *The Lady of the Camellias*. Translated by Liesl Schillinger. New York: Penguin, 2013. Originally published as *La Dame aux camélias* (Brussels: Alphonse Lebègue, 1848).

Eaksittipong, Sittithep. "Textualizing the 'Chinese of Thailand': Politics, Knowledge and the Chinese in Thailand during the Cold War." PhD diss., National University of Singapore, 2017.

Fanon, Frantz. *Black Skin, White Masks*. Translated by Richard Philcox. New York: Grove, 2008. Originally published as *Peau noire, masques blancs* (Paris: Éditions du Seuil, 1952).

Fasseur, Cees. "Cornerstone and Stumbling Block: Racial Classification and the Late Colonial State in Indonesia." In *The Late Colonial State in Indonesia: Political and Economic Foundations of the Netherlands Indies, 1880–1942*, edited by E. Nathaniel Gates, 37–56. New York: Routledge, 1997.

Firpo, Christina Elizabeth. *The Uprooted: Race, Children, and Imperialism in French Indochina, 1890–1980*. Honolulu: University of Hawai'i Press, 2016.

Fowler, George A. Introduction to *The Rose of Cikembang*, by Tek Hoay Kwee. Jakarta: Lontar Foundation, 2013.

Freedman, Maurice. *Chinese Family and Marriage in Singapore*. London: H.M. Stationery Office, 1957.

———. *Chinese Lineage and Society: Fukien and Kwangtung*. New York: Athlone Press, 1971.

Furnivall, John S. *Colonial Policy and Practice: A Comparative Study of Burma and Netherlands India*. Cambridge: Cambridge University Press, 1956. https://doi.org/10.1017/CBO9781107051140.

Geertz, Hildred. *The Javanese Family: A Study of Kinship and Socialization*. New York: Free Press of Glencoe, 1961.

Ghosh, Durba. *Sex and the Family in Colonial India: The Making of Empire*. Cambridge: Cambridge University Press, 2006. https://doi.org/10.1017/CBO9781139878418.

Goody, Jack. *The Development of the Family and Marriage in Europe*. Cambridge: Cambridge University Press, 1983. https://doi.org/10.1017/CBO9780511607752.

Gooszen, Hans. "The Marriage Market for Chinese Girls in Batavia: Some Exploration in Its Territorial Boundaries." In *The Archives of the Kong Koan of Batavia*, edited by Leonard Blussé and Chen Menghong, 69–79. Leiden: Brill, 2003.

Gouw Giok Siong. "Segi-Segi hukum Peraturan Perkawinan Tjampuran (Staatsblad 1898 No. 158)." Djakarta: Perjetakan Express, 1955.

Govaars-Tjia, Ming. *Dutch Colonial Education: The Chinese Experience in Indonesia, 1900–1942*. Translated by L. L. Trytten. Chinese Heritage Centre, 2005.

Groeneboer, Kees. *Weg tot het Westen: Het Nederlands voor Indië, 1600–1950* [Way to the West: The Dutch Indies, 1600–1950]. Leiden: KITLV Uitgeverij, 1993.

Haryono, Steve. *Perkawinan strategis: Hubungan keluarga antara opsir-opsir Tionghoa dan "Cabang Atas" di Jawa pada abad ke-19 Dan 20* [Strategic marriages: Familial relations among Chinese officers and the "Upper Branch" in Java during the 19th and 20th centuries]. Indonesia: Steve Haryono, 2017.

Heryanto, Ariel. "Ethnic Identities and Erasure: Chinese Indonesians in Public Culture." In *Southeast Asian Identities: Culture and the Politics of Representation in Indo-*

nesia, Malaysia, Singapore and Thailand, edited by Joel S. Kahn, 95–114. Singapore: Institute of Southeast Asian Studies, 1998.
Ho Engseng. *The Graves of Tarim: Genealogy and Mobility across the Indian Ocean.* Berkeley: University of California Press, 2006.
Hoadley, Mason C. "Javanese, Peranakan, and Chinese Elites in Cirebon: Changing Ethnic Boundaries." *Journal of Asian Studies* 47, no. 3 (1988): 503–17. https://doi.org/10.2307/2056972.
Hoogervorst, Tom. "What Kind of Language Was 'Chinese Malay' in Late-Colonial Java?" *Indonesia and the Malay World* 45, no. 133 (2017): 294–314.
Hooker, M. B. "English Law and the Invention of Chinese Personal Law in Singapore and Malaysia." In *Law and the Chinese in Southeast Asia*, edited by M. Barry Hooker, 95–130. Singapore: Institute of Southeast Asian Studies, 2002.
Hsieh Bao Hua. *Concubinage and Servitude in Late Imperial China.* Lanham, MD: Lexington Books, 2014.
Hsu, Francis L. K. *Under the Ancestors' Shadow: Kinship, Personality and Social Mobility in China.* New York: Columbia University Press, 1948. Reissued with a new chapter. Stanford: Stanford University Press, 1967.
Hughes-Hallett, Lucy. "The Beautiful Corpse." In *Violetta and Her Sisters: The Lady of the Camellias: Responses to the Myth,* edited by John Nicholas, 93–98. London: Faber and Faber, 1994.
Hui Yew-Foong. *Strangers at Home: History and Subjectivity among the Chinese Communities of West Kalimantan, Indonesia.* Leiden: Brill, 2011.
Ikeya, Chie. *Refiguring Women, Colonialism, and Modernity in Burma.* Honolulu: University of Hawai'i Press, 2011.
Jones, Eric. *Wives, Slaves, and Concubines: A History of the Female Underclass in Dutch Asia.* DeKalb: Northern Illinois University Press, 2010.
Jones, Gavin W., Endang Sulistyaningsih, and Terence H. Hall. "Prostitution in Indonesia." Vol. no. 52. Working Papers in Demography. Canberra: Australian National University, 1995.
Kan, S. Y. "Personal Data Tjoe-Hong Lie (1846–1896), Stamboom Kan, Han En Tan—Genealogy Online." www.genealogieonline.nl/en/stamboom-kan-han-en-tan/.
Kelly, John D. *A Politics of Virtue: Hinduism, Sexuality, and Countercolonial Discourse in Fiji.* Chicago: University of Chicago Press, 1991.
Kesastraan Melayu Tionghoa dan kebangsaan Indonesia. Vol. 2, *Kesastraan Melayu Tionghoa.* Jakarta: Kepustakaan Populer Gramedia (KPG), 2001.
Khan, Sher Banu A. L. *Sovereign Women in a Muslim Kingdom: The Sultanahs of Aceh, 1641–1699.* Ithaca, NY: Cornell University Press, 2017.
Kuiper, Koos. "The Early Dutch Sinologists: A Study of Their Training in Holland and China and Their Functions in the Netherlands Indies (1854–1900)." PhD thesis, Leiden University, 2015.
Kuo, Margaret. *Intolerable Cruelty: Marriage, Law, and Society in Early Twentieth-Century China.* Lanham, MD: Rowman & Little, 2012.
Kwartanada, Didi. "Bangsawan Prampoewan: Enlightened Peranakan Chinese Women from Early Twentieth Century Java." *Wacana* 18, no. 2 (2017): 422–54. https://doi.org/10.17510/wacana.v18i2.591.
Kwee Hui Kian. *The Political Economy of Java's Northeast Coast, c. 1740–1800: Elite Synergy.* Leiden; Boston: Brill, 2006.
Kwee, John B. "The Many Implications of Name Change for Indonesian-Born Chinese." In *The Chinese Diaspora: Selected Essays*, Vol. 2, edited by Wang Ling-chi and Wang Gungwu, 50–54. Singapore: Times Academic Press, 1998.

Kwee Tek Hoay. *The Origins of the Modern Chinese Movement in Indonesia*. Translated by Lea E. Williams. Ithaca, NY: Cornell University Press, 1969.

——. *The Rose of Cikembang*. Translated by George A. Fowler. Jakarta: Lontar Foundation, 2013. Originally published in serial form as *Boenga Roos darie Tjikembang* in *Panorama* (1927).

Kwee Thiam Tjing. *Menjadi Tjamboek Berdoeri: Memoar Kwee Thiam Tjing*. Depok: Komunitas Bambu, 2010.

Lee, Peter. *Sarong Kebaya: Peranakan Fashion in an Interconnected World, 1500–1950*. Singapore: Asian Civilisations Museum, 2014.

Lee, Y. K. "The Grand Jury of Singapore (1819–1874)." *Journal of the Malaysian Branch of the Royal Asiatic Society* 46, no. 2 (224) (1973): 55–150.

Lewis, D. J. "A Requiem for Chinese Customary Law in Hong Kong." *International and Comparative Law Quarterly* 32, no. 2 (1983): 347–79.

Lim How Seng, "Social Structure and Bang Interactions." In *A General History of the Chinese in Singapore*, edited by Kwa Chong Guan and Kua Bak Lim, 115–34. Singapore: World Scientific, 2019.

Lindsey, Tim. "Reconstituting the Ethnic Chinese in Post-Soeharto Indonesia: Law, Racial Discrimination, and Reform." In *Chinese Indonesians*, edited by Tim Lindsey and Helen Pausacker, 41–76. Singapore: ISEAS–Yusof Ishak Institute Singapore, 2018. https://doi.org/10.1355/9789812305442-007.

Liu Oiyan. "Creolised Confucianism: Syncretism and Confucian Revivalism at the Turn of the Twentieth Century in Java." *Journal of Southeast Asian Studies* 51, no. 1–2 (2020): 154–74. https://doi.org/10.1017/S0022463420000272.

Lohanda, Mona. *Growing Pains: The Chinese and the Dutch in Colonial Java, 1890–1942*. Jakarta: Yayasan Cipta Loka Caraka, 2002.

——. *The Kapitan Cina of Batavia, 1837–1942: A History of Chinese Establishment in Colonial Society*. Jakarta: Djambatan, 1996.

Loos, Tamara. *Subject Siam: Family, Law, and Colonial Modernity in Thailand*. Ithaca, NY: Cornell University Press, 2006.

——. "Transnational Histories of Sexualities in Asia." *American Historical Review* 114, no. 5 (2009): 1309–24. https://doi.org/10.1086/ahr.114.5.1309.

Lowrie, Claire. *Masters and Servants: Cultures of Empire in the Tropics*. Manchester: Manchester University Press, 2016.

Maier, Hendrik M. J. *We Are Playing Relatives: A Survey of Malay Writing*. Singapore: ISEAS, 2004.

Mandal, Sumit K. "Strangers Who Are Not Foreign: Pramoeday's Disturbing Language on the Chinese of Indonesia." In *The Chinese in Indonesia: An English Translation of "Hoakiau di Indonesia,"* by Pramoedya Ananta Toer, edited by Mary Redway and Tan Dan Feng, translated by Max Lane, 2nd ed., 35–54. Singapore: Select, 2007.

Mani, Lata. *Contentious Traditions: The Debate on Sati in Colonial India*. Berkeley: University of California Press, 1998.

Mann, Susan. *Gender and Sexuality in Modern Chinese History*. Cambridge: Cambridge University Press, 2011.

——. "Grooming a Daughter for Marriage: Brides and Wives in the Mid-Ch'ing Period." In *Marriage and Inequality in Chinese Society*, edited by Rubie S. Watson and Patricia Buckley Ebrey, 204–30. Berkeley: University of California Press, 1991.

Marle, Hans van. "De groep der Europeanen in Nederlands-Indië Iets over ontstaan en groei." *Indonesië* 5 (1951).

McClintock, Anne. *Imperial Leather: Race, Gender, and Sexuality in the Colonial Conquest*. New York: Routledge, 1995.

Ming, Hanneke. "Barracks-Concubinage in the Indies, 1887–1920." *Indonesia* 35 (April 1983): 65. https://doi.org/10.2307/3350866.

Moeis, Abdoel. *Never the Twain*. Translated by Thomas M. Hunter. Jakarta: The Lontar Foundation, 2010.

Nandy, Ashis. *The Intimate Enemy: Loss and Recovery of Self under Colonialism*. Oxford: Oxford University Press, 1983.

Overbeck, H. O. "Malay Animal and Flower Shaers." *Journal of the Malayan Branch of the Royal Asiatic Society* 12, no. 2 (119) (1934): 108–48.

Palmier, Leslie. *Social Status and Power in Java*. London: Athlon Press, 1960.

Pan, Lynn. *When True Love Came to China*. Hong Kong: Hong Kong University Press, 2015.

Pearson, Stuart. *Bittersweet: The Memoir of a Chinese Indonesian Family in the Twentieth Century*. Singapore: NUS Press, 2008.

Pijper, G. F. *Studiën over de geschiedenis van de Islam in Indonesia, 1900–1950*. Leiden: E. J. Brill, 1977.

Post, Peter. "Profitable Partnerships: The Chinese Business Elite and Dutch Lawyers in the Making of Semarang." *Journal of Southeast Asian Studies* 52, no. 2 (2021): 214–45. https://doi.org/10.1017/S0022463421000448.

Post, Peter, and May Ling Thio. *The Kwee Family of Ciledug: Family, Status, and Modernity in Colonial Java Visualising the Private Life of the Peranakan Chinese Sugar Elite*. Volendam, The Netherlands: LM, 2019.

Raben, Remco. "Batavia and Colombo: The Ethnic and Spatial Order of Two Colonial Cities 1600–1800." PhD diss., Leiden University, 1996.

Raffles, Thomas Stamford. *The History of Java*. Vol. 1. London: Printed for Black, Parbury, and Allen, Booksellers to the Hon. East-India Company and John Murray, 1817.

Ravensbergen, Sanne. "Courtrooms of Conflict. Criminal Law, Local Elites and Legal Pluralities in Colonial Java." PhD diss., Leiden University, 2018.

Reddy, William M. "The Rule of Love: The History of Western Romantic Love in Comparative Perspective." In *New Dangerous Liaisons: Discourses on Europe and Love in the Twentieth Century*, edited by Luisa Passerini, Liliana Ellena, and Alexander C. T. Geppert, 1st ed., 33–58. New York: Berghahn Books, 2010.

Reid, Anthony. "'Closed' and 'Open' Slave Systems in Pre-colonial Southeast Asia." In *Slavery, Bondage, and Dependency in Southeast Asia*, edited by Anthony Reid and Jennifer Brewster, 156–87. New York: St. Martin's Press, 1983.

——. "Flows and Seepages in the Long-Term Chinese Interaction with Southeast Asia." In *Sojourners and Settlers: Histories of Southeast Asia and the Chinese*, edited by Anthony Reid, Kristine Alilunas-Rodgers, and G. William Skinner, 15–50. St. Leonards, New South Wales: Allen and Unwin, 1996.

——. *A History of Southeast Asia: Critical Crossroads*. Chichester, England: Wiley Blackwell, 2015.

——. *Southeast Asia in the Age of Commerce, 1450–1680*. 2 vols. New Haven, CT: Yale University Press, 1988–1993.

Reyes, Raquel A. G. *Love, Passion and Patriotism: Sexuality and the Philippine Propaganda Movement, 1882–1892*. Singapore: NUS Press, 2008.

Rush, James R. *Opium to Java: Revenue Farming and Chinese Enterprise in Colonial Indonesia, 1860–1910*. Ithaca, NY: Cornell University Press, 1990.

Sai Siew-Min. "Mandarin Lessons: Modernity, Colonialism and Chinese Cultural Nationalism in the Dutch East Indies, c. 1900s." *Inter-Asia Cultural Studies* 17, no. 3 (2016): 375–94.

Salmon, Claudine. "Ancestral Halls, Funeral Associations, and Attempts at Resinicization in Nineteenth Century Southeast Asia." In *Sojourners and Settlers: Histories* of *Southeast Asia and the Chinese*, edited by Anthony Reid, Kristine Alilunas-Rodgers, and G. William Skinner, 183–203. St. Leonards, New South Wales: Allen and Unwin, 1996.

———. *Literature in Malay by the Chinese of Indonesia: A Provisional Annotated Bibliography*. Paris: Editions de la Maison des sciences de l'homme, 1981.

Salmon, Claudine, and Denys Lombard. "Confucianisme et esprit de réforme dans les communautés Chinoises d'Insulinde (fin XIXe—début XXe siècle)." In *En suivant la voie royale: Mélanges offerts en hommage à Léon Vandermeersch*, edited by Jacques Gernet and Marc Kalinowski. Paris: EFEO, 1997.

Sangren, P. Steven. *Chinese Sociologics: An Anthropological Account of the Role of Alienation in Social Reproduction*. New York: Routledge, 2020.

Savage, Gail L. "The Operation of the 1857 Divorce Act, 1860–1910: A Research Note." *Journal of Social History* 16, no. 4 (1983): 103–10.

Seng Guo-Quan. "Fujianese Pioneers and Javanese Kings: Peranakan Chinese Lineage and the Politics of Belonging in West Java, 1890s–2000s." *Indonesia* 104, no. 104 (2017): 65–89. https://doi.org/10.1353/ind.2017.0011.

———. "The Gender Politics of Confucian Family Law: Contracts, Credit and Creole Chinese Bilateral Kinship in Dutch Colonial Java (1850s-1900)." *Comparative Studies in Society and History* 60, no. 2 (2018): 390–414. https://doi.org/10.1017/S0010417518000099.

Sharafi, Mitra June. *Law and Identity in Colonial South Asia: Parsi Legal Culture, 1772–1947*. Cambridge: Cambridge University Press, 2014. https://doi.org/10.1017/CBO9781107256545.

Sidharta, Myra, ed. "The Making of the Indonesian Chinese Woman." In *Indonesian Women in Focus: Past and Present Notions*, edited by Elsbeth Locher-Scholten and Anke Niehof, 58–76. Dordrecht, Holland: Foris, 1987.

———. *100 tahun Kwee Tek Hoay: Dari penjaja tekstil sampai ke pendekar pena* [100 years of Kwee Tek Hoay: From textile peddler to warrior of the pen]. Jakarta: Sinar Harapan, 1989.

Siegel, James T. "Early Thoughts on the Violence of May 13 and 14, 1998 in Jakarta." *Indonesia*, no. 66, 1998, 74–108.

———. *Fetish, Recognition, Revolution*. Princeton, NJ: Princeton University Press, 1997.

Simmel, Georg. "The Stranger." In *The Sociology of Georg Simmel*, translated and edited by Kurt H. Wolff, 402–8. New York: Free Press, 1950.

Skinner, G. William. "Chinese Assimilation and Thai Politics." *Journal of Asian Studies* 16, no. 2 (1957): 237–50. https://doi.org/10.2307/2941381.

———. *Chinese Society in Thailand: An Analytical History*. Ithaca, NY: Cornell University Press, 1957.

———. "Creolized Chinese Societies in Southeast Asia." In *Sojourners and Settlers: Histories of Southeast Asia and the Chinese*, edited by Anthony Reid, Kristine Alilunas-Rodgers, and G. William Skinner, 50–93. St Leonards, New South Wales: Allen and Unwin, 1996.

Spivak, Gayatri Chakravorty. "Can the Subaltern Speak?" In *Marxism and the Interpretation of Culture*, edited by Cary Nelson and Lawrence Grossberg, 271–313. Urbana: University of Illinois Press, 1988.

Stenberg, Josh. *Minority Stages: Sino-Indonesian Performance and Public Display*. Honolulu: University of Hawai'i Press, 2019.

Stoler, Ann Laura. *Carnal Knowledge and Imperial Power: Race and the Intimate in Colonial Rule*. Berkeley: University of California Press, 2020.

———. *Race and the Education of Desire: Foucault's History of Sexuality and the Colonial Order of Things*. Durham, NC: Duke University Press, 1995.

———. "Sexual Affronts and Racial Frontiers: European Identities and the Cultural Politics of Exclusion in Colonial Southeast Asia." In *Tensions of Empire: Colonial Cultures in a Bourgeois World*, edited by Frederick Cooper and Ann Laura Stoler, 198–237. University of California Press, 1997. https://doi.org/10.1525/california/9780520205406.001.0001.

Suryadinata, Leo. *Peranakan Chinese Politics in Java, 1917–1942*. Rev. ed. Singapore: Singapore University Press, 1981.

———. *Pribumi Indonesians, the Chinese Minority and China: A Study of Perceptions and Policies*. Singapore: Marshall Cavendish, 2005.

Sutherland, Heather. *The Making of a Bureaucratic Elite: The Colonial Transformation of the Javanese Priyayi*. Singapore: Heinemann Educational Books (Asia), Asian Studies Association of Australia, 1979.

Sutrisno, Evi. "Moral Is Political: Notions of Ideal Citizenship in Lie Kim Hok's Hikajat Khonghoetjoe." *Wacana* 18, no. 1 (2017): 183–215. https://doi.org/10.17510/wacana.v18i1.577.

Tan Chee-Beng. *The Baba of Melaka: Culture and Identity of a Chinese Peranakan Community in Malaysia*. 2nd ed. Petaling Jaya: Strategic Information and Research Development Centre, 2021.

Tan, Mely Giok-Lan. *The Chinese of Sukabumi: A Study in Social and Cultural Accommodation*. Ithaca, NY: Cornell University Press, 1963.

Taylor, Jean Gelman. *The Social World of Batavia: European and Eurasian in Dutch Asia*. 2nd ed. University of Wisconsin Press, 2009.

Theiss, Janet M. *Disgraceful Matters: The Politics of Chastity in Eighteenth-Century China*. Berkeley: University of California Press, 2005. https://doi.org/10.1525/j.ctt1ppz0p.

Thung Liang Lee. "The Unreality of Chinese Nationalism in Indonesia: An Apologia and a Reorientation." *Indonesia Review* 2, no. 1 (1954): 69–75.

Tjiook-Liem, Patricia. *De rechtspositie der Chinezen in Nederlands-Indië, 1848–1942: Wetgevingsbeleid tussen beginsel en belang*. Amsterdam: Leiden University Press, 2009.

———. "Feiten en ficties bij het ontstaan van de Japannerwet" [Facts and fiction surrounding the emergence of the Japanese law]. *Themis* 4 (2005): 192–208.

Toer, Pramoedya Ananta. *The Chinese in Indonesia; An English Translation of "Hoakiau di Indonesia."* Edited by Mary Redway and Tan Dan Feng. Translated by Max Lane. 2nd ed. Singapore: Select, 2007.

Tran, Lisa. "Concubines under Modern Chinese Law." PhD diss., UCLA, 2005.

Vickers, Adrian. *Bali: A Paradise Created*. 2nd ed. Tokyo; Tuttle, 2012.

Wallerstein, Immanuel. *The Modern World-System: Capitalist Agriculture and the Origins of the European World-Economy in the Sixteenth Century*. New York: Academic Press, 1974.

Wertheim, W. F. "Political Status of the Chinese in Pre-war Netherlands Indies." *Indonesian Law and Administration Review* 3, no. 2 (1997): 6–27.

Wheeler, Charles. "Interests, Institutions, and Identity: Strategic Adaptation and the Ethno-evolution of *Minh Hương* (Central Vietnam), 16th–19th Centuries." *Itinerario* 39, no. 1 (2015): 141–166.

Williams, Lea E. *Overseas Chinese Nationalism: The Genesis of the Pan-Chinese Movement in Indonesia, 1900–1916*. Glencoe, IL: Free Press, 1960.

Willmott, Donald E. *The National Status of the Chinese in Indonesia, 1900–1958*. Ithaca, NY: Modern Indonesia Project, Southeast Asia Program, Dept. of Far Eastern Studies, Cornell University, 1961.

Wolf, Margery. *Women and the Family in Rural Taiwan*. Stanford, CA: Stanford University Press, 1972.

Worsley, Peter. "Gouw Peng Liang's Novella, *Lo Fen Koei*: Patrons and Women; An Account of the Peranakan Chinese Community of Java in the Late 19th Century." *Archipel* 68, no. 1 (2004): 241–72.
Wu Fengbin, Nie Dening, Xie Meihua. *Yajiada Hua ren hun yin: 1772–1919 nian Bacheng Tangren chenghun zhuce bu*. Xiamen: Xiamen da xue chu ban she, 2010.
Yahaya, Nurfadzilah. *Fluid Jurisdictions: Colonial Law and Arabs in Southeast Asia*. Ithaca, NY: Cornell University Press, 2020.
Yen Ching Hwang, "Early Chinese Clan Organizations in Singapore and Malaya, 1819–1911." *Journal of Southeast Asian Studies* 12, no. 1 (1981): 62–92.
Zhou Taomo. *Migration in the Time of Revolution: China, Indonesia, and the Cold War*. Ithaca, NY: Cornell University Press, 2019.

Index

Locators in *italic* refer to figures and tables.

abduction:
  excessive lust (M: *birahi*) motivating it, 122–123, 136
  kidnapping plots in *Song from Seven Heavens* by Ong Ping Lok, 140–141
  protections against in verifications for marriage certifications, 25
  of slave women, 19
  See also pingitan (seclusion of post-puberty young women)
Abeyasekere, Susan, 19
adat. *See* marriage law–customary (*adat*) law
Albrecht, J. E., 34–35
Algemeen Handelsblad, Caroline Tan's speech on the front page of, 153
Andaya, Barbara Watson, 17

Baay, Reggie, 172
Baba. See peranakan–local born.
Bao Jiemin, 8, 193
Batavia:
  divorce rate among the Chinese in 1820–1890, 60–61, *60*
  location in Southeast Asia, *xvi*
  marriage rate among the Chinese of, 164–165, *164*
  marriage rate for Europeans in (1920–1940), 164, *164*
  protest again the draft of Indies Chinese marriage law (1892), 152
  registration of illegitimate births in, 173–174, *173*
  as a slave town of the Dutch VOC trading empire, 18
  See also Sin Po
Batavia Chinese marriage registry. *See* Chinese Council of Batavia (Kong Koan)–marriage registry
birth registration:
  acceptance among the Chinese of Java, 171–172, *171*
  civil registry established by the Chinese Council (Kong Koan), 159

  as a form of de facto marriage ceremony, 177, *177*
  legal category of illegitimacy created for children born to native mothers, 13, 169, 174, 187
  opportunity to pass on the father's patrilineal name facilitated by, 143, 169–171
  racialized legal apartheid between Europeans and Asians justified by, 143, 169
  registration of illegitimate births, 172–174, *173*
Blussé, Leonard, 12, 24–25
Bogor:
  Dutch missionary school in, 104
  generational changes in attitudes toward marriage in, 39–40
  location of, *xvi*
  Phoa brothers from, 112, 160
  spread of "male retributive" moral tales in, 136
  THHK branch in, 109, 214n19
  Thung lineage group of, 196
Bok Tok weekly based in Surabaya, Tan's speech translated and rebutted in, 153–156, 222n53
Boomgaard, Peter, population estimates, 164, 207n16, 223n83
Borel, Henri, 149, 220n17
Bowen, John Richard, 181

Carey, Peter, 12
Chan Faye Yik-Wei, 12, 226n53
Chandra, Elizabeth, 12, 135, 136
Chen Menghong, 12, 42, 197
Chinese Council of Batavia (Kong Koan):
  authority as ritual master of the Chinese, 110
  cased recorded in the minutes of the proceedings of, 13
  cases involving native concubines, 209n85
  cases of *nyai* in Chinese civil trail records, 19–21, 28–31, 47, 202nn25–26

243

Chinese Council of Batavia (Kong Koan) (*continued*)
civil trial records on transactions for slave girls, 19, 201n8
"Collection Guide Archive of the Kong Koan of Batavia," 14
endogamous vows in trials of, 50
interior set up of, 57, *58*
Major Tan Eng Goan as head of, 37, 38, *39*, 217n40
Chinese Council of Batavia (Kong Koan)–marriage registry:
ages at marriage of Chinese women, 42
calls to boycott it, 162–163
case of Tjoa Kiat Beng, 25, 202n38
Chen Menghong's study of, 42, 197
data from the 1930 records of, 176, *176*
decline in numbers of, 207n15
divorce procedures, 57
divorce records, 207n16, 223n84
knowledge of Confucian marriage rituals reflected in testimonies recorded by, 25–26
names of go-betweens no longer recorded in (1912), 110
rate among the Chinese of Batavia, Semarang, and Surabaya (1920–1940), 164–165, *164*
rules for marriage, divorce, birth, and death, 159
upholding of the Six Rites, 26
Chinese families in Java:
Chinese man depicted with his *nyai*, 1, *2*
portrait featuring a Chinese wife-cum-mother, 1, *3*
See also peranakan (M: local born) and peranakan families
Chu, Richard T., 192
Chung Hwa Hui:
annual meeting on 20 October 1913, 152, 221n35
formation of, 152
Fromberg's keynote speech for their annual meeting (1912), 152
Fromberg's lecture "The Indies-Chinese Family and Legislation" (1916), 159–160
scholarship fund for young people of Chinese descent, 221n35
Caroline Tan's keynote speech for their annual meeting (1913), 153–154
Claver, Alexander, 12
concubines:
bini moeda, 123, 178, 180
de-sinicizing by Ong Ping Lok's *Song from Seven Heavens* (1931), 140–141
Eurasian women as concubines for Asian men, 220–221n9
interethnic concubinage relations, 187, 192
"philosophical basis for concubinage" in Fromberg's draft code, 148
prices paid for, 74–75
separate residences from primary wives, 75–76
concubines–*goendik/gundik*:
as the derogatory term for kept women, 125–126, 160
gundik (mistresses) in the adultery law (Art. 256) of the Native Criminal Code, 150
gundik used as a term by Nio Joe Lan, 180
laws concerning children of, 178
mid-1950s campaign against Chinese men's fostering of *gundik* (mistresses), 175, 181–182
concubines–native concubines (*nyai*):
association with the Dutch colonial social milieu, 177
custody disputes, 27–31, 46
definition in the *Encyclopaedie van Netherlandisch-Indië*, 120
depiction with a Chinese man, 1, *2*
as the dominant female head of Chinese settler households, 18, 31–32, 49
example of Nyai Gambir, 21, 29
example of Nyai Marsiti, 185, *186*
example of Nyai Roem, 178–179
examples of cases in Chinese civil trail records, 19–21, 28–31, 47, 202nn25–26
exclusion from Confucian marriage, 10, 12, 18, 23–27, 32, 187–188
goendik as the derogatory term for kept women, 125–126, 160
in Kwee Tek Hoay's *The Rose of Cikembang*, 1–3
liminal zone inhabited by, 15, 27, 32, 191
as a term of respect, 177
Confucian Associations (Khong Khauw Hwee):
congress on marriage rites (1924), 166
Poey Kok Gway on marriage rites reforms, 165–166
Confucianism:
ancestral worship, 9, 170
basic learning and literacy of young men aspiring to careers in business, 34–36, 41
Confucianizing framing of Dumas's Christian "love" in Thio and Tjan's translations and adaptations, 130–132
creole Confucian patriarchal resistance to women's equality, 151, 153–158

rise of Confucian cultural nationalism, 170
Tjhoen Tjhioe periodical, 112, 113, 128, 129, 222n51
See also wife-initiated Creole Confucian divorces
Confucian marriage:
  exclusion of Indonesian women from, 10, 12, 18, 23–27, 32, 187–188
  go-betweens, 24, 25–26, 35, 110, 189
  love marriage contrasted with in novels by Dutch-educated Chinese authors, 120, 122–128
  match-made marriage, 125, 159
  middle-class respectability associated with, 33, 37, 44, 51
  persistence after 1919 of, 165
  practices of Islamic marriage law hybridized with, 60
  role in the creation of racially endogamous communities, 15, 128, 187, 188
  Six Rites of, 24, 26–27, 75, 166, 168, 202n44
  See also wife-initiated Creole Confucian divorces
Confucian reformers:
  gender equality and women's rights resisted by, 13
  new moralities invented to discipline creole bourgeois subjects, 10, 119–120
  new patriliny reconstituted to counter the Dutch colonial civilizing mission, 12
  revivalist movement first born in Batavia, 14
  revivalist organizations. *See* Tiong Hoa Hwee Koan (THHK)
Coppel, Charles A., 12, 104, 165, 194, 200
Cordes, J. W. C., monogamous marriage law proposed by, 149

divorce:
  civil law divorce in England (1857), 207n18
  delaying of wives' divorce pleas, 65
  divorce rate among the Chinese in Batavia, 1820–1890, 60–61, *60*
  proceedings initiated by women, 1820–1890s, 60, *61*
divorce–abuse, as one of five causes cited in divorce pleas, 55, 198
divorce–abuse pleas, as one of five causes cited in divorce pleas, 55, 61, *62*, 63, 198
divorce–concubine jealousy:
  alleged transgressions, 76–77
  as one of five causes cited in divorce pleas, 55, 61, *62*, 70–74, *73*, 198

divorce–desertion pleas:
  another source of tension as the trigger for, 198
  case of Liem Yam Nio, 66–67
  case of Lie Soen Nio, 210n23
  case of Oeij Lai Nio, 69
  case of Sofijah, 57
  case of Tan Djie Nio, 66
  case of Tjeng Tjoe Nio, 58–59, 61
  case of Tjia Hong Nio, 69–70
  concubine favoritism related to, 59, 61, 71–74, *73*, 77
  filings by women in uxorilocal marriages, 68–70
  husband's misappropriation of the wife's personal property, 68
  as one of five causes cited in divorce pleas, 55, *62*, 65–67, 198
  women's conception of spousal dependence, 63–65, 67–68, 70
divorce–eviction, as one of five causes cited in divorce pleas, 55, *62*, 198
divorce–jealousy pleas, as one of five causes cited in divorce pleas, 55, 198
divorce–tensions with in-laws, as one of five causes cited in divorce pleas, 55, 61, *62*, 198
Djamour, Judith, 207n15
Duara, Prasenjit, 184
Dumas, Alexandre–*Lady Camille*:
  Pho Tjoen Hoay's translation and serialization for *Li Po*, 128, 217n47
  reception in China, 128, 129, 130, 217n46
  Sie Tjaij Kim (*Nona Kim*) adaptation by Thio Tjin Boen, 128–129, 130–131
  translation and adaptation by Tjan Kim Bie, 129
Dutch colonial sinologists:
  authoritative positions on questions of family law and Chinese women's property rights, 86, 91, 92, 108
  Chinese mandarin tutors brought to the Indies as personal secretaries, 211n34
  Lie Kim Hok's reliance on, 105
Dutch colonial state:
  Governor-General Idenburg's gradual elimination of concubinage, 120–121, 148–149
  race management through family law, 7–8, 108, 174, 189–190, 214n16
  recognition of Chinese customary marriage, 23–24
  slave trade, 18
  See also van Limburg Stirum, J. P.

Dutch-educated Chinese:
  Anna Tan Sian Nio's recounting of concubinage after 1919, 178
  championing of women's rights, 13
  femme fatale genre associated with the specter of Dutch-educated Asian women by Chandra, 135, 136
  love marriage contrasted with Confucian marriage in novels by, 120, 122–128
  Oey Beng Liong's announcement of the "free marriage choice," 132
  See also Lie Kim Hok; Loe Ping Kian; Tio Tek Hong
Dutch Vereenighde Oost-India Compagnie (VOC):
  ban on marriage between Chinese and Muslim subjects, 24
  collapse of, 15, 163

Faber, Godfried von, 108, 214n16
family law:
  Tan, Siok Tjwan's calls for reforms, 156–157
  unification of European and Asian subjects under the civil code, 146–149, 220n16
  upholding of Confucian-colonial family law associated with manhood, 34
  See also birth registration; marriage law; Dutch colonial state
family law–child custody:
  assimilation of nyai-reared children as a concern, 29, 203n57
  case of Emak Kwiesa, 28–29
  custody rights claimed by a nyai, 27–31
  Semarang case of Nauru's claims to her sons, 28
  transfer to a patrilineal kin, 29, 203n58
  transitory law on the guardianship of children born outside of wedlock, 178, 225n29
Fasseur, Cees, 168
Freedman, Maurice, 70, 206n2
Fromberg, Pieter Hendrik:
  arranged marriage viewed as "bordering on slavery" by, 148, 153
  championing of causes of the Indies Chinese and emergent Indonesian nationalist groups, 151–152, 161, 221n33, 221n35
  The Chinese Movement in Java (1911), 151–152
  feminist critique against patriarchal practices launched with Caroline Tan, 152
  on gender equality and monogamous marriage, 145–146
  on the illegal status of children born outside of marriage, 178
  "The Indies-Chinese Family and Legislation" (1916), 159–160
  keynote speech for Chung Hwa Hui, 152
  "New Regulation of the Private Legal Status of the Chinese" (1897), 86–87, 89, 148, 211n50
  six notes (1915) concerning Republican China's provisional civil code, 149–151
Furnivall, John S., 7

Geertz, Hildred:
  on the age of Javanese girls at marriage, 42, 179
  on women-initiated divorces in Java, 63
gender:
  as a central to how men conceptualized racial difference before the 1850s, 189
  impact of the Confucian renewal movement on, 101, 103–104, 122–123
gender–manhood:
  class distinctions, 37
  as a fluctuating ideological construct, 188–189
  marital expectations of virginity, 16, 33, 42–44, 51, 74, 135, 137
  middle-class respectability associated with Confucian marriage, 33, 37, 44, 51
  political status embodied in, 34, 37
  polygamy associated with, 8, 38
  upholding of Confucian-colonial family law associated with, 34
gender–womanhood:
  Chinese women's property rights, 80–88, 96
  as a fluctuating ideological construct, 188–189
  impact of prohibitions against inter-religious marriage on, 49–51
  proportion of Chinese probate case set up for women (1840s to 1930s), 80, *81*
  sources of women's wealth in Java, 80–84
  in Southeast Asian port cities, 201n1
  uterine family alliances, 80, 84, 92–97, 99–100
  See also concubines; Jo Heng Nio; Paginio, Tan–property rights lawsuit; slave women; wife-initiated Creole Confucian divorces
Goody, Jack, 79
Gouw Giok Siong, 180, 226n43

Gouw Peng Liang:
    background of, 112, 114, 216n11
    involvement in THHK, 114–115
    Lo Fen Koei, 122, 123, 124, 216n11
    marriage guide, *The Life of Husband and Wife*, 114, 115, 116–117
Groeneveldt, W. P.:
    argument for great legal recognition of Chinese women's property rights, 88
    background of, 86
    draft legislation on property rights (1892), 86, 88, 89
    rejection of Kapitan Oeij's plea, 96

Haagsche Courant, Caroline Tan's speech on the front page of, 153
hartawans, as a focus of reform-minded Chinese writers, 122–123, 129, 136–137, 140
Haryono, Steve, 93, 134, 170
Heryanto, Ariel, 171–172
Ho Engseng, 7–8
Hoogervorst, Tom, 12
Hsieh Bao Hua, 74
Hui Yew-Foong, 10, 12

Ikeya, Chie, 7
Indonesian state
    patrilineal racial identity of Chinese accentuated by name-changing policy, 193, 195
    racial discrimination via civil registries, 189–190, 214n16
    racial labeling under Suharto's rule, 193, 196
interethnic relationships:
    Chinese women's elopement with native men, 49–51
    family-law racial criterion added to the new Indies Constitution (1925), 168
    Gouw Giok Siong study of mixed marriages in Jakarta, 180, 226n43
    interethnic marriage in the Philippines, 192
    interethnic marriage prohibitions, 7–8, 24–25
    in Kwee Tek Hoay's *The Rose of Cikembang*, 1–3, 182–187
    Lau Jie Nio's proposed remarriage with a Muslim (1847), 49
    Loos on the need for research on international intra-Asian liaisons, 7
    rights of mixed-race children, 172–173
    See also race (ethnicity)

interethnic relationships–mestizos and mestizas:
    defined, 202n43
    domestication and sinicization in the Straits Settlements, 190
    impact of colonial-imposed ethnic segregationist policies on mestizas, 45–46
    impact of prohibitions against inter-religious marriage on mestiza daughters, 49–50
    knowledge about Confucian marriage rituals passed to mestiza women, 26
    lukjin (Chinese mestizo) descendants, 7–8, 192–193
    mestizo Chinese wives of *lukjin* men, 192–193
    nyai-mothers' custody of their mestizo children, 27–29
    pingitan evaded by mestiza Chinese girls, 43
    responsibility of nyai to raise mestizo children, 12, 15, 18, 27, 32, 191
    treatment of their "absorption" in histories of overseas Chinese, 188
intermarriage:
    cautionary tales about love marriage related to, 157–158
    colonial prohibitions against inter-religious marriage, 51
    interethnic marriage in the Philippines, 192
    between South Asian men and Burmese women, 7
Islam. *See* Muslims and Islam

Japan, "European" racial-legal status granted to, 146, 219n5
Java, location in Southeast Asia, *xvi*
Jo Heng Nio:
    as a Chinese landowner, 97–98, 213n81
    cross-cousin adoption of a grandchild, 97–99, *99*
Jo Ping Nio, divorce plea (1856), 43
Jones, Eric, 20, 47

Kelly, John D., 9
Khoe Siauw Eng:
    as an officer on the Chinese Council, 108
    on THHK marriage and funeral rites reform committees, 108, 214n17
Khouw Kim An, Major, 110, 159n64
Ko Kimko (C: Gao Genge), 21–23, *22*
Kollewijn, R. D., 178
Kong Koan. *See* Chinese Council of Batavia

248   INDEX

Kuiper, Koos, 86
Kwartanada, Didi, 12, 152
Kwee Hing Tjiat:
  editing of Confucian journals, 112–113, 222n51
  reaction against Caroline Tan's autocritique of Chinese traditions, 155, 158
Kwee Hui Kian, 12
Kwee Kang Tik:
  cautionary tale about love marriage, 158
  reaction to Caroline Tan's talk, 155
Kwee Seng Tjoan, *Templates for Love Letters*, 135, 218n78
Kwee Tek Hoay:
  background of, 182, 184
  Tan's gender-equal ideas rebutted in *Sin Po*, 154, 221n44
Kwee Tek Hoay–*Boenga roos dari Tjikembang* (*The Rose of Cikembang*):
  Chinese patriliny in Java critiqued in, 182, 184–187
  classified as "tragic" by Nio Joe Lan, 184, 226n57
  excerpt from, 1–3
  kin relations among major protagonists, 186, *186*
  publication of, 183, *183*
Kwee Thiam Tjing, 133, 224n8
Kwee Yat Nio (aka Tjoa Hin Hoei), on marriage in *Maandblad istri*, 117, 141

Lauw Giok Lan:
  background of, 215n44
  involvement in the THHK movement in Batavia, 114
  Laws and Mysteries, 114, 115–116, 215n51
Lee, Peter, 201n1
Li Po. *See* Tiong Hoa Hwee Koan (THHK)–*Li Po*
Lie Kim Hok, *104*
  association with *Li Po*, 104, 112
  background of, 39–40
  Kabar Perniagaan (later *Perniagaan*) edited by, 109, 112
  marriage to Oey Pek Nio (aka Roti), 40
  on moral enlightenment, 105–107
  Pembrita Betawi Confucian periodical of, 112, 214n31
  poems on husband-wife relations, 40–41
  polemical debate with Tiemersma in *Li Po*, 104–106
  reliance on European sinologists to assert the theological superiority of Confucian texts, 105
  rites reform campaign, 107–110
  on THHK marriage and funeral rites reform committees, 108
Lie Tjoei Khai [pseud. Tjoekat Liang], 166–167
Lindsey, Tim, 196
Liu Oiyan, 213n10
Loe Ping Kian, 117–118
Lohanda, Mona, 12
Loos, Tamara, 7, 193
love and love marriage:
  anxieties about intermarriage related to, 157–158
  Confucian marriage contrasted with in novels by Dutch-educated Chinese, 120, 122–128
  Kwee Thiam Tjing on adolescent romance, 133
  local-themed love stories as a new literary genre, 119–120
  Oey Beng Liong's announcement of the "free marriage choice," 132
  in Tan Boen Kim's *Gan Liang Boen*, or *A Scary Night!* (1924), 140
  Teddy Kan Hway An's diary documenting adolescent romance, 133–135
  Templates for Love Letters, 135
  in Tjoe Bou San, *An Obstructed Match* (1917), 138–139, 140

McClintock, Anne, 5
manhood. *See* gender–manhood
Mann, Susan, 23–24
marriage law:
  cautionary tales against love marriage, 157–158
  civil marriage law offered to Chinese Subjects of the Straits Settlements (Singapore, Melaka, and Penang), 145
  conflict between Islamic and civil law definitions of marriage, 181–182
  Hadrami practice of *kaa' fa* (rule of sufficiency), 7–8
  "legal marriage" defined in terms of the Confucian Six Rites of Marriage, 24
  Mixed Marriages Act (1898), 24, 121, 147, 220–221n9
  race management of family law as its base, 108, 174, 189–190, 214n16
  VOC ban on marriage between Chinese and Muslim subjects, 24
  See also Chinese Council of Batavia (Kong Koan)–marriage registry; Muslims and Islam–Islamic law

marriage law–cases:
  Lau Jie Nio's proposed remarriage with a Muslim (1847), 49
  Liem Djan Nio, 47, 48, 50
marriage law–customary (*adat*) law:
  case of Jo Heng Nio's cross-cousin adoption of a grandchild, 97-99, *99*
  comparative study from the 1990s, 108
  customary institutions (*peradatan*), 138, 165
  favoring over Islamic textual law, 85
  lack of customs on giving birth outside of wedlock, 179
  as part of Lie Kim Hok's conception of the moral ego, 106
  viewed as outdated in *Tambahsia,* 126
marriage law–monogamous marriage laws:
  Article 27 of the Dutch Civil Code discussed in *Sin Po,* 160
  concept of civil law (1919), 143, 146Wording okay here?
  in Hong Kong (1971), 145
  Phao Tjoen Hoay's "Prohibitions on Men," 162
  Republican China's Article 27 monogamy clause (1914), 149
  Republican China's law on monogamous marriage (1931), 145
  in Republican China's provisional civil code (1912), 149, 159, 220n17
  in Singapore (1961), 145
  in the Straits Settlements, 191
  uniform monogamous marriage law (1957-59), 182
marriage law–polygamy:
  abolition of, 158, 159
  concubinage tolerated under Chinese adat law, 149, 220n23
  manhood associated with, 38
  perpetuation in the Chinese law code for Java, 89, 148, 151, 152, 189
  polygamous relationships counted in the 1920 census, 38-39
  Caroline Tan's critique of, 153
marriage–love marriage. *See* love and love marriage
marriage registration:
  lack of universality of, 207n15
  marriages and marriage rate for Europeans in Batavia, Semarang, and Surabaya (1920-1940), 164, *164*
  the Singapore Muslim marriage registry, 57, 207n15
  See also Chinese Council of Batavia (Kong Koan)–marriage registry

Meeter, P.:
  citing of his characterization of Indies-Chinese customary law by Van Deventer, 91, 92
  enforcement of patriarchal norms in colonial law, 88-89, 96, 212n72
Malacca:
  location in Southeast Asia, *xvi*
  See also Straits Settlements (Singapore, Malacca, and Penang)
Mimi [Lim Kim Lip], *Boenga Rajah,* 136
Muslims and Islam:
  conflict between Islamic and civil law definitions of marriage, 181
  divorce as part of the law in Islam, 78
  Hadrami practice of *kaa' fa* (rule of sufficiency), 7-8
  Muslim personal law "granted" to Siamese vassal states, 7
  VOC ban on marriage between Chinese and Muslim subjects, 24
Muslims and Islam–Islamic law:
  Confucianized "Islamic law" divorce in the Straits Settlements, 190
  Parsi law in British India contrasted with, 85
  Singapore Muslim marriage registry, 57, 107n15
  women-initiated divorce under, 56-57
  women's right to separate estates from their husbands, 82

native concubine (*nyai*). *See* concubines–native concubines (*nyai*)
naturalization policy in Indonesia:
  assimilationist name-changing policy, 194-196
  outlines of, 194
  terms for "alien" residents, 193-194
Nederburgh, I. A., 147-149, 220n16
Nemo [pseud], *The Story of What Young Ladies Did in Secret* (1919), 137
Nio Joe Lan:
  classification of Chinese Indonesian literature as "romantic," 139
  gundik used in references to the concubine, 180
  history of Tiong Hoa Hwee Koan (THHK), 159, 218n65
  The Loan Eng described by, 139
  The Rose of Cikembang classified as "tragic," 184, 226n57
nyai. See concubines–native concubines
Nyonya. *See peranakan*–local born.

Oeij Hap Ho [also known as Tambah]:
marriage certificate, 217n37
murderous exploits of, 217n34
retelling of his story in *Tambahsia,* 126
Ong Hok Ham, on "Bhinneka Tunggal Ika" (M: Unity in Diversity), 195
Ong Kwie Nio:
interlocking alliances between the Ong and Oeij families of Batavia, 94–95, *95*
suit to retain control of uterine familial property, 94–97
Ong Ping Lok:
Just for One (1927), 140
Song from Seven Heavens (1931), 140–141

Paginio, Tan–property rights lawsuit, 90–92
marriage alliance of the Tan and Liem families, 93–94, *94*
Palmier, Leslie, 42
Pan, Lynn, 130, 217n46, 217n46
Panorama:
Chinese women's causes addressed in, 184, 226n53
Kwee Tek Hoy's *Boenga roos dari Tikembang* published by, *183*, 184
running of, 184
patriliny:
Chinese patriliny in Java critiqued in Kwee Tek Hoay's *The Rose of Cikembang,* 182, 184–187
creole Confucian patriarchal resistance to women's equality, 151, 153–158
enforcement of patriarchal norms in colonial law, 88–89, 91–92, 96
feminist critique against patriarchal practices launched by Fromberg and Tan, 152
new patriliny reconstituted by Confucian reformers to counter the Dutch colonial civilizing mission, 12
patriarchal character of love stories in the 1920s and 1930s, 139
patriliny-inflected racial identity of Chinese settlers in Indonesia accentuated by the VOC, 193, 195
the Thung line of Bogor, 196
traditional Chinese patriliny theorized by Sangren, 9
transfer of child custody to a patrilineal kin, 29, 203n58
women's resistance to, 9, 10, 52
See also birth registration; marriage law; marriage registration

Penang:
location in Southeast Asia, *xvi*
See also Straits Settlements (Singapore, Malacca, and Penang)
peranakan (M: local born) and peranakan families:
assimilationist politics of, 12, 194, 200
"Baba" and "Nyonya" as honorific forms of address, 203n57
"creole" as an alternative to the term "peranakan," 11
portrait of, 1, *4*
Perniagaan:
discussion of colonial civil law in, 159, 161
Gouw Peng Liang as editor of, 112, 114–115
Lauw Giok Lan as editor of, 114
Lie Kim Hok as editor of, 109, 112
Phoa brothers' association with, 112, 160
Thio Tijin Boen's contributions to, 112
Philippines:
Chinese family law interpreted in, 192
interethnic marriage in, 192
location in Southeast Asia, *xvi*
Phoa Keng Hek, Confucian reformation activities of, 104, 222n73
Phoa Tjoen Hoat, background of, 112, 160
Phoa Tjoen Hoay:
background of, 112, 160
Lady Camille translated as serialized for *Li Po,* 128
law codes translated for the *peranakan* Chinese by, 160–163, 172, 224n14
legal status as Th. H. Phoa, 224n8 Wording okay here
"Prohibitions on Men," 162, 222n79
Pijper, G. F., 57
pingitan (seclusion of post-puberty young women), 42–43
case of Go Tjoe Nio, 43
case of Lie Jan Nio, 48
case of Pang Fo Nio, 43
case of Tan Ho Nio, 44
case of Tio Teng Nio, 43–44
plotting of in Lim Kim Lip's *Bunga Raya,* 136
polygamy. *See* marriage law–polygamy
Pramoedya Ananta Toer, 10

Qing Code:
criminal code of, 87, 149
silence on women's status, 89
use by Dutch colonial jurisprudence in the Indies, 159

race (ethnicity):
  Confucian proto-racial boundaries in Semarang and Surabaya, 14
  European imperial race management, 7–8, 108, 174, 189–190, 214n16
  "European" racial-legal status granted to Japan, 146, 219n5
  nominal status as "European" granted to Chinese converts to Christianity, 191
  patriliny-inflected racial identity of Chinese settlers accentuated by colonial rule, 193, 195
  racial status of Indies Chinese as "Native," 146
  religion-based interethnic divide of the colonial state, 28–31
  rights of mixed race children, 172–173
  separate civil registers for the Chinese as the legal basis racial management, 23, 158–159, 189–190
  See also interethnic relationships; naturalization policy in Indonesia
Raffles, Thomas Stamford, 56
reform-minded Chinese writers:
  male ego of the hartawan as a focus of, 122–123, 129, 136–137
  Tjerita Njonja Lim Pat Nio, 112, 124
  See also Gouw Peng Liang
Reid, Anthony:
  on the marriage ages of daughters of elites, 205n45
  on women's autonomy in Southeast Asia, 71
Rush, James, 36

Sai Siew-Min, 12
Salmon, Claudine, 217n49, 219n95
  on the building of ancestral and funeral halls in colonial cities on Java, 169
  on the patriarchal character of love stories in the 1920s and 1930s, 139
Sangren, P. Steven, on traditional Chinese patriliny, 9
Schlegel, Gustasf:
  background of, 86
  Confucianist dictum about women's incapacity to own property (1865–72), 87–88, 96
  draft private law code (1872), 88
Semarang:
  case of Major Tan Hong Yan's marriage of his daughter to Be Ing Tjioe, 36
  case of Nauru's claims to her sons, 28
  Chinese councils modeled after the Batavia council, 14
  Confucian proto-racial boundary in, 14
  location of, *xvi*
  marriage rate among the Chinese of, 164–165, *164*
  marriages and marriage rate for Europeans in (1920–1940), 164, *164*
  protest again the draft of Indies Chinese marriage law (1892), 152
  registration of illegitimate births in, 173–174, *173*
  Selompret Melajoe, 111
  slave population in, 18
  Tan Paginio's property rights lawsuit in, 90–92
  THHK-affiliated newspapers in, 112
  van Deventer's work based in, 89–90, 91–92
  See also Sie Hian Ling
sex and sexuality:
  excessive lust (M: *birahi*) motivating abduction, 122–123, 136
  marital expectations of virginity, 16, 33, 42–44, 51, 74, 135, 137
  racial division of sexual labor, 73, 124
  sexuality as moral duty, 113–118
  slave women as sex slaves for Chinese men, 19–20
  See also concubines; love and love marriage; *pingitan* (seclusion of post-puberty young women)
Sharafi, Mitra June, on Parsi law in British India, 85
Sidharta, Myra, 41–42
Siegel, James T., 129, 132
Sie Hian Ling:
  background of, 112
  Bintang Semarang edited by, 214n31
  Story of "Yang Soen Sia," 125
  Tamboor Melaye founded in Semarang, 214n31
Simmel, Georg, stranger theory or, 8, 199n19
Singapore:
  acceptance of concubinage in, 70
  divorce in, 206n2
  location in Southeast Asia, *xvi*
  monogamous marriage law in (1961), 145
  Muslim marriage registry in, 57, 107n15
  See also Straits Settlements (Singapore, Melaka, and Penang)
Sin Po:
  "Privaatrecht bagi orang Tionghoa" (Private law for the Chinese) published by, 160
  Tan's gender-equal ideas rebutted by Kwee Tek Hoay, 154, 221n44
  Tjoe Bou San as editor of, 113, 138

INDEX

Skinner, G. William:
assimilationist study of the Chinese in Thailand, 9, 12, 27, 192–193
Cold-War-oriented politics of Skinner's social science intervention, 200n21
on the creolized Chinese of Java, 79, 80, 190
estimate on the number of women, 200n32
Mely G. Tan's fieldwork in Indonesia guided by, 180
slaves:
from Bali and southern Sulawesi brought to Batavia, 18
decline in numbers after the British interregnum, 18
slave women:
case of Ong Hae's slave, 20
of Ko Kimko, 21–23, *22*
Opera Singer Slaves, 77–78
runaway slaves, 20, 47
as sex slaves for Chinese men, 19–20
transactions for, 19, 201n81
Spivak, Gayatri Chakravorty, 9
Staatsblad van Nederlandsch-Indië [Statutory Laws of Netherlands India]:
design of Chinese monogamous marriage (1917 no. 129), 151
pass and quarters system law (1835), 45, 205n61
permission from a penghulu required, 225n36
statute on marriage validity (1929), 24, 202n34
statute on the guardianship of children born outside of wedlock, 178, 225n29
statute on the settlement of foreign orientals, 45, 205n62
Stenberg, Josh, 77
Stoler, Ann Laura, 5
Straits Settlements (Singapore, Malacca, and Penang):
civil marriage law offered to Chinese Subjects of, 145
labor migrants in, 200n31
Lim Kim Lip's *Bunga Raya* set in, 136–137
monogamous marriage law granted in, 191
numbers of immigrants from China in Java compared with, 10
Sukarno, 182, 193
Surabaya:
Bintang Timur, 111, 214n31
Chinese councils modeled after the Batavia council, 14
civil marriage registry figures for, 223n84
Confucian proto-racial boundary in, 14
location of, *xvi*
"male retributive" moral tales in, 136
marriage rate among the Chinese of, 164–165, *164*
marriages and marriage rate for Europeans in (1920–1940), 164, *164*
protest again the draft of Indies Chinese marriage law (1892), 152
registration of illegitimate births in, 173–174, *173*
slave population in, 18
THHK-affiliated newspaper, *Pewarta Soerabaja*, 112
Tjhoen Tjhioe based in, 112, 113, 128, 129, 222n51
Tjoa family of, 170
See also Bok Tok
Suryadinata, Leo, 194, 227n12, 227n16
Sutherland, Heather, 38
Sutrisno, Evi, 106

Tambahsia:
retelling of the story of Oeij Hap Ho (Tambah), 126–127
Thio Tjin Boen likely the author of, 217n33
Tan Boen Kim:
Gan Liang Boen, or *A Scary Night!* (1924), 140
Tjhoen Tjhioe edited by, 112
Tan Ging Tiong:
elite Kapitan background of, 112
Li Po founded with Yoe Tjai Siang, 111
translation of Confucian texts with Yoe Tjai Siang, 107
Tan Kittjoan, 123, 216n19
Tan, Siok Tjwan:
"Long Live the Emancipation (of Chinese women)!," 158
reaction to Caroline Tan's talk, 155–156, 158
reforms to Chinese family law in the Indies called for, 156–157
Tan Souw Lien, Caroline:
arranged marriage viewed as "moral murder" by, 153
background of, 152, 221n35
feminist critique against patriarchal practices launched with Fromberg, 152
talk for Chung Hwa Hui (1912), 151, 153–158, 160, 222n53
Tan Eng Goan, Major, 37, 38, *39*, 217n40
Tan, Mely Giok-Lan, 180n44

Taylor, Jean Gelman, 6, 27
Thailand:
  location in Southeast Asia, *xvi*
  monogamous Family Registration Act passed in Siam (1935), 193
  Skinner's assimilationist study of the Chinese in Thailand, 9, 12, 27, 192–193
Thio Tjin Boen:
  Cerita Oey Se by, 217n33
  contributions to local newspapers, 112
  Sie Tjaij Kim (*Nona Kim*) adaptation of *Lady Camille*, 128–129, 130–131, 218n59
  Tambhasia likely written by, 217n33
Thung Liang Lee, 195, 227n17
Thung line of Bogor:
  patrilineal identity of, 196
  Thung brothers of West Java, 170Okay to have this subentry here
Tio Tek Hong:
  background of, 216–217n27
  Confucian marriage match-made marriage described by, 125
Tiong Hoa Hwee Koan (THHK):
  Chinese medium THHK schools, 133
  establishment of, 103, 222n73
  marriage rites reform, 109
  newspapers affiliated with, 112
  Nio Joe Lan's history of, 159, 218n65
Tiong Hoa Hwee Koan (THHK)–*Li Po*:
  founding of, 111–112
  Lie Kim Hok's association with, 104, 112
  Phoa Tjoen Hoay's translation of *Lady Camille* for, 128, 217n47
  polemical debate with Tiemersma in *Li Po*, 105–106
Tjan Kim Bie:
  Lady Camille first encountered by, 128
  reformist credentials of, 129, 131–132
  Tjhoen Tjhioe edited by, 129
  translation and adaptation of *Lady Camille*, 129–132, 218n38
Tjioe Tik Lien, reaction to Caroline Tan's talk, 157

Tjiook-Liem, Patricia, 12, 87
Tjoa Boe Sing, *Story of Lim Tjin Sioe*, 123–124
Tjoa family of Surabaya:
  Nyai Siri Gambir's testimony as a slave of, 21
  Tjoa Tjoan Lok, 214n31
Tjoa Kiat Beng, 25
Tjoe Bou San [pseud. Hauw San Liang]:
  An Obstructed Match (1917), 138–139, 140
  campaign to oppose Dutch-Indies nationality led by, 138
  The Loan Eng (1922), 139

van Deventer, C. Th.:
  "debt of honor" coined by, 147
  Tan Paginio's property rights defended by, 90–92
van Heekeren, C. W., 91
van Limburg Stirum, J. P.:
  legal unification under one civil code pressed for, 146
  prohibition on concubines in the army barracks, 147
van Wettum, B. A. J., 149, 159

Wichers, H. L., 87
wife-initiated Creole Confucian divorces:
  divorce rate among creole Chinese in Batavia, 59–60, *60*
  five commonly asserted complaints, 55
Williams, Lea E., 12, 109, 213n13
Wolf, Margery, 80
womanhood. *See* gender–womanhood

Yahaya, Nurfadzilah, 57
Yoe Tjai Siang:
  equation of the Confucian God with Nature, 115
  Li Po founded with Tan Ging Tiong, 111
  translation of Confucian texts with Tan Ging Tiong, 107
Young, J. W., 108

Zhou Taomo, 12

Printed in the USA
CPSIA information can be obtained
at www.ICGtesting.com
CBHW031538150624
10141CB00006B/564